Sympathetic Sentiments

The WISH List
(Warwick Interdisciplinary Studies in the Humanities)

Series editors: Jonathan Bate, Stella Bruzzi and Thomas Docherty

In the twenty-first century, the traditional disciplinary boundaries of higher education are dissolving at remarkable speed. The last decade has seen the flourishing of scores of new interdisciplinary research centres at universities around the world and there has also been a move towards more interdisciplinary teaching.

The WISH List is a collaboration between Bloomsbury Academic and the University of Warwick, a university that has been, from its foundation, at the forefront of interdisciplinary innovation in academia. The series aims to establish a framework for innovative forms of interdisciplinary publishing within the humanities, between the humanities and social sciences and even between the humanities and the hard sciences.

Also in The WISH List:

Sympathetic Sentiments

Affect, Emotion and Spectacle in the Modern World

John Jervis

Bloomsbury Academic
An imprint of Bloomsbury Publishing Plc

B L O O M S B U R Y
LONDON • NEW DELHI • NEW YORK • SYDNEY

Bloomsbury Academic

An imprint of Bloomsbury Publishing Plc

50 Bedford Square	1385 Broadway
London	New York
WC1B 3DP	NY 10018
UK	USA

www.bloomsbury.com

BLOOMSBURY and the Diana logo are trademarks of Bloomsbury Publishing Plc

First published 2015

British Library Cataloguing-in-Publication Data
A catalogue record for this book is available from the British Library.

ISBN: HB: 978-1-4725-7637-8
PB: 978-1-4725-3560-3
ePub: 978-1-4725-3561-0
ePDF: 978-1-4725-3562-7

Library of Congress Cataloging-in-Publication Data
A catalog record for this book is available from the Library of Congress.

Typeset by Fakenham Prepress Solutions, Fakenham, Norfolk NR21 8NN

Contents

List of Illustrations

Chapter 2, p. 31:
Bartolomé Esteban Murillo
Invitation to a Game of Argolla (c. 1670)
© London, Dulwich Art Gallery

Chapter 3, p. 53:
Jean-Baptiste Greuze
Le Fils puni (1778)
Paris, Musée du Louvre
© Musée du Louvre/Agence Photographique de la Réunion des Musées Nationaux et du Grand Palais

Chapter 8, p. 197:
War photograph (1991)
(for details, see text)
© Kenneth Jareke/Contact Press Images

A Note to the Reader

This book is for students, in a properly broad sense of the term: academics, undergraduates, graduate researchers and the educated general reader (there are a few of those around, hopefully). This already indicates a problem of level: potential readers will have different degrees of knowledge. Further, it is a book positioned within cultural studies, again in the properly broad sense: it may get readers from backgrounds in literature, art, philosophy, film studies, media studies, sociology, history, cultural theory. The book uses examples from the novel (Stowe, Dickens, George Eliot, Proust), and art (Murillo, Greuze); it draws on philosophers (Spinoza, Hume, Kant, Deleuze) and cultural theorists (Adam Smith, Benjamin). Hence there is also a problem of range: potential readers will have differing areas of knowledge (and ignorance). If all this poses a challenge for readers, it has certainly posed one for the writer: an impossible one, many would say. Clearly there are risks, but at least the rationale for some of my stratagems – such as smuggling in elements of plot synopsis in discussing the novels – will now be apparent. And it is important to emphasize that the book is not just a collection of case studies: it is also – in aspiration, at least – a more integrated essay in applied cultural theory. I would add that all readers would be well advised to read the first half of the Introduction, so as to be aware of the relation between this book and another I am publishing simultaneously, also intended to further this project; and, most important, the concluding page of the Introduction, clarifying the overall organization and direction of the book. Beyond that, specialists can look after themselves, but I would suggest that less specialist readers be ready to skip one or two of the more difficult sections that occur in most chapters, at least on a first reading; in particular, the second half of Chapter 5 (on Spinoza and contemporary affect theory) could certainly be omitted. In the end, if the book stimulates thought and discussion then it will have achieved its main aim.

Acknowledgements

I would like to thank Jo Collins, for introducing me to Mary Hays (Chapter 3), persuading me to read Žižek (Chapter 8), and, most of all, for reading early drafts of the book and being a wonderfully sustaining influence throughout this venture. I would like to thank Mary Evans, for stimulating my interest in George Eliot (Chapter 6), and for invaluable advice and support. And thanks are above all due to Naoko, for recognizing and accepting the strangely important role that writing this stuff seems to have in my life.

Foreword

The reader of this and John Jervis's companion volume, *Sensational Subjects*, holds in their hands a veritable challenge to the iconoclastic tradition of Western cultural aesthetics. But 'iconoclastic' here is used quite literally to describe those modes of critical inquiry in the humanities and social sciences that are weary of the image, of the icon, and, with that, are weary of sensorial experience as a source and resource for understanding. Indeed, I might go so far as to suggest that Jervis's volumes are a challenge to the methodological pursuit of understanding in the social and human sciences. In this respect, these volumes aren't exactly transdisciplinary efforts, in the same way as the other volumes in The WISH List series. Jervis does engage and inform a variety of political, aesthetic, cultural and social disciplines, and his two books will prove crucial to scholars in a diverse range of fields from political science to cultural studies; from geography to film studies; from literary studies to economics. But although Jervis's work is informed and informs these diverse areas of academic inquiry, it isn't born from any one of them. Rather, in *Sympathetic Sentiments* and *Sensational Subjects*, Jervis's ambition is to unsettle our expectations regarding the outcome of inquiry itself: namely, comprehension. Jervis puts pressure upon our inherited common sense that a critical attitude begins with establishing the proper distance between subject and object of inquiry so as to achieve comprehension. In short, the issue regards our faith in the existence of mediation, and the collective trust we put in both the temporal and spatial distance of spectatorship.

In *Sympathetic Sentiments*, this ambition takes on the modern tradition of sentimental culture and the eighteenth-century discovery of 'sympathy' (and therefore spectatorship) that became central to modern political, economic and moral considerations. This was the birth of the modern discourse on value, and with it came an exploration of value as an event of relation between peoples, objects, spaces and times. Sympathy, value and spectatorship were interrelated concerns of sentimental thought. These and other relational impulses emanate from our corporeal dispositions, creating events of attraction and repulsion. Thus, whereas in *Sensational Subjects* Jervis is interested in exploring the collapse of spaces of intervention between subjects and objects by insisting on the immediacy of experience, in this volume Jervis considers the intervals of in-betweenness that allow the emanation of sympathetic sentiments. As he affirms quite clearly, 'Sensation engages us primarily as organic and physical beings, through energy, force and flow; sympathy engages us as cultural beings, through the power of reflexive awareness, imaginative engagement with images and visions of self and other' (p. 5).

In short, and as Adam Smith had affirmed in his *Theory of Moral Sentiments*, sentimental life is impossible without spectatorship – without, that is, the separation that makes one aware that we are not an other. We shudder at an other's pain, or joy, or sadness only because there is a distance between us that makes it impossible to occupy the source of their sensations. This enables a curious turn of events in that the experience of sympathy makes doubt – that critical impulse of modern thought – irrelevant. The consciousness that allows us to raise questions of doubt regarding the suffering of an other, for instance, is irrelevant to our sympathizing with an other. That is, we do not need to satisfy our doubt and know an other is in pain in order to sympathize with them. We merely have to witness their suffering.

Like *Sensational Subjects*, *Sympathetic Sentiments* is a challenge to contemporary cultural, political, aesthetic criticism in the humanities and social sciences. Jervis is not afraid of the society of the spectacle, nor does he bemoan it. On the contrary, the spectacular is put front and centre as an everyday source for sympathy. In doing so, he also puts front and centre the inadequacy of our epistemological attitudes and our habits of critical judgement. By making doubt irrelevant – or, at the very least, secondary to sentimental life and cultures of the spectacle – Jervis disposes of the hermeneutics of suspicion as a moral prerogative of critique. His methodological development of an *immersive* approach is thus precisely the point: immersion is what reification theory, ideology critique and hermeneutics have always sought to escape via a critical epistemology suspicious of sentimental life.

Thus we return to the foundational challenge for humanities and social science research: is critique exclusively oriented towards understanding? Jervis doesn't give us an explicit answer, nor does he ask the question explicitly. And yet it is there, palpable, on every page of his WISH List volumes. *Sympathetic Sentiments* and *Sensational Subjects* both challenge us to question our inherited motivations about the purposiveness of inquiry, the exclusivity of epistemology as the basis of critique, and our attachments and aversions to the spectacle of everyday life.

Davide Panagia
University of California, Los Angeles

1

Introduction

This book began from my being intrigued by the way we seem to live in a 'culture of feeling' that is ill at ease with itself, and has indeed been intermittently but persistently in a state of denial, with *any* public show of feeling risking denunciation as 'sentimental' – and this in turn led me to wonder whether sentimentality is simply a derogatory term for feelings one 'feels' unhappy to acknowledge (and why is this?), or whether there is a distinctive 'structure of feeling' here that can be distinguished from other, perhaps more conventionally acceptable, patterns of sympathetic engagement with the plight of others, patterns that are implicitly gender-coded. So the aim here is to try to constitute such a matrix, a structure of feeling in a virtual state, realizable in different historical contexts and cultural configurations, and inherently allowing for, and even encouraging, the controversy that seems central to it. Whether 'the sentimental' is really distinguishable here, and what would follow from this, is a central theme of this book, but for now we can tentatively say that sentimentality involves an immediacy of emotional response, which can be embedded in powerful collective currents, whereas what will emerge as the other key term here, sympathy, is more nuanced, involving the feelings in a broad sense that is inclusive of elements of reflection, and assumes a degree of distance from the other even as it seeks to overcome it.

When one traces this back it does indeed seem that the problem of feeling is always linked to relations with others. A question of central importance raised by theoretical debates around sympathy is whether we sympathize most with those we most resemble. It is often assumed that we sympathize with people because we like them, and we like them because we are alike; and that, additionally – but overlapping with this – we are more likely to sympathize with those who are 'closest' to us. Sympathy can readily get elided here into notions of identification and identity, based on a spontaneous immediacy of affective contact. This whole book will involve taking a critical distance from this, as an adequate account; for now, it will suffice to say that this orthodox view downplays the relation between emotion, imagination and judgement in our responses to the suffering of others, the way these involve a distinctive culture of the self as an imaginative construct that is both internal yet also manifest in those public dimensions of gesture and narrative that have come to constitute selfhood *as* a relation to the other in the modern world.

What is 'modern' about all this, then, seems to develop out of what we can identify as a 'spectacle of sympathy' in the eighteenth century, in which sympathy seems inherently to entail public forms of expression whereby being 'on show' is both a condition of the authenticity of such feelings *and* of their capacity to be masked and simulated. Hence a culture of theatrical display actually underlies and renders possible the interiority of the self as it comes to be recounted in the novel. One form of being 'on show' indeed involves narrative, whereby the sympathetic self narrates its 'sentimental' involvements with others, as an emotional being, thereby revealing also the distortions and misunderstandings that such apparent 'transparency' entails. Feelings seem to call for narration, for embodiment in stories through which they are revealed, intensified and explored. They can also be pictured, whether in the imagination or externalized in paintings. If we put more emphasis on the present day, another implication of this is significant. We are continually confronted, in the media, with assorted disasters, traumas and forms of suffering, both personal and collective, and these are always liable to engage our emotions, just as we may also try to defend ourselves and block off these responses. But we may also seek out a vicarious engagement with such experiences, as in film or the novel; and this has been apparent since the origins of the novel in the eighteenth century. Such vicarious involvement can raise the disturbing possibility that we could take pleasure in suffering – even, conceivably, our own – or that at any rate we could become inured to it.

In elaborating this, it would be useful to go back in time once again, to get some perspective. The concept of 'sensibility' was of central importance to eighteenth-century culture and its patterns of behaviour. Sensibility always faced both ways: towards the body, the realm of affect and sensation; and towards other people, thus displaying a public face, and an embeddedness in codes of civility. It was about physiology *and* ethics, individual psychology *and* social interaction. As such, one can say that an engagement with 'suffering' was basic to it, since suffering, particularly as pain, is both the most funda-mental 'sensation' and also what most dramatically involves us when perceived in other people. Sensibility was, one might say, fundamentally 'aesthetic', in the foundational sense of the term, encompassing our embodied, evaluative response to the world, a response that could be said to ground the moral, too, even though subsequently the two have been kept distinct: aesthetics, that is, as a response that was as much to do with everyday culture and behaviour as with what was already becoming the more specialized arena of art and its pleasures, which has, of course, since become the primary zone of application of 'aesthetics' in its narrower sense. Sensibility, then, incorporated a distinctively 'sensational' physiology and a 'sentimental' capacity to respond to the predicament of the other, an 'other' who would in principle be 'the same' only as the putative possessor of an equivalent capacity but could otherwise be very different (gender, race, culture).

Encounters with 'other cultures' would, of course, increasingly both stretch and challenge this perspective. Alongside this implicitly egalitarian capacity for 'feeling with' the other – central to the Enlightenment vision – was the possibility that this could turn out to be more imposition than dialogue, the emergent cultural emphasis on self-identity and forms of social exclusion risking either an identification with an other who was thereby drawn *too close*, too like oneself, or, if this failed, was expelled altogether from the purview of the sympathetic engagement that defined this affective universe. Here is the source of the criticism, still frequently encountered, that notions like 'sympathy', 'pity' or 'compassion' are inherently patronizing, too embedded in relations of inequality they do nothing to challenge – alleviating distress maybe, but implicitly only on the agent's terms, and quite possibly more to do with guilt than genuine concern.

Returning to the idea of 'spectacle' in the context of sensibility, we can see that the latter manifestly implies a semiotics, a way of treating the body as a sign system, to be 'read', just as sympathy involves reading the signs of distress in the sufferer. Such signs involve a staging of the body, with the body on display just as surely as if it were on the stage; and indeed theatricality provided a range of figures for self and body in their public acts, and society as essentially an arena for performance, just as all this naturally provoked controversy around issues of sincerity and manipulation, concerns central to the motivational patterns of market-oriented behaviour. Thus, in the cultural dynamic of sensibility in relation to the suffering other, we can reinforce our sense of a 'spectacle of sympathy' that has widespread ramifications, but carries with it built-in tensions.

This eighteenth-century world of 'spectacle' positions observer and observed, stage and audience, spectator and spectacle, as necessarily *separate*. This element of distance, inherent in spectacle, poses various problems and possibilities for the sympathetic relation to the other, but it must necessarily pose a potential problem of voyeurism, of positioning the spectacle itself as object of fascination, and – potentially – enjoyment. The apparently paradoxical notion of 'pleasure in (contemplating) suffering' raises its head here, but so does the wider resonance of spectacle, the way it becomes implicated in popular culture, presupposed in the idea of 'entertainment' that emerges as central to the latter. All this is inseparable from the great innovations in the technologies of the visual that enable the late nineteenth century to transform the spectacle into the ever-more spectacular, converging with the increasingly sophisticated use of such technologies as capitalism enters the era of mass-market advertising. Photography and electricity – particularly used as lighting – ensure that by the early twentieth century the spectacular has become a new mode of spectacle, and the scene is set for what will duly become the new century's central innovation in popular cultural forms: film. Spectacle – particularly as spectacular – therefore manifests what can appear to be a degree of autonomous cultural power. It is enthralling, seductive, not in any way inherently compatible with norms of rational action and response, just as its links to the mass media could be taken to imply that it is us, in our guise as 'the masses', that would be most subject to its influence, would be its essential 'audience'.

At this point, it is important to point out that this book is one of a pair, published simultaneously, the other one being entitled *Sensational Subjects: The Dramatization of Experience in the Modern World*. While each stands on its own, and can be read independently, it will be apparent that there are significant links and overlaps. Indeed, they started off as one project, only gradually being separated as it became clear that two strands were being conflated, pointing to two distinct discourses and modes of embodiment that have been central to the relations between mind, body and culture (especially mediated culture) in the world of Western modernity. As key triggers, 'sympathy' and 'sentiment' seemed to point one way, and 'sensation', and a word that has become fashionable in recent years, 'affect', seemed to point the other. In effect, it is claimed that we can tentatively identify two distinctive cultural configurations here, referred to, in a shorthand way, as the spectacle of sympathy and the circuit of sensation. 'Sensation' suggests the more overtly physical side of feeling, and the links between this and the 'sensational', as it comes to feature in media 'sensationalism', are the central topic of the other volume. In effect, it is argued there that the two senses of the term 'sensation' – embodied feeling and dramatic media event – are interlinked from early on in the history of the modern.

Sensation involves quasi-physical circuits and breaks, shocks, and defences breached, a culture of nerves, stress and nervous energy, linked to desire and release. Sensations involve processes and cycles: within a cycle, sensations have a built-in tendency to inflation; one seeks 'newer' or 'better' sensations. The spectacle of sympathy is more passive, more visual (although by no means exclusively so), more about interpreting imagery and engaging the other through imagination, rather than responding to stimuli, in their immediacy. Where sensation threatens to flood the spectacle of sympathy, overwhelm it by obliterating distinctions between subject and object, sympathy separates them, hence maintaining a degree of distance, allowing for judgement to be brought into play. Sensation engages us primarily as organic and physical beings, through energy, force and flow; sympathy engages us as cultural beings, through the power of reflexive awareness, imaginative engagement with images and visions of self and other. These latter features remain crucially embodied, but in a way that emphasizes the cultural shaping and interpretation of the body, rather than the body as testifying directly to physical processes and powers that may well *appear* to work through culture but apparently do so in some immediate way, *without* cultural mediation. As disjunctive aspects of the modern world, they are both central to our constitution *as* moderns, subjects of modern experience.

In tracing the origins of the spectacle of sympathy in the eighteenth century, then, we also encounter the way 'sensibility' lies at the source of both of these strands, and an important theme of this book – particularly in the second half – is to consider the later history of the processes whereby they evolve as different, often in tension, yet also interrelated, so that analysing particular cultural materials, texts or pictures challenges us to tease out these strands as they exist in uneasy coexistence, even threatening the integrity of the object of analysis itself.

Pursuing this on into the nineteenth century, we can say that consciousness, as a condition of rational action in the world, is always potentially threatened by physiological responses, drives and desires, whether capricious or obsessive, and an interest in these 'unconscious' elements of mind and culture increasingly becomes a feature of science and cultural debate generally. With the cultural perception of time and change as it has developed over this period, this can be mapped onto the temporal dimension whereby selves and cultures can be said to have histories. 'Memory' thus becomes problematical: both an important source of identity and an inherently contestable resource, something that can indeed break down and fragment, all of which contributes powerfully to the cultural background, and content, of modernism in the arts and psychoanalysis.

Hence the characteristic pathologies of feeling, from hysteria to trauma, along with the cultural dynamics of late twentieth-century 'identity politics' in which trauma, in particular, has been embedded, and which pose further problems for the possibility of sympathetic engagement, and the terms in which this is debated.

It is worth developing this, because it can help tease out the often obscure ways in which sensation and sympathy could work their way through different cultural contexts and forms. However it may be theorized, the unconscious is not just a dynamic cauldron of energy; it is also a dramatic scenario in which self and other enact strange fantasies of disturbing difference, which can, in turn, be reflected in everyday behaviour. If the pathology of sensation is trauma, the pathology of sympathy is hysteria. Both involve over-identification, whether as traumatic repetition or hysterical mimesis: the other as insistent force, threatening the self in its relation to itself over time, the sense of self as self-development; or the other as inescapable image, of loss or plenitude, trapping the self in the delusions of identity, unable to constitute the difference and distance that makes relations of belonging and sympathetic engagement possible. Trauma recycles the eternal return of the traditional, in the modern age of shock and sensation; it collapses present into past, in the repetition of the past as crippling present, with the subject unable to 'move on'. Identity as identification – with persons and objects, the celebrities of the ordinary – threatens to subvert the frameworks and boundaries that can permit sympathetic engagement with the other, *and* the reflexive distancing from self that is a condition for this, while encouraging the immersion in sensationalism and sentimentalism that permits the intensity and excess of 'feeling' so central to modern hedonism.

In the light of this, we can return, one more time, to sympathy itself. The developments we have been referring to enable us to ask about the fate of the spectacle of sympathy in the contemporary world. Mass media accounts and presentations of scenes of suffering, frequently involving graphic images, can intensify the awareness of it, 'bring it home' in a way not possible before. But the corollary could be a lessening of *imaginative* engagement: too much work is done for us, too much is put in place for us. It is easy to assume that we can be more affected by the Haitian earthquake of 2010 than contemporaries were by the earthquake that destroyed most of Lisbon in 1755, but this is not necessarily the case. And just as the 'spectacular' aspect of spectacle could be said to heighten the impact, so it could also distract us all the more from the ostensible object of our gaze; the 'aestheticization' of suffering could take us away from the possibility of response through feeling. But here, it will be important to interrogate not just the notion of spectacle but also the way aesthetics has been repositioned as autonomous, and separate from ethics to the point of running into conflict with it. When the spectacle of sympathy itself becomes spectacular, has aesthetics anaesthetized the moral sense, the capacity to engage with the other? Could it, conversely, be the case that the contemporary spectacle could indeed *engage* the spectator in ways that remind us of that earlier balance between distance and closeness, now 'simulated' in a postmodern era of new media developments?

We can recall here the case of the Asian tsunami of Christmas 2004. In this case, the initial impact – undeniably 'sensational' – was speedily followed by the sympathy response (record donations poured in to the aid agencies). There was a conspicuous lack of interest in possible perpetrators (very unlike 9/11). One might think that was hardly surprising: it appeared to be a textbook case of a 'natural' disaster, and no clever thesis about any possible distant human contribution (global warming?) could detract from that. This suggests a kind of emotional bedrock here, that the sympathy response is most likely where a basic dimension of human suffering comes into view, where no questions of blame can readily be raised: and this, again, is broadly continuous with the eighteenth century, as is the potential for 'blame' discourses to move us into more directly political responses (though doubtless still presupposing some notion of 'fellow-feeling'). Historically, the politics of modernity has crucially involved this latter dimension, where a prospective underlying sympathy produces a collective anger or resentment, which can be channelled into public debate, ideological commitment and mass political involvement. At the same time, the interpretations of 'sensation' and 'sympathy' developed here would indeed contribute to a critical perspective on the ways the capacity for sympathetic engagement opened up by aspects of modern experience and reflection can nonetheless be stymied and corrupted by other features of that same world, particularly those associated the self-interested motivational patterns associated with capitalist individualism – though never irretrievably so.

We can conclude that while the era of mass media sensationalism simultaneously brings suffering closer while subtly distancing us from it, the potential for sympathetic involvement is still there. 'Feeling', reconstructed as a kind of 'emotional intelligence', need not be antithetical to reason; and this may lead us to a sense in which 'sympathy' and the network of ideas around it (empathy, compassion, fellow-feeling) can point to aspects of the 'humble narratives' of modernity, and the patterns of everyday interaction, that are positive sources of value in people's lives, that are often unnoticed, and that, when noticed, can easily be disparaged by critics and theorists. This can be distinguished from self-interested rationality on the one hand, and, more tentatively, from senti-mentality on the other, though the latter remains an irreducible and essential aspect of the cultural politics of the modern. All this may appear to be in some tension with our awareness of the increased development of the spectacular in spectacle and the impact of the mass media generally, but any such tension should be *productive*. For example, it has already been suggested that there is a sense in which sympathy was, even in the eighteenth century, *already* implicated in spectacle; nor is the idea of 'belonging', implicit in the notion of sympathy developed here, incompatible with emergent notions of network communities, or indeed of 'community' as extending beyond the human. And all this reveals the importance of understanding modernity as the history of the contemporary and history *in* the contemporary: just as we are (also) living in the eighteenth century, so they were (already) living in the twenty-first ...

Overall, then, this is a multi-layered cultural history of modern feeling as it has been conceptualized and represented over the period since the eighteenth century, particularly through literature, art, the media and theoretical reflection. The book questions the tendency to assimilate modernity to 'the contemporary', attempting instead to reveal the patterns of repetition and reconfiguration in Western culture that can be seen to underlie the very real changes that have occurred over this period.

General approach and assumptions

How are we to write about 'modern culture' when we are inevitably positioned, at least partly, within it? This is a book about the experience of the modern that has to be in some sense situated both within and beyond it, in a reflexive move that straddles the boundaries: an uncomfortable place to be, but one in which we may all at times find ourselves. This in turn suggests that the modern is always liable to be also 'postmodern'; that perhaps the potential for this is found deep within the modern, always associated with it. This must also affect the status of the claims that can be made: bold but tentative, exploratory, condi-tional, situated; and this necessarily poses reflexivity as fundamental both as problem and as resource. There is inevitably a practice of world construction and reconstruction as one inhabits the world and reflects on it, a sense of the essential multiplicity of what we nonetheless – reasonably enough – think of as *one* world, on which we have a range of viewpoints. Writing, then, affects the written-about, at least in the sense that it carries a complex message of its own involvement, its own contribution to the reflexivity of the world, implying both distance and embeddedness.

Modernity itself can anyway be taken to question the very idea of 'boundaries', with their implication of fixity; as an alternative, porousness and fluidity can be seen both to incorporate an awareness of the relativity of limits and categories, and to suggest ways of pursuing and presenting the substantive issues. The method of approach adopted here is *immersive*, as if donning a guise, appearing (dis)guised as whatever or whoever is being expounded, thereby both extending and interrogating that other position, questioning its boundaries, indeed showing that its implications are frequently 'other' than what it wants or purports to be. Hence, while 'style' is often treated as a feature of surface rather than substance, it is considered here as a way in which content is 'formed' in a way immanent to it. It carries dimensions that are immersive and reflexive, and also syncretic and centrifugal.

Syncretic links, centrifugal movements and the use of figures respond to the connectedness of the world; and so does throwing together several differing uses of a word, as an invitation to consider connections beyond the confusions that can possibly result. And this 'throwing together', in juxtaposition, is an *active* process, an intervention, reorganizing the world-as-understood. At the same time, it can be *responsive*, sensitive to the tensions and inadequacies of existing taken-for-granted assumptions and categories as they (fail to) fit experience. This is to say that concepts – and indeed images – can appropriately be *inclusive* rather than, or as much as, exclusive; they can break down their own boundaries, flow into adjoining regions, incorporate distinctions within themselves. This is important because while analytical distinctions are intended to resolve problems, they can characteristically bring their own problems with them: distinctions solidify into separations, fragmentation, a loss of connection; and also the implication that something has been solved when it may merely have been put out of view, or swept under the carpet. A strict and specialized division of labour can be as troublesome and counter-productive in language and thought as elsewhere in the world. (None of this should be taken to imply, *per contra*, a metaphysics of holism, replacing an empiricism of fragmentation with an idealism of totality.)

There may, in short, be good reasons for *not* making distinctions, just as there may be good reasons for making them *within* the range of application of a concept, and only tentatively: that should help ensure the concept's reflexive inadequacy, its necessary (and desirable) *in*sufficiency in grasping itself in its extensions and applications. To take an example central to this book, this could apply to the terms 'sympathy' and 'empathy'. Today, it is often thought important to distinguish them, but this can lose a sense of their mutual imbrication, their shared history, indeed the fact that the latter term has only come into use relatively recently. It is not that it is necessarily wrong to distinguish them, but that it may also be right not to, depending on the context and the unfolding of the connections and implications of the discourse in which the term or terms are embedded. One danger in making the distinction is that we try to hive off what we see as the 'bad' aspects of the sympathy tradition, as suggested in the previous section, leaving empathy as the term to designate the 'good' side, which can lead to a complacent and uncritical use of the latter, just as insensitive to context and situation as the original frequently can be. Using sympathy as the inclusive term reminds us of the historical resonance here, as the word flits in and out of use, sometimes explicit, often implicit. Smooth temporality, the process of gradual change, is intersected by moments of reflexive upheaval, when criticism and explicit rethinking can shift the terrain in ways large or small.

Even on a cursory glance it will be apparent that 'feeling' and 'thought' are two further terms that play a central role here. Feeling is often bracketed with emotion, and thought with reason. The implicit or explicit dualism here has been central to the Western tradition since the eighteenth century, but has been widely refined and criticized; indeed, 'sensibility', as an originating moment of this tradition, can be seen as both asserting and refusing this distinction. In more contemporary terms, feelings and emotions can be said to be 'intentional' in a sense related to the phenomenological: they can give us an orientation, a sense of awareness, along with embeddedness in what we do not directly understand or control. Forgetting the latter risks making emotions *too* rational, assimilating them to cognition. Feeling can itself be seen as a bridging term, between the senses on the one hand, and emotion on the other. As for 'thought', however, when elided into 'reason', the problems become particularly acute when the latter is in turn given a rather narrow connotation: logical argument or following rules. This has serious effects when we consider 'judgement', a term which deviates greatly in its everyday use from its use in the Kantian philosophical tradition, where, again, subsumption under rules is taken as basic. In everyday life, judgement involves a balancing act between reason, feeling, experience, and – the joker in the modernity pack – the imagination.

It will be a central theme of this book that the imagination has indeed been central to modern thought and culture, from well *before* the Romantics got hold of it. In effect, there is a process of translation or transfiguration here, as the affective in feeling or emotion becomes imaginatively transposed into language and imagery, into the conceptual grasp of awareness. Indeed, in the case of emotion, the imagination enters into the very constitution and formulation of it. As they loom out of the hinterland, emotions are shaped, figured, by the imagination, and this 'hinterland' can be conceived as 'outside' or 'inside', and perhaps as 'unconscious'. In encountering the deep structure of modern selfhood, we thereby encounter an element of projection, of the theatrical, as if involving a stage, an actor and an audience – frequent sources of imagery in the eighteenth century and since. Inner space emerges as the theatre of the self and the play of others, with transfigured feelings, rather than reason, providing the dynamism. One assumption that governs this book is already apparent then: that there can be too great an emphasis on rationality, at the expense of judgement and imagination. And this is linked to a second: that it is the culture of everyday life itself that can often provide the resources needed to correct this bias. One does not have to take some highly abstract or philosophical road, deriving critique from an unaccountable 'elsewhere'; it is there, ingrained in the culture and experience of life as it is lived and reflected on both in everyday contexts *and* the more specialist areas of cultural practice and debate.

Actually, the whole realm of practical everyday moral choice and judgement can be subsumed under a broad sense of the term 'feeling', and often is. This is feeling as it is rooted in orientation, in our responses to the challenges posed by the world as we meet it in daily life. This is an aspect of, or perspective on, the arena of 'experience', of reaction to what are often the effects of the modern project of rational appropriation and manipulation of the world, but never exclusively so. When we remember that aesthetics caused problems for the contours and categories of Kant's system, that it operates both as a bridge between the first two *Critiques* and as a precarious summation, always liable to expand into subverting rather than confirming their autonomy, we can perhaps see how an aesthetically tinged conception of everyday life can take up some of this inheritance. This is particularly so when we incorporate the imagination, thought 'in excess' of reason, positioning it in the production of fantasy, fiction and imagery: the world as representation, both as and beyond mimesis. Modern culture reveals an 'interest' in the world that is not just pragmatic, self-interested or rational, but which is prior to these interests of an already-constituted subject, and has a basis in what can indeed be called 'aesthetics', related to that originating eighteenth-century sense of the term, as embodied discourse, of thoughts imbricated with feelings, of an involvement in the world that is sensory as well as intellectual, 'aesthetic' in a way that grounds the moral and political rather than being auxiliary or derivative. First and foremost, aesthetics involves an *encounter*, a response to the difference of the 'other' (whether object, person or culture). This difference, whether as a sense of involvement with, or belonging in, is *felt*, registered as feeling and grasped *as relation*, as pattern, through imaginative figuration, in a process which 'expresses' the culture that is simultaneously constituted or reconstituted by such experiences and their framing. In this sense, this book is an essay in 'cultural aesthetics', a contribution to the elaboration of theoretical understanding in cultural studies. The term itself is given some elaboration in *Sensational Subjects*, but some of its further implications can be spelt out here, in the context of the central concerns of this volume.

Whether or not these ways of situating the unity or multiplicity of our experience of this world have any clear philosophical rationale, they do seem implicit in, or suggested by, such a world. (Doubtless for most philosophers, up to and including Deleuze, this whole way of putting it would seem topsy-turvy, as if *doxa*, 'opinion', were being called on to interpret, even correct, the rational principles of philosophical argument; but, as will be seen in the book, philosophy does have a place, even if not quite the elevated position many of its practitioners claim for it.) Furthermore, the concepts we invoke here may or may not have any purchase beyond this world of modern experience – quite likely not – and one must, in principle, accept their complete historical contingency. The cultural imaginary of the modern West, then, encompasses this broad field of the humble narratives of everyday life, and the images through which they are reflexively figured as they are grasped, and also the more specialist (or speculative) narratives of science and politics, some of which conjoin to form the ideological grand narratives that give the civilization its distinctive 'flavour', just as their relation to the humble narratives of the everyday in which they are partially and problematically implicated is always one of tension and dissension, and frequently repudiation. Here we can return briefly to content, for it could be said that 'sensation' and 'sympathy' are aspects or transpositions of the two most fundamental dimensions of the humble narratives of the modern: the polarity between the everyday, experienced as banality and routine, and the world of shocks and sensations; and the significance of love and suffering in interpersonal relationships, in the light of the modern cult of individualism and individual feeling.

To 'inhabit culture' is also to belong to one or several cultures, however defined, and the cultural imaginary can be said to pose the questions and possibilities of what is involved in this, how to navigate these worlds. It maps the structure of relations between actual, virtual and possible that open up and frame the contours of experience, experience as it is lived and reflected on. In the modern world, the cultural imaginary draws on the full resources of the media-inflected narrative and imagery through which such experience is reflexively appropriated as discourse and figuration, embedded in cultural forms (specific media and art forms) and cultural practices.

To take this framework further, it might be useful to return briefly to an example that is central to this book, namely 'the sentimental'. As a genre, this can occur across different media and art products (novel, film, play), all of which retain their own distinctive cultural positions and histories but in this respect are all instances of 'the sentimental'. At the same time, the sentimental as genre points towards the experiential dimension. One can act, or feel, 'sentimental'; and one can live at a time when 'feeling sentimental' can be culturally validated or devalued and when, additionally, it can be more, or less, gender-coded. So it is here that one might perhaps encounter what we referred to above as a 'structure of feeling', a pattern or code of affective experience that colours the interactions between subjects in a range of contexts, and that thereby in turn partially constitutes and strongly influences the self as subject of experience, mediating between body and consciousness. In the case of the sentimental, this seems indeed to be a legacy of the dispersion of eighteenth-century 'sensibility', reconstructed as an 'excess' widely perceived as thereby available for critique and denunciation.

This, in turn, implies the possibility that this structure of feeling has intimate links to the cultural forms that both express and transmit it, and that in this sense modern experience does indeed become heavily 'mediated'. Indeed, if we regard the novel as media form, as well as art form, as we surely must, this 'mediated' quality becomes coterminous with modernity itself. Facing one way, one has a structure of feeling; facing the other, one has a 'cultural configuration', a distinctive fusion of cultural form and content, including the signifying practices of text-based and image-based representation, in turn taken up in reflexive discourse. Such cultural configurations embody the effects of the modern project, of representation and experience interacting in mediated form, the grounds out of which modern subjectivity is constructed. Of course, as indicated previously, none of this enables the world to be mapped into our categories in any straightforward way. 'The sentimental' can be treated as one pole of sensibility, implicitly being contrasted with other possible applications of the latter term, all on the terrain of a 'structure of feeling'; but one of the problems with 'sensibility' is that the term can have a wider purchase, as a relation between feeling, civility, public spectacle, and reflexive thought, hence emerging as a cultural configuration, incorporating the sentimental as one of its modes – particularly likely given that we have no readily available adjective to accompany sensibility, so that 'sentimental' can be called on to play this wider role. Such 'terminological' problems are never *merely* such; they are content-laden, and have to be handled with a sensitivity to context.

The unfolding of the themes through the chapters

The book starts with contemporary 'sentimentality', examining its underlying structure and tracing it back in time to probe its origin in eighteenth-century 'sensibility' and the controversies over sympathy, which together reveal the sources of this pattern and the conflicts it engenders. After exploring the theoretical aspects of sympathy itself, the fifth chapter – which serves as the turning point, the hinge of the book – sets up a duality between two key theorists, Adam Smith and David Hume, enabling us to locate, more clearly and explicitly, a 'spectacle of sympathy', along with a cultural configuration that comes to exist in some tension with it, that of sensation and sensationalism, which we have called the 'circuit of sensation', both of which can now be seen as phenomena central to the evolution of the modern world in its codes of feeling and their expression and transformation through culture and the media. We conclude this chapter by suggesting that contemporary 'affect theory' is in effect a development of *one* of these, the circuit of sensation, and that this gives grounds for questioning its adequacy as an approach to these issues more broadly. The book then retraces a path back towards the contemporary world, via nineteenth-century culture, showing how the ramifications of these two strands work their way through the newer concerns with unconscious influences in – and on – mind and history, and the implications of this for the understanding of creative processes of art and memory, along with those key 'pathologies', hysteria and trauma. A concluding chapter revisits earlier themes through a consideration of the impact of the mass media and reinvigorated capitalism on debates about sympathy, sentiment, sensation, and alleged 'compassion fatigue'. Historically, then, the book unfolds as a series of episodes, from the origins of Western modernity in the eighteenth century, through to developments in the contemporary world; but it does not unfold *as* history, as a historical narrative. The book uses history, but is not itself history. Rather, it moves strategically, to reveal the underlying patterns, the discontinuities as well as the continuities, out of which we construct what can often be rather rationalizing and simplifying historical narratives, and thereby accepts the reflexive paradox inherent in writing a history *of* the modern that is also a history *in* the modern.

2

Cloying Sentiments

Sentimentality occupies a strange place in our culture: apparently pervasive, superficially attractive, yet widely disparaged, despised and denounced. Sentimentality is sweetness, it seems. One critic complained of 'the torrent of sentimentality that poured out of the media's treacle well' after Princess Diana's death.[1] Others referred to a 'sickly confection'[2] and 'sugared sadness'.[3] So it is hardly the sweetness of 'sweetness and light'; rather, it is sweetness to excess, threatening nausea, sickness. And if the senses of smell and taste seem to be engaged here, so too does the sense of touch. As treacle, sentimentality is sticky, viscous. Sentimentality is *cloying*, and clinging: it can get onto you, into you; it can pollute you, melt your boundaries, threaten your integrity. If we succumb to temptation, and wallow in it, we become like hippos in a mudbath. 'Faked feelings!' protested D. H. Lawrence, denouncing sentimentality: 'the world is all gummy with them'.[4] This reminds one of Sartre's discussion of the ontology of the slimy, the viscous, halfway between solid and liquid.[5] It is 'sticky baseness', he writes; it is like a leech, 'it draws me, it sucks at me'. I can sink in it, get lost in it, may even dissolve in it. Initially seductive, it quickly becomes repulsive, horrible. And it 'transcends all distinctions between psychic and physical': mind and body, thought and feeling, slide together. Then there is that sweetness again, now more openly gender-coded: it is 'a sickly-sweet, feminine revenge …'.[6] And, like Lawrence, he associates it with a kind of bad faith. Not only is sentimentality dangerously invasive, in a quasi-physical sense, but there is danger also in its dishonesty, in that it is not what it purports to be: its façade of genuine concern for the other, or grief over loss, is just that – a façade.

For its critics, then, sentimentality could be said to manifest the traps and temptations of everyday life, in condensed, almost corporeal form, a congealing flow that both drags us down and sticks us together, drugged by its syrupy sweetness. In this gluey flow, we are both immobilized and swept along, losing our individuality, all capacity to 'think differently' gone; in becoming part of this glutinous mass, we also succumb to a state in which the public arena is swamped by the private world of irrational feeling. Sentimentality, one might say, is the everyday as *tacky*: both sticky and substandard, dragging us down, down and away from the illumination of light and reason.

'Recreational grieving' for the 'people's princess'?

In the recent British context, it is the death of Diana that has proved to be the most potent focus for these concerns. A massive investment of popular sentiment was apparent right from the start – and so was the strength of the reaction against it, by critics and intellectuals, denouncing not only the contagion of sentimentality but also what they saw as outbursts of mass hysteria, in the very virulence of their attack sometimes appearing to fall into the latter themselves. And the relation between popular emotion and the mass media was always a crucial issue. If the emotion on display was, as critics alleged, second-rate and second-hand, this either derived from, or was reinforced by, the media. Graham Little refers to the claims about manipulation, 'the so-called grief being the product of the same tabloid minds that brought us the celebrity queen they lived off',[7] and quotes a journalist: '... it was largely a tabloid crowd and I was struck by the general kitsch of it ...'.[8] That there could be a circular process involved here is implied by the ambiguity of these quotes: the 'tabloid minds' in the first may well be the editors, but they could also be part of a 'tabloid crowd', who could in turn both be readers of the tabloid press and creators of the celebrities they read about, by their active willingness to participate in this creation: no public, no celebrity. Who is manipulating whom may not be so clear-cut; but, behind all this critical paranoia about 'manipulation', there could lie an accurate enough perception that involuntary participation in a 'society of the spectacle' may imply a deep substratum of assumptions, hopes, fantasies, emotions, a 'structure of feeling' that is drawn on, in a general and taken-for-granted way, by everyone – readers, viewers, editors and producers alike. This is what will need to be explored.

In this specific case, it is worth observing that Diana's death took everyone by surprise: most institutions, newspapers and broadcasters (except for the BBC) had no contingency plan in place, and for at least the first few days it was 'the people' who set the pace; and through the subsequent development of events, the media reflected, as much as contributed to, the general mood.[9] And we are reminded of a now-forgotten historical parallel, useful for comparison: the death in childbirth of Princess Charlotte of Wales, the only child of the Prince Regent (soon to be George IV), in 1817. Perceived as pure and caring, hugely popular in contrast to her father and the rest of a royal family seen as arrogant and out-of-touch parasites, her death triggered an immediate powerful wave of communal mourning, with crowds turning out not merely in London but also in other towns and cities, business life suspended on the day of the funeral, and a huge market emerging for assorted memorabilia and stories. Yet this, of course, *preceded* the development of what we would conventionally call the 'mass media'; even the telegraph was some years away.[10] It is hardly evidence of 'media manipulation', then, but would be perfectly compatible with the 'structure of feeling' emphasis outlined in the Introduction.[11] And, to return to Diana, it is worth remembering that there was also a degree of overt popular hostility to the media, and sometimes to Diana, too; Christie Davies documents the intriguing phenomenon of 'Diana jokes', which began circulating almost at once, and which he presents as a protest against 'the abrupt canonization of a well-meaning but rather ordinary person whom the press had previously derided, mocked, hounded and harassed'.[12]

This also raises the issue of Diana's relation to her audience: who, precisely, were 'the people' here? Clearly some groups were more affected than others, though the range of her appeal across different groups could make the diversity of mourners indeed look like 'the people'. Her own image, after all – a combination of rejection and marginalization on the one hand, and of active involvement in 'caring' on the other – made her a marketing dream. Her brother, Earl Spencer, referred to her affinity with 'the constituency of the rejected',[13] and this seems very relevant to her appeal to gays, ethnic minorities, and the disabled and stigmatized. In the background here lies the suggestion that the excluded, in their amorphous, undifferentiated state, can embody a certain power, that 'what is socially peripheral is often symbolically central',[14] and Diana emerges as a figure of mediation between this 'other' world and that of conventional power and politics, particularly in her readiness to display feeling herself. Little alludes to the suggestion that public figures should be seen to be 'emotionally representative', that they should 'turn into public emotion the private feelings shared by the community';[15] and since she could apparently master the unusual skill of appearing to be both royal and 'ordinary', she could become 'a conduit between royalty and commoner, society and the individual ...'.[16] She managed to appear both image and substance, celebrity and 'genuine person', an actor in the soap opera of real life. And her death was a jolt partly because it disturbed this precarious unity: it was simultaneously real, all too real, yet also – inevitably – a media event. She was both the occasion for the sentimental flow, and the channel whereby it could connect people, drawing unwittingly on this deeper source, this amorphous mass of feeling, excluded yet potent. Dramas of rejection and identification, central to Diana's own life, were just as central to her relation to her own audience, testifying to the power of the vicarious both in distancing us, and in enabling us to draw together, in the contemporary world of spectacle and simulacrum.

In the light of this, we can return to the issue of emotion itself, the display of sentimental feeling that was such a feature of it all. It could indeed appear capricious: people in the crowds seemed to switch readily between being mourners and tourists, participants and observers. While this is a structural feature of life in a society where spectacle and sympathy have become enmeshed, almost an adaptive response, it could also be taken as further evidence that the display was superficial or insincere. After all, the vast majority of those who grieved had never met her. One of 'those who felt differently' referred to it as 'recreational grieving', adding that even if the grief was genuine, it was 'grief with the pain removed, grief-lite'.[17] Another commentator claimed that the tears at Diana's lakeside shrine at Althorp seemed to be willed, produced artificially, evidence of emotional suggestibility. Now, apart from the fact that there is anyway plenty of cross-cultural evidence to suggest an element of cultural shaping and individual volition in any production of tears, however 'natural' they might seem, one might have thought that 'suggestibility' was precisely the point: only in the tradition of Western Protestant individualism is it assumed that grief should be purely personal and, indeed, preferably not really *displayed* at all, and that only close relations, the 'bereaved', should mourn; anything beyond is vulgar display, 'bad taste', the public sphere invaded by the private. On all this, a thoughtful comment by a mourner at the time is worth consideration: 'Diana told "me" (and many others) of her dreams and disappointments – and despair; my grandmother never did. So for whom should I really mourn?'[18] The 'me' in quote marks is highly suggestive – clearly the writer was aware that there was a multiplicity of subjects here, each able to *feel* a special relationship with Diana. Like Little Eva in *Uncle Tom's Cabin* distributing locks of her hair before dying, Diana, too, had shared herself, parcelled herself out; and if, in the age of vicarious identification, this occurs through emotional display in the media, it doesn't alter the fact that the basic pattern is still in place. The vicarious world of celebrity identification, with its own potential for distancing and fragmentation, for the expression of hopes, longings and anguish, can be, in its own way, just as real as the 'real'.

This will all need further exploration, but for now we will merely note that there could, anyway, be a trap in the condemnation of sentimentalism itself. The critic, who claims such skill in identifying self-indulgence and self-deceit in others, could fall victim to them himself. Impurity of motive can be infectious. Thus Deborah Knight argues that when the condemnation of sentimentality is self-congratulatory, so that one enjoys 'the pleasure of feeling that one is the sort of person who recognizes the unworthiness of the sentimental', then, since this response 'masquerades as reasoned and reasonable, and thus conceals its potential to be both self-gratifying and self-deceiving, it is sentimentality of the most vicious sort'.[19] Lawrence may fall foul of his own critique. Sedgwick concludes, in turn, that 'antisentimentality can never be an adequate Other for "the sentimental", but only a propellant for its contagious scissions and figurations'.[20] Indeed, we find that occupying positions within the conventional discourse of sentimentalism, whether for or against, may produce much abuse and scapegoating but rather limited insight.

Framing feeling: Dilemmas of popular culture

Knowing how to express emotion in socially acceptable forms, in a society which often downplays or disparages it, is difficult enough, after all. In a measured defence of the popular reaction at the time, Linda Grant argued that 'wanting to express our feelings and having a voice for them are not the same thing ... Expressing emotions in words is one of life's trickiest exercises. Get it wrong and you're finished. This is why we develop rituals ...'[21] In this everyday context, the ritual form words take is, in effect, the cliché, precisely because clichés are standardized and repetitive – which in turn, of course, renders them vulnerable to being dismissed as trivial, second-rate and derivative. And, of course, some of it inevitably arouses ridicule. The problem here is real enough: somehow, words and gestures never seem adequate; the piles of floral bouquets make their point, but, even as the piles rise higher, their inadequacy cries out all the more.

This repetitiveness of popular cultural forms can be further illustrated by another example – nearly contemporary – this time from the US. In 1994, Susan Smith drowned her two young sons in a South Carolina lake. There was an immediate outpouring of popular sympathy for the two boys; a shrine by the lakeshore (with teddy bears, flowers, photos, poems); and frequent use, in the poems, of the idea that God plucks 'rosebuds' to brighten up heaven. In her discussion, Kirsten Gruesz points out that Smith's own confession used much the same language as that of the popular mourning, so that the same sentimental conventions appeared to govern both the act and the public response.[22] As for the 'rosebuds', the imagery may derive from a widely known poem by Longfellow (1839), 'The Reaper and the Flowers', a staple of consolation literature; the suggestion is that Jesus needs the flowers, as they remind him of his time on earth:

> And the mother gave, in tears and pain,
> The flowers she most did love;
> She knew she should find them all again
> In the fields of light above.
>
> Oh, not in cruelty, not in wrath,
> The Reaper came that day;
> 'T was an angel visited the green earth,
> And took the flowers away.

Directly addressing the reader is, of course, a well-known ploy in sentimental fiction, so I will now ask: how do you react to that, Reader? Are your tear-ducts engaged? Or are you closer, in spirit, to Oscar Wilde's reaction to a famous example in Dickens: 'One must have a heart of stone to read the death of Little Nell without laughing.' Or – like me – do you tend to veer indecisively between them? Emotional response need not be straightforward, after all. It is as though one reacts partly to one's own reaction, with a mixture of simultaneous fascination and revulsion. One gets caught up in it – that treacle again – but tries to escape it, too. One is embedded – partly, at least – but reflexively aware, even critical and self-critical.

This example also, of course, engages with a favourite scenario of sentimental reaction, not just in the form it takes, but the occasion for it: the death of children, who are, in this context, always coded as innocent and pure. Indeed, it is as though there is a surplus of purity here, so – particularly in the nineteenth century – the all-too-frequent death of children was appropriated culturally as a 'purification' of other aspects of the social order, as Karen Sánchez-Eppler shows in her study of the prevalence of photos of carefully posed dead children in the Victorian period, especially in the form of the post-mortem *carte de visite*: 'The family, as locus of love and feeling, constitutes itself sentimentally as an act of memorialization.'[23] In the case of two of the most famous literary examples – the deaths of Little Eva, and of Little Paul in *Dombey & Son* – we know the authors had recently suffered bereavements: in the case of Harriet Beecher Stowe, her infant son had died shortly before the novel was written, and it is clear that she was very distressed; and in the case of Charles Dickens, the death of his young sister-in-law, Mary Hogarth, just before, had affected him deeply. In a letter, he promised not to shrink from speaking of her, but rather 'to take a melancholy pleasure in recalling the times when we were all so happy';[24] and 'melancholy pleasure', an apparently paradoxical fusion of loss, desire and recall, of absence as presence is, as we shall see, central to sentimentalism. So: if it is the case, as most readers feel it to be, that these two novelistic deaths come over to us as highly sentimental, this merely emphasizes, perhaps, that major writers, too, have recourse to popular forms in articulating emotion that can, evidently, be deeply felt.

Grant's argument is that the alternative to sentimentality in such situations is artistic originality, images that are fresh and unexpected, and 'which force us to think and see in new ways while simultaneously inducing deep recognition, as if we have been told something about ourselves we have always known but has been unaccountably obscured'. And one might add that if this culminates in modernism, which emphasizes the novelty of word and image at the expense of this 'deep recognition', ultimately producing the eloquent silence that closes in around the words in a Beckett play, or in postmodernism, which gives this up in favour of a play on the garrulous promiscuity of words and meanings we always already recognize, then neither can ultimately deliver the goods. As Grant puts it: 'What it comes down to is whether or not you prefer words to silence, each a failure in their own way.'[25] And here we can rejoin Diana; for if there were words – plenty of them – there was also silence, for long periods: the profound, resonant silence of the crowds at the funeral, as the cortège passed …

It is surely significant that many of these examples of sentimentality and sentimental response involve the world of popular cultural forms.[26] 'Weepies' have constituted a very important strand in cinema since the earliest days of silent film; popular fiction is replete with sentimental situations; and music, particularly the tunes and lyrics of popular song, has perhaps been the most frequent precipitant of sentimental response. Here we might recall a line from Noël Coward's *Private Lives* where Amanda falls prey to the strong feelings that well up as she catches the notes of an old popular tune being played by a band: 'Strange how potent cheap music is'. Indeed so; and just recently, listening to the radio, the first few lines of a song I had not heard since my youth arrested my attention and tore through my emotional defences: 'Pale Hands I loved beside the Shalimar, / Where are you now? Who lies beneath your spell? …' An old recording, in mono, with a distant-sounding male voice audible through the old-fashioned accompaniment, with a slight hiss or crackle, singing what I later learnt was called 'Kashmiri Song': it was the fusion of the lines themselves, the aching tune, and the very process of transmission itself, that seemed to do it for me.

Naturally I did some research. This turns out to have been one of four poems 'from India' by Adela Nicolson (1865–1904), set to music as 'The Indian Love Lyrics' by Amy Woodforde-Finden (1860–1919), published in 1902, to considerable success. Both of them had spent some time in India, and had Indian Army connections. I could imagine the song being addressed by some British officer in India to an Indian girl he would love and leave; a more downmarket version of Puccini's opera *Madame Butterfly*, perhaps, from the same era. In short, a long-obsolete Edwardian song with a somewhat dubious colonial pedigree – and learning all that does not, of course, affect the immediacy of my sentimental response in the slightest. Doubtless it must originally have been a record in my parents' collection, or for some reason it remained in my memory from some long-forgotten radio programme – and, either way, it was probably already on the way to oblivion. So the distance here, the distance of nostalgia, of 'loss remembered', is crucial too: nostalgia is, after all, a mode or aspect of the sentimental.

The comparison with Puccini raises an important issue. It is more acceptable for us to be affected sentimentally in this case, though it would probably be described as 'being moved'. Opera, after all, is Art, definitely at the high end of culture. Is it possible to distinguish the quality of the responses here? Characterizing one response as 'sentimental' and the other as 'being moved' may simply reflect one's greater degree of embarrassment in the one case in comparison to the other. In other words, someone from the appropriate social and educational background, exposed to opera and classical music from an early age, could easily find that the sentimental response could later kick in, for some of this material – but might well see this as being 'moved' by art, which is culturally encoded as an 'appropriate' response. In this sense, describing one's response as 'sentimental' is really to describe one's reaction *to* one's response, indicating a degree of unease, of critical distance, reinforcing the suggestion made above: 'tears came to my eyes, but I feel embarrassed by it and wish they hadn't'. The label becomes merely an exercise of internalized, taken-for-granted notions of taste.

However, writing 'merely' here is not to deny that, in another way, this is a very important dimension. After all, the distinction between 'good' and 'bad' taste carries a powerful identity charge: this is the sort of person I am, or want to be seen as. It is a reminder of the civilizing process, whereby my public image, manifest in my choices in these matters, becomes a sign of my personal character, my quality as a person. But this has a further implication. In the absence of any other sufficient grounds for making these distinctions – any 'rational' basis for distinguishing between 'good' and 'bad' taste – then my exercise of these cultural judgements has no rationale beyond the mere fact of the hold they have over me. In other words, I would have no good grounds for continuing to *disparage* a reaction as 'sentimental' (rather than merely describing it, in value-neutral language). And that would raise the issue of whether what remains of 'sentimentality' would continue to amount to a distinctive pattern of feeling, or whether it would dissolve back into some more generalized feeling, such as sympathy – with which it has had close historical links – thereby raising more general issues around the nature of feeling and emotion in relation to cultural life and the exercise of individual judgement. Any adequate account of the place of 'the sentimental' in modern culture must therefore be able to provide for both the appearance that 'sentimentality' *is* a distinctive category of feeling, and the rationale for the relative stigmatization that *often* accompanies it, but also for the possibility that this distinctiveness is illusory, that sentimentality may not ultimately be distinguishable from other feelings or aspects of feeling. We must try to outline or uncover a matrix, a 'structure of feeling' existing in a virtual state that can be realized in different cultural configurations and hence allows for these possibilities as sites of cultural controversy.

One central theme in all this – whether we take film, opera or popular song – is revealed both in the content, and in relation to listener or audience: the theme of loss, of separation. *Goodbye Dolly Gray*, a song forever associated with the First World War but actually originating a decade earlier, is both *about* separation and has itself come to signify separation and loss – in this case, the loss of a whole generation. And doubtless this repertoire has in turn been added to, by subsequent generations. With loss, as we've seen, goes nostalgia, a potent part of the sentimental brew. The songs of the 1960s girl groups, with their three-minute odes to lost or unrequited love, would feature on many lists. The Shangri-Las, in *Leader of the Pack*, add the 'bad boy' motif, the gang leader from the 'wrong side of town', killed in a motorcycle 'accident' when they were forced to split up ... Here, it is adolescent loss, all the more poignant in its transience. Love as such isn't sentimental: it is the association with loss, separation, absence (actual, anticipated or remembered), that makes it so, that contributes the distance that is filled with the longing, the yearning, the nostalgia, the ache of desire.[27]

And this brings us back to the Noël Coward quote. What makes 'cheap' music cheap, what makes it 'common', vulgar, ordinary, is that we don't have to work at it, 'suffer' in acquiring an appreciation of it, as we are supposed to with 'art'; we can just sing along, or get carried along. It is like relaxing among friends. And this relates to the theme of loss, too: friends can be 'absent' friends. Sooner or later, there is always separation, loss; indeed, there was, for each of us, right at the start of life. Community *involves* loss. Yet this need not contradict pleasure: the reaction to loss, insofar as it involves both sharing and acknowledgement, recognition, can be affirmative. We do not – normally – take pleasure in loss, pain or suffering as such, but we can take pleasure in the way we deal with them, the way we cope. As a final example of this mix, let us return to Grant, recalling the sentimental songs from her Jewish family background, songs like *Mein Yiddishe Mamma*, sung by Sophie Tucker, with its 'tear-jerking rendition of all Jewish mothers as selfless, devoted angels who sacrificed everything for our children. In our hearts we knew the songs were rubbish, but they held within them some kind of truth ...', some connection to ideals about motherhood:[28] here, loss becomes the self-sacrifice of love itself, in the simultaneous abjection and idealization of mother as motherhood.

Leaving to one side our ambivalence about sentimentality, let us return to that *initial* response, in terms of the immediacy of the feeling involved. Here, too, there could be grounds for disquiet. After all, what we encounter here is what Ed Tan and Nico Frijda call the 'submission response': tears of joy or grief 'occur in situations that are experienced as overwhelming, as situations that one feels unable to control, to deal with, to retain one's distance from'. The sentimental forces us to 'yield to the overwhelming',[29] and this helplessness is a problem for us; it does not conform to the ideal of the autonomous self, one in which 'self-control' is a virtue, or just a taken-for-granted presupposition of adult life. Although the nature and extent of this cultural emphasis on self-discipline and firm boundaries has varied at times over the last two or three centuries, this has not disturbed the importance of this in the structure of modern selfhood.

It can seem as though feeling, in its impact on us, features as a sort of undifferentiated field of force which then assaults us in concentrated form; it is likely to break out unpredictably, and to be difficult to control when it does. Once again, 'mass hysteria' seems to be an ever-present danger. Writing a few months after Diana's death, Decca Aitkenhead identified a 'darker wave of mob brutality' whereby 'the faintest whisper of a paedophile will bring crowds out, and have grandmothers screaming for castration', so that 'One minute Britain is a weepy nation clutching teddy bears, the next a snarling mob throwing stones'; and her argument is that these are two sides of the same coin, a logical outcome of 'emotional politics' and irrational thought. Emotional currents swill around, uncontrollably, seeking outlet, and producing 'phoney tribal attachments' in the process.[30] We may recall other examples of this ambivalent significance of emotional release, such as the case of a leading Nazi, Rudolf Hess, who is alleged to have wept at an opera performance put on by condemned Jewish prisoners during the Holocaust.[31] And, in a sense, it is perfectly reasonable for this to fuel the criticisms of a 'culture of feeling': if indeed 'feeling' is to be presented as an alien, all-conquering force, then it can only be amoral in itself, resulting in political, cultural and individual consequences that can as easily be evil as the reverse. But the way this problem is set up in the first place should make us pause. The whole cultural rhetoric of 'self-restraint' and 'self-control' embodies and projects this sense of 'the body' as alien and dangerous, and 'feeling' as necessarily antithetical to reason and thought; and this helps to ground both the cultural distrust of feeling and the specific stigmatization of 'the sentimental' in the narrower sense.

The mere fact of 'losing control' can be a problem, then, and it is a *gendered* problem; there has been more tolerance for women to show feelings – particularly the sympathetic feelings – and succumb to them. Let us indeed linger with gender for a moment. This was clearly a factor in the reaction to Diana's death – there were more women mourners than men – and it divided the commentators: some feminists celebrated Diana as an iconic figure, others dissented. Claims about a 'feminisation' of British culture, protested Elizabeth Wilson, 'reaffirmed a reactionary stereotype of women as the only sex with tear ducts, the only ones who "care"'.[32] Indeed, the historical data give other grounds for caution here, too. A 1994 issue of *Time* magazine carried an article, under the title 'Annals of Blubbering', listing occasions when George Bush (Senior) cried during his time of office as president. One or two such occasions involved the military, reminding us of George Washington's tearful resignation from his command in 1783, accompanied by an appropriately tearful response from his fellow officers. Thus did a 'foundational national moment' involve a 'fluid affective exchange between men', as Mary Chapman and Glenn Hendler put it. Their book does indeed claim to establish that 'masculinity and sentimentality are mutually constitutive discursive formations'.[33] This would conventionally be seen as elite male bonding, whereby an elite differentiates itself by engaging in normally proscribed behaviour, though it is worth adding that the *form* the behaviour takes – the 'letting go' – is also a paradoxical mimicry of what would be (more) acceptable among women.

Away from elite military contexts, one can mention that in 1842 substantial numbers of American men could be found weeping in public, in front of large crowds, at meetings of the Washington Temperance Society, as they gave their alcohol abstention pledges.[34] Hendler goes so far as to argue that 'Washingtonianism was the first massively popular movement organized around the experience of sympathy'; the movement was built around 'a compulsively repeated primal scene of tearful, sympathetic identification with another *man's* suffering'.[35] Clearly this would be a classic example of the sentimental mode of a 'spectacle of sympathy'. One can tentatively suggest, then, that while sentimentality has indeed frequently been *seen* as a feminine and a feminizing attribute, and may frequently have been stigmatized on this basis, so that Luc Boltanski can claim, in his historical account, that it is 'above all the feminisation of sentiment' which entails its discredit and the accusations of sentimentalism',[36] it has nevertheless at times been associated with *men*, and not *necessarily* in stigmatized contexts.[37] 'Sentimentality' is always a gendered label, but in ways that can complicate our understanding of gender itself.[38]

All this suggests that questions about the meaning and constitution of the sentimental become deeply entwined with its historical construction and reception, to the point where one can wonder, again, whether there is anything 'there' at all, beyond the problematical label and the battles around its use. We can pursue this more directly through the work of an artist whose changing fortunes exemplify these issues, namely Murillo.

The eye of the beholder

Starting life in late seventeenth-century Seville, a city in severe economic decline, where large masses of people had become dependent on the charity of powerful Catholic institutions – a theme reflected in Murillo's own portrayals of beggar boys and street urchins – a trickle of Murillo's paintings penetrated the English art market where they were seen as fitting well enough into the relatively secular atmosphere of the eighteenth century, influencing some of the leading painters, notably Gainsborough. After the Peninsular War, the trickle became a flood, and by the middle of the nineteenth century Murillo was well known, through reproductions, even in the parlours of middle-class homes. But the signs of trouble were already present. Mass reproductions were of poor quality, and too often indiscriminately mixed up with inferior imitators; and some of his own works were still being confused with those of Velázquez. Both factors counted against him with the art elite: as Velázquez's reputation rose, Murillo's declined, and has never recovered, even though reproductions of his work on cards, posters, even wallpaper, were still selling well even into the 1920s. But it is above all for one reason that this undoubtedly very skilful artist remains out in the cold: his alleged sentimentality.

A Murillo Madonna – and there are certainly plenty of them – has two immediately apparent features: a beauty that tends towards a certain sweetness; and a naturalism that makes it abundantly clear that, as with his genre portraits of children, they are based on real-life models, real women. As for the latter, it is rather unusual in religious painting, as it plays down the iconographic typification that has been taken as an essential requirement within the traditions of the ecclesiastical framework of sponsorship, in favour of expressions and gestures that situate the person in ways that bear the hallmark of what we have come to see as 'individual personality'. Whatever their traditional trappings, those Madonnas do not point us 'beyond', towards the transcendental; rather, they emphasize the manifestation of the transcendental in the here and now, in the embodied materiality of that specific person. This is not body transfigured by spirit, already rising towards the ethereal, but spirit as immanent in the very materiality of the body; it is the very definition of the modern person, the self 'in' the body. As Suzanne Stratton-Pruitt puts it, when Murillo was regarded in England as the greatest Spanish painter, it was because 'his religious narratives had an immediacy, a genre like quality, a feeling of everyday reality',[39] and Xanthe Brooke adds that in the eighteenth century his images appealed through the combination of sentiment and naturalism, 'perfectly adapted to a secularized Anglican audience'.[40] Murillo's art prefigures, as much as it embodies, this momentous shift, the onset of the modern conception of the individual; and it is this that makes possible his seamless incorporation in the structure of feeling we know as 'sensibility'. And here, the combination of naturalism with sweetness is significant: these are young women who could be appropriate objects of love, and it was indeed the eighteenth century that put the modern ideal of love, as a secularization of spiritual love, individualized into an affective tie between two specific persons, on to the social and cultural agenda of the modern age.

If we move more specifically to the childhood scenes, the depictions of urchins and their games, and their (unsurprising) obsession with acquiring and consuming food, we can perhaps suggest that spiritualism is mediated into naturalism via purity, and purity is *not*, in this context, a matter of perfect behaviour, elevated thoughts and sexual abstinence. Rather, it is about a certain kind of naturalness, of 'innocence' coded as naturalness, again prefiguring a staple of Enlightenment views of childhood: the Christ child thereby mediated, through naturalistic depiction, into images of real children. Of one of his paintings, Peter Cherry suggests that 'the infant Christ is no mere ideal cipher but seems endowed with an individual character',[41] and his portrayals of familial domestic contentment reinforce this. And whereas, in the case of the Madonna, such 'innocence' is likely to be represented in terms of a certain sweetness, in the case of children this can well be complemented by playfulness, even mischievousness, without contradicting this allegorical residue of the sacred. These elements are present, for example, in *Invitation to a Game of Argolla*, one of the most widely reproduced of Murillo's images in the nineteenth century, turning up on postcards and wallpaper designs.

For all this to work, both the naturalism and the hint of the sacred have to be present together; yet the sacred, as manifest only in and through the innocence of the ordinary, the humdrum, the everyday, can simultaneously hint at its absence, at its withdrawal as a transcendent source of power or signification – and this, in turn, adds an element of nostalgia, a sense of 'homeliness' as an origin that may need to be precariously recreated in the permanent context of its own threatened disappearance. By the nineteenth century, then, for many of the more militant or avant-garde secularists, any religion is too much, and the sweetness and light a distraction from the imperatives of a hard-nosed realism, just as for Victorian evangelicalism the naturalism was too gritty, even vulgar, swamping the religious pretensions altogether. The possibility of viewing Murillo's paintings as revealing the historical, constitutive *components* of the sentimental, rather than as being 'sentimental' *in themselves*, is thus lost.

So far, then, one might say that there is plenty here to indicate the possibility of the sentimental, but nothing to *necessitate* invoking it. The very variation in the historical reception of these pictures suggests that if they can be read as sentimental, they can equally be read as only mildly so, or not as sentimental at all; commenting on Gainsborough's paintings that include children, Ann Bermingham contrasts 'the sweet, wistful sentiment' of the children with 'the more robust expressions' of Murillo's.[42] Only an age hostile to *any* expression of sentiment would insist on denouncing Murillo's pictures as 'sentimental'. The label would be merely an indication of our unease with the display of feeling, nothing more. So far, then, sentimentalism is in effect constituted by our own denunciation – with the corollary that those who complain loudest about it are contributing most to spreading it.

We must, however, return to the sunny aspects, the sweetness – for these do indeed seem to be central to Murillo's art. There are, in particular, a lot of smiles.

Bartolomé Esteban Murillo, *Invitation to a Game of Argolla* (c. 1670) London, Dulwich Art Gallery

Cherry writes, of the smile, that it has been 'long regarded as the most difficult expression to catch';[43] and there is certainly a case for arguing that Murillo catches it better than anyone. We would all like to believe that a spontaneous human smile is possible and that, as such, it would constitute a 'natural' signifier of fundamental goodwill or goodness, hence manifesting an immediacy of feeling that can simultaneously count as morally expressive. As a test case for human sentiment, for spontaneous joy or pleasure with a hint of benevolence, the smile constitutes a grounding for the possibility of any community based on 'natural feeling'. A more cynical age, attuned to the possibility of deception and manipulation, to the artificial shaping of even the most apparently 'natural', may understandably distrust all this, even to the point of doubting its possibility, in which case Murillo's art becomes complicit with a pattern of assumptions readily dismissed as 'sentimental'. And we again encounter that assumption, a dual legacy of Romanticism and modernism, that art should involve the serious, the difficult, the challenging: it should be hard work, bracing, for artist and viewer alike. In the end, art revolves around forms of suffering. Murillo is too easy, too mired in 'superficial' emotions, in happiness and the sentimental. Murillo is a problem because he reflects the limitations of our own assumptions back at us, in a way that actually reinforces their hold.

A further point is made by Pérez Sánchez. He refers to the 'joyful, warm component' in Murillo's genre scenes, usually incorporating a laugh or a smile, and adds that they 'offer a vision that is like a snapshot of something about to happen whose meaning and subsequent unfolding is only implicit, so that it is our gaze that completes it'. Hence, he concludes, the 'joy of life which becomes contagious and engages the sympathy [affection] of the spectator'.[44] This is, indeed, a feature of many of these paintings: they seem to reach out to us, they seek to incorporate us in a relationship, a community, through a figure depicted as addressing us, or looking at us. This can incorporate – but is not reducible to – an invitation to sympathetic engagement in the narrower sense, invoking the kind of sympathy that could lead to making charitable donations. But, once again, this means that we are running up against another strong modernist dictum: that of the autonomy of the artwork, its self-contained self-sufficiency – in particular, in the strong hint of an emotional involvement at the level of demonstrative feeling, rather than interior appreciation, self-transformation by being 'moved' internally, which again conjures up the evil demon of the sentimental.

Hence, by the mid-nineteenth century, with sentimentality strongly established in Victorian culture, but also increasingly stigmatized, as vulgar, feminine, overflowing proper boundaries, and therefore endangering good taste and fine art, the scene was set for the increasing denigration of Murillo's work, just as this work forces us to confront the uncertainties of sentimentalism's own boundaries and the importance of the ascription of the label as a move in the cultural politics of the modern age. The issues raised here – the relation between affective involvement and contemplative or reflexive detachment, and the further relation between sympathetic engagement and the sense of belonging – remain central to our understanding of the whole place of 'sentiment' both in art and in social life. But to pursue a discussion of sentimentalism itself, we need to plunge into what would more clearly count as key exemplars.

The sentimental at home

The sphere of the sentimental situates the person as 'subject of affect', encompassing intimate (romantic, familial, domestic) contacts and situations, and thereby setting up a dynamic of presence and absence, fullness and loss, linked through desire, hope, or anguish. To sentimentalize – however distant the object – is to 'bring home', bring into affective proximity to the subject. The 'homely' has a simultaneously spatial and affective sense; it refers to wherever I feel 'at ease', relaxed, off duty. Home is a place where the self spreads itself, unguarded; it is not unbounded, but its boundaries diffuse outwards; and the boundaries between the self and those persons or things felt to be closely related become more fluid and flexible. (This is, in effect, a less loaded version of the description given at the beginning of this chapter.) In this sense, the homely is fundamental to our experience of identity, of selfhood and relationship, but in this distinctively diffuse and unfocused way; it thereby exists as a contrast to an equally important mode of selfhood, more bracing, concentrated, focused, self-consciously rational, project-oriented.

To bring out these points, and some of their wider ramifications, we can take two classic texts of literary sentimentalism, roughly contemporary: from the more political end of the spectrum, Stowe's *Uncle Tom's Cabin* (1852), and the more apparently lightweight but, in its own way, just as moralistic *A Christmas Carol* by Dickens (1843). Both have not only been widely read on their own account, but have subsequently produced a long string of souvenirs, plays, assorted spectacles and films, becoming firmly embedded in the traditions of popular culture.[45] It is hardly surprising that the most intensive investments of the sentimental in *Uncle Tom's Cabin* involve recurrent arrivals at, returns to or simply being present in, the home;[46] and much the same is true of the domestic scenes in *A Christmas Carol*, very similar in tone.[47] Conversely, Uncle Tom's arrival at the slave-owner Legree's estate[48] – the 'home' that is the antithesis of a true home – exudes a similarly powerful but wholly negative affect, as indeed does Scrooge's return, on Christmas Eve, to his 'gloomy suite of rooms, in a lowering pile of building up a yard', with their darkness and coldness reflecting the state of the soul of their owner.[49] Places exude feelings, just as surely as people experience them; but this is because 'place' and 'person' become indissolubly linked in the image and fantasy of the home, where even the most ordinary and menial tasks or objects can be ennobled and purified in the light of the sentimental.

What we encounter here, then, is what Lori Merish describes as 'a model of sentimental possession that both animates objects and constitutes sentimental subjects'.[50] And we can cite Stowe herself, who writes elsewhere of the way things in domestic spaces come to life and 'have a sort of human vitality in them'; they express 'homeliness'.[51] Even the furniture comes alive. In the Quaker household, we encounter a rocking-chair, 'motherly and old, whose wide arms breathed hospitable invitation, seconded by the solicitations of its feather cushions'.[52] This is a good example of what Merish appropriately christens 'sentimental animism'.[53] And this 'homeliness' is manifest in a sense of fecundity, of abundance, both of household commodities and of 'good feeling'. Now, food itself can be supremely expressive of all these domestic (and maternal) virtues, and the form of sentimental animism appropriate to food would seem to be that it evince its own need to be consumed. And so indeed it does. In the Quaker household, at breakfast time, there was 'good fellowship' everywhere, and 'the chicken and ham had a cheerful and joyous fizzle in the pan, as if they rather enjoyed being cooked than otherwise'.[54] In a parallel fashion, we find ourselves, in *A Christmas Carol*, among the happy but busy Christmas shoppers, in a fruit shop, where the apples, 'in the great compactness of their juicy persons' were 'urgently entreating and beseeching to be carried home in paper bags and eaten after dinner'. A few sentences later, in an intriguing formulation, we learn that 'the blended scents of tea and coffee were so grateful to the nose';[55] here, an uncommon usage of 'grateful' (whereby objects are 'pleasing') is subtly used to convey a hint of the more frequent usage, so that the objects again appear to take on animate attributes. And these particular objects demand to be *bought*, to be 'consumed' in the commercial sense before they can be 'consumed' organically. As we will see, sentimentalizing the market and marketing sentimentality can easily slide together.

In such environments, suggests Merish, one can encounter 'a deepening of sympathy through the revelation of mutual vulnerability and imperfection',[56] but this is not to deny that issues of conflict and power are raised. Drawing on writings on domestic economy of the time, as well as *Uncle Tom's Cabin*, Lynn Wardley observes the 'middle-class preoccupation with the civilizing mother and the spirit of the house'; her own conclusion is that 'the aesthetics of sentiment survives in Stowe's fiction as a stratagem for redressing the asymmetries of cultural power'.[57] Exploring the relation between abolitionist political goals and domestic values, Sánchez-Eppler argues that the wider context of these 'asymmetries' makes the political project of sentimentalist abolitionism inherently problematical. Abolitionist fiction purports to offer values based on domestic sentimentalism in order to critique slavery, but the problem is that 'these standards are implicated in the values and structures of authority and profit they seek to criticize'.[58] This is certainly true – how could it be otherwise? – but the outlines of an arena of oppositional sentimental values and practices are not hard to find. There is a recalcitrance about this arena; it is not easy to impose order on it, to subordinate it to conventionally rational imperatives. Attempting to do this can provoke resistance or a sense of futility – or both – and this is most notably apparent in Miss Ophelia's doomed efforts in the St Clare household, where the zone of the domestic is the zone both of the feminine and of the slave, and where Dinah's alternative dis/order proves more than a match for her.[59] This may be true more generally, in that this zone of 'sentimental autonomy' conveys a sense that 'affective efficiency' is more to do with habit, eclecticism, contingency and tolerance than with more obviously 'rationalist' values and practices. Wardley is right to imply that Stowe develops an implicit critique of the aesthetic practices of rational modernism and, as part of this, seeks 'to recuperate the decorative as an instrument of feminine influence'.[60]

In order to clarify the moral imperatives of all this, it is worth returning to the issues raised in relation to consumerism and the market. In her discussion of Stowe, coming from a broadly Marxist perspective, Merish refers to a 'bourgeois discourse of sentimental proprietorship' and points to the 'humanizing exchanges between the material and the affectional that sentimental consumption both promises and promotes'.[61] It certainly seems fair to point to homologies between domestic and wider public networks of circulation here. The conclusion drawn by Sánchez-Eppler, on the basis of her study of child mortuary photographs, seems very pertinent: 'If commodification exploits feelings to yield profit, it is equally possible for emotions to use the commercial as a means of expression and a form of circulation.'[62] In *A Christmas Carol*, too, the whole language of sympathetic engagement with others is the language of consumption, of objects become commodities. Nevertheless, these parallels must not be pushed too far, and we can bring out some of the tensions here by examining the case of Scrooge in a bit more depth.

Scrooge's problem is that he is too self-enclosed; he lacks 'spirit', embodied in the parallel worlds of circulating phantoms and circulating commodities that tie people together through gestures of sympathy. 'Spirit', claims Audrey Jaffe, thus names 'an inexhaustible fund of sympathetic capital'. And the manifestation of his 'cure', at the end, is that he is now, suddenly, everywhere, dispensing *bonhomie* and goodwill in all directions. 'The gift is a visible manifestation of spirit ...', as Jaffe puts it.[63] But 'gift' and 'capital' do not exist together quite so harmoniously. Gifts dispensed *as* gifts subtract from the circulation of money and capital used 'productively' to generate further capital, but thereby gain *moral* efficacy. After all, Marley's Ghost explains that if spirit 'goes not forth in life, it is condemned to do so after death', when it is 'doomed to wander ... and witness what it cannot share, but might have shared on earth, and turned to happiness!'.[64] Hell is the eternal anguish of witnessing need that one could have helped relieve, and can no longer. The 'real' spirit is the spirit of the gift; the spirit of commodity circulation is only a pale reflection. Yet the text suggests the ultimate impossibility of emancipating good deeds from the nexus of commodity exchange that nevertheless *also* reinforces the need for such behaviour in the first place. The intensity of the sentimental vision of plenitude cannot displace its simultaneous insufficiency, just as it reinforces the impetus for the vision to be constantly replenished. And all this has a significant moral for sentimental homeliness: this is not about being self-contained, self-sufficient, complacent; it must be outward-looking, expansive, incorporative. There must always be room for guests, for good deeds, for a welcome to the needy other – as there always is, in both these texts, thus exhibiting some of the conditions under which a 'spectacle of sympathy' can emerge.

By contrast, we can throw further light on all this by considering the 'unhomely'. As remarked above, Legree's home is most definitely not homely. Indeed, he used it, like everything else, merely as an 'implement for money-making'. We also learn that Legree, 'like most godless and cruel men', was superstitious. To be 'godless' is still to inhabit the sacred, in its antithesis; it is by no means to escape it. And consequently, his home now becomes even more 'unhomely': 'ghostly legends were uncommonly rife, about this time, among the servants on Legree's place'. We have entered the realm of the uncanny, the unhomely in the homely. And there is a particular object, or token, that carries this symbolic load. When a scrap of paper is handed to him, out of it falls a 'long, shining curl of fair hair – hair which, like a living thing, twined itself round Legree's fingers'. This lock of Little Eva's hair, which Tom had kept tied around his neck as one of his most treasured sentimental possessions – possessions of the kind the unsentimental Legree had thrown out as mere 'trifles' – and which was originally a gift of protective love, has now turned into something feared, into witchcraft, a malevolent power, a 'devilish thing': 'sentimental animism' returning with a vengeance ... And Legree is doubly cursed. This has happened before: a lock of his mother's hair, sent from her deathbed, too, had 'twined about his fingers'.[65] And he had burnt it. On its return, as the sentimental turned uncanny, devilish, its power is redoubled by his betrayal of Little Eva's gift to Tom. And it is *female* hair, as if female hair, shorn and distributed just before death, becomes alive, powerful or empowering, for good or evil.[66]

What comes into focus here, then, is both the intense moralism of the sentimental universe, but also its perhaps unexpected kinship with the uncanny. While there are significant differences between these texts – *Uncle Tom's Cabin* is embedded in a deeply Christian world view, whereas *A Christmas Carol* manages to appear strikingly secular, even though the ghosts clearly imply an afterlife and some notion of hell – there is a similarity not only in the intensity of the moral imperative, but in the aesthetics of the imagination in both texts, manifest in their intensely visual quality, their pictorialism. And this is worth lingering over, as this pictorialism resonates with the spirit of the sentimental. In the former case, visions, dreams, premonitions, feature extensively – and these are not clearly differentiated, either from each other, or from the 'real'. They may, indeed, be experienced as intensely real. At the religious pole, for example, we find Tom, in his hour of deepest despair, being granted a vision of the face of Christ on the cross, a transfiguring experience which leaves him renewed and reinvigorated, able to go forward willingly to his fate. But we also find Eliza, in her secure retreat in the Quaker settlement, having a dream in which she and her child are reunited with her husband, only to find, on waking, that it was 'real': her husband is by her side.[67]

In the other text, we encounter Scrooge looking through a window to find that the window both provides access to another, ghostly, reality – 'The air was filled with phantoms, wandering hither and thither in restless haste, and moaning as they went' – and that it also *frames* that reality, captures it as picture. But earlier, Scrooge had himself been framed, fixed in a picture: we learn that the 'gruff old bell' of a nearby church was 'always peeping slily down at Scrooge out of a Gothic window in the wall'.[68] If he subsequently lives in the world of representations provided by his ghostly escorts, he has already been positioned there anyway. So it is not surprising that Scrooge can 'lose' himself so readily in the reality of the visions he is shown, for it is also true that he 'finds' himself there; the uncertain status of this 'other' world of representations does not in any way compromise, but rather facilitates, his dawning capacity for sympathetic engagement (as we saw earlier, in the mourner's relation to Diana). So Jaffe can argue that 'The reality Dickens re-presents is, thus, already encoded as spectacle'. And clearly it is a spectacle in which the spectres of Scrooge's own past play a crucial part: 'In several ways, then, the story ties the ability to sympathize with images to the restoring of a past self to presence.'[69] If this 'past self' is initially engaged in the register of the uncanny, it is ultimately recovered, comprehensively enough, in the sentimental.

Each of these scenes is also a tableau, a picture for the reader, transforming narrative scene into pictorial scenario. Both texts are full of these, reaching their most intense form in the household scenarios of domesticity, the sentimental theatre *par excellence*, where 'home' in all its manifestations is lovingly displayed before our eyes, the minutely detailed descriptions threatening to burst through or overflow their frames, in the excess of their plenitude. And in *A Christmas Carol* it is the ghosts themselves who organize the tableaux, of past, present and future, tableaux which gain so strong a hold on our imagination of the real that the intervening narrative flits by as quickly and spectrally as the ghosts do, on their wanderings. Although she is writing of the eighteenth century, particularly with reference to the painter Greuze, Emma Barker's definition of 'tableau' seems entirely appropriate here: 'a pictorial device that arrests time by isolating the key features of the narrative for contemplation … the tableau's function is to condense the underlying emotional truth of a given situation and thereby allow it to discharge its full affective power.'[70]

There is, indeed, a distinctive relation to the experience of time here. The passage of time, linear time, collapses into presence, experienced as intensified immediacy. This is most dramatically the case for Scrooge. His travels in time, into past, present and future, all involve travel to other places, sometimes far away, so it is already extraordinary that these supposedly take place over just three successive nights; yet we then learn that they actually take place, in 'real' time, in just *one* night. These phantasmatic experiences of the self occur out of time, just as they must return to it. And what they return to has been reconstructed: the future has opened out, freed from the endless oppressive repetitions of 'time enslaved'. So, for Scrooge, 'the Time before him was his own, to make amends in!'[71] And for Eliza and George, time is freedom, too, to make their new life in Canada. Freedom from enslaved time is not freedom from all temporal repetitions and cycles; purposive projects, often centred on the individual, will unavoidably be embedded in 'sentimental time', the presence of the 'eternal in the homely', as an essential – if often unacknowledged – presupposition of the modern cultural imaginary. And if this may involve elements of fantasy and illusion, so does the idea of freedom as the escape from all preconditions and constraints. Time flattened, past or future made vividly present, the time of image as picture, in the moment of the imaginative grasp, which can carry a dramatic affective power: this is sentimental time, loss resolved or denied, absence rendered into presence.

At this point, the sentimental and the uncanny can touch each other. The whole spectrum of visual experiences, from Scrooge's phantoms to Uncle Tom's visions, involve tableaux of the self, its projections, figurations and involvements; and these can as easily strike us as disturbing as redemptive. If the uncanny finds the unhomely in the homely, the sentimental will always find the homely in the unhomely; however distant, however 'other', anything can be sentimentalized. This is what can be both fascinating and disturbing about it. And just as the self can waver uncertainly in its status here, so can the objects it confronts in the world; the uncanny de-materialization of the subject goes hand in hand with an uncanny fetishism of the object, linked, in the domestic context, to a simultaneous sentimentalism.

The sentimental universe

An important part of the background of all this is the problematical history of modernity in its relation to the sacred, a history that can by no mean be seen simply as the decline and fall of the latter. The Christian religion has certainly proved readily compatible with the development of sentimentalism, *Uncle Tom's Cabin* of course being the classic example. Something of the problems this can pose for the non-religious reader is brought out in the following passage from Jane Tompkins, describing the typological narrative typical of the novel. She suggests that truths:

> can only be reembodied, never discovered, because they are already revealed from the beginning. Therefore, what seem from a modernist point of view to be gross stereotypes in characterization and a needless proliferation of incident, are essential properties of a narrative aimed at demonstrating that human history is a continual re-enactment of the sacred drama of redemption ... its characters, like the figures in an allegory, do not change or develop, but reveal themselves in response to the demands of a situation.[72]

Thus, everything has its place. Take the death of St Clare.[73] It is an accident, the result of a meaningless act of violence: he was in the wrong place at the wrong time. Yet it is, also, *not* a meaningless accident. It is deeply expressive, of his character, and of his part in the unfolding drama of Tom's death and redemption. He has been well-intentioned, but effete, ineffectual; he was going to set Tom free, but hadn't got around to it – so Tom is doomed. Sentimentalism here reveals an expressive totality, in which object or event can be read as inherently, 'naturally', signifying. That this can also apply in more obviously secular contexts is suggested by Roland Barthes in his discussion of the lover. For the 'amorous subject', he writes, a fact about the beloved is transformed into a sign, and 'it is the sign, not the fact, which is consequential'.[74] And since, for someone outside the relationship, or for the non-sentimentalist generally, this link is necessarily going to appear arbitrary, rather than inherent and necessary, it invites 'corrosive irony', as Jonathan Culler puts it. In Culler's discussion, we find modernity characterized both by this ironic anti-sentimentalism while simultaneously 'the sacred has become practically submerged by the sentimental'.[75]

Ordinary tasks, objects, situations: all can be invested with the aura whereby sacramental can become sentimental. At the same time, this transfiguration works in two directions, and the way these operate together takes us into the heart of the sentimental universe. There is the process of transcendence, purification, pointing outside and beyond the materiality of the body; but this is paradoxically located *in* the body, which is thereby simultaneously positioned as *abject*. In effect, this is a modern transformation of the Christian mystery of the Incarnation; and indeed, one could suggest that the survival and intermittent resurgence of religion in modernity may be as much a reflection of this purification/abjection dynamic in relation to the modern body as it is a source of it. Immersion in abjection reveals a fascination with the otherness of the body in the all-too-physical reality of flesh and pain. There is a bringing-near, a vicarious identification with the fundamental realities of the body from which the self normally exiles itself. So at this pole, sentimentalism is a mode of involvement in the very otherness of the unacceptable, abject self: distance-in-proximity, emotional involvement with boundaries that are threatened but not ultimately subverted. Sentimentalism thus involves abjection as projection into the other, vicarious identification with the normally proscribed dimensions of modern identity, the body in its materiality – from tears to pain – challenging cultural appropriation through its very excess. For Little Eva, suggests Athena Vrettos, 'there is a moral imperative to feel pain when confronted with pain and a hermeneutic imperative to suffer in relation to stories of suffering'.[76] And

Marianne Noble sees this as central to the promise of sentimentalism, which 'does not simply idealize the compassionate observation of another; it offers an intuitive and visceral understanding of the other's fear and anguish'.[77]

There is, indeed, a history here, a recurrent history of the modern body, crucially positioned as the public face of the civilizing process, yet distrusted, controlled, always excessive, perpetually a threat to 'reason'. And this body as other, as rejected, can also be coded as maternal, the site of originating differentiation. In her thoughtful exploration of the relations between sentimentalism, modernism and feminism, Suzanne Clark points out that 'the process of delineating borders between an undifferentiated self and the maternal other is marked by horror and disgust',[78] linking this to the 'purification' of reason during the eighteenth-century Enlightenment and subsequently. Here, Clark draws on Julia Kristeva's concept of abjection, as 'What does not respect borders, positions, rules. The in-between, the ambiguous, the composite.'[79] What is 'abjected' cannot simply be ejected; it remains uneasily present or nearby, threatening precarious boundaries, treacly …

Out of the eighteenth century emerge both the abject and the sublime (only the latter being theorized explicitly at the time). These are, on the face of it, polar opposites that nonetheless can be seen to feed off each other; indeed, Kristeva claims that 'The abject is edged with the sublime'.[80] And this feeds into the sentimental. So, on the one hand, sentimental expression displays 'a rupture of narration by static tableaux evoking the melancholy and the sublime', as Clark puts it, while on the other it 'participates in the psychology of abjection'.[81] Both the sublime and the sentimental can indeed be said to involve the 'submission response', the sense of being overwhelmed. Nevertheless, the differences here are just as important. While both the sublime and the sentimental entail proximity to the other, to ensure engagement, the sublime maximizes distance (proximity-in-distance), to encounter the other in all its immensity and majesty, the sentimental minimizes it (distance-in-proximity), to explore the other in its fellow-suffering. Both must maintain the boundaries of the self, to make the experience possible; but the sublime tests them, strengthens them, through a bracing, strenuous encounter, whereas sentimentalism relaxes them, seeking a 'letting go', an emptying-out of the self that threatens its boundaries. The adventures of the sublime, of the self in its integrity, give priority to imagination and reason; the sentimental is more body-focused, exploring imagination and feeling through emotional discharge. Although the shared 'submission response' complicates this, the sublime is more readily encoded as masculine, the sentimental, feminine.

In the light of all this, and discussing rationalist-oriented critiques, Clark makes the interesting claim that 'Reasonable histories have produced the sentimental retroactively as the effect of their judgments about emotion in discourse, and their efforts to eject it'.[82] We can perhaps place this alongside Kristeva's suggestion that 'I expel *myself*, I spit *myself* out, I abject *myself* with the same motion through which "I" claim to establish *myself*'.[83] Taken together – relating the abject to the sentimental – these could imply that abjection could be said to exist on two levels. At the first level, abjection is a response to the projection of self into the alienated body figured as other; at the second level, abjection responds to this first level of involvement by spitting out the complicit embodied self that – despite 'itself' – was 'moved' in the initial sentimental response. This second level, then, corresponds to the stigmatization of the sentimental that is, as we have seen, a powerful influence in modern culture, and hence in our own individual feelings and attitudes as well.

And then, the other pole, the purification and idealization of the self – in some cases, through death. We can recall Sedgwick's claims for the sentimental potency of images of the crucified Christ in modern culture.[84] The person who looks at these images of the redemption of the abject body, the body transfigured even *in* its suffering, can engage emotionally with these images, become purified, redeemed, rendered 'whole' through this vicarious experience of suffering. The scenario of Tom's vision dramatizes this, telescoping the process: Christ's face first reveals pain and anguish, but then comes radiance ('the sharp thorns became rays of glory'). This has a direct impact not only on Tom's spirit, but its effects can also be *seen*, in his body: 'All noticed the change in his appearance.'[85] And of course the Virgin Mary can be a potent focus for the love/loss dynamic, in her capacity as *mater dolorosa*, figuring our own losses, whether of mother or lover, with the added potential of nostalgia and its promise of vicarious resolution-in-recollection (in contrast to the return of an unresolved, unquiet past, in the uncanny).

To return to the abjection dimension: how is it manifested, what is its mark? The idea of the *wound* can be invoked here. For Noble, the 'sentimental wound' is 'a bodily experience of anguish caused by identification with the pain of another', and she reveals its workings in *Uncle Tom's Cabin*. Here, it implies a critique of disembodied, abstract notions of person and identity: knowledge comes *through* the body, not despite it. For example, Stowe appeals directly to her readers, reminding them of the anguish of separation, particularly from dead children; she 'thrusts into readers' pre-existing wounds', ruthlessly seeking to produce sympathetic feeling despite or across boundaries of gender, class and race.[86]

For Barthes, sentimentality presents itself as a language of the body in its immediacy, as the wound of the suffering subject,[87] but it is in relation to photography that he develops these ideas most extensively. He explains that, as a spectator, 'I was interested in Photography only for "sentimental" reasons; I wanted to explore it not as a question (a theme) but as a wound ...'. When a picture 'works', it pierces him like an arrow, and 'these marks, these wounds' are what makes the picture's appeal sentimental, personal to him, incommunicable – and, for him, it is particularly a lost picture of his mother that has had this effect. 'For you', he writes, addressing the reader – that sentimental gambit again – 'it would be nothing but an indifferent picture ... In it, for you, no wound.'[88] The wound opens up a gap in the self, a gap towards the other that promises a communication it may not be able to deliver. And this wound may well be a foundation of the 'culture of trauma', to be explored later, locking us together in communities of mutual inaccessibility, frantically trying to construct identity out of what separates us ....

Hints at another dynamic here are implied in Noble's observation that, at the climax of *Uncle Tom's Cabin*, 'wounding is so intimately linked with desire that torture seems to express longing and intensity of imagined pleasure more than it does literal physical agony'.[89] Eroticism is, after all, in some sense heir to the sacred, and the pleasures of vicarious identification with abjection as pain or suffering can take on darker hues. Masochism and sentimentalism are culturally and historically linked. One can point to a range of influences here: the construction of the body as alien, subordinate, dirty, in need of domination; the work ethic, asceticism, self-sacrifice; ethereal femininity as ideal, purified, abstracted from the body; and the resultant fantasies of martyrdom, fulfilment through suffering, the paradoxical quest to escape the body through bodily excess.[90] Both masochism and sentimentalism could be said to converge in a search for plenitude, for ecstatic union through pain. Some of the best-selling novels of the nineteenth century exemplify Tompkins's claim that 'Learning to renounce her own desire is the sentimental heroine's vocation ...',[91] such renunciation sliding readily into a yearning for submission to domination, with more than a hint of the sexual humiliation/pleasure dynamic of *The Story of O*.[92] And, whether as fantasy or practice, this can of course readily enough swing over to the sadism pole. Nor can the reader escape getting enmeshed in this sado-masochistic potential. Leo Bersani argues that sympathetic involvement implies these illicit pleasures, hence 'the risk in all sympathetic projections: the pleasure that accompanies them promotes a secret attachment to scenes of suffering or violence'.[93] Whether this risk is actually or necessarily *realized* is an issue to return to; but it is certainly inherent, as risk, in the spectacle of sympathy.

On the one hand, then, we find these tableaux and the spectacles in which they are embedded – spectacles which imply a certain distance from the reader or viewer: 'Spectacle depends on a distinction between vision and participation, a distance that produces desire in a spectator', as Jaffe suggests.[94] Yet, on the other, the whole drift of sentimentalism seems to go against this. Solomon notes that, for its critics, sentimentalism is objectionable precisely because it 'violates the reader's sense of self by provoking these unwelcome emotional intrusions at an intensity that cannot be controlled'.[95] In her study of anti-slavery fiction, Sánchez-Eppler argues that:

> Sentiment and feeling refer at once to emotion and to physical sensation, and in sentimental fiction these two versions of *sentire* blend as the eyes of readers take in the printed word and blur it with tears. Reading sentimental fiction is thus a bodily act, and the success of a story is gauged, in part, by its ability to translate words into pulse beats and sobs. This physicality of the reading experience radically contracts the distance between narrated events and the moment of their reading, as the feelings in the story are made tangibly present in the flesh of the reader.[96]

This hints that the sentimental is the sensational mode of the spectacle of sympathy, a 'contagion of tears' washing over the distinction between the two bodies of text and reader. Barker concludes, in turn, that 'The sentimental aesthetic is thus communicative, its fundamental aim being to dissolve the barriers between the work of art and the observing subject, between fiction and reality'. And, both for the Enlightenment tableau and for the nineteenth-century anti-slavery novels, there was intended to be a moral impetus to all this: 'the tableau holds out the possibility that the entire human species can be united in virtue ... a perfect communion of innocent hearts',[97] and, for Sánchez-Eppler, 'The tears of the reader are pledged in these sentimental stories as a means of rescuing the bodies of slaves'.[98]

There are two issues here: the relation between the work of art, or the situation, and the response of the spectator; and the implications of the latter for our sense of the moral and political implications of sentimentalism. As for the first: is the reader or observer a witness, or a protagonist? The resolution of this dilemma involves going decisively for the witness option, and suggesting that sentimentalism *intensifies* this sense of being a witness, and hence *involved* as a witness, yet necessarily 'outside', and therefore unable to affect events. It does this by piling on the emotional pressure, hence *forcing* the witness to respond emotionally precisely because – given the distance – no other response is possible. It is as though sentimentalism pushes the witness position to the limit: any gap that remains – and there always *is* a gap – is excessive, and 'excess' is what flows in to bridge the unbridgeable. One distinctive way this is brought about is by direct authorial appeals (particularly frequent in the case of *Uncle Tom's Cabin*, as has been seen). And if this works, it does so precisely through the vicarious identification-in-distance that has been discussed above ('how would you feel if …?'); and hence the process whereby witness becomes – vicariously – protagonist.

As for the second issue, the 'unity in virtue' is only possible initially as a vicarious sense of community-through-witness; this immediacy of response, as passivity, necessarily produces its own gap, a momentary interregnum before there can be action, or the affirmation of moral commitment that could lead to it. This need not inhibit such action or commitment, but it may do so, as it opens up the possibility that the former could *substitute* for the latter, by producing its own self-satisfaction through the feeling of virtue itself. 'Feeling good' could provide its own sufficient motivation, subtly supplanting 'doing good'. This again revisits the terrain of earlier controversies around sentimentalism, and will necessitate a more thorough examination of the cultural politics of 'sympathy', in due course.

The concept of the vicarious has been used extensively here, and giving it some more explicit attention, particularly in relation to spectacle, may help clarify all this. For Sedgwick, sentimentality is not so much a distinctive subject matter as 'a structure of relation, typically one involving the author – or audience – relations of spectacle', and she argues that vicariousness is crucial to this.[99] Ellison observes that the term 'vicarious' itself has theological, political and psychological dimensions, in that it 'links the notion of the vicar, or surrogate (as in Christ the vicar) to long-distance, virtual, or figurative identifications between self and other'.[100] In elaborating these links between vicarious involvement and the audience–spectacle relation, Tan and Frijda argue that sentimentality 'tends to be associated with the response to cultural products rather than real-life situations', an interesting point that seems to be in some tension with a later comment, in the context of discussing sentimentality in film:

Film-elicited emotion … consists largely of *witness emotions*. That is, the major affects in film viewing correspond to affects in daily life when we watch people to which we relate in one way or another, who are involved in an emotional situation, but under conditions in which we cannot act, be acted upon, or otherwise participate in the situation except as onlookers. We are concerned about their fate, but have to wait for the outcomes.[101]

Perhaps, in the light of the significance of the vicarious, we can resolve this by suggesting that indeed we can, of course, respond to real-life situations, but we do so *as if* they were in some sense cultural products. And this sense of participation in a sentimental spectacle of vicarious involvement, where the 'involvement' involves an inherent distance and an impotence, an inability to act, is central not just to understanding the nature of the reaction to Diana's death, but to the fundamentals of spectacular sentimentality more widely. Thus, we can follow Howard's suggestion that 'The vicariousness so often criticized in sentimentality is here more neutrally seen as one of its structural elements'.[102]

To conclude, we have seen that the sentimental seems to constitute an irreducible aspect of modern experience, a structure of feeling that can be defined through the simultaneous presence of the two poles of purification and transcendence, on the one hand, and pain and suffering, on the other, and that its manifestations of unconstrained feeling always render it liable to stigmatization and denunciation. In tracing out the ramifications of this, we have found the terrain to be criss-crossed by further tensions: between the visual, embodied in tableau, and narrative; between the spectral image and the material, embodied aspects of the self; and between the moral extremes, the melodrama, of good and evil. We have also seen that this terrain of the sentimental, which so intimately involves relations with the other, can itself only be approached through its relation to its own others, with which it overlaps and from which it is separated by fluctuating and uncertain boundaries: in particular, the abject, the uncanny and the sublime. Finally, the 'spectacle of sympathy' comes into focus as the framework through which there can be 'spectacular resolution' of these tensions – insofar as that is possible – just as it adds another element: that of an excess beyond representation, the affect that draws in the spectator, enforcing vicarious participation.

All this raises an important theme that has so far remained latent. Sentimentality, as a response, is characteristically precipitated by scenes of otherness, in relation to misfortune. This is not always true: it may be one's own sense of loss (or joy), in relation to oneself. Even here, though, it is as though it is the otherness to self that is involved, the imagined or remembered past, via loss or 'recovered presence'. In order to explore this engagement with the other, involving the response of sympathy, we need to open up the discussion of the latter; and to do that most effectively, we need to go back in time. It is to this task that we now turn.

3

Sensibility and Sympathy in the Theatre of Tears

Writing in 1790, Anne Radcliffe, the novelist of Gothic adventure fiction, offered this characterization of what she referred to as 'the sentimental', and which was also often referred to at the time as 'sensibility':

> Conversation may be divided into two classes – the familiar and the senti-mental. It is the province of the familiar, to diffuse cheerfulness and ease – to open the heart of man to man, and to beam a temperate sunshine upon the mind. – Nature and art must conspire to render us susceptible of the charms, and to qualify us for the practice of the second class of conversation ... To good sense, lively feeling, and natural delicacy of taste, must be united an expansion of mind, and a refinement of thought, which is the result of high cultivation ... In sentimental conversation, subjects interesting to the heart, and to the imagination, are brought forward; they are discussed in a kind of sportive way, with animation and refinement, and are never continued longer than politeness allows. Here fancy flourishes, – the sensibilities expand – and wit, guided by delicacy and embellished by taste – points to the heart.[1]

While this is ostensibly 'only' about conversation, it actually reveals this as an embodiment of a whole culture of sensibility, and hints at some of the accompanying tensions. To cut through the terminological complexities implicit here, and referred to in the Introduction, we can use 'sentimental' both as the adjective that can accompany 'sensibility', and as a problem term that can hint at the presence of a province of feeling not always easily contained within the latter. What seems to be suggested in this piece, then, is that a more 'cultivated' or 'refined' sensibility grows out of, and presupposes, a basic framework of social life that already permits or implies an 'open-hearted' involvement with others. Indeed, 'heart' occurs three times here: in the second and third cases, what 'interests' the heart contributes to 'expanding sensibilities', a process which works hand-in-hand with 'expansion of mind'. Sensibility is presented as a fusion of nature and art: nature as feeling, as the untutored potential that can be realized through art – both art in the form of paintings and novels that can represent this in concentrated or idealized fashion, and as the 'art of life', its 'cultivation' as 'taste'. We can say that as a structure of feeling, sensibility aspires to express nature, construed as 'the natural', a spontaneous language of gesture, passion and feeling; yet this goes hand in hand with an awareness that feeling, if it is to be expressed at all, necessarily calls on form, which must shape or structure it without betraying it, and the evident tension here is never really resolved, indeed it provides the energy that fuels the debates about the whole viability of 'sensibility' as a basis for a civilized social order. The expression of feeling needs to be artless if it is to be genuine, but such expression, in the very irreducibility of its element of cultural encoding, slides towards the artfulness of artifice.

As for nature transformed into an 'art of life', this seems here to involve a social framework of manners, of civility, manifested in a concern with performance and display. Feeling is always shaped and structured in some way. In practice then, writes Anne Vincent-Buffault, sensibility was 'not an unmastered expression of the body, it presented itself rather like an *art de vivre* which one should know how to follow while avoiding dangerous excesses'.[2] The ideal of sensibility is clearly that it manages to be both expressive of community, of 'open-hearted' relationship, and of the person; since sensibility is supposed to manifest itself in a person's 'quality', including the quality of interactions with others, so a social order of sensibility would manifest a combination of 'good manners' and benevolent behaviour towards the less fortunate.[3] And just as the relation to the 'suffering other' is the litmus test of 'real' quality here, so it highlights the problem of integrity and form: is 'demonstrating concern' a matter of displaying 'appropriate' feeling, or something more? There is always a risk – exhaustively explored in eighteenth-century fiction and theatre – that the suffering other will come to exist merely as a means for demonstrating the purity of feeling of the man or woman of feeling, the sentimental subject. Colin Campbell points to 'the tension which is bound to arise between being sensitive to the actual plight and real feelings of others, and being oneself susceptible to displays of intense emotion';[4] in effect, each of these can interfere with the other, a situation that constantly threatens to push sensibility into sentimentality, even though the latter merely displays the tension even more vividly. The alternative, which is to slide into restrained emotional display as mere propriety, 'correct form', threatens to lose the imperative to sensibility altogether.

'Sentimentalism', then, responds to the tension by intensifying it. The issue here, after all, is the public presentation of private feelings, and the significance attached to such inner states. Thus tears, for example, become indicators of 'heart', emotion, depth; they appear spontaneous, and this is how they 'ought' to be, in their cultural role as immediate manifestations of a person's 'sympathetic' quality; they signify 'letting go', being 'overwhelmed', dominance by the emotions, particularly those coded as 'uplifting'. And all this is, in turn, what exposes them to criticism for florid excess, indulgence, betrayal of true sensitivity, both because they involve a dangerous, irrational subordination to 'nature', *and* for the opposite reason – that they can be 'rehearsed', manipulated, not really spontaneous at all. The signified can become too 'natural', and the signifier too cultural, too artificial, a pretence rather than a true expression.

Yet these problems can be presented as their own – albeit always precarious – solution. If sensibility can only exist through display, if sympathy has to be shown as well as felt, suffering too exists as displayed, in 'scenes': in each case, there is an audience, hence spectators who are both at some distance yet are also *involved*. That this all entails an intense sense of a theatrical aspect of life, of life *as* theatre, is apparent enough in eighteenth-century texts. Hence the two, related dimensions of aesthetics come into their own here; for if 'sensibility' is itself an everyday aesthetic category, and raises issues of authenticity, of proximity, distance, and involvement, similarity and difference, in relation to the other, so these are raised also in the context of representation and narrative in art and literature – and the arts can be said to rehearse or anticipate, as much as reflect, this situation. This also implies a key role for the imagination. Feeling as response, and judgement as reflection, are brought into relation via imagination, indeed imagination *as* the simultaneous grasp and constitution of 'relation' itself, whether of body and mind, or self and other.

We can here rejoin sensibility itself: in summary, what could be said to be most distinctive about it, in this eighteenth-century context, is precisely that it expands the sense of 'feeling' to *incorporate* these other dimensions, giving the term a very broad sense – yet also raising the spectre of feeling in its narrower sense, the threat that it will sweep all before it, in turn provoking an 'othering' of the sentimental in a culture that nonetheless insistently produces and reproduces it, remaining insidiously attached to it.

But this is all very abstract. We will elucidate further by discussing two products of the time: a painting and a novel.

The grief of the prodigal son

Exhibited in 1778, we are told that 'all Paris' flocked to see the latest painting by Jean-Baptiste Greuze, *Le Fils puni*. It depicts the return of a prodigal son (doubtless the one shown being expelled from the domestic hearth in a picture a year earlier, *La Malédiction paternelle*) to the deathbed of his father, whose fate has, by implication, been brought about by grief at the son's wrongdoing.[5] The son is shown entering the room, appropriately grief-stricken, and there he finds the women and children of the household in postures of intense emotional display. Indeed, the viewer today may find rather too much display. The woman on the far side of the bed, with her arm stretched forward over the dead man's head, does not actually look at him (or us); she might seem to be more concerned to express her emotion in dramatic form than with the ostensible object of her grief. Actually, *nobody* looks at the father, or indeed at anyone else; the intensity of the emotional displays, while marking them as public, through the appropriateness-to-excess of the displays themselves, also marks them as private, self-centred, with each participant locked paradoxically in this shared universe of private sorrow. What David Denby writes of the literature of the time would seem to be just as apposite here: 'sentimental texts bear witness to the semi-public process whereby a new private space is defined'.[6]

It is the body, through its demonstrative gestural economy, that has to bear the full weight of signification: no words seem to be spoken. The woman who brings in the returning son says it all with her outstretched arms, displaying the results of his sin; words would have nothing to add. Ostensibly conveying truth, words betray it; the body, in its immediacy, can alone express it, through the very inarticulacy of its gestures, its involuntary expressions of pain and pleasure. And if, in the conventions of the time, this is coded as 'natural', a foundation of human solidarity in pre-verbal sympathetic response, we confront not only the paradox of the constitution of the self-centred individual facing the other, but also the endless doubling of nature *as* convention, the gestural as manifesting 'aesthetic form' – that reliance on expressiveness through convention that is likely to seem, to us today, so very *un*-natural, histrionic and manipulative. Hence James Elkins can say of a Greuze that it is 'an utterly sincere painting, and at the same time it is utterly contrived'.[7] Understanding how these opposed qualities can both be present reminds us of this key insight of sentimentalism: that feeling, however 'natural', stands in need of form, that it can only be manifested, shaped, through frames or conventions; and that any culture of sensibility that gives due weight to feeling and emotion both presupposes and

Jean-Baptiste Greuze, *Le Fils puni* (1778) Paris, Musée du Louvre

reproduces an 'aesthetics of community' through which paintings and texts can communicate their meanings, and their cultural power.

These aesthetic forms can, of course, shift. If Greuze, so influential in the 1760s and 1770s, now seems so distant to us, this is partly because we perceive gestural form as taking the place of genuine emotion, rather than shaping it; and we thereby repeat the anti-sentimental reaction widespread in the period after Greuze, whereby ostentatious rejection can be accompanied by disavowed, unacknowledged continuities.[8] In a recent scholarly re-examination, trying to recover a sense of the impact of this art, Emma Barker links his work to Enlightenment concerns with poverty, progress and plans for social reform, while suggesting that there are irresolvable tensions present: 'Greuzian sentimentalism was not only uplifting and consolatory but also sombre and reflective in its consciousness of the gulf between the innocent world of the paintings and the corrupt one inhabited by the viewer', so that 'even as it seeks to restore unity and harmony, Greuzian sentimentalism inscribes the impossibility of its own project.'[9] In the context of this specific painting, the 'innocence' can be taken to refer to the implicit moral simplicity of the scenario, and the spectator's reaction, just as the 'corruption' is *also* featured in the implicit narrative of the painting, as well as the world outside where the spectator is positioned; and this fracturing of *both* subject and object contributes to the sense that the corruption is not to be easily resolved, that there is no privileged position from which 'unity' can be ensured. Denby, too, alludes to this Enlightenment context, here pointing up the optimism: 'an aesthetic feature (the foregrounding of non-linguistic forms of communication) parallels and supports the moralising project of establishing and celebrating sentiment as the basis of social solidarity.'[10] In examining these claims – not only with regard to Greuze, but more generally – we will find that tensions around narrative, image and spectatorship in painting and theatre, and the relation of representation to loss (particularly loss of innocence), bring to a head problems of community, art and representation that suggest that sensibility, as a fundamental condition of social interaction, implies an 'aesthetic community of loss', the ramifications of which work their way through the subsequent development of both modernity as culture and modernism in the arts.

The art of tableau, the theatricality of culture

Dr Johnson suggested that sensibility was not just a mode of feeling but also of perception, 'a way of seeing that found in ordinary scenes and events occasion for deep reflection.'[11] In exploring the relations between feeling, seeing and reflection, the ethics and aesthetics of sentimentalism, it is useful to consider the significance of the 'tableau', which will in turn have ramifications for our notions of community and spectacle. The concept itself was central to the theoretical and critical writings of the Enlightenment philosopher Diderot, at the time, and has been taken up more recently by the art historian and critic Michael Fried. It refers to a scenario of emotional display, characteristically depicting an encounter between innocence and misfortune (though guilt and punishment can also feature), generally in a familial or domestic context. As such, depictions of tableaux – or tableau *as* picture – were particularly significant in relation to painting and theatre, though resonances in literature are not hard to find.[12] Clearly *Le Fils puni* would count as an exemplary instance.

Diderot develops the concept, in the context of theatre, by making a key distinction: 'An unexpected incident that happens in the course of the action and that suddenly changes the situation of the characters is a *coup de théâtre*. An arrangement of these characters on the stage, so natural and so true to life that, faithfully rendered by a painter, it would please me on canvas, is a *tableau*.'[13] The former – the arena of plot and narrative – needs to be complemented by the latter, potentially more profound and moving. In Fried's words, Diderot was calling for 'expressive movement or stillness as opposed to mere proliferation of incident', an emphasis on the self-sufficiency, unity and affective potential of the object of the gaze; hence, the challenge is 'to reach the beholder's soul by way of his eyes'.[14] For Carolyn Williams, writing of the subsequent adventures of the tableau in nineteenth-century drama and culture generally, 'the tableau interrupts and punctuates the ongoing action with its silent, composed stillness – calling for the audience to be likewise arrested yet all the while to be actively feeling and interpreting'.[15] There is a necessary element of tension here, yet of course tableau and narrative are – and have to be – interdependent: every picture tells a story, we say, but every story also implies arrested moments of descriptive, reflective picturing. In freezing narrative, suspending time in the immobility of the moment, the effect of tableau is that 'the set of forces which the narrative has brought together in a particular moment may be allowed to discharge their full affective power', as Denby puts it.[16] The tableau could be said to repeat but also to concentrate the narrative, as synecdoche. It 'rises out of the action, yet detaches from it to turn around and function as commentary on it', adds Williams; yet the sense of repetition and/as intensification remains, for the tableau is 'critically double: terrifying and sentimental, otherworldly and domestic, extravagant and realistic, outward and inward turning'.[17] If tableau is the moment of reflexivity in the arts it could also go beyond this: the reflexive moment, aiming to grasp the whole, is projected into tableau, as figural intensification.

All this has wide-ranging implications, not least for our concept and experience of selfhood. Using 'soul' in the new, Enlightenment sense as the 'inner principle' of selfhood, Diderot writes that 'Our soul is a moving tableau which we depict unceasingly; we spend much time trying to render it faithfully, but it exists as a whole and all at once. The mind does not proceed one step at a time as does expression.'[18] Fried thus suggests that he found in the tableau 'an external, "objective" equivalent for his own sense of himself as an integral yet continuously changing being'.[19] In effect, there is a homology here between narrative and tableau in the arts and the reflexive development of self-identity, one that reveals a shared tension. Just as any attempt by the self to picture its 'essence', to imagine ('image') its fundamental character, is bound in some degree to impose, rather than find, the unity it seeks, losing as it must the very sense of its own unfolding, so too the image of unified wholeness projected in the tableau cannot summarize, without remainder, the unfolding of a narrative that is, also, necessarily, ongoing, facing the future as well as recalling the past. The timeless present, and experience as/of succession, remain mutually recalcitrant; and thus the intensity of the reflexive grasp is as much evidence of its failure, of its own absence to itself, as it is of testimony to its success.[20]

This sense in which the power of tableau lies in its ability to convey a sense of wholeness requires further elaboration. Returning to Diderot's figuration of selfhood as soul, one could say that manifesting the soul *as* a whole requires tableau, a pictorial image, while narrative can only display the doings of the soul in time. And here the imagination is centrally involved, in that what is entailed is the production of an 'ideal whole' rather than – or as much as – finding a 'real' one. *Framing* is critical here, isolating the scenario against its background, fixing it *as* whole – indeed, the 'whole' may be no more than the effect of this framing, and the 'composition' thereby made possible. The tableau, suggests Barthes, is 'a pure cut-out segment with clearly defined edges, irreversible and incorruptible; everything that surrounds it is banished into nothingness …'. In its self-sufficiency, the tableau has something to say and knows how to say it: it is 'reflexive, moving and conscious of the channels of emotion'.[21] Yet one might add that this very fact necessitates an 'other place' from which it speaks, precisely through the reflexive move whereby it tries and fails to project itself in pure transparency, and which results in the concentration of meaning in parts of the tableau, objects within it, in the process of figuration that is also a fetishization, and testifies to the presence of absence even in the heart of the dramatic unity of the tableau. And when Diderot describes tableau as 'a whole contained under a single point of view',[22] this perspectivism invites one to ask: *which* or *whose* point of view? Debates around 'reception aesthetics' loom … If – to anticipate the argument somewhat – we are present here not only at the birth of the modern subject but of modernism in the arts, we can see that the 'self-contained' nature of the tableau, its pretension to autonomy, is to some degree forced, artificial, its necessary hinterland thereby disavowed.

Here we can return to the dramatic 'excess' that seems to be present, both in the tableau and in the reaction to it. The 'excess' of the tableau has the effect of reinforcing its autonomy, its self-integration, by providing a dimension of rhetoric, dramatizing its unity in and as passion, with specific gestures, expressions and flourishes, and indeed objects – notably tears – acting as signs and triggers, carrying this affirmation of meaning as emotional involvement and display. In this sense, the tableau is always inseparable from melodrama, indeed can be positioned as an originating instance of it; Diderot himself drew attention to links between the family misfortune scenario and melodrama, a connection that has continued through to Hollywood and beyond.[23] Susan Manning indeed argues that we can regard sensibility as 'the repressed face of melodrama'.[24]

This melodrama is then, in part, a dramatization of the autonomy of form itself, insulating its content, proclaiming the autonomy of the artwork, an autonomy that is never sufficiently manifest in itself, hence can only ever be excessive, the 'excess' serving to define its boundary through exaggeration – and thereby, in a sense, *also* overflowing the boundary. And this also produces or confirms the spectatorial involvement, in reacting to the excess, the gap between spectator and object simultaneously affirmed and denied. But we can see more in play here. If the tableau's relation to its hinterland is problematical – denying it as it proclaims its wholeness and autonomy – this is analogous to the situation of the self in relation to *its* hinterland: self-identity in its public face calls for excess, whereby self-autonomy can be both manifested and defined. Pointing to what are often seen as the distortions induced by sentimentalism, Campbell indeed suggests that 'the intensity of expression tends to be somewhat in excess of that which the occasion would "naturally" demand'.[25] Leaving aside the obvious problem here – can we be sure of what is 'naturally' demanded in these cases? – we can see how this would come about. When a felt emotion is in turn felt to be a significant manifestation of self, and likely to be so regarded by others, it calls for display, for public form – otherwise how can anyone know it is there? And given that emotions are to an extent *cultivated*, and part of an inter-subjective culture of the vicarious, there may be a tendency towards inflation of expression, so as to enhance the 'reality-effect' – which in turn means that the degree of emotional expressiveness can become a likely source of conflict, and subject to fashion (as in the denunciations of 'sentimentalism', then[26] and now). The drama of self-projection can slide readily enough into melodrama.

The relation of tableau to a spectator or audience is indeed crucial here, and exploring it will help clarify the nature and problems of this 'autonomy'. Diderot writes, provocatively: 'in a dramatic representation, the beholder is no more to be taken into account than if he did not exist.'[27] So, in the context of Greuze, Fried suggests that what is usually seen, today, as 'appealing most egregiously to the beholder functioned largely to neutralize the latter's presence', and it was precisely this attempt to portray the scene in its own self-sufficiency, to refuse to allow the audience 'to impinge upon the absorbed consciousness of his figures', that led the audience to be transfixed by – and before – the spectacle. The emotionalism is not there to seduce the audience, as it were, but to exclude it, in the interest of the self-contained pictorialism of the scene *as art* – its possible *effect* being all the more intense. In short, Fried suggests that what Diderot is calling for, and may be exemplified in Greuze, was 'the creation of a new sort of object – the fully realized tableau – and the constitution of a new sort of beholder – a new "subject" – whose innermost nature would consist precisely in the conviction of his absence from the scene of representation'. And we encounter 'an implicit apprehension of the beholder's alienation from the objects of his beholding (and therefore, in a manner of speaking, from himself, both in his capacity as beholder and as a potential object of beholding for others)'.[28] One might indeed postulate a formal equivalence of the autonomy of the artwork, its imaginative unity, and the self and its own autonomy (and the sense in which both are 'imaginary' as well as imaginative).

Barthes makes the ambitious claim that 'the whole of Diderot's aesthetics rests on the identification of theatrical scene and pictorial tableau', aligning the term 'theatrical' with Diderot's sense of a new aesthetic of the theatre.[29] If we take the case of the stage, we can indeed recall Diderot's 'paradox of acting', glossed by Jay Caplan as the claim that 'what is proper to a great actor is that nothing is properly his'.[30] He *becomes* the character he acts. An actor's stage presence is entirely 'other', and an actor should manifest no awareness of this fact, or of the presence of an audience, since both of these would endanger the self-absorption in the role, in the character portrayed, that makes it so 'real' for the spectator. And hence the apparent paradox that it is when characters are most self-absorbed, locked in their own emotional responses, that they are of most interest, and the beholder's emotions and imagination are most engaged. For the beholder, being excluded *and* being absorbed go together.

In exploring Diderot's own writings, Caplan adds a further, decidedly more controversial twist, arguing that 'the absence of the beholder is so crucial to the structure ... that we must speak of the beholder as a character in it'.[31] Here, it is useful to introduce Diderot's claim that virtue is 'a form of self-sacrifice'[32] whereby one has to give up the time of one's self-interested projects in order to acknowledge duties to others.[33] In the light of this, Caplan argues that 'The beholder's tear repeats the sacrifices that the represented characters have made and also represents the beholder's own sacrifice'; hence, tears '*relate* a sacrifice, *repeat* it, and *represent* or *signal* it'.[34] It is as though the beholder becomes a vicarious member of the family whose 'loss' is represented in the tableau (in whatever form it may take): author, character, beholder, all become substitutable, superimposed, and hence their implicit dialogue makes the tableau, just as they simultaneously become its topic. Citing Richardson, Diderot exhorts us: 'Come, we shall cry together over the unhappy characters of his fictions, and we shall say, "If fate should overwhelm us, at least decent folk will cry over us".[35] The community of tableau is the community of tears, just as 'Virtue requires a sacrificial representation – it requires a tableau'. And the beholder? In an important passage, Caplan writes of 'a desire that this loss in the family that was at the origin of the tableau be mourned and compensated for by the beholder whom the tableau summons forth', and that the family would thereby be reborn at another level: 'The family's fragmentation would once again be made whole at the level of the family of Man.' Yet representation and beholder can never completely overlap: 'A desire for wholeness never alters the fact that the tableau is always incomplete.'[36] Aesthetic unification is bound to fail, it cannot heal the absence in the real; all that is possible is a 'momentary unity in tears', as Jochen Schulte-Sasse puts it.

This whole line of argument has, in effect, led us naturally into what can be called the 'compensation model', so influential in interpretations of the position of art in modern culture. If fragmentation and conflict in the modern world deny us this longed-for sense of harmony, perhaps art can supply it, if only by keeping the dream alive. Hence it is not by chance that a newly separate aesthetic realm coincides with 'the emergence of a new desire for intimacy and a valorization of human sensibility and sympathy', in Schulte-Sasse's words. Unfolding in time, the modern experience produces 'an infinite cycle of desire and partial fulfilment that can never be arrested in a timeless moment of fulfilled presence', and this tension between desire and its adequate realization leads to 'an imaginary sublation of that tension in the institution of art'.[37] Given that this sense of absence or loss, geared to a notion of progress through amelioration or revolution, also drives the Enlightenment project, Barker usefully summarizes all this by suggesting that the historical interest of Greuzian sentimentalism derives 'from its position on the cusp between an Enlightenment model of art as useful and potentially reformist and an autonomy model that suppresses art's emancipatory potential by offering a purely aesthetic compensation' for the ills of the modern world.[38]

There are clearly insights here, but this overall approach is open to serious criticism. Art as 'imaginary sublation' is – among others – the standard Freudian or Marxist view, reducing art to function, to the satisfaction of need, whether individual or social. To dismiss the power of art – or culture generally – to move people as mere 'compensation' is always, ultimately, a form of reductionism, however sophisticated the argument's garb. This all reflects – rather than analyses – too much of the governing rationalist and utilitarian biases *within* the modern way of looking at the place of culture; and this would be true both of the narrower version of this approach, keeping alive the hope embodied in 'high' art, or the version that emphasizes that art, too, must inevitably succumb to market pressures, becoming 'merely' another aspect of consumerism. Either way, culture becomes functionally determined, in relation to an 'other', whether psyche or economy, postulated as external, needy and determinant – a perspective that hardly goes beyond an elaborate redescription of those alienated aspects of modern experience it purports to explain or understand.

With this in mind, let us return to the tableau, and try a different tack. Caplan himself refers to the fact that it requires the beholder to 'bear witness to a spectacle'. Clearly there is a hint here that if the tableau is in some ways a founding moment of modernism, celebrating the self-absorption not just of the figures depicted but of the artwork itself, firmly positioning the beholder *outside* it, as spectator, this also suggests that such a work, *in* its very distance, can join the world of other visual spectacles, even those it might not otherwise resemble. In effect, we return to the issue of the disavowed hinterland, developing a particular aspect of this. Whatever the distinctive forms and attributes of modernism, it is also true that it cannot escape the world of spectacle; and if tableau emerges as significant here, it is because it can prefigure modernism while remaining embedded within the spectacle of sympathy.

Now, Caplan does seem to position the beholder rather too close to the tableau, at some risk of losing Fried's original insight. The beholder is *witnessing*, not 'sublating' or 'compensating'. Nor is it the case that the beholder either wants to be or can be a participant, at least not in any reasonably straightforward sense. This claim is not necessary to explain the emotional reaction, the fact that the beholder reacts *as if* a participant. Rather, tableau as self-absorption corresponds to – reflects and encourages – the beholder's self-focused sense of the immediacy of his own emotional response to situations, of 'other' situations as *analogous* to those of self, as *imaginable* in terms of his own possible experiences. The relation between them and their loss or lack is analogous to the relation between the beholder and his own loss or lack, and it is this superimposed analogy that permits the underlying sense of 'involvement', without ever denying the difference or distance that makes it possible. Any sense of 'community' here is as much to do with absence as with presence; community does not exist as a potentially real 'resolution' of this absence, or a compensation, either in the aesthetic realm now or in some possible real future. *Pace* Caplan, there is no question of the family being 'reconstituted', at this or any other level. The 'perfect family' may exist as sentimental presupposition or aspiration, either in the 'as if' of the vicarious or a past realm of (partly imagined) nostalgia, and *this* absence is quite sufficient to generate emotion, whether for painter or beholder. The 'involvement' of the latter is thus 'real enough', but still distant, still exiled from the scenario itself. What is involved here is aesthetic *realization*, not a *resolution* of anything. There is no satisfyingly teleological closure here. And Diderot's claim that 'self-sacrifice performed in imagination creates a predisposition to sacrifice ourselves in reality'[39] may or may not be over-optimistic, but has the virtue of recognizing the power of imaginative involvement in, and difference from, the plight of the other. But this, in turn, raises broader issues and tensions that can be pursued if we turn to the second case study, the novel.

The tribulations of Emma

One of that courageous band of 'Jacobin feminists' around Mary Wollstonecraft in the 1790s, Mary Hays, published *The Memoirs of Emma Courtney* in 1796, at a time when the reaction in Britain against the 'excesses' of the French Revolution was increasingly being used to block any kind of progressive Enlightenment reform, inaugurating a period of conservatism that would indeed last for the rest of her long life. At best a minor success in its own time, the novel – along with its author – has long been forgotten, although its republication two centuries later suggests a revival of interest.[40] A genre-defying mix of fiction, epistle, autobiography, political polemic and philosophical disputation, the relatively slim volume manages to encompass a passionate tale of the miseries of obsessive desire and unrequited love; a rational analysis of the social and cultural conditioning that makes women, in particular, the victims of such misfortune; and a reflection on the adequacy of her own account, showing how easily reason can become mere rationalization when disconnected from the springs of feeling which lie ultimately in the bonds of sympathy between us. These springs have to be accessed through the links between feeling and imagination that are embodied in literature and art, and that produce the self itself as a work of 'fiction', with the accompanying dangers of that term. There is quite a lot going on, then, beneath a veneer that can easily lead it to be dismissed – yet again – as 'mere sentimentalism'.[41]

The relation between disclosure and the truth of sentiment is an important theme in the novel, and can lead us towards both the author's critique of Enlightenment and her underlying assumptions about sympathy.[42] Disclosure becomes an index of sensibility, proof of integrity: 'the sensible heart yearns to disclose itself', Emma tells Augustus. Such sincerity is 'artless'; it is not shaped in any way, at least not by any deliberate, conscious interference, so no question of strategy, or possible deceitfulness, can arise in relation to it. There is also the implication that it is not distorted by imagination or passion. And this has an immediate corollary, namely that the other, to whom the heart is thus disclosed, cannot be unaffected by this revelation, on pain of itself being revealed as a being incapable of 'sensibility' at all. The other, then – 'a mind with which my own proudly claimed kindred' – is necessarily embedded in this sympathetic connectivity, and hence must react in a way consistent with that.[43] Reinforcing this, Emma's later willingness to accept that she had been wrong about Augustus cannot be allowed to reflect on this basic logic: she blames the imagination, or, alternatively, his own lack of openness, since 'concealment' necessarily impedes the flow of sensible revelation.

Can this pure, autonomous, immediate revelation of sensibility, both index or sign and the reality that is thus manifested or designated, perform the task required of it? For Emma, it can seem straightforward enough: 'genuine effusions of the heart and mind' are 'easily' distinguished from the 'vain ostentation' of 'lip deep' sentiment, because the latter leaves no emotional trace, either in its own manifestation or in its effect on the other. Depth is integrity: mere surface is not enough; it can be 'art', factitious or superficial. This indeed seems to imply a critique of sensibility as *mere* taste, good form, since such 'form' can be empty or deceitful. The 'genuine' effusions are described, in this passage, as 'energetic', hence darting from person to person, and it is this quality that seems to differentiate them. But in another letter, she refers to the 'mild current of gentle and genial sympathies', and indeed now describes the opposite as a 'destructive torrent',[44] so it seems that the forcefulness of their manifestation cannot suffice to distinguish them. Passion has the power to sweep all before it, as Emma knows all too well. So we are forced back onto the idea of 'artlessness'. But this, too, presents problems. Since it is clear that distortions due to the imagination, particularly linked to passion, can and do occur, can they be so easily detected and avoided? Simulation is the stock in trade of the imagination, after all. And Emma herself, trying to wriggle out of the charge of hypocrisy – she has, after all, partially concealed the truth about her relationship with Augustus from her correspondent, Mr Francis – regrets that she cannot disclose the full truth, she can only 'paint' it, portray it, indirectly; and if this is so, how can we be sure that such 'painting', necessarily 'artful', may not in fact be frequent in such expressions of sensibility, indeed may be *inherent* in sensibility insofar as it *is* expressed, exists *as* expression? The role of the imagination in 'shaping' these manifestations could turn out to be central both to it and to them, raising the whole question of the place of the imagination in experience and judgement. And the 'artless', direct, exhibition of sensibility seems to have become inseparable from its own imaginative 'artfulness'.

In this particular case, Emma's tentative defence of her secrecy amounts to the claim that sensibility itself dictates a degree of concealment out of the very 'sympathy' that binds her to the object of her love, even though such concealment is in principle never desirable. Hence we find that the particularity of the sympathetic bond carries with it a degree of tension with the rational universalism of abstract, normative discourse, an element of selectivity and exclusion; and in itself, for Emma, this may be a tension we have to live with. But, conversely, concealment *within* relations of sensibility and intimacy is disastrous: she points out to Augustus that his mysterious silences made matters worse; the absence of mutual sympathetic engagement leaves scope for passionate excess, particularly as passion is 'roused and stimulated by obstacles'.[45]

Here we encounter, again, that eighteenth-century fascination with the idea of a universal language of feeling, of the body-as-sign, the 'community of sentiment' that underlies apparent diversity: signs as manifestations of bodies that are also figurations of the social. 'Because feelings were deemed natural, they united people rather than isolating them; they were shared by all, a public resource', as William Reddy puts it.[46] Hence the encouragement for these emotional outpourings, each one 'an outpouring which proved one's existence through the sensations which it excited', as Vincent-Buffault argues, in her study of the ultimate manifestation of this – those tears, whether of sadness or joy, or both at once, that drench texts and bodies alike.[47] As we found with Greuze, however, there are real problems here.

As Emma comes to realize, language itself can be both inadequate and deceptive. For Janet Todd, sentimentality reveals the inadequacy of language: novels supposedly reflect good manners, yet their language is fractured by repetition, hyperbole, rhetorical intensity, and a tidal wave of exclamation marks, italics and capital letters – in short, an overabundance of words and punctuation that strain to convey the immediacy of feeling yet actually undermine it.[48] Language and feeling fly apart: each is in excess of the other, forced together yet mutually incommensurable. The novel thereby constructs 'a sensitive and socialised body', writes John Mullan, 'the site where the communicative power of feeling is displayed, but also where sensibility can become excessive or uncontrollable'.[49] Hence the preoccupation with 'signs' as direct expressions of feeling, signs that communicate messages *through* their very expressiveness. Exploring

this, David Denby suggests this reveals 'the possibility of sentimental transparency: words may betray, but other signs permit others to know the inner life
of the subject, and the signs of sensibility figure high among the elements of
this universal language'. He shows how tiny textual details can be loaded with a
powerful affective charge, a 'sentimental effect' that concentrates the circulating
meanings in the particular feature, by a kind of synecdoche.[50] Yet, as already
suggested, it is not so easy to be sure of the 'artlessness' of the body.

Image, imagination and the narrative of feeling

We have seen that Emma aspires to 'paint' the truth, in her account. Images,
indeed, play an important part in the novel. At the very start, Emma complains,
in writing to her stepson, of having to 'renew images' of harrowing memories,
just as other memories, recalled through images, can of course carry pleasure.
And the initial 'connection' with Augustus, after all, was through his image, as
captured in his portrait; she saw this before she saw him. This portrait, indeed,
seems to have a life of its own. Later, ill and depressed, when she sees it again,
the smile seems to have been replaced by 'an expression of perplexity and
sternness'; but later again, in a calmer state, after Mrs Harley's death, 'the cold
austerity, the gloomy and inflexible reserve' had gone.[51] Like Dorian's picture in
the eponymous Wilde novel, it seems to become a physical manifestation of an
inner state. But *whose* inner state? Here the parallel with Wilde may be inexact.
In this miasma of sympathetic connections, it is too easy to see it simply as a
projection of Emma's state of mind. After all, her initial readiness to fall for the
portrait is, on her own admission, linked to the 'sympathy' existing between
Mrs Harley and herself, just as the later assumption of 'negative' features could
in part reflect Mrs Harley's state of physical decline, or indeed the state of the
relationship between Emma and Augustus. But these sympathetic networks can
be too readily psychologized, perhaps: the 'inner state' could be as much to do
with *relations* as with 'mind' or 'heart'. It may be more a matter of currents and
contexts out of which selves are constructed, rather than already-constituted
internal contents or attributes of the latter. And what is involved here, in this
production of images and portraits out of these currents and connections
whereby the emergent self reflexively constitutes itself, seems – appropriately
enough – to be a process of *painting*. This is referred to on several occasions.
When she asks, 'How shall I paint the sensations ...', Emma seems to imply that
this can only be partial, that much escapes; whereas, writing later to Mr Francis,

saying she cannot tell her secret, but can try to 'paint' her sensations instead,[52] the emphasis is more positive: one can, to an extent, paint what cannot be said. Depiction is indirect, but none the less important for that.

Crucially, however, it is the *imagination* that actually has to 'paint the picture'. Images are not in any straightforward way products of feeling; sensibility in this narrow sense is not enough. Its necessary element of passivity, its dependence on perception and sensation, means that without a 'shaping power' it is not able to form (or formulate) feelings, figure them in a way that makes the truth they promise actually knowable as such. That 'shaping power' is the imagination, which by the late decades of the century – years of nascent Romanticism, with Coleridge and Schiller, in particular, exploring the potential of the Kantian imaginary for aesthetics and creativity – has come to represent both the strains or deficiencies of the broadly Lockean empiricist tradition that had dominated Enlightenment thought, and to signal possible ways forward.

For much of the time, the impression given in the novel is one of hostility towards the imagination, emphasizing its dangers. It can be too easily dominated by passion. Such a conjunction typically produces what Emma refers to, intriguingly, as 'a pernicious, though a sublime, enthusiasm', suggesting a hint of admiration for such an excess, however rationally dubious it may be. Indeed, this linking of terms couples the long-established Enlightenment distrust of 'enthusiasm' – a fusion of popular credulousness, superstition and religious fervour – with the Romantic fascination with the sublime, the fusion of the awesome and the dangerous, encapsulating the very evolution of one into the other, while reminding us that its source, in elements of popular consciousness, cannot wholly be assimilated into a specialized realm of art. And here we begin to encounter the potentially positive dynamic of the imagination. Her problems, she suggests, may be due to 'the imagination capable of sketching the dangerous picture'.[53] And the 'dangerous picture', as an idealization that reveals the power of the imagination to shape the discrete phenomena of experience, figure them *through* art, is thus necessarily transformative, for good or ill. Mary Hays herself adds, in a letter, that the individual with 'strong mental powers', like the revolutionary, 'transcends temporality and creates new worlds in imagination'.[54] What can in some contexts be misleading can also be creatively (and politically) potent; and this creativity can lead us to a kind of truth, just as it can result in error. Emma claims, tellingly, that 'without some degree of illusion, and enthusiasm, all that refines, exalts, softens, embellishes, life – genius, virtue, love itself, languishes'.[55] Thus we learn that semblance itself can embody, or result in, a kind of truth: art *as* semblance is an aspect of the potential of aesthetic truth itself.

In the context of the novel, one would think that the imagination would work primarily through narrative, though, as we have seen, *Memoirs* is particularly appropriate for raising questions about the relation between narrative, reflection, and the manifestation of 'sympathetic connection' in ways that keep issues of imagery and truth constantly in play. In a novel that is written *as* a letter, from Emma, and largely draws on letters for its narrative, we find that the most extensive episode of self-reflection – Chapter VI in Part II – is written *as if* it were a letter, a letter to herself, her self.[56] By implication, one writes to oneself as one writes to others. This epistle to the self, as the form of self-reflection, becomes simultaneously an exercise in self-constitution, again posing difficult questions of presence and revelation, of truth and self-knowledge. She reflects on her self-deception in pursuit of Augustus; but if she was wrong then, what proof that she is right now? If she can conceal the identity of Augustus from Mr Francis, what can she conceal from herself? There is a sense, it seems, in which reflexive knowledge actually reflects an inability to be fully self-present, or, more positively, a process of figuring self as other that simultaneously eludes and grasps it.

Incorporated in writing, this process enforces narrative interruptions, as the reflexive mode disrupts the narrative while simultaneously, subtly, continuing it by other means. Wishing she had followed her aunt's advice, regretting her excessive enthusiasms, Emma writes: 'But I check this train of overwhelming reflection, that is every moment on the point of breaking the thread of my narration, and obtruding itself to my pen.' 'Narration' here implies a certain *lack* of reflection, the 'getting on with it' aspect of telling a story, and living a life, hence the partial lack of self-understanding inherent in this everyday process. In an early scene, after first meeting Mr Francis, she writes, after he has left, of 'the solemn stillness, so grateful to the reflecting mind, that pervaded the scene ...'.[57] Here, Emma emphasizes the *difference* of the reflexive mode, the way 'reflection' *stops* life, stops time, entailing a kind of 'stillness' in our response to life, our capacity to live it, as though we are in part out of it, beyond it. And, corresponding to the emphasis on sensibility, in its broader sense, and sympathy, this is life itself, as a feeling, or mood, experienced in part as response to nature, to be located as much 'outside' as 'inside', a sense of harmony, as stillness, all around and within. Action and process become stasis, available for appropriation or projection as *image*, as spectacle. The scene asks to be painted, to be preserved as tableau. Yet of course the reflexive mode is problematical here, too: in the novel, it is necessarily recuperated *as* narrative, even while implicitly questioning this.

Mary Hays, too, is writing to her readers, and this is inseparable from her self-reflection; and she does not necessarily expect a reply, though at some level doubtless hopes for one, some 'public' response. This writing, this 'letter', then, is straddling boundaries that are constituted as inherently problematical: not only self and other, but private and public, in that the 'private' – indeed intimate – letter is both addressed to the other and put on public display, exhibited, written and written *about*, an element in the spectacle it helps to constitute. And just as the self, through text and body, is always, in principle, on display, so also this whole process questions or straddles another boundary, that of fiction/reality, since imaginative figuration is inherent in this whole process whereby the self grasps or projects its essential otherness to itself, and which necessarily raises issues around 'fiction' in the broader sense (truth, falsity, deceit).

This can be placed in a wider cultural context. Denby argues that fiction has 'both an especially self-conscious focus on the sphere of feeling and a generic appropriateness in presenting it'. This is because the 'examined life of feeling' is 'like a lived fiction in that its object is always mediated by imagination, conditioned by context, and modified by time'.[58] And all this has an interesting implication, drawn out by the eighteenth-century aesthetic theorist Henry Home, Lord Kames: 'if, in reading, ideal presence be the means by which our passions are moved, it makes no difference whether the subject be fable or reality'.[59] The phrase 'ideal presence' was intended, suggests Michael Bell, as a 'careful balance between immediacy of the response and the imaginative status of the object', and as such 'must not collapse into being perceived too simply as either fact or as fiction'.[60] In short, as Reddy puts it, 'because feelings, whether inspired by fiction or by life, were the same ... the difference between art and life was attenuated'.[61] Nor is emotional response to fiction necessarily any less intense because of this element of the vicarious: Margit Sutrop argues that the imagination, directed towards fictional objects, can provoke such emotion even if we 'know', at some level of awareness, that the object is a work of fiction,[62] which reinforces the sense that the standard fiction/reality distinction can be tenuous or unhelpful in this context. Coleridge's phrase 'willing suspension of disbelief' seems pertinent here: we may not straightforwardly believe in the reality of the object, but it is not make-believe or pretence, either. Finally, Bell adds – ambitiously and controversially – that 'the sentimentalist assumption of emotional continuity between the living reader and the fictional object lies at the heart rather than the periphery of the response to fiction'.[63]

In the light of this, we can return to the text – and the body. Tilottama Rajan points out that *Memoirs* is a 'textually self-conscious work' which seeks to 'position experience within textuality and relate textuality to experience'.[64] And this 'experience' is particularly the experience of the body, coded as 'feeling'. The body, in turn, is not a totally self-contained entity, but part of a network of sympathy, in which such 'sympathy' manifests connectedness, spills beyond the self and, indeed, through 'feeling', becomes partially constitutive of the latter. The body can be seen as facing both ways, subject and object of feeling, self and other uneasily superimposed. It is 'nerves' – simultaneously mental and physical – that show this most effectively: 'nerves' and 'distempers' seem to affect imagination and body alike, and are affected by them, in this generalized circuit of the forms of dis-ease.[65]

But the dis-ease seems to go deeper here. Peter Logan has noticed that Emma seems to experience narration as a violation: retelling her story requires 'involuntary self-violence'.[66] Indeed, right at the start Emma addresses her stepson by pleading '… why do you tear from my heart the affecting narrative'; yet, she cannot 'keep back the recital, written upon my own mind in characters of blood'.[67] Logan argues that since, for Hays, women are 'uncertain of reason, denied agency, and unable to trust their own feelings', pain is left as the only sign of narrative authority: not a guarantee of reason, but at least a sign of distance from desire, from passion. It is as though 'the only time a woman can know she has something to say is when her body tells her not to say it';[68] only thus can narration become a *response* to the nervous body, rather than a symptom or aspect of it. If passion and reason both fail, pain alone remains.

This is insightful – and raises gender issues for us to return to – but there is a risk of falling for the simplistic dichotomy of Enlightenment reason versus passion: it is an implication of what has been argued before that Emma is struggling towards a broader sense of narrative understanding that goes beyond this distrust of the body, and tries to find a place for the imagination as an important aspect of this. At the start, framing her account for her stepson, she advises: 'be not the slave of your passions, neither dream of eradicating them', for they are the basis of our 'talents'. She elaborates the point in her rhetorical question, later on, in a letter to Mr Francis: 'What are passions, but another name for powers?'[69] Passion, properly harnessed, is a creative force. Hence rationality needs to be 'embodied', via sensibility, and linked to passion, via the imagination, making possible a creative response to the world, whether as action or as art. In this sense, what traps Emma, what gives her pain, is that she can find no clear, objective way of distinguishing between the latter, positive model, and the flawed model, in which that very rationality that sets itself *against* the body can so easily end up as rationalization, prey to the body and its desires, so that, in Emma's case, in thrall to her passion for Augustus, 'the certainty of her own rationality becomes the primary symptom of its absence', as Logan puts it.[70] Having lived this failure, now forced to return to it, through recalling, narrating and reinterpreting it, she can have no guarantee that her account can be any more reliable, and it is hardly surprising if this re-membering, which is also a dis-membering, brings pain with it. And if this is Emma's tragedy, it may not be hers alone.

There are several Emmas present here, then; can they ever achieve any final synthesis? Emma in the throes of passion gives way to Emma analysing her passion, getting an understanding of it; she in turn gives way to Emma analysing her analysis, realizing that her supposedly rational understanding was a rationalization, reaching thereby the important insight that those who proclaim their rational grasp of a situation are often those most in thrall to psychological drives and the distortions of self-interest. But can she be sure that her later self-understanding, framing her whole account from her current vantage point as narrating subject, is adequate? We appear to be in a regress, one that is in principle insoluble, raising as it does the whole issue of reflexivity, an issue raised earlier in reading Diderot, but now returning with renewed force. If Emma remains *herself*, if there *is* a subject there, then it cannot simultaneously reflect on itself, without remainder; and if there are several selves, it is difficult to see how the current one can claim any final authority over the others. There are, of course, external limits to this process, the contingencies of life – and death – but these can only be arbitrary.

There is, however, an internal limit – or, more strictly, one that bridges the internal/external dichotomy – and this is given by the very fact of 'framing' itself, a point where narrative again engages with the pictorial and with emergent notions of the autonomy of art. Here, authorial decision becomes its own justification, as it were: the point at which closure seems appropriate to Hays is quite sufficient to justify it. For what we encounter thereby is the work as *work of art*, defined by the frame that sets it off in its own apparent sufficiency, through its own internal principles of organization; and 'truth' becomes coloured by aesthetic criteria – criteria defined by the relation of feeling and imagination – as well as cognitive and ethical ones. And in this particular case, the *Memoirs* carries the profound truth of the discourse of sensibility, the ultimate refusal of any absolute distinction between 'mind' and 'body', with 'feeling' as the crucial linkage, reminding us of the work of art that is life itself. It also suggests that 'narrative' cannot close itself off from image, tableau, and participation in the world of spectacle, hence also implying the ultimate impossibility of the work of art (and art itself) separating itself off from the rest of life. For Emma herself, closure comes at a point where she 'feels' a degree of understanding – but it is also precipitated by the demand of her stepson for an account of her life. The contingencies always have the last word …

Reason, sensibility and the critique of gender: Problems of Enlightenment

For Emma, modern civilization is above all a culture of 'semblance', of disguise, deception and deceit. And this intensifies a problem that has become apparent: if such 'semblance' is everywhere, if the 'spell' is all-pervasive, what are its sources, and how can anyone claim to see through it? We have seen that distortion is always potentially present through the very dependence on images as a central component of the language of sympathy. Such images are, after all, inherently at the level of appearance, rather than depth, hence the realm of 'semblance' as an irreducible aspect of the very means by which sympathy makes itself manifest. Sympathy appears to carry the permanent possibility of delusion with it. But we need to dig deeper.

The potential relevance of gender has been alluded to, and sensibility seems to be the key here. Sensibility is presented as both accessing and revealing a kind of truth; hence Emma can, in principle, see through the semblances, penetrate behind appearances. Feeling as revelation (by the subject) is paralleled by feeling as insight (into the other, into the object). But it is hardly surprising if this appears as a kind of arrogance: first as an excess of confidence in one's own integrity, purity of feeling and motive, and secondly as a sweeping claim to insight into the truths of others, indeed into the nature of modern civilization itself. Feeling becomes the key to the truths of feeling, because feeling seems to access the network of sympathy in some direct, unmediated sense, while the truths of reason are more detached, distant, abstract: truth as rule and principle. (And they are not, of course, necessarily the worse for that: it depends on domain of application, and context of use.) But, actually, we have found grounds for thinking that this network of sympathy, transmitted and known through and as feeling, is simultaneously a world of insight *and* deceit, of truth *and* semblance, always in the context of specifics, the presence of persons, memories, and images. If Emma is as much trapped by this as she is perspicacious about it, this is hardly so surprising; here, the eighteenth-century structure of feeling seems to be concentrated with particular intensity, the tensions in the cultural configurations through which it is articulated becoming particularly apparent.

While not herself claiming to be a philosopher, Mary Hays moved in 'Enlightened' philosophical circles, and was familiar with the ideas of Helvétius and the Lockean tradition. Her novel implies both a critique of gendered aspects of this tradition, and an attempt to point to a way of 'doing philosophy' that would avoid some of the pitfalls, those of over-abstraction in particular. Feeling relaxed after having met Mr Francis, and finding her feelings reflected in objects around her, Emma suggests that 'After having bewildered ourselves amid systems and theories, religion, in such situations, returns to the susceptible mind as a sentiment rather than as a principle'. This is not so much praise of religion as a complaint that abstract systems of thought that lose touch with feeling are missing some essential dimension of human life; and we have already suggested that feeling always has an element of the particular and the specific about it. And her stepson is urged to learn from the particular incidents of her life 'a more striking and affecting lesson than abstract philosophy can ever afford'.[71] The word 'lesson' implies that there needs to be a way of mediating the particular and the abstract or general: looked at in the right way, a particular becomes an exemplar, not merely particular but not subsumable under a rule either; it involves judgement, sensitivity to both poles of the dichotomy, a refusal to let the dichotomy exhaust the possibilities.[72] But it is an exchange of letters with her philosopher friend Mr Francis – who is almost certainly modelled on the philosopher and political theorist William Godwin – that brings all this into sharpest focus.

Proclaiming that 'independence' is 'the first lesson of enlightened reason', Mr Francis develops the point: 'The system of nature has perhaps made me dependent for the means of existence and happiness upon my fellow men taken collectively; but nothing but my own folly can make me dependent upon individuals'. He adds that this does not, of course, prevent one from 'admiring, esteeming, and loving' individuals who are worthy of such responses. Emma is having none of this: such admiration, esteem and love must imply a degree of dependence on the individual concerned, which in turn must imply an acute sense of lamentation if the object of our affection is lost to us, for whatever reason – which is, of course, precisely her own personal situation *vis-à-vis* Augustus. The difference here is critical, for it is not just about feeling. Mr Francis is arguing from the existence of already constituted selves, the subjects of Enlightenment philosophical speculation, and the citizens of emergent 'civil society', orienting themselves to their own interests in the light of reason;

Emma is arguing from a point at which such selves and subjects are in process of constitution, perhaps in a *never-ending* such process, one that gives a certain priority to the network of sympathies out of which these bounded individuals arise, in their perhaps imaginary independence. And, in a revealing aside, she adds that 'love in the abstract, loving mankind collectively, conveys to me no idea'[73] – a 'confession' that could be taken, by a later age, either as revealing her own failings, perhaps reflecting a broader cultural inadequacy, an as-yet inadequate grasp of the possibilities of human emancipation, inseparable from precisely this ability to 'think mankind collectively' and 'in the abstract'; or, conversely, as a prescient *critique* of an Enlightenment project that accurately pinpoints one of its central flaws, its *in*ability to think abstraction through concrete particulars, specific contexts and hence its potential for totalitarianism. These points link up: an adequate philosophical position must encompass the particularities of feelings and relationships, *in relation to* broader principles; and this in turn, for the author, opens up a terrain for fiction, a role, for example, in 'delineating the progress, and tracing the consequences, of one strong, indulged passion, or prejudice' since this can 'afford materials, by which the philosopher may calculate the powers of the human mind, and learn the springs which set it in motion'.[74]

To come to Emma's own claim, then, she argues that it is not nature but 'the barbarous and accursed laws of society' that have denied independence to women.[75] Her critique could be seen to lay itself open to counter-attack, however. She appears to be calling for a revaluation of the relation between reason on the one hand, and the 'non-rational' sphere of sentiment and passion on the other; yet she herself also aspires to the 'independence' that alone makes rational judgement possible, is clearly envious of the freedoms it brings, and can at times seem to present the 'other' realm, in part at least, as compensation for, or unfortunate by-product of, that very *lack* of independence that characterizes the status of women, of which she is so acutely and perceptively aware. Although this tension is not explicitly resolved in the text – and may in some ways be irresolvable – we can at least try to get a clearer view of the terrain on which it arises, and the hints of a way beyond it.

Emma's critique has several dimensions. One can start from the fact that the oppression of women has adverse consequences for *both* sexes. Men are reduced to pursuing their interests, thus becoming the 'wretched, degraded victims of brutal instinct'; women, conversely, remain 'insulated beings', able only to watch, to witness, the drama of life, and if they manage to avoid sinking into 'mere frivolity and insipidity', do so by being 'sublimed' into 'refined, romantic, factitious, unfortunate' beings. Women are thereby rendered 'feeble and delicate by bodily constraint and fastidious by artificial refinement'[76] – all of which amounts to a highly prescient and insightful account of the fate of the sexes during the century to come, and beyond. Emma's critique is thus deepened by pointing simultaneously to the egocentric, driven quality of independent male 'rationality' under these social conditions, and to the impotence and artifice of the feminine part of the now strongly gendered realm of sensibility, in which women, only able to witness rather than participate, can only be aware of each other as witnesses to witnessing, manifested in the artificial conventions of surface and display. This, then, grounds a critique of sensibility that also seeks to rescue it, in a stronger sense: that is, sensibility as a form or language of sensitivity, responsiveness to others, connectivity – in short, sensibility as the face of sympathy, testament to its presence.

We can see that 'sympathy' is posited here both as a ground, and as a potential; both a condition for meaningful social intercourse, and a call for it, or promise of it, beyond those social conditions that systematically negate its potential through this reified, impoverished gender polarization. Hence Emma's claim that the 'vain ostentation' of 'lip deep sentiment' can be distinguished from the real thing – alluded to above – can at least be given a clearer rationale. But we can also see what happens to sympathy in this situation. When it is embedded in the egocentric 'rationality' of patriarchy, it in turn is rendered liable to justifiable criticism as a self-centred feeling of superiority and patronizing disdain for the afflicted other even as help is being – or may be – offered. And, in this case, the 'other' may be woman herself, hence Emma's contemptuous claim that 'the men who condescend to flatter our foibles, despised the weak beings they helped to form'.[77] A corollary that would seem to follow is that feminine sympathy also suffers here, liable either to ineffectuality or to excess, being overwhelmed by passion, hence both rather undiscriminating and socially ineffectual, unconnected with possibilities for meaningful action – thus unwittingly reinforcing the plausibility of 'rational' male critique (as we have seen with Mr Francis).[78] And the upshot is a model of sympathy and sympathetic giving in which the omnipresent influence of a corrupt social order renders motives of self-interest – including the need to feel good about oneself – ever-present, and difficult to separate from the operations of the very sympathy that purports to escape them.

All this inevitably has consequences for Emma personally. She is as much victim as critic. She protests her virtue – 'I have all along used, and shall continue to use, the unequivocal language of sincerity' – but also has to admit, in self-criticism, to her 'weakness and vanity', to 'the illusions of my self-love', to the fact that 'my views were equally false and romantic'.[79] And this is precisely the consequence that one might have predicted, if her critique of patriarchy were to have any validity: namely, the likely confusion of sensibility and self-love, and the distorting effects that excess passion can have in producing a 'romantic' misreading of her situation, and of the feelings of Augustus. It also, again, illustrates the author's thesis about the appropriateness of the literary form for social and philosophical reflection.

And here, for now, we must leave Emma – but not her concerns, and her passion for change.

Community, sensibility, observation

Can there be a 'community of feeling'? Can sensibility be the foundation of a social order? Enough has been said already to suggest that the sentimentalist pathos of the present as loss gives a distinctive flavour to all this: community always seems to involve separation, even from the truth of experience itself. Mullan goes so far as to argue that the vocabulary of feeling ultimately 'elaborates society as a capacity of the self', and that, in the end, 'There is no social space for sensibility',[80] but this may take the bounded self of the modern ideology of individualism too much at face value. Manning figures 'tears' as the negative emblem of change: sensibility embodied 'loss and melancholy as the inevitable price of progress in the world of civil society'.[81] Ostensibly about connection, it actually embodied rupture. Vincent-Buffault refers to the 'liquid circulation' of tears, a kind of economy of sorrow, which appeared to bind people in transient but meaningful social situations. She writes: 'This participation through tears in the suffering of others ... this more general emotion concerning the ills of humanity indicated a new relationship with others regulated by emotional identification.'[82] And while one can observe a tension between sentimentalism and the 'philosophical history' of the Enlightenment, with its emphasis on rationality and progress, the two could also complement each other, as is particularly apparent in the French case, producing a potent brew crucial to the ideology of revolution.[83]

We can explore the implications of all this by looking in more detail at newly emergent social practices and institutions of the early to mid-eighteenth century in Britain. The old system of parochial relief had left the poor relatively invisible, whereas the new charitable organizations reversed this, seeking to display – and thereby create – a category of 'deserving poor', or 'deserving cases' of misfortune more generally. The process of presenting particular 'cases' as instances of 'types' of misfortune to the public, to the gaze of the more fortunate, would of course be expected to produce the charitable contributions that would in turn testify to the sensibility of the latter.[84] We thereby encounter a process whereby 'the humanity of the excluded'[85] is reconstructed, with the universal located in the morally relevant particular, in that distinctive mix of visibility, sensibility and theatrical display that constitute the central features of the emergent 'spectacle of sympathy'. In her illuminating account, Jessie Van Sant takes the instance of Magdalen House, in London, an institution for penitent prostitutes; sermons would be preached in front of the women and their benefactors, recounting individual instances of distress, and resulting in plentiful tears all round, a 'theater of pathos'[86] that simultaneously certified the institution's viability and legitimacy.

We can detect an interesting link here, between curiosity and pity, science and sympathy, in that both focus on particulars, and both place an emphasis on observation; and we can detect an oscillation between pathetic and investigative observations of suffering. And science – by then, a widespread practice and an object of public fascination – requires not just observation but also experiment, the controlled intervention in nature to produce results which would prove hypotheses. Something of this can also be found in Magdalen House: the display of virtuous suffering and its relief would prove the efficacy of intervention; and the display would, in turn, stimulate further intervention, by affecting the emotions of the spectators. Both victims and spectators can thereby prove their status as sensitive beings. Thus sensibility calls for active intervention, proof, and this can slide into manipulation of the other to *produce* suffering: to study suffering, and test one's reaction to it, it may be necessary to stimulate it, and the 'drama of sensibility ... caused by misfortune, evil agents, an author, or a scientist, can invite either objective scrutiny or sympathetic identification', as Van Sant puts it,[87] and the one approach can flip easily into the other. Science and literature can be oddly reflective of each other's methods and concerns.

James Boswell is known to have visited the hanging grounds of Newgate and Tyburn – a not infrequent occurrence among the socially respectable of the time. He was aware that his behaviour could be regarded as callous, even cruel, but asserts that it was actually 'proof of sensibility':[88] it was an exercise in self-observation and sympathetic identification, participation in dramatic spectacle and scientific observation, an experiment in feeling. As with Yorick in Sterne's *A Sentimental Journey* (1768), we again find that there can be as much interest in the self's responses as in the suffering that is the ostensible object of sympathy.[89]

The capacity for other-identification, sympathy for the predicament of the sufferer, is constantly threatened by this immediacy, this reflexive lingering on the moment of emotional response that can produce self-absorption; and hence, again, the 'excess' of feeling, obscuring the object, that is such a feature of the culture of sentimentalism.[90]

This combination of detached objectification and sympathetic engagement can also be turned back on the self, then, simultaneously creating or recreating a sense of self as object and as emotional resource: the self becomes reflexively constituted *through* this experience of engagement with the other. In this drama of sympathy, the self too can become other, object of curiosity alternating with subject of emotional experience, as we saw with Emma's story, thus producing a tension that is also central to modern self-management and to the power of 'selfhood' as the basis of our individually centred engagement with the world, whether in terms of reason or emotion, science or aesthetics. In one of his sermons, Hugh Blair claimed that sensibility 'lays open the heart to be pierced with many wounds from the distresses which abound in the world',[91] such 'wounded hearts' – a favourite figure of the time – testifying to this revers-ibility of pain whereby subject and object could change places, as response and provocation, cause and effect, in this theatrical spectacle of suffering in which narrative and tableau are both deeply implicated.

Novelists do indeed play their full part in this drama of sensibility in which sympathy, curiosity and manipulation feed off one another. The novelist as experimentalist systematically manipulates both characters and readers, devel-oping scenarios in which both can reveal themselves through the engagement of their feelings, particularly sympathy, the inter-subjective feeling *par excellence*. Cruelty becomes a method of revelation, in the spirit of Oliver Goldsmith's advocacy of 'torturing' nature, by experiment, forcing 'her' to give up her secrets.[92] And in these respects, and as hinted in the previous chapter, the sadomasochistic scenario is really only an extreme version of this pattern, revealing its logic. In *Clarissa* (1747–8), the heroine becomes such through trials and tests, in which the author, Richardson, seems to identify as much with the villain, Lovelace, as with the observer, Belford; Clarissa thereby becomes the 'persecuted maiden' who recurs endlessly in pornography, with Sade's Justine as merely the best-known version.[93] Nor is Clarissa's own positioning so straight-forward; Laura Hinton argues that 'Clarissa's own subject is bound up in the sadomasochistic contradictions between autonomy and dependency, aggression and desire', documenting her 'unacknowledged masochistic aggression'.[94] And this dialectic of distancing and involvement renders the reader, too, subtly complicit in Clarissa's fate, and fascinated by his or her own responses, as the very objectification inherent in the authorial relation to the novel is mapped onto the reader's own relation to self. Through this, ethical and aesthetic categories and responses are disturbed, and Van Sant argues that 'The aesthetic detachment necessary in order for the creation of suffering to be acceptable as a source of pleasure is analogous to scientific detachment'.[95] And we can also note the paradoxical, parodic nature of the culminating 'experiment', the rape, when the administration of laudanum has rendered Clarissa insensible and uncon- scious: the essence of the feminine revealed in its very absence ...

This spectacle of sympathy clearly presents problems, then. Some different implications are spelt out in this letter to a magazine, from 1791: 'Let us beware of becoming spectators in scenes of cruelty, lest by repeated and horrid spectacles of this kind, we lose the sympathetic sense which vibrates at the pain of another.'[96] The influential physician Benjamin Rush agreed with this: purely 'passive' sympathy threatened society by breaking the link between experience and action, observation and involvement.[97] In effect, these are already pointing to what has, of course, been the very influential argument that sympathy as spectacle has a morally anaesthetizing effect: this argument, far from being a late development, has been in place from the very beginning. And we can point to the emerging paradox that the spectacle of sympathy can produce objections both because of the slide between observation of suffering and the production of it – as discussed above – and because of the breaking of that link in the pure passivity of contemplation. Whether this is a double bind, inherent in the situation and in the discursive possibilities opened up by it, or whether there can be a response that is properly 'responsive', and can be active without being manipulative, is of course a crucial issue to return to; but for now we can take up the more specifically political aspects of this spectacle of involvement and detachment, whereby the community of suffering is constituted.

Sympathy and the politics of pity

The suggestion, then, is that this vicarious community of the spectacle of suffering might be one that actually *needs* suffering, as its own source of energy, that it might have a vested interest in perpetuating it, as much as in ameliorating it, and that 'sympathy' is part of this process of production, rather than an 'innocent' response. This tradition of sympathy critique reached its culmination in the influential work of Hannah Arendt. Given that the focus of her work in this area is on the French Revolution and its consequences, it seems particularly appropriate to consider it here.[98]

Basic to her argument is an attempt to distinguish between compassion and pity. For Arendt, compassion is an immediate response to the plight of a particular person; it is not primarily a feeling or emotion, indeed may not involve these at all. As act or reaction, it is essentially mute, more a matter of gestures than words. Above all, it cannot be generalized: 'Because compassion abolishes the distance, the worldly space between men where political matters, the whole realm of human affairs, are located, it remains, politically speaking, irrelevant and without consequence.' Jesus, as portrayed in Dostoevsky's 'The Grand Inquisitor', is the classic exemplar: he has compassion for each and every one of us, in our irreducible singularities, manifesting an ability to comprehend all, as individuals, that can only be divine. For Rousseau, on the other hand, '... while the plight of others moved his heart, he became involved in his heart rather than in the sufferings of others, and he was enchanted with its moods and caprices as they disclosed themselves in the secret delight of intimacy'; and this slide, she adds, proved crucial in 'the formation of modern sensibility'.[99] This is Arendt's version of the argument that one's feelings can all too easily supplant the other as focus of attention, and from this she generates a critique of pity.

When 'compassion becomes talkative', pity is discovered. With pity, generalization becomes possible; pity keeps its 'sentimental distance' and can 'reach out to the multitude'.[100] As Luc Boltanski glosses it, pity 'generalises in order to deal with distance, and in order to generalise becomes eloquent, recognising and discovering itself as emotion and feeling'.[101] Here we have an interesting reaffirmation of the idea that 'narrating emotion' can develop it and encourage self-centredness, that 'narrative' and 'emotion' can feed off each other in an endless spiral. Reading – or writing – the novel can indefinitely defer the compassionate action that may ostensibly be called for, even though it may *also* contribute to a general awareness of issues that can be shaped into a political response. But Arendt, true child of the rationalist Enlightenment, distrusts all such passion in the public sphere, and sees only the dangers: 'without the presence of misfortune, pity could not exist, and it therefore has just as much vested interest in the existence of the unhappy as thirst for power has a vested interest in the existence of the weak'. And because, as has been seen, 'pity can be enjoyed for its own sake ... this will almost automatically lead to a glorification of its cause, which is the suffering of others'.[102] Inspired by Enlightenment ideals, the French Revolution, that ultimate sentimental event, proclaimed '*le peuple toujours malheureux*'[103] as the fount of virtue, and the need to relieve suffering as its essential drive. Yet this grandiose experiment revealed – more clearly perhaps than Magdalen House – that the display and the relief of the 'deserving poor' in turn generated a vast category of the 'undeserving', shading from the merely apathetic over to the seditious and the counter-revolutionary, just as the activities of the revolutionaries themselves swelled the ranks of both groups. Hence the slide to Robespierre's Terror, wherein pity 'has proved to possess a greater capacity for cruelty than cruelty itself'.[104]

So: the central charge is that pity *needs* its victims, endlessly recreates them. Pity always carries with it the implication of separation, distance, even superiority. To pity someone requires, or indeed reinforces, a degree of autonomy. In this sense, pity could unwittingly serve the interests of the self, strengthen it, just as it could serve the interests of the socially powerful. And this could be true even of that characteristic eighteenth-century scenario where the beholder breaks down in tears: appearances to the contrary notwithstanding, this can reflect a self-interest that is confident about putting itself at some apparent risk, and could be further strengthened in the process. It is more about testing the self, or validating the self-respect of the group, than any real concern for the other. And if the structural asymmetry is unaffected by the emotional display, it becomes easy to disparage or distrust the latter. The danger, then, is that this brings about an *interest* – a possibility of self-interest – in the existence of pity, and the object of pity. The pitfalls of sentimentalism are manifest: that in responding to your suffering by my own feelings of sadness, thereby showing my sensitivity, I may gain a vested interest in your suffering. I need it, so that I can feel good about myself. And the upshot is the disappearance of your pain in my self-indulgence. And – as we saw with Emma – a further problem is that it is difficult to see how one could ever be really sure that this was *not* the case, that one's motives were indeed sufficiently pure and unsullied, particularly in a culture in which functionalist stereotypes about selfhood and the drive to self-interest have become so pervasive – assumptions that are, of course, reproduced in this critique itself.

The idea of powerful 'unconscious' aspects of mind and self-identity, and their influence on social groups, reinforced or reproduced ideologically, is of course one that only becomes influential *after* the eighteenth century; and what it leaves us with here is the theme of motivational complexity, and the consequent irreducibility of self-understanding to self-conscious awareness. This complexity, though, is arguably just as damaging to the critique as it is to the possibility of pity as a positive force in human relations. It is true that the 'pity response' is no guarantee that morally appropriate action will result, or that such action would be motivationally pure – but this is true of the relation between reaction and response in other contexts, too. And if sentimentalism is flawed here, or can be naïve, this is also true of rationalism: subsuming the instance under the morally appropriate law does not, of itself, guarantee an appropriate outcome either; motivational complexity can just as well interfere here, too. The relation between these two perspectives is significant, though, for our understanding of sympathy, and will be returned to in the next chapter, in the discussion of sympathy theory.

In the meantime, we can observe that it is too easy to dismiss the very possibility of emotional distress at the other's suffering, or to imply that the element of the vicarious present in the spectacle necessarily vitiates the quality, or even the likelihood, of the response. As for self-interest, we have to start from the fact that we do not – generally – feel good about the other's suffering; crucially, what we may feel good about is our capacity to respond sympathetically *to* the other's suffering. In this sense, the other's distress may be a condition for our feeling good about ourselves, but because that distress, in itself, is still distressing, we can in principle still respond to it appropriately. The fact that a slide in focus from the other to the self is possible does not make it inevitable; and if I suspect that I have made that slide, that in turn will counteract the complacency of my self-image – I will not feel so good about feeling good – and push me back towards the claims of the other. If the focus can be kept *there*, the situation is not morally irretrievable, whatever the motivational complexity. This does, of course, imply a (culturally reinforced) capacity for reflexivity, even though this cannot guarantee the outcome – and, as we have seen, this interest in reflexive awareness was certainly present here, both as discourse and pattern of experience. In short, Boltanski's claim that one of the constitutive tensions in a politics of sympathetic engagement is the tension between egoistic self-realization and self-realization through action oriented altruistically – however difficult this distinction may be in practice, and however likely it may be that elements of both will be present – remains more appropriate and useful than the attempt to dismiss the tension present here by reducing the latter alternative to the former.[105]

What this altruism might entail, in terms of a sentimental politics, is of course notoriously difficult to pin down. It seems fair to say that it can run from essentially conservative charity, geared to maintaining the status quo, through to radical action to overthrow it: historically, sentimentalism can be found to have been both an apology for hierarchy and its enemy.[106] Yet the ostensible universalism of sentimentalist themes, the focus on feeling, love, individual aspiration, as somehow more basic, more strong and positive than the restrictions imposed on them by traditional hierarchical forms, always implies the possibility of life beyond these forms. What Denby claims in the context of French literature surely resonates more widely: 'Sentimental love, the spontaneous expression of the heart, dictated by nature, is pitted against the social prejudice which sets obstacle of birth and fortune in its way, and the sentimental identification of the text is all on the side of the victims.'[107] One might say that the logic of sentimentalism is to push towards the subversion or abolition of contingent historical and social forms of human oppression, so as to highlight a more basic theme in human life: that of the fundamental equality of the human condition in the face of misfortune, those adversities of life and death that can be considered as, in principle, recurrently possible, probable or irremediable. If it is human to suffer misfortune, this recognition should bind us to one another, as the foundation of human community.

And we can return to Arendt here: for there is indeed a relation between sentimentalism and Enlightenment, but one that she misreads. There *is* an opposition, but it is between 'reason' and 'feeling', a polarity shared by the rationalist Enlightenment and the more extreme form of sentimentalism that sets up the mute body as the sole source of the 'language' of truth; as indicated previously, other strands of Enlightenment thinking converge with mainstream sentimentalism in trying to modify or overcome this polarity.[108] And the convergence extends to the Enlightenment project to reduce or remove socially induced suffering, so that only what is left *after* these political projects of reform are carried through could be truly regarded as inherent in the human state. The high points of Enlightenment and sentimentalist influence coincide: sentimentalism and reformism go hand in hand.

Just as the politics of modernity, stemming from the more ambitious versions of the rationalist Enlightenment, was dedicated to the elimination of all suffering, whether natural or social in origin, calling on the full resources of science, technology and the state to achieve this, so a politics of the postmodern might recognize a sense in which the sentimentalist emphasis at least points to limits as well as possibilities of human endeavour. The attempt to control the world to eliminate all suffering produces negative unintended consequences of the process itself. It is not primarily sentimentalism that produces suffering, through some mysterious teleology (it 'needs suffering to feed on'); the world of the project of modernity contributes plenty of its own, thereby in turn producing and reproducing the possibility of sentimentalist politics.[109]

But there is an important reservation to be made here. Sentimentalism, embedded in the spectacle of sympathy, is not basically a political or even an ethical, project. Sentimentalism is not, in itself, primarily about 'doing good', about charitable actions or gifts, in response to the plight of the other. That has always been there, in the Christian tradition. The plight of the other can always trigger sympathy, but what is basic here is the sense of a 'fellowship of selves', of 'fellow-feeling'. And this implies a kind of equality – not, now, an equality of souls before God, but of human selves encountering the misfortunes of life. And not necessarily just humans, either, for this seems to imply a relation to 'nature' as something both 'beyond' and 'within', also involved in this network of 'feeling', again a perspective that sentimentalism shares with influential strands in Enlightenment thought. As Taylor suggests, nature is seen as 'attuned' to our feelings; it can 'reflect and intensify those we already feel or else awaken those which are dormant'. Hence it can 'awaken us to feeling against the too pressing regulative control of an analytic, disengaging, order-imposing reason'.[110] We can say that 'nature' serves to encode this sense of a diffuse otherness, the experience of a world *recalcitrant* to control, the sense in which 'experience' *as* experience evades control and subverts the coherence of the self as agent of control. So all this, then, is more a matter of mutuality, of feeling, rather than a moral response, though of course it may perfectly well *result* in the latter. Such 'responsiveness' to the other can readily incorporate doing good; and here the issue of pleasure returns. Diderot claims that 'we need do nothing more in order to be happy than be virtuous'.[111] Misfortune recognized, acknowledged and, to that extent, *shared*, takes us outside ourselves, affirms our commitment to the other, and, in that respect, is bound to be experienced as pleasurable – which is not, of course, to say that the original experience in itself is, or that we can experience it other than vicariously. The community of loss incorporates pleasure, without that loss thereby being either redeemed or compensated.

But let us give the tableau the last word on this. In the Greuze picture, we see a communal drama of suffering unresolved. We also see action, but action as display, action that apparently negates itself, has no outcome beyond itself. Sentimentalism, one might say, always tends towards the immobilism of tableau, the timelessness of the moment in which we come together in pain, in the separation that locks us together. If we reveal our inner state, our expressive truth, in this moment, and read it in the other, it is simultaneously truth as loss, the truth of loss. But if this is both there, in the picture, and in our relation to it, the loss is also present as absence, our absence *from* the scene inherent in the spectatorial relation. And we know that this distance *can* enable an *active* response – through, rather than despite, emotion – and was frequently intended to do so, in a context in which such depictions were part and parcel of an Enlightenment vision, one in which sympathy played a significant part. And, finally, this whole relation, between feeling and representation, distance and involvement, can be taken to imply the possibility of a cultural aesthetics of sympathy, a perspective that we will explore further, in the next chapter.

The bonds of sympathy

But let us return to Emma once more, for the last time. In doing this, we repeat something she does twice in the novel, after the deaths of her father and of Mrs Harley. After the latter, she wanders once more through the rooms, 'to view, for *the last time*', the scenes of past 'affections'. The objects and places – the 'scenes' – now have emotional resonance, and seem as if enveloped by a 'mysterious and sacred enchantment'.[112] Since they previously lacked this, it is as if they are only invested with it because of this being the 'last time': it is this that gives each of them its uniqueness, as a coalescing of separate memories and experiences into a specificity that is grasped, here, as a manifestation of 'sympathy', that sense of a bond that is only there as, or immanent in, this very experience of it in these terms. And since, in this context, this 'sympathy' necessarily involves memory, the fact that it is not clear from the text whether Emma's 'wandering' over these past scenes was literal or metaphorical hardly seems to matter. Insofar as experience involves any element of reflection or conceptual appropriation, this is the element that is 'lost' in remembering; and since this is essential to the constitution of time, of time-as-experience, the effect is to abolish temporal distance in ('sentimental') presence, while overlaying the latter with the mysterious veil of the past regained. And this veil, this web, of sympathy, clearly extends beyond humans: it incorporates places, objects, even 'circumstances', insofar as these can get involved – as indeed they do – in our 'affections'. It is constantly described in the novel in the language of 'attachment' and 'connection', and involves the idea of a bond, which in turn, in the primary case of relations between people, involves mutuality (*shared* feeling, rather than feeling *for*).

What is clear, in all this, is that the 'mutuality' of sympathy implies a priority of relation, in some sense 'interpersonal' or communal, over entity or self.[113] And as for 'feeling', it is, once again, notoriously difficult to pin down, manifesting what Bell calls 'categorial elusiveness'.[114] It subverts or overflows any strict notion of subject boundaries, of an isolated self. And here, a further clue is given by Emma's suggestion, in a conversation with Augustus, that the affections are 'generated' by sympathy;[115] for this would imply that part of the problem with locating 'feeling' is that it is embedded in relations, connections, but emanates from these, and is not reducible to them. To put it the other way round, sympathy is not primarily feeling, or *a* feeling – though we can often think of it in this way – it is, rather, the condition, or virtual state, that is realized *in* feeling. Sympathy is affect in its virtual state, somehow prior to its manifestation in any particular feeling, but only accessible *as* or *through* the latter, with all the problems of image and interpretation that must imply. And that, perhaps, is as far as Emma can take us …

4

Sympathy Theory

The implication of the discussion so far is that sympathy can be viewed as the grounding of the social in the 'community of the self', an aesthetic of feeling which responds to the impossibility of making sense of feeling purely in terms of the embodied individual. The combination of feeling and imagination whereby the self is grasped is simultaneously a grasp of the self in relation to the other, of the modern sense of community in its virtual state. In this sense, sympathy was at the heart of eighteenth-century concerns with these issues, just as it has returned to feature in contemporary debates. In neither area can we anticipate terminological consistency, but some formulations point in helpful directions. Solomon tells us that 'Sympathy is neither a pleasant nor an unpleasant feeling. Sympathy is *about* the other person, a role that no sensation can play.'[1] This usefully highlights the social significance of sympathy, as does Boltanski's version, putting a more obviously Kantian gloss on it, claiming that sympathy is 'the natural faculty without which an individual could not know or be interested in someone else'.[2] Sympathy is not, then, on these formulations, so much a specific feeling or emotion, as a capacity for emotional response in the presence – real or imagined – of the other, and a response that is somehow affirmative of the other's existence as a fellow-subject. From this point of view, Ferguson's description of sympathy as 'a spontaneous "fellow-feeling" in the spectacle of life'[3] is very apposite.

Feeling sentimental

In the light of all this, we can return to the specific grounds on which sentimentality itself has been condemned, and examine them more closely. D. H. Lawrence claims that 'Sentimentalism is the working off on yourself of feelings you haven't really got.'[4] Elsewhere he adds: 'Sentimentality is the garment of our vice. It covers viciousness as inevitably as greenness covers a bog.'[5] More recently, in her sensitive exploration, Sedgwick has listed the attributes of the sentimental as it has been stigmatized and devalued: 'the insincere, the manipu- lative, the vicarious, the morbid, the knowing, the kitschy, the arch'.[6] Most of the items on this list incorporate the idea of *deception*. If we return to the model of the modern self as alienated from its feelings, its body, we can make sense of this by observing that this self-consciously 'rational' self is indeed able, in imposing itself on 'feeling', to manipulate the latter, even to the extent of simulating feeling that isn't really there. At the same time, ideas of an 'unconscious' mind, as these have developed since the nineteenth century, paradoxically *reinforce* this sense of the 'knowing' self as a producer of deception – this time, precisely because it is *not* sufficiently master in its own house, does not have the requisite self-understanding (it 'unconsciously' deceives itself *and* others). Again, this manifests a problem about feeling more generally, as we have known since the eighteenth century: that the display of feeling is no automatic guarantee of its authenticity. This line of criticism can perhaps be summed up in this quote from the philosopher Mary Midgley: 'Being sentimental is misrepresenting the world in order to indulge our feelings ... the central offence lies in self-deception, in distorting reality to get a pretext for indulging in *any* feeling'.[7] And the point here is not so much whether one agrees with this, but that one can see how the very issue itself is a cultural product, a manifestation of the 'feeling wars' made possible by an underlying structure of feeling that characterizes both the site of our problematical ability to relate to each other and to the world, and our discursive options in thinking and arguing about it.

At the same time, a criticism from the other direction is possible. This would emphasize not the quality of the feeling, but its strength: feeling that overwhelms the self, the 'submission response' outlined previously. Thus Tan and Frijda characterize the sentimental as 'an urge to cry or a state of being moved with a strength in excess of the importance we attach to its reason'.[8] This is the source of the idea that sentimentality is too easy, a superficial response. It makes no demands on us. In an interesting critique of critiques of sentimentalism, Deborah Knight points to the gender dimension again: for its critics, 'Sentimentality is a womanish – and at the end of the day, a sluttish – attitude: indulgent, cheap, shallow, self-absorbed, excessive ...'.[9] And its 'self-absorbed' character entails a deficit of self-understanding: the feeling washes over us, but afterwards, when the tide recedes, may leave us unchanged. So it can, in its way, be deceptive, too, for these rather different but parallel reasons. Only apparently innocent, this seductive feeling is more of a *femme fatale* ...

This, then, is where the two strands of criticism converge: in a thesis about motives. Sentimentalism, it is alleged, purports to involve wider concerns, particularly concerns for the suffering of the other, but it is actually a perversion of this; it is really about the pleasures of emotional self-indulgence, whether brought on deliberately or simply as a by-product of the feeling itself. In the latter case, the potential of the experience for reflexive appropriation makes it more likely that, in future, it will be 'cultivated', for example by placing oneself in a situation that is thought likely to elicit the desired response. Hence, suggests Boltanski, the possibility of 'deliberately seeking out the spectacle of suffering, not in order to relieve it, but in order to obtain from it the precious moment of emotion and … the happiness it arouses'.[10] And we here rehearse and reproduce the denunciations of sentimentalism that became commonplace in the later decades of the eighteenth century as the 'Age of Feeling' came in for increasing criticism.

All this does, of course, assume that this *is*, indeed, the motivational structure of sentimentalism, and that in condemning it as an alleged abuse of feeling, it is possible to identify a valid alternative, 'proper', location and role for feeling. This may not be so easy, particularly if the alternative again turns out to postulate the simplistic polarity of 'thought versus feeling' that has helped produce the problem in the first place.[11] All this suggests, however, that the notion of 'feeling' here, and its relation to other related terms, needs some further examination, particularly in the light of the tension between 'feeling' and 'reason' that has been prominent in modern discourse since the eighteenth century.

Words and problems: Feeling, emotion, thought, imagination

In this culture of sensibility, in this world of subjects and objects related through emotion, feeling and sensation, what is the place of thought? Now, there may be a strong sense – stemming from everyday life over this whole period, then and since – that this is not a problem that has to be posed; that thought and feeling may overlap seamlessly, and even be aspects of a common experience. 'My sentiments, too', can mean 'I agree with you' or 'I feel the same way', and the two are hardly distinguishable, any more than they would have been by eighteenth-century writers, including some philosophers. Hume, for example, uses 'sentiment' to refer to feelings, opinions and judgements, as occasion demands.[12] Even in contexts where these terms are not interchangeable, there can in practice be extensive overlap. This relationship is expressed well by Bell:

The word 'feel', as a near synonym for 'think', suggests, half subliminally, the mixture of the affective and the conceptual in what we call 'thought'. Feeling seems an obscure antecedent to, and therefore perhaps a necessary part of, conceptualization; as if thought has an affective component, or feeling is a form of understanding.[13]

And Michelle Rosaldo adds that 'feeling is forever given shape through thought, and ... thought is laden with emotional meaning'.[14] Clearly it is important to maintain this insight that there are everyday contexts in which these terms can be mutually implicated, rather than opposed, and that there can be an element of *necessary* overlap.

At the same time, the tension is there, particularly when 'thought' becomes narrowed to 'reason'. The term 'sentiment' could be seen as useful for containing the tension between the particularity, the situational specificity, of 'feeling', and the attempt to outline more general principles of human action implicit in the idea of 'reason': in Bell's words, 'Sentiment as "principle" was invoked as if it had the intuitive and spontaneous impact of feeling, while sentiment as "feeling" assumed the universal, impersonal authority of principle'.[15] Increasingly, as this tension became difficult to contain, the distinction came to embody the principle and the practice of separate spheres, with 'reason' coded as public and masculine, and 'feeling' as the arena of the domestic and the feminine, and this can lead us to situate the modern sense of alienation here, in one of its manifestations. The significance of reflexive thought, self-consciousness, as the attempt to understand the basis of our own actions, is both an essential implication of this rationality and a clue to T. S. Eliot's claims about a modern 'dissociation of sensibility', in that it 'embodies' this constantly recreated distancing of feeling,[16] which becomes 'alienated' as that which must be understood, even mastered, even while the impossibility of doing this in any conclusive way reinforces the sense of feeling as fundamental, albeit recalcitrant. Part of this is captured by Charles Taylor's thesis that the modern self is characterized not just by 'the power of disengaged rational control' but also by 'this new power of expressive self-articulation', and that these are in tension, since the first requires the disengagement from feeling that the second refuses.[17]

We thus return to the idea of feeling as a 'form of life', a structure or pattern of feeling that we inhabit prior to making analytical distinctions between feeling and thought, and which can be lost to view when we become reflexive and self-consciously 'rational'. From this point of view, exhortations to 'act rationally', for example, can be seen as covert calls to change the emotional register, rather than as implying any real possibility of giving up feeling altogether; and indeed

Hume argued that what we call 'reason' is often just a calmer state of feeling.[18] However much it may ostensibly be exiled, feeling always returns, as it were, even reminding us that it never really went away. Bell concludes that we are encouraged 'consciously to distrust feeling while implicitly depending on it', and that 'There is no alternative within a self-conscious modernity to the primordiality of feeling'.[19] If this position can be sustained, then clearly the eighteenth century is still powerfully present ...

'Feeling' can readily be diffuse, unfocused; so let us take the issue further by looking at emotion, which tends to be more concentrated, and more clearly 'psychological', and consider its relation to thought. One way of trying to move round, or beyond, the dualism outlined above is to argue that emotion *is* thought. This has been an influential approach in the cognitivism so influential in psychology in recent decades, an influence apparent in Reddy's formulation, whereby an emotion is presented as 'a type of activated thought material too broad to fit into attention all at once'.[20] This converges with the definition offered by Rosaldo, an anthropologist: 'Emotions are thoughts somehow "felt" in flushes, pulses, "movements" of our livers, minds, hearts, stomachs, skin. They are *embodied* thoughts, thoughts steeped with the apprehension that "I am involved"'.[21] These are both insightful, but we need to develop the implications with care. There is always the danger of rationalist distortion: emotion becomes merely a slightly indirect manifestation of the workings of reason, as it were. A tendency to slide in this direction can be detected in many of these recent approaches. Far from being 'dumb and blind', claims Simon Williams, emotional shifts can be seen as 'intentional, purposive adaptations engaged in by individuals, as embodied sentient and sensible agents';[22] Solomon presents emotions as 'ways of coping, products of assessment and evaluation, modes of rational action';[23] and Reddy argues that emotions are goal-oriented, and enable feedback and control, as well as being performative, ways of doing things.[24] Clearly there are some important truths here, notably the implication that emotions involve an *active* response to the world; but capturing this as 'intentional', in the sense of 'purposeful', risks merely reflecting the rationalist obsessions and priorities of the modern project.

There is also a risk of this in Campbell's illuminating account of the growth of modern 'autonomous' hedonism, the cultivation of the emotions as sources of pleasure that can provide more diverse and prolonged pleasure than the sensations sought in traditional hedonism.[25] This requires the skill and the habit of emotional self-control, the emancipation of emotion from mere reaction to external events. Since 'an emotion links mental images with physical stimuli', a stronger role for the imagination, whether in day-dreaming, fantasy or reading novels, gives us the power to 'conjure up stimuli in the absence of any externally generated sensations', hence permitting the pleasure of emotional involvement and release, and the intensity of emotional experience, to be enjoyed in a person's own time and own way.[26] In this account, reminding us of the 'experimental' approach to selfhood discussed in the previous chapter, there is a danger that too great an emphasis on the element of control, as such, might make this too rational and instrumental, the self's 'internal' version of the project of modernity, part of a 'project of the self'[27] that misses the sense in which emotions are *responses*, and cannot be wholly 'determined' by the subject on pain of losing this effect. An element of *lack* of control, of encounters across the borders of self and other, an acceptance of the unpredictability of the onset and development of emotion, also seem crucial. What is present here is a tension, an emphasis on learning selfhood through self-direction and reflexive understanding, attempting to control experience even as one is displaced by it, experience *being* that very displacement. One may learn to 'cultivate' emotional release, just as one learns of the perils and complexities, as well as the pleasures, of the outcome. Certainly one can agree with Campbell and Taylor on the significance of the growth of literacy and the spread of the novel as ways in which this emotional structure of modern selfhood was furthered; literature, after all, shapes and intensifies the capacity for emotional immersion and involvement in the pleasures and pains of the other.

Here, we can draw on a different sense of 'intentional', stemming from the phenomenological tradition. Sara Ahmed suggests that 'Emotions are intentional in the sense that they are "about" something: they involve a direction or orientation towards an object … or a way of apprehending the world', and this sense of being directed 'towards' or 'away', of being 'oriented', is not just feeling; in its immediacy, it involves a kind of appraisal, an attitude of selection, which itself implies thought, or at least 'being aware'. One doesn't just 'feel' angry; one has an awareness of reasons, and implicitly, of justifications. Thus, she continues, 'whether something is beneficial or harmful involves thought and evaluation, at the same time that it is "felt" by the body …'.[28] Thus Crossley can conclude that 'Our emotions form part of our point of view on the world; we do not just have them, we exist in and by way of them'.[29]

One way of developing this is to suggest that emotions involve *judgements*. Thus Solomon, observing that 'practical reason is circumscribed and defined by emotion', argues that emotions entail a framework of judgement: 'Anger involves judgments of blame; jealousy includes judgments about a potential threat or loss. Love involves evaluative judgments, typically overblown, but so does hatred ...' Such judgements can themselves, in turn, be evaluated as well or ill-founded, rational or irrational, but what is important is this initial element of appraisal, this sense of an *active* response. And while this obviously includes the basic sense of judgement as positive or negative evaluation, it also includes a more subtle dimension: that of initial *focus*, of reacting to something as *worth* reacting to, selecting something as being of 'interest'. Feeling isn't just an appraisal in terms of good and bad; it also discriminates experience in terms of important and unimportant. This is where it is so easy to overlook the sense in which 'calm' emotion is nonetheless still emotion. A good sense of this is conveyed by Solomon: 'Through our emotions we edit a scene or a situation in such a way that it *matters to us* ...'[30] Emotion as a kind of pre-rational 'editing' suggests that it makes no sense to think of rationality even as a possibility without this element of emotional involvement in setting the agenda in the first place, and providing the motivation to seek the resultant goal. Our sense of purposive, goal-directed action is dependent on this, not productive of it. And if we note that, on Bateson's interpretation, Kant's starting point in the *Critique of Judgement* is that 'the primary act of aesthetic judgement is selection of a fact',[31] then we can see that these 'felt judgements' provide a clue to how aesthetics is basic to thought and indeed our immersion in the world, our sensory, embodied experience of it.

Yet it cannot be left here: an active response is still a *response*. At this level, one *suffers* an emotion; it is something that happens to one, not something one does. One can try to 'get it under control', but that acknowledges that there is indeed something *there*. Emotion and feeling testify to an essential passivity in experience, to experience as something one lives through, endures. And this has carried considerable resonance in modern culture. At the beginning of *Sense and Sensibility*, Jane Austen informs us that 'Elinor's disposition was affectionate, and her feelings were strong, but she knew how to govern them': feelings are inherently disruptive, unpredictable, in need of 'government'.[32] Solomon points to the way emotions can be said to 'violate' our autonomy: 'The presumption is that our emotions, unlike our reason, are not truly our own, and they are humiliating rather than ennobling.'[33] Fear of passivity and fear of emotion tend to go together, with emotion seen as somehow 'beneath' thought or reason; and this has reinforced the powerful gender coding that has surrounded the contrast.[34]

It is also important not to lose the sense that emotion may be in some sense 'inside', but is also, crucially, *embodied*. This, too, produces problems for 'control', because emotion may seem difficult to locate. Ahmed argues that 'emotions create the very effect of the surfaces and boundaries that allow us to distinguish an inside and an outside in the first place'; they are not simply something we 'have' – in 'having' them, we find it difficult to *place* them. They are part of the very grounding of the categories of modern experience, contributing to our sense of the other as object, and hence, also, of ourselves as subjects. Such 'objects' become 'sticky', 'saturated with affect', which can carry past histories, of association, tension and communication. Overall, emotions work 'through signs and on bodies to materialise the surfaces and boundaries that are lived as worlds'.[35]

Drawing these aspects together, then, we might want to characterize emotions as 'expressive judgements', 'felt thoughts', expressing an orientation; and we might add that this expressive dimension seems to come from 'within' the self[36] – the 'I am involved', in Rosaldo's formulation, above, or Norman Denzin's description of emotion as 'self-feeling'[37] – while yet being 'intentional', pointing 'beyond', other-directed. And (in turn revisiting Reddy) we might suggest – rather speculatively – that when the scanning activity of consciousness is swamped, overwhelmed, we have emotion; or, emotion is what is excessive to consciousness yet somehow present to it, as power or energy, disparate, different in kind, the difference enforcing an orientation (positive or negative). Emotion brings into play the hinterland of consciousness. It may also be that, as Reddy suggests, this sense of being swamped by something 'different' can usefully be seen as involving 'translation', so that what we find here is a failure to translate 'the flow of coded messages an awake body generates',[38] a way of putting it that is nicely reminiscent of the 'nervous body' of eighteenth-century science, as we shall see. And it could be pointed out that while there is much sliding around between the three terms 'emotion', 'feeling' and 'sensation', and while there are indeed continuities and overlaps – 'feeling', in particular, seems to embrace either or both terms, depending on context – one might nonetheless want to emphasize a point of contrast between emotion and sensation, as polarity rather than continuum. While of course 'embodied', emotion carries an essential, albeit implicit, reference to a depth model of the self, along with this imputed link to an outside, an 'other', while sensation is more strongly body-focused, primarily a matter of physical impressions, perceptions and reactions.[39]

What matters at this point, then, is not so much what emotions are, or where they come from, but this very process whereby they are shaped or figured – and, since the eighteenth century, this has been characterized as the arena of the imagination, a mysterious 'place' or 'power' which clearly requires further discussion. This power only exists as embodied, in the shapes and figures that loom up out of the hinterland: a puppet theatre with nobody pulling the strings.

And this hinterland can be 'outside' or 'inside' the self – characteristically, indeed, it implicitly questions or subverts this distinction, inhabits the nebulous boundary zone that makes the distinction both possible and problematical. The eighteenth century witnessed an increasing focus on experience as experience of and by a subject, and the hypostatization of this subject as 'self', with 'mind' as its seat of consciousness, constructed as an internal space that could most appropriately be figured as 'theatre'. Then, and perhaps now, this seemed the term which best captured that sense of process unfolding within a space, a frame, involving a dynamic relation between appearance, semblance, illusion and reality, a drama of sentimental self-construction in which the self is called on to manifest itself through inescapable signs of its own truth, just as those signs are forever unable to deliver incontrovertible proof. Denby describes the mind as 'the theatre of the imagination',[40] which also reminds us again of the importance of *not* equating 'thought' with 'reason': within the context of thought, it is the imagination, rather than reason, that figures this underlying sense of subjective experience as involved in, even based on, feeling.

In short, the imagination shifts the emphasis away from sensation, towards the imaging of feeling as experience, making sense of what is in us and yet what we are part of, the otherness within that is also the otherness of those we encounter and address as fellow subjects of the community of sensibility. 'Inner space' thus emerges as the imaginary theatre of the self, a figuration through which we encounter the play of others, and the self as other, projected as image, simultaneously inside and outside, the legible but always disputable 'sign' of the inner theatre. It is a space of precarious autonomy, 'guaranteed' by the self-reflection that also renders it provisional, inconclusive – a 'work of art' like the tableau it can readily contemplate, criss-crossed as it is by the same constitutive relations and tensions.

We can let Bell conclude, by returning us to sympathy, and thereby pointing us forward. Following Adam Smith, he suggests that sympathy is 'an imagined arena in which the subjectivities of all human others, and of the self, are reconstructed in a manner which has to be both emotional and judgemental at once ...'.[41]

Adam Smith and the sympathetic imagination

Along with his older colleague, David Hume, one of the twin pillars of the Scottish Enlightenment, and the author of *The Wealth of Nations*, the founding text of political economy: until recently, that was the entirety of Adam Smith's reputation. Over recent decades, however, that has been changing. There is even a case for arguing that the earlier *Theory of Moral Sentiments* is the key text, providing the essential context for the later one: the economy is one part, albeit crucial, of modern life, but the latter has to make prior sense in 'moral' (we might say, social and cultural) terms. This is the Adam Smith we draw on for this discussion.[42]

An initial challenge about the very definition of 'sympathy' needs to be confronted here. In both Hume and Smith, the term seems to be used in a way that contrasts with standard usage today; and both authors are aware that they are diverging in some degree from standard usage in their own time, too. Hume suggests that the 'soul or activating principle' of other passions, of whatever kind, is sympathy;[43] hence sympathy is not just one feeling or emotion among others, it is the lynchpin. Smith suggests that while sympathy may originally have meant something like pity or compassion, now it may legitimately be used 'to denote our fellow-feeling with any passion whatever'. Later on, however, he writes that the word sympathy, 'in its most proper and primitive signification, denotes our fellow-feeling with the sufferings, not with the enjoyments, of others'.[44] The immediate contradiction here can perhaps be viewed strategically: that is, Smith is implicitly acknowledging the 'normal' use of the term, and accepting that the bulk of his discussion and examples must therefore be drawn from this area. Indeed, we do generally invoke the term in contexts where people are experiencing difficulties or disasters, and this *practical* (moral, political) use of the term has been central to its everyday cultural significance.

I can feel sorrow at your grief, even to the point of shedding tears; this would seem to be a textbook case of sympathetic fellow-feeling. But I can also feel joy at your good fortune, again even to the point of shedding tears; and there is an evident similarity of response here, whatever the obvious difference in the precipitating cause or context. Both seem to qualify as manifestations of 'fellow-feeling'. This could reinforce the idea that, in this broad sense, perhaps sympathy simply *is* 'fellow-feeling', feeling *as* other-oriented; it is a condition for, and an aspect of, more specific other-oriented feelings – other-oriented feeling in its virtual state, perhaps. It is both a general capacity, and a more specific realization, although even in the latter form it retains its more unclear, unspecific associations: 'grief', 'fear', 'joy', seem specific enough emotions, but 'sympathy' hardly fits in the list. In discussing Smith, Alexander Broadie makes the interesting suggestion that 'sympathy' indicates 'the way that the spectator has the feeling – he has it *sympathetically*. It is the way he is angry, or is joyful, and so on …' He adds that, as in Hume, 'it is a feeling to which the mechanism of sympathetic communication has made an essential contribution', as in the spectator's anger or joy.[45] And the 'other-orientation' can perhaps be clarified here. There seems to be an element of mimesis, or at least of sharing, in what is involved. If you are grieving, my sympathy will be expressed in similar terms; if you are joyful, my sympathetic reaction will also be upbeat. (Of course, I may also react unsympathetically, in either case.) Hence Sutrop's prescient suggestion that 'Sympathy is for Smith not an emotion but the correspondence of emotions'.[46] Sympathy, one might say, is the affect of homology, a perspective that will need further elaboration. It is both the capacity, and the underlying pattern, that permit the more specific emergence of sympathy as the feeling of mutuality, of a 'being together', rather than being locked into totally separate subjectivities, even though this is expressed indirectly, through other feelings and emotions. It is important, then, to respect these insights of Hume and Smith into the wider resonance of 'sympathy', which may give insight into links with other cultural experiences that are not immediately apparent.

What, then, is involved in this act of sympathy? To ensure 'some correspondence of sentiments' when witness to misfortune, Smith suggests that the spectator should try to 'put himself in the situation of the other', adopt the 'whole case' of the sufferer, and 'strive to render as perfect as possible, that imaginary change of situation upon which his sympathy is founded'.[47] If sympathy 'does not arise so much from the view of the passion, as from that of the situation which excites it', as Smith puts it, this makes it clear that what is crucial here is the capacity of the imagination to grasp the position of the other, rather than the ability of our feelings to share in, or be directly influenced by, the other's feelings. Indeed, until we know more, anger may merely exasperate us, rather than provoke sympathy, and lamentation may merely provoke curiosity at first.[48] In a celebrated passage at the beginning of his book, Smith expands on this:

> As we have no immediate experience of what other men feel, we can form no idea of the manner in which they are affected, but by conceiving what we ourselves should feel in the like situation. Though our brother is upon the rack, as long as we ourselves are at our ease, our senses will never inform us of what he suffers. They never did, and never can, carry us beyond our own person, and it is by the imagination alone that we can form any conception of what are his sensations. Neither can that faculty help us to this any other way, than by representing to us what would be our own, if we were in his case. It is the impressions of our own senses only, not those of his, which our imaginations copy. By the imagination we place ourselves in his situation, we conceive ourselves enduring all the same torments, we enter as it were into his body, and become in some

measure the same person with him, and thence form some idea of his sensations, and even feel something which, though weaker in degree, is not altogether unlike them.

Thus it is by 'changing places in fancy' that we can have 'fellow-feeling for the misery of others'. In one of his examples, Smith refers to a mother with a sick infant, superimposing her own imaginative consciousness on to the sense of its helplessness to form 'the most complete image of misery and distress'.[49]

Perhaps we can say that to *try* to share the other's feelings, in some direct and purposeful way, is to court failure: the 'trying' interferes with the objective. It is the indirectness of the imagination that is important here, coupled with the emphasis on situation: it is not the other so much as the *place* of the other, the other *in relation to* context. So, on this approach, it is the imaginative grasp of situation that is critical, not because it draws us away from feeling, but because it can produce or deepen it. It is likely to have this result because – as we just saw with Smith's example – it can be said to superimpose an element of understanding, working to strengthen feeling, and increasing the likelihood of some *shared* feeling. And it is the understanding, projected *within* the imagination, an aspect of it, that does this, by bridging – not closing – gaps, by imaging relationships: in this case, self and other. And this helps make sense of the productive tension in Smith's account: in sympathizing with the other, to what extent do we remain ourselves?

Smith suggests that what is involved is both an 'imaginary change' of circumstances and something more fundamental, a change of 'persons and characters'.[50] This seems to make it both not-real and real, yet the paradox is only apparent; taken with the 'as it were' of the extended passage above, it is clear that we are in the realm of the vicarious, in the guise of the other. In this realm, distance is maintained, both self-distance and distance in that we are not 'really' being the other; it is a reflexive 'knowingness' rather than knowledge as such. The boundaries that separate may be in abeyance, but the 'distance' remains; we are not on the other side, either. Hence Howard can appropriately claim, of Smith's formulation, that 'The vicariousness so often criticized in sentimentality is here seen more neutrally as one of its structural elements'.[51] And the (external) circumstances are relevant here in that the vicarious gives us *perspective*, a view of the world from a different angle, relative to the difference in position. The vicarious both exhibits and lives this experience of distance, of distance *as* experience, thereby enacting the simultaneous inseparability and mutual irreducibility of self and other.

This also reminds us that there is a fictive dimension to the expression of emotion and feeling, together with the implication that 'expression' is not a mere extra, but an essential dimension to their culturally embodied reality. In short, two formulations by Charles Griswold, discussing Smith, point up the tension here effectively: '"Sympathy" articulates the fundamental fact of our already being, at least to some degree, "in" each other's world', while 'Our fundamental separatedness ... is not obliterated by the imagination.'[52] The term 'distance', after all, has both spatial and emotional connotations; and 'sympathy' attempts to show how the individuals of our modern world can both 'be together' while yet 'standing apart'.[53] And here, in this sense that the sympathetic imagination involves a degree of distance, rather than identification, we find a certain convergence with another influential writer on these themes: Rousseau – at least in Derrida's interpretation of the latter. Derrida argues that, in Rousseau, pity requires a degree of non-identification, that 'we neither can nor should feel the pain of others immediately and absolutely', and this in turn invites the imagination to play a crucial role. It is the power of imagination that raises mere affect to emotion: 'Without imagination, this pity does not awaken of itself in humanity, is not accessible to passion, language, and representation.'[54]

When can I sympathize? Under what conditions is the sympathetic imagi-nation most likely to engage? Using the term 'passion' in a broad sense, to encompass the range of emotions, desires and feelings (as did Hume), Smith argues that the 'passions of the body' either do not provoke sympathy, or only do so to a limited extent.[55] The classic case would seem to be physical pain. 'I feel your pain' has become an expression that is widely used satirically because it is so difficult to give it credence if taken literally.[56] And if I can't feel your pain, it is difficult to see how I can imagine it, either; the experience of severe pain, for either of us, just seems to block out 'imagination' altogether. Smith implies that pain is *pure* body, hence inaccessible to imagination; and certainly it is true that our culture, with its strong tradition of mind–body dualism, insists upon pain as the unmediated voice of body, often linked to claims about embodiment as the grounding reality of the individual and individualism. The 'cultural work' of pain is to emphasize our separateness, our irreducible individuality, our identity *as* body.[57] Thus, the spectacle of sympathy addresses feelings through imagination, imagined roles, situations and predicaments, not the embodied reality of pain and suffering as such. The latter, we might say, is appropriated by the language of the circuit of sensation, and is more likely to produce 'visceral' reactions (terror, horror, revulsion) that may well be unaccompanied by sympathy. It is not that pain defies our capacity to connect with it, but that any such connection is direct, unmediated, a visual or visceral stimulus (as 'sensation'). And indeed the 'unmediated' voice of the body is all too available for media appropriation in the spectacle as it becomes sensationalized. To *emphasize* pain, or pain as *body*, is *already* to sensationalize it, encouraging a visceral impact on us, while making it readily available for spectacle as the thrill in horror: sensation as *entertainment*.[58] Conversely, if we encompass pain as feeling or emotion, embodied but also available to us as a resource for imaginative thought, we can engage with it 'sympathetically'. Pain accompanied by feeling and emotion is pain situated, contextualized, available for incorporation in the spectacle of sympathy.

It is 'passions which take their origin from the imagination', argues Smith, that produce the conditions for 'normal' sympathetic response. 'A disappointment in love, or ambition, will, upon this account, call forth more sympathy than the greatest bodily evil. These passions arise altogether from the imagination.' These passions characteristically include grief, anxiety, fear and joy. I can readily sympathize with a friend who has lost a son; and whereas pain may pass quickly, this is not so with an unguarded word from a friend. 'What at first disturbs us is not the object of the senses, but the idea of the imagination.' And this can linger. If we sympathize with Tom when he is beaten by Legree in *Uncle Tom's Cabin*, or with Sethe's 'tree of scars' in Toni Morrison's *Beloved*, it is the anguish, fortitude and resilience of the sufferers, rather than the pain itself, that engages us; and it can also be when pain is coupled with danger, and hence provokes fear, that we are more likely to sympathize with it, as the fear gives our imagination something to work on. In a somewhat different example that is, shall we say, delightfully of its time, Smith suggests that while the loss of a mistress is less grave than the loss of a leg – mistresses are clearly two a penny, while the loss of a leg is serious stuff, a 'more real calamity' – it is the loss of the mistress that would provoke the writing of a fine tragedy, whereas one based on the loss of the leg would be merely 'ridiculous'.[59] But finally, such 'passions of the imagination' also need to fall within the broad bounds of the 'reasonable': the passions of two lovers can appear ludicrous to everyone else, whereas secondary passions that can arise from this (such as envy or remorse) can be more readily sympathized with, as can qualities inherent in the situation when not pushed to excess (generosity, kindness).[60]

The imagination, one might say, is best equipped to explore itself, within certain broad limits that we might recognize as 'normal'. There is, in effect, some model here of a range of comprehensible human responses to problems and situations, 'normality' characterizing the relation between feeling, emotion and thought that occurs here, 'thought' in turn encompassing a relation between imagination and reason that provides for the appropriate exercise of judgement. This is also implied by the requirement that the imagination not be slave to the passions, that it have the necessary independence to respond to the latter rather than be in thrall to them. When these conditions are met, our capacity for sympathetic engagement in the other's situation is enhanced. And while there is an obvious risk of social or cultural bias in this category of 'normality', it is important to register the fact that this is intended to refer to the relationship between the faculties, as indicated, *not* to cultural values, which will of course vary considerably, without necessarily challenging the fundamentals of the model. One must remember that the aspirations of Smith, as of his fellow Enlightenment theorists, was to ground the possibility of response to the predicament of the other in ways that are *not* restricted by particulars of class, status or culture – responses that could indeed rise to the challenge of 'difference' itself.

Approaching the heart of Smith's theory, we can now take up the part that pleasure plays in sympathetic response. What is at stake here is important, and the issue comes to the fore rather dramatically in a footnote to the second edition of the *Theory of Moral Sentiments*, in which Smith replies to a criticism of his position made in a letter from Hume. Directing his fire at Smith's assumption that sympathy is *always* a pleasurable feeling, Hume argues that it may actually be experienced in negative terms by the spectator: one is affected by the other's feeling, for good or ill, in an immediate way, rather like catching an infection. He takes the instance of 'An ill'humord Fellow … always *ennuié*, sickly, complaining', someone who 'throws an evident Damp on Company, which I suppose wou'd be accounted for by Sympathy; and yet is disagreeable'.[61] In response, Smith accepts that while it is agreeable to sympathize with joy, we struggle against 'sympathetic sorrow' when seeing a tragic play at the theatre, since 'it is painful to go along with grief, and we always enter into it with reluctance', but then proceeds to defend his main point in a passage that requires extended quotation:

> I answer, that in the sentiment of approbation there are two things to be taken notice of; first, the sympathetic passion of the spectator; and secondly, the emotion which arises from his observing the perfect coincidence between this sympathetic passion in himself, and the original passion in the person principally concerned. This last emotion, in which the sentiment of approbation properly consists, is always agreeable and delightful. The other may either be agreeable or disagreeable, according to the nature of the original passion, whose features it must always, in some measure, retain.[62]

On this account, the 'original passion' in the agent is reflected, in some quasi-automatic way, in the 'sympathetic passion' of the spectator; in effect, this retains something of the element of immediacy, even contagion, that Smith has absorbed from Hume but is generally trying to play down. The 'second' emotion, however, derives from observation, a self-observation that is also an observation of the relation *between* one's own emotion and that of the other person. This shift in emphasis is momentous. It seems to introduce a distance into the situation, the distance of observation (in contrast to involvement, participation) emerging after or beyond the initial impact, or somehow super-imposed on it. And it is a moment of *reflexive* awareness, simultaneously constitutive of the self and incorporating a relation with the other. This second emotion is said to be what the 'sentiment of approbation' properly consists of. This is a feeling of approval, carrying an element of judgement with it, that is, in effect, a response to a *relationship*, a harmony, a 'perfect coincidence' between self and other. My feelings about your situation are mapped on to your feeling about your situation: this is a relationship between two relationships; there is a homology between these two relationships, between two sets of 'intentional' feelings. The response is a response to form, to congruence beyond content: it can thus be characterized as a properly *aesthetic* response. It is this that provides the rationale for Smith's universality assumption, that 'agreeableness' is inherent in this second-order response. At its most basic, this is *disinterested* pleasure;[63] it is 'response', as such; issues of motivation are not raised. As Griswold summarizes it, 'The pleasure we take in mutual sympathy is understood by Smith aesthetically, as a disinterested attraction to harmony, concordance, system, and balance. It is not "mere pleasure".'[64]

Nevertheless, we can observe here that this second level of response is one that can, in principle, be lingered over. Since it is a source of pleasure, this feeling can be indulged. Here lies the source of one of the most widely observed features of sentimentalism, as it is also one of the most widely criticized. Hume's party pooper, apparently spreading melancholy, could also be spreading the possibility of *pleasure* in melancholy, as a response to this second-order congruence. The pleasures of lamentation – Diderot's 'sweet pleasure of being moved and shedding tears'[65] – apparently so paradoxical, can be seen in this light. Indeed, this enables us to account for the way in which the person *not* suffering the original distress can, through rehearsing it, repeating it vicariously, get something out of it.[66]

To return to Smith, one can recall his insistence that sympathy involves putting ourselves in the place of the other, in the other's *situation*: that is, it is the relationship between the other and his problems or circumstances that we are trying to grasp, rather than the essence or distinctiveness of 'the other' as such. Sympathy is inherently *structural*. 'Fellow feeling' does not require that we 'know' the other person; it is simply that we can have a meaningful relationship, based on responsiveness to his predicament. The element of 'distance' is irreducible. But there is also a sense in which this distance is a distance from self, incorporated into the self. The process whereby the self grasps itself *in* this relation to the other, is mapped on to the process whereby the self expresses its own feelings, 'manifests' them in recognizable, culturally variable ways. And this grounds the dimension of the *vicarious* in feeling, the process whereby feeling is given imaginative form, is projected, clothed, in the vestments that constitute its public garb; in this spectacle of sympathy, the self in its public guise manifests itself as inherently theatrical.[67]

The impartial spectator

This space, or tension, between reflection and passion, mapped onto the relationship between self and other in the context of sympathy, has wider ramifications. Smith presents us with a distinction between what he calls the 'amiable' and the 'respectable' virtues, between 'indulgence' and 'self-command'. To understand this, we need to develop the rather static account given so far, remembering that sympathy involves a process of interaction. Just as the spectator tries to meet the feelings of the potential recipient of sympathy, in an expansive move of self towards other, so too the latter moderates his feelings so as to meet the spectator halfway: 'while the spectator seeks to approve, the agent seeks his approval', as Broadie puts it,[68] and the two can evolve towards a position of mutuality. In the first case, that of the spectator, Smith argues that we encounter 'the soft, the gentle, the amiable virtues, the virtues of candid condescension and indulgent humanity'; in the case of the sufferer, we find 'the great, the awful and respectable, the virtues of self-denial, of self-government', showing the need to 'command' the passions, in the light of 'honour' and 'propriety'.[69] After all, 'clamorous grief', for example, counts for less than 'noble and generous resentment' in swaying the spectator. Overall, then, we are called on to 'restrain our selfish, and to indulge our benevolent affections', thus revealing the 'perfection of human nature' and potentially producing 'harmony of sentiments and passions'.[70] The amiable virtue, 'humanity', thus consists in 'exquisite fellow-feeling', and actions based on this require no self-denial; in contrast, the respectable virtue, 'generosity', calls on us for self-sacrifice.[71] Yet there is no ultimate incompatibility here: sensibility to the feelings of others is the principle on which self-command is founded, after all. Thus does Smith attempt to fuse the nobility of ancient Stoic ethics with the sentimentalism of the eighteenth century, in the process further revealing the potential tension within the dichotomous self, carrier of the civilizing process and emergent modernity.[72]

This reflexive dimension, with its implied self-division, enables us to consider the nature of spectatorship in relation to judgement. In self-examination, argues Smith, 'I divide myself, as it were, into two persons', and 'I, the examiner and judge, represent a different character from that other I, the person whose conduct is examined and judged of'. This latter 'character' is referred to as the 'man without', motivated by desire for actual praise, and the avoidance of blame; but we can appeal beyond him, to the 'man within', who desires 'praise-worthiness' and is averse to 'blame-worthiness'.[73] Thus can men listen to 'the appeal of their own consciences, to that of the supposed impartial and well-informed spectator, to that of the man within the breast, the great judge and arbiter of their conduct'. Only in this way can we make 'any proper comparison between our own interests and those of other people'.[74] It is only this 'impartial spectator' who can show us 'the propriety of generosity and the deformity of injustice', who can persuade us, through 'reason, principle, conscience', that we should be concerned about the victims of an earthquake in China; who can, in short, show us 'the real littleness of ourselves' and lead us to realize that 'we are but one of the multitude, in no respect better than any other in it ...'.[75]

This line of argument could appear to be quite strongly rationalist, an impression that could be strengthened by Smith's claim that 'Our continual observations upon the conduct of others, insensibly lead us to form to ourselves certain general rules concerning what is fit and proper either to be done or to be avoided'.[76] And some of the glosses by commentators could be seen in these terms, such as: 'To become the spectator is not to be possessed by the passion of others, but to be the arbiter of all sentiments'.[77] But the whole way Smith has set the situation up should make us pause. He refers, after all, to 'persons' or 'characters', and to the spectator as 'representing' one of these characters. This is not the language of rationalist philosophy; it is the language of role play, of the theatre, of actor and audience. It can certainly, without contradiction, include elements of the drama of the courtroom ('judging'). It is Griswold who notices this most clearly: 'The theatrical relation is thus internalized; we become our own public'.[78] Hence 'the spectator is the personification of the public'.[79]

In effect, we can see two alternatives polarized here. First, rationalism: judgements about whether cases deserve sympathy should be based purely on general principles, applied through universally valid rules to the cases in question. On this model, feeling becomes essentially irrelevant; the Age of Sentiment has truly disappeared into the Age of Reason. Second, it is our passionate response to particular people in particular situations that is our sole guide; the language of tears, the dictates of the heart, tell us all we need to know. This is full-blown sentimentalism, the foundation of our present-day notion of sentimentality, allowing no place for thought at all. Clearly Smith rejects the latter, but it is important to see that he also rejects the former. In effect, Smith inverts the rationalist argument, and radically transforms it in the process; we go from particular cases to more general rules, but the former cannot, anyway, be derived from, or subsumed under, the latter. The process is actually inductive, not deductive. Virtue does indeed entail 'conformity to reason'. And reason is indeed the source of the 'general rules' of morality, and hence of our moral judgements. Yet, crucially, reason is not the starting point.

Confronted with a situation that is one of potential moral engagement, our initial response depends on *feeling*, not reason. It is feeling that responds to the particularities of person, action, and context. Our 'first perceptions', as Smith calls them, 'cannot be the object of reason, but of immediate sense and feeling', since 'nothing can be agreeable or disagreeable for its own sake, which is not rendered such by immediate sense and feeling'.[80] This is a significant formulation: such immediate response to an object or situation *in itself*, without reference to utility or other goals, can appropriately be characterized as *aesthetic*, in the broad, foundational sense of the term, whereby feelings that are positive or negative include a potential for an ethical response, as yet undifferentiated. And, as we have seen, this arena of feeling, of emotional response, includes an implicit element of judgement, in that it registers *what really matters*, what is of central relevance in the situation. One might add here that the imagination, too, must have an active involvement, through that initial grasp of the specificity and integrity of the situation-in-itself.

It is at this point – and it is only at this point – that reason becomes important, in that it enables *reflective* judgement to weigh in, considering the wider context and other similar cases.[81] Feelings, then, are *basic*, but not *decisive*; they are in principle open to assessment and re-evaluation. If we sympathize with someone's actions, we take pleasure both in his actions and in the response of others his actions benefit, but we also, argues Smith, 'observe that his conduct has been agreeable to the general rules by which these two sympathies generally act'. And these 'general rules' function as generalizations about 'appropriateness' in 'types of situations', rather than as premises in an inflexible rationalist deduction. In the end, the 'impartial spectator', the 'demigod within the breast',[82] can only do his best: as demigod, he remains part-mortal, and hence, in principle, fallible.[83] Even so, this might qualify him to be regarded as 'a hero of the Enlightenment', in Broadie's striking phrase.[84]

Overall, then, it seems fair to say, with Griswold, that 'sentiment, imagination, and understanding, not philosophical reason, are the basis of sympathy',[85] and hence the spectator emerges as the 'reasonable' person, 'the person of reflective and informed imagination and appropriately engaged emotions, suitably detached from the actor ... so as to allow perspective'.[86] This 'perspective' again reinforces the point that detachment from the viewpoint of the actor does not mean detachment from *any* viewpoint. This is not a transcendental spectator, free of any conceivable role. Rather, spectatorship *is* a role: that of the 'concerned citizen', the actor in the 'public' sphere, in the broadest sense of the latter – the sense in which it implies our general rights and responsibilities in society. Boltanski takes the argument further, by noting that the figure of the 'impartial spectator' permits and encourages the possibility of communication *about* sympathy and suffering. I react to the situation of the other; then, in my capacity as 'impartial spectator', I also react *to* my reaction, and can gain 'perspective' on it. This is inherent in what has been said about the role of the imagination and reflective judgement. The introduction of reflexivity here, suggests Boltanski, 'makes it possible to introduce a symmetry which reduces the tension between an aperspectival objectivism and moral involvement',[87] and the outcome is that compatibility between the responses of different spectators becomes more likely, just as it may also make it more likely that there will be greater convergence between the perspectives of the spectator and the sufferer.[88] Precisely because the 'impartial spectator' is *not* just a synthesis of the opinions of others, it follows that 'Coordination between the reactions and emotions of distinct spectators cannot then be imputed solely to the gradual contagion of opinions and affects'.[89] And this implicitly provides us with a model of 'involvement plus distance' that could serve to guide the reporting of situations that provoke sympathetic engagement in a world that has become increasingly one of media spectacle.

Sympathy and the critique of modernity

We can explore this further by elaborating what is, in effect, Smith's theory of modernity. In a powerful, prescient passage, he writes:

> The poor man goes out and comes in unheeded, and when in the midst of a crowd is in the same obscurity as if shut up in his own hovel ... The man of merit and distinction, on the contrary, is observed by all the world. Every body is eager to look at him, and to conceive, at least by sympathy, that joy and exultation with which his circumstances naturally inspire him ... Scarce a word, scarce a gesture, can fall from him that is altogether neglected ... and if his behaviour is not altogether absurd, he has, every moment, an opportunity of interesting mankind, and of rendering himself the object of the observation and fellow-feeling of every body about him.[90]

The amendment one might want to make to this, as an age of established social ranks slides towards an age of spectacle and celebrity, is to substitute '*particularly if his behaviour is altogether absurd*', but then we find that Smith himself seems to do this, as he moves into more overtly critical mode. He observes that 'this disposition to admire, and almost to worship, the rich and powerful, and to despise, or, at least, to neglect persons of poor and mean condition' is 'the great and most universal cause of the corruption of our moral sentiments'. The rich can thereby set 'what is called the fashion', and the rest of us follow, slavishly. 'Even their vices and follies are fashionable; and the greater part of men are proud to imitate and resemble them in the very qualities which dishonour and degrade them.' Finally, we note that, in comparison to the pleasures of basking in the public gaze, 'all other pleasures sicken and decay'.[91] Thus do we encounter a world in which the spectacle of sympathy slides readily enough into the spectacle of consumerism.

What seems to happen is this. Initially we respond, through feeling, to the joys or griefs of others. Both the situations we respond to, and how we respond, have already been shaped – but not determined – by previous experience. Then an element of reflection kicks in, providing the stage on which the impartial spectator can make his appearance. This figure enjoins us to sympathize with the joys of those who are entitled to them, and with the griefs of those who do not deserve their misfortune. This sympathy can be manifested as admiration or as indignation, respectively; in other words, once again, sympathy characteristically reveals itself in the guise of other emotions. Now, in the first case, admiration, it is all too easy to mistake sign for substance – this, as we have seen, being an abiding problem both in the culture of sentimentalism and in the civilizing process. It is as though we feel that those whose situations are pleasurable, the rich and powerful, those of 'rank and distinction', must surely, in some broad sense, deserve their positions; hence we can justifiably engage the sympathetic response. The apparent 'merit' can be read backwards, as it were: effect becomes cause, and the signs become the substance. We forget that actually it is not wealth or greatness *in themselves* that we should admire, but wisdom and virtue; and 'inattentive observers are very apt to mistake the one for the other'.[92] The superficial signs are there for us all to see, after all, in the age of publicity and the mass media, whereas the reality 'behind' – which may involve obscure motives, etc. – can be mysterious, difficult to penetrate. Indeed, Smith takes this further, looking forward to a later cult of 'authenticity' that is already emergent in the culture of his time. Commenting on the importance of a 'free communication of sentiments and opinions' he adds: 'We all desire ... to know how each other is affected, to penetrate into each other's bosoms, and to observe the sentiments and affections which *really* subsist there.' In producing the theatre of manners, the civilizing process also reminds us that manners can be deceptive, and this, too, reinforces Smith's point.[93]

It is the 'parade of our riches',[94] the spectacle of consumerism, that dominates, though, and seems to invite us in, suggesting that we can all share in it. Sympathetic participation slides into vicarious identification: if we can vicariously share our friends' good fortune, take pleasure in their pleasure, then no great step is needed to ensure our participation in this wider spectacle. If they have worked to achieve the pleasures of their position, then this result is not unmerited. We can thereby legitimize our aspirations, allowing our own emulation of their lifestyle. And the imagination plays a significant role here. 'Our imagination', writes Smith, 'which in pain and sorrow seems to be confined and cooped up within our own persons, in times of ease and prosperity expands itself to every thing around us.'

Here, in 'the mysterious veil of self-delusion', where we encounter 'self-deceit, this fatal weakness of mankind',[95] a further crucial slide can occur, from an accurate perception that there is frequently a link between the possession of objects, riches and status, and the life of pleasure, to the assumption that the latter consists *in* the former, is reducible to it: that luxury possessions bring happiness, and that mere contentment is necessarily inferior. In Griswold's words, 'The deception consists in the belief that by attaining all of those good things we strive for we will be happy and tranquil', whereas actually we are merely condemning ourselves to hard work, both directly and indirectly: work to maintain the appearance, the image of success that will enable us to keep our place in the 'parade of riches' and give us the illusory esteem we seek, and perpetuate our hope that there is happiness at the end of the rainbow. Thus is social improvement accompanied by self-deception; a potential for dissatisfaction and unhappiness both drives and results from social progress. Hence 'The pleasure of vulgarized sympathy leads to the nearly universal toils of emulation'[96] and the resulting culture of frantic but ultimately ineffectual hedonism. And thus does Smith's dissection of the possibilities and tensions of the spectacle of sympathy propel him into the front rank of critics and theorists of the modern condition.

And the other side of the picture, the griefs and miseries of the poor? Just as we can slide to an unjustified assimilation of riches and virtue, so we may despise the poor, as if their poverty is a result of their *lack* of virtue or wisdom. Hence, while we parade our riches, we conceal our poverty.[97] This relative invisibility can reinforce the sense that poverty is shameful, along with decreasing our awareness of its extent. But another scenario is possible here. Suppose we see the poor not as victims of their own inadequacies, but as victims of the system; not just as poor, but as *oppressed*, wronged, suffering injustice. In this case, our sympathy with them – feeling and the impartial spectator working together – will mean that we sympathize with the *resentment* they feel, their justified sense of grievance. Resentment at harm done produces or reinforces a sense of injustice. Indeed, the poor could justifiably expect us to *share* their resentment.[98] We do not rush to do this, since in general 'resentment' is not a pleasant feeling; but this very fact can contribute to the strength of the feeling, under the reinforcement provided by the impartial spectator. And from this stems a major strand in the subsequent politics of modernity, whereby the Enlightenment tradition spawns grand projects of social reform and political movements of the oppressed, through to socialist movements and beyond.[99]

The extension of sympathy

This leads us to a final problem. Both Hume and Smith imply that we are more likely to be able to sympathize with those who resemble us and who are closest to us; the shared experience of small-scale groups such as families seems to be the model here, as it seems to be for sentimentalism generally. Smith suggests that getting agitated about distant suffering of which we know nothing is artificial and unreasonable, and does nobody any good;[100] and Hume goes so far as to argue that 'In general, it may be affirm'd, that there is no such passion in human minds, as the love of mankind, merely as such, independent of personal qualities, of services, or of relation to oneself'.[101] The possible implication of all this, given the significance of spectacle, is spelled out by Griswold: '"Sympathy" may foster, rather than counter, selfishness and self-love; the pleasure of mutual sympathy seems transformed into the pleasure of mutually reinforcing vanity.'[102] I can sympathize most with those who most resemble and reinforce my own – frequently self-deluding – self-image, and society becomes a series of fragmented networks of nervous narcissists.[103]

Yet this is, of course, precisely the situation the 'impartial spectator'[104] is there to try to prevent; and we have referred to Smith's example of an earthquake in China to suggest that this figure can have some success. Indeed, Smith claims that 'The plaintive voice of misery, when heard at a distance, will not allow us to be indifferent'. More radically still, he asserts that 'our good-will is circumscribed by no boundary, but may embrace the immensity of the universe. We cannot form the idea of any innocent and sensible being, whose happiness we should not desire'.[105] And Hume adopts a strikingly similar position. Having just dismissed the possibility of a 'love of mankind' in the abstract, he proceeds to assert the power of sympathy to range even beyond the confines of the human: '... there is no human, and indeed no sensible, creature, whose happiness or misery does not, in some measure, affect us, when brought near to us, and represented in lively colours.'[106]

This is a highly significant twist in the argument. For a start, it reinforces the idea that it is feeling, 'sentience', that provides the grounding of moral response, hence the extension of the range of sympathetic engagement beyond the human. But it also suggests that the 'closeness' needed for this engagement is, again, a matter of 'situation' and, crucially, how that situation is *represented* (in 'lively colours'). Far from being necessarily in tension with sympathetic engagement, the spectacle is a presupposition of its operation. Vivid representation amounts to a kind of proximity, while in no way abolishing the distance of difference. One needs the vividness of proximity, to engage us in the first place, but also distance, as the space within which the imagination can work. Effective witnessing has an element of indirectness about it. And this also reminds us that sympathy reacts not to universals and abstractions, but to particulars, *within* this broad, overall presumption of sentience. Except, in this sense, such particulars are not instances of universals, although they may be exemplars of analogous situations. As Jamie Ferreira puts it, in a discussion of Hume: 'What is morally relevant is what is brought home to us imaginatively – namely, the particular we engage with when we abstract from *our* particularity only'. He argues that this calls for 'concretizing engagement' in which 'imagination is clearly used to generate a distance'; but this is a distancing that seeks to 'engage fully with the relevant other', rather than to universalize or reconstruct the other as a 'representative' or 'typical' human.[107] Again following Hume, Davide Panagia concludes that 'there is an ethical priority in learning to relate to difference rather than sameness', born from 'an aesthetic experience that generates a capacity for sympathy – an attunement, that is, to difference as such'.[108]

If it is *difference* that drives all this, then this can, of course, include difference of class, race and gender; and it is essential not to reduce such 'difference' to the discriminatory, stigmatizing 'otherness' that has been such a central feature of so many modern constructions of self-and-other, serving to legitimize inequality, oppression and exploitation.[109] And difference is not *primarily* a matter of identity, but of situation, ranging from culturally and socially restricted 'positions', that do have serious implications for self-identity, through to current contexts, predicaments and problems, which may well be transitory and only contingently linked to identity, whether individual or cultural. As we saw earlier, for Smith sympathy could be said to involve a relationship between differences: the conversion of difference into relationship, or difference *as* relationship; as an idea, it enables us to think 'relationship-in-distance'. And, from this point of view, if we do sympathize with those 'close' to us ('closeness' defined in Hume's terms, as proximity plus resemblance), then this is not because of, but despite, the closeness: it is the *difference* that is relevant. I am not you, however much I may resemble you; the difference in our situations can be converted into a sympathetic response on my part if the relationship between my response and your situation can be mapped on to your response to your situation. Fundamentally, this analysis is not about identity politics and identification with the same in the other, however much it can be appropriated *ideologically* for the elaboration of stereotypes of identity and community, and frequently has been, from the eighteenth century onwards (with nation being added to gender, family and class as bases for this process of group identification). Such stereotypes are indeed the 'other' side of the coin to discrimination against the 'other'. They are mutually reinforcing.[110]

In an arresting formulation, Hume claims that 'the happiness of strangers affects us by sympathy alone'.[111] It might appear that, as sentient beings, we recognize a kinship with them only through the shared sentience that makes sympathy possible as a relation of similarity between differences. But this initial recognition poses a problem: we might have extended the range of sympathy, but we still seem to encounter similarity or identity again, at this point of furthest extension. Perhaps we should return to the fact that they are *strangers*, after all – how do they become candidates for sympathetic response in the first place? We may indeed be bumping up against the limits of the discursive possibilities available within this framework, but we can perhaps just remember the key role of the sympathetic imagination here. McCarthy claims that 'Sympathy is only truly itself when there is a challenge to the imagination'.[112] This challenge occurs, as Ferreira suggests, via 'interestedness – sentiment catching us, captivating us, engaging us'.[113] And this 'interest' is not the telos, the 'purposiveness' of the self-interested subject, with its 'vested' interests to defend, but rather refers to the curiosity of the outgoing self in its responsiveness, its openness to 'other' experiences, an orientation towards the other *as* other, in its difference. This is the 'extension' of sympathy – not just its range, but its capacity to extend outwards, towards the experience of difference.[114] And this imaginative engagement with the other is *felt*; it captivates us, our senses and feelings. It is indeed sympathy itself, at its most basic.

5

From Sensibility to Affect?

Theories of sympathy, as they develop out of reflecting on sensibility, encourage us, in turn, to consider the roots of the latter; and, in doing so, we will find that we are led into an intriguing miasma of cultural currents, out of which loom early signs of what was tentatively distinguished, in the first chapter, as a 'spectacle of sympathy' and a 'circuit of sensation'. We will not find theoretical unification here – but, in pursuing this, we may find the endlessly recreated origins, the originating instances, of spectacle and sensation as they have been so prominent in the cultural life of the modern. And this, in turn, may help illuminate the revival of interest in embodiment and feeling in our own time, particularly in the context of the debates over the so-called 'affective turn', since affect, too, proves to have been a significant part of this early modern mix.

Making sense of sensibility is a challenge. For a start, sensibility does indeed 'make' sense, both in that it shapes the senses and, in doing so, is productive of culturally meaningful sense: it is the public face of the body. But it also faces inwards, both as expression of selfhood and as embedded within the organic. This 'embodiment' of sensibility produces and reproduces the body both as publicly legible and as deeply mysterious, both cultural and physical, both spectacle and sensation. The language of sensibility seems to combine feeling and emotion with physiology, a language of nerves and bodies, seemingly at once literal and metaphorical. 'Sensibility is both the subjective awareness of experience and the organic sensitivity through which that awareness occurs', suggests Van Sant. These analogies do indeed vividly criss-cross this language of body and mind: 'touching the heart' becomes electric, and involves 'thrilling the nerves', and 'the structures of feeling (nerves and delicate fibers) become the location for experience'.[1] We can recall *The Memoirs of Emma Courtney*: here we learn that 'energetic sympathies' go 'darting from mind to mind' with 'electrical rapidity'; and one's heart can be 'touched, electrified', just as one can catch the 'soft contagion' of tears.[2] All this is profoundly anti-Cartesian, and Christopher

Lawrence too notices this emphasis on monism, with 'the nervous system itself as the bridge which possessed attributes of both mind and body', and a term like 'sensibility' being used interchangeably to refer to properties of the nervous system or the 'soul'. Nervous systems, perceptions and manners – all alike could be characterized as 'coarse' or 'refined'.[3] The absolute quality of the distinction between literal and metaphorical that we often – too often? – take for granted should not be transposed too readily into the eighteenth-century cultural context: the boundaries are unstable, the distinctions unclear, the resulting 'figures' of uncertain ontological status.

It was surely the Scottish Enlightenment, centred on Edinburgh and Glasgow in the middle years of the century, that was the prime centre for the source and diffusion of these intellectual currents as they became embedded in the discursive formations of the age, and came both to influence and to reflect cultural life and experience more generally. It was feeling, rather than reason, that was postulated as the basis of human actions, and of morality, and the nervous system mediated between self and other, body and environment. History itself emerged as a process of 'gradual refinement of feeling', with body and mind playing their integrated part in this development. And at this point we might appropriately return to Hume and Adam Smith, to deepen the elements of tension between their perspectives, presenting this as a clue to these deeper 'currents'.

Intensity and reflection: Hume, Smith and their difference

Observing that our capacity to sympathize with distress is strong, Smith observes that 'we weep even at the feigned representation of a tragedy',[4] and Hume's account of our responses to the same situation can help sharpen our awareness of the implications of our emerging sense of the difference between them. Hume points to the puzzle here: 'It seems an unaccountable pleasure which the spectators of a well-written tragedy receive from sorrow, terror, anxiety, and other passions that are in themselves disagreeable and uneasy.' Disputing Fontenelle's claim that such tragedy can appeal because we know it is unreal, occurring 'merely' on the stage, Hume takes a speech of Cicero in which he gives an account of an episode of butchery of prisoners, and of the profound effects this has on his listeners, to argue that what matters is not that we know an event to be unreal – clearly it may not be – but, as in this case, the 'force of oratory' whereby it is communicated. In painting too, and the arts generally, we can thus see how 'The affection, rousing the mind, excites a large stock of spirit and vehemence; which is all transformed into pleasure by the force of the prevailing movement'.[5] For Hume, our capacity for sympathy resides in the easy communicability, the *power*, of passion: 'The passions are so contagious, that they pass with the greatest facility from one person to another, and produce correspondent movement in all human breasts'.[6] The emphasis here seems clear enough; by contrast, here we have a passage from Smith, which is actually discussing the case of how one takes pleasure in the mirth, rather than the distress, of one's companions:

> Neither does his pleasure seem to rise altogether from the *additional vivacity* which his mirth may receive from sympathy with theirs, nor his pain from the disappointment he meets with when he misses this pleasure ... this correspondence of the sentiments of others with our own appears to be a cause of pleasure, and the want of it a cause of pain, which cannot be accounted for in this manner.[7]

In effect, we can say, in line with the analysis developed in the previous discussion, that it is the *relationship*, the pattern of 'corresponding sentiments', that is crucial – not the extra force that accrues from the process whereby the other's feelings are transmitted. 'Vivacity' is the word to trigger our attention here; vivacity is not a Smith word, but it – and its cognates, such as vividness, liveliness and force – spatter the pages of Hume,[8] and it is difficult not to see Hume as the target at this point.

Hume's approach here comes close to the rather crude contagion model for the transmission of feeling which was widely influential in the eighteenth century, and clearly reflects, or implies, an adherence to sensationalist empiricism, whereby an identity of content is transmitted as a kind of imprinting (the 'impress' in 'impression') – hence Hume's view that sympathy requires that one share the same feelings as the other.[9] This can all be seen as an early philosophical formulation of an emergent cultural configuration, a powerful structure of experience and ideas, that emphasizes the significance in human life of the transmission of sensation. Nor can this configuration – particularly in its emergent or virtual stage – be mapped exclusively onto particular thinkers, artists or authors. For example, the emphasis on direct contact, immediacy, the physical or tactile dimension of transmission, also occurs in some examples used by Smith very early on in his account. He remarks that some people complain that 'in looking on the sores and ulcers which are exposed by beggars in the streets, they are apt to feel an itching or uneasy sensation in the correspondent parts of their own bodies', and cases like this suggest that passions 'may seem to be transferred from one man to another, instantaneously' – which would also include sympathy.[10] These are clearly *not* examples of 'thinking oneself into the situation of the other', which is how they are presented, and indeed Smith quickly proceeds to surer ground; but they well illustrate how texts can – and should – be read as complex cultural documents, indicators of conflicting cultural currents, as well as supposedly unitary philosophical treatises.

Of course, Hume's own development of this is philosophically sophisticated. So far, it may seem as if the mystery of representation – how to decode the signs of emotion in the other – is being 'resolved' by dissolving it into a kind of mechanical transmission, so that the 'idea' (of sympathy) is essentially just another (sensory) 'impression', and, as such, it can be made as instantaneous as possible, thus negating the distance that makes representation possible even as it makes it troublesome. Hume favours the image of a stringed instrument here: 'As in strings equally wound up, the motion of one communicates itself to the rest ...' Nonetheless, there is an activity of mind present here, a capacity to copy, intervening as we move from the level of impression to that of ideas. Arguing that 'no passion of another discovers itself immediately to the mind', but only indirectly, via causes and effects, which in the latter case means 'those external signs in the countenance and conversation, which convey an idea of it', Hume suggests that it is these that give rise to our sympathy. In this process, "Tis also evident, that the ideas of the affections of others are converted into the very impressions they represent, and that the passions arise in conformity to the images we form of them'. That is to say, we form images or ideas of the feelings of others, and these ideas or images are converted back into feelings that *we* now possess, hence the sharing we characterize as 'sympathy', such sympathy being 'nothing but a lively idea converted into an impression'.[11]

Laura Hinton can therefore suggest that, in Hume, 'The sympathetic device works not only through "vibration", but mimetically, through visual resemblance and identification'.[12] These two modes are not, after all, so far apart. Both operate so as to reduce distance; both operate in a quasi-mechanical way, giving little role to thought in general, or the imagination in particular. Ideas are copies of impressions, and mimesis interpreted as copying brings representation as close as possible to an immediate, physical, automatic process; it emphasizes the visual as an organic capacity, the eye as an organ, one sensory channel among others, and 'feeling' as an essentially 'unthinking' response to the power, the vivacity, of impression-as-idea. Indeed, while 'impression' and 'idea' are seemingly distinct in Hume, they are actually rather closely assimilated; they are only distinguished by 'force and vivacity'[13] – that favourite Hume pairing – hence only by a difference of degree, ideas being really just weak impressions. Thus closely linked, similarity (mimesis, idea) and contiguity or proximity ('vibration', impression) are indeed important aspects of Hume's analysis generally.[14] We might cite Hume's use of the mirror as a figure to capture all this, showing – in its revealing awkwardness, the tension of its imagery – the convergence of these two aspects of the circuit of sensation: 'In general, we may remark, that the minds of men are mirrors to one another, not only because they reflect each other's emotions, but also because those rays of passion, sentiments and opinions may be often reverberated, and may decay away by insensible degrees.'[15]

Smith, too, uses the mirror, but with a significantly different emphasis. In one of those characteristically eighteenth-century speculative experiments, he invites us to imagine a 'human creature' growing up in 'some solitary place'. Lacking a mirror, he could acquire no sense of his own character, or any norms of behaviour. Yet, 'Bring him into society, and he is immediately provided with the mirror which he wanted before'. Previously, he could think only of the external objects of his passions; he could not reflect on these passions themselves. Nor could he anticipate new pleasures or sorrows. Once in society, however, his passions will become the causes of new passions, and he will observe that 'mankind approve of some of them, and are disgusted by others'. Smith reflects on this process, and draws out the implications: 'We suppose ourselves the spectators of our own behaviour, and endeavour to imagine what effect it would, in this light, produce upon us. This is the only looking-glass by which we can, in some measure, with the eyes of other people, scrutinize the propriety of our own conduct.'[16] For Smith, argues Griswold, 'we always see ourselves through the eyes of others and are mirrors to each other. We are not transparent to our own consciousness; indeed, without the mediation of the other, we have no determinate moral selves "there" waiting to be made trans-parent.' Self-knowledge depends on our understanding of others: 'Sympathy is key to our self-conception.'[17] And this, as David Marshall points out, is a two-way process: 'the mirror of sympathy in which the spectator represents to himself the feelings of the other person and places himself in the position of the other is itself mirrored in the experience of the person who knows he is being viewed.'[18] In these uses of the mirror to figure the sentimental foundations of society, then, the rays and reverberations of minds have been supplanted by the mutual gaze of self and other, selves *as* self and other to each other.

Thus Smith's myth of origin institutes a gulf between reflection and passion, a fundamental discontinuity rather than a difference of degree. And this discontinuity between thought and feeling is simultaneously constitutive of the self in relation to others. Passions no longer reverberate freely; a crucial element of distance is introduced. With Smith, 'spectatorial aloofness is made the condition of the operation of sympathy', claims Mullan, so 'the metaphor of spectatorial scrutiny is simply at odds with a version of sympathy which allows for the natural mutuality of passions and sentiments'.[19] This practice of reflection involves both judgement and imagination, thinking ourselves into the situation of the other. And as the imagination manoeuvres in this gap, this discontinuity, so re-imagining the self in relation to its own passions becomes feasible, and new desires can emerge. The self-reflective imagination images – projects – our desires, thereby potentially transforming them.[20] Merish suggests that this model of social life requires 'a certain self-consciousness in one's emotional self-presentation, a certain theatricalization of one's inner life'.[21] These selves are not integrated, not coherent, either in themselves or in relation to each other. This hall of mirrors refracts and distorts, and the reflected images may function as masks. Thus Griswold: 'We are not ourselves without the masks that sociality imposes, but that mask both reveals and conceals'.[22] This Smithian myth of origin looks more and more like a thesis on the constitution of modernity ...

This imaginative engagement of the self, in 'becoming-other', is central to the possibility of sympathy, inviting vicarious identification, the play of identity across the gap, but we need to be careful in our interpretation of this. In this spectacle of sympathy, 'spectacle' is not about mimesis as mimicry, but as *theatricality*; vicarious identification is identity-in-difference, not identity per se, and any 'mirror' present here incorporates *distortion*, inherent in the idea of perspective, not narcissistic self-sufficiency.[23] One could say that spectacle is about incorporation (into relationship) rather than identification (with the other) and, given difference as distance, can readily encompass the idea of 'self' and 'other' as *scenario*, a place of theatrical enactment wherein feelings exist as manifested, as *shown*, available to an audience.[24] The 'showing', with a certain emphasis on the visual, is significant here, as the means whereby the 'inner' theatrical space of selfhood is mapped into the 'outer' scenario, the public persona (and vice versa). And, both as presented and appropriated in public, this involves the world of appearances and representations, the world of 'images' (in the several senses of that term).

And we can return here to the difference between Smith and Hume: the difference that may only be a hair's breadth, the minimal difference that makes a difference, the difference of emphasis or focus that has such wide-ranging ramifications.[25] Smith is struggling towards a perspective in which feelings are always already 'worked up' by the imagination, as representations, for it is only thus that they become evidence of emotions and passions, the object of our sympathy. That is not to deny their status as bodily experiences, but to point out that they are not *only* that. In Hume, though, the emphasis tends to be on the original sensation or impression, seen as the founding moment, the 'originating force' in the origin. But even in Hume, passions themselves are impressions, sensations, that have been impregnated by ideas; they are the results of memory and imagination, working on 'original' sensations. Hume calls them 'impressions of reflexion', showing our emotions to be 'impressed' with our ideas, our images.[26] From this point of view, it is not a matter of 'original' impressions or sensations, direct, unmediated – nature rather than culture; rather, any 'original moment' here could be seen as a retrospective construct *we* impose, hence an intervention, a reflective distancing. This is the move Smith makes. And the point of this intervention, or its effect, is to mark a constitutive difference of perspective, whereby the immediacy of sensation and the reflective appropriation of sentiment can be moves *in* the circuit of sensation and the spectacle of sympathy, respectively.

For Smith, the reflective grasp of the imagination is crucial here; it institutes the very gap that it can then bridge vicariously and assess or contemplate 'objectively'. It is within the imagination, working on the data of sensory experience, that the sense of *pattern* can form itself or be recognized. This is a pattern of superimposed homologies, similarities or relations between differences: other in relation to self; idea or image in relation to impression or feeling; the other's response to his situation in relation to my response to mine.[27] It is the sense of these correspondences, 'felt' reflectively, that gives – or *is* – pleasure. It is this *aesthetic* dimension that emerges as basic to sympathy.

For Hume, though, the imagination is really just an aspect of the process of sensory transmission in which continuity is emphasized; differences are ultimately differences in degree, as in his claim that impression and idea differ only in intensity. And this points to the dynamic in Hume's system: his emphasis on force, vivacity, with sympathy as the intensive power to convert idea into impression, feeling. To put it like this, invoking 'intensity' in this central role, is to give it a rather Deleuzian gloss; but it is also true that, in saying that the imagination in Hume is not active but that it nevertheless 'rings out, and reverberates',[28] Deleuze is colouring it in decidedly vivid, Hume-inflected prose. Influenced by Deleuze, Panagia writes that sympathy in Hume is 'the principle of composition that relates things through intensity – that is, on the basis of their difference', with 'difference' to be seen here, one might add, as something like an original differentiation between quanta of energy. Difference is still crucial, but it is intensity that does the work: it is the 'differentiating force that allows dissimilars to coincide'. Hence 'The social is the domain of sympathy where the intensity of difference makes its appearance'.[29] With intensity, suggests Boundas, 'force overtakes form',[30] a phrase that encapsulates this difference of emphasis between Smith and Hume. And intensity, one might add, runs back through to the shock of the initial sensory experience itself, the initial 'encounter'.[31]

Let us now trace these differences – or these traces of difference – further back through the maelstrom of the eighteenth-century culture of sensibility, particularly as appropriated by the language of science and medicine, and see if any further sense can be made of them.

Nervous bodies

The suggestion that 'sensibility draws on the fundamental analogy in the language between physical and psychological feeling, an analogy that suggests cause without ever entirely giving way to it' alerts us to underlying problems; so does Van Sant's further hint that 'physical structures are the location of responsiveness, and their delicacy determines the delicacy and immediacy of feelings; but nerves do not *cause* the emotions, passions, etc.'[32] Via sensations, nerves provide 'occasions' for feelings and emotional responses, one might say, without determining their content or mode of expression. And covering this gap with the language of 'vibration', much favoured at the time, is merely to substitute a figure for a mystery – not that this in any way diminishes its vividness, the power it derives from this very obscurity at its core. We are beginning to touch on tensions fundamental to the whole tradition of sensationalist empiricism stemming from Locke, and this is basic to our understanding of the source not only of the circuit of sensation but the spectacle of sympathy as well.

This may become clearer if we suggest an analogy with a related tension that is apparent in an influential work by one of Locke's followers, Hartley's *Observations on Man* (1749).[33] For Hartley, an idea is an 'internal representation' of some sensation, and 'simple' ideas give rise to more complex ones through a 'coalescing of vibrations', hence 'association', and indeed the 'associative power of words' is central to this.[34] Again, the language of 'vibration' and 'power' alerts us to the problem: the gap between sensation and its appropriation as representation, which cannot plausibly be accounted for by 'cause', yet points to the necessity for this as the price of not allowing any idea of mind as faculty, or a capacity for representation, with systematizing attributes, to play a part here. The problematical role of language in this appropriation is critical: words seem to have mysterious properties ('associative powers') irreducible to the impact of particular sensory experiences. Indeed, if there are relations, 'analogies', between these problems, this very mode of expressing it may well be a significant clue.

Relations, connections: as suggested previously, it is above all through the language and imagery of 'nerves' that these terms and these problems in the understanding of feeling, emotion and the body come to the fore in eighteenth-century culture, and provide a route into how the culture tries to make sense of its own assumptions. What we find is that 'The nervous connection of different parts and organs produces the body as an analysable whole', as Mullan puts it.[35] Newton had originally provided sensational psychology with its understanding of nerves, arguing that they were solid and transmitted sense impressions by vibrations; and the language of nerves had increasingly replaced that of humours. 'Sensibility' itself, as a cultural construct, 'connoted the operation of the nervous system, the material basis for consciousness', a consciousness 'responsive to signals from the outside environment and from inside the body',[36] and Barker-Benfield's point can be exemplified by the way novelists like Richardson, Fielding and Smollett, along with theorists like Burke, drew extensively on 'nerves' in their work. Along with 'vibrations' and 'impressions', this shared language of expression testifies to the spread of this paradigm in literary culture. For the influential physician Alexander Munro, sensibility could be located in the physiological organization of the nervous system; in his *Structure and Function of the Nervous System* (1783) he claimed that the 'great sympathetic nerve' transmitted messages from all round the body.[37]

By the end of the century, the language of electricity is proving highly compatible with this dominant paradigm, and Vincent-Buffault suggests that 'It was by transposing the discoveries about electricity into the human body that doctors adopted this idea of a nervous fluid which sometimes came close to magnetism', and sensitivity was like a fluid which 'ebbed and flowed' in channels.[38] 'Electricity' is indeed an appropriate resource for the language of sensation here, posited as a figural reality that may not be entirely metaphorical; as a principle of attraction, it was widely seen as a 'current' and indeed, by Benjamin Franklin himself, as a 'subtle fluid diffused through all bodies'.[39] Drawing on a lifetime of research in this area, George Rousseau could conclude that 'the nervous system became the battlefield on which civilization and its discontents would be played out'.[40]

If the Scottish Enlightenment was indeed influential, Scottish medicine was at the core of this. According to Lawrence's survey, it emphasized 'the total integration of body function, the perceptive capacity or sensibility of the organism, and a preoccupation with the nervous system as the structural basis for these properties'. Robert Whytt, physician to George III and professor at Edinburgh in mid-century, had been formulating these doctrines from the 1740s and became their major source, though his successors through the century adapted and developed the general approach. Rejecting the Cartesian reduction of body to mere mechanism, Whytt argued that only if 'soul' was reintroduced, on a scientific basis, so as to be seen as extending through the whole nervous system, could the whole range of the body's emotional capacities and responses be accounted for. Hence his postulation of a 'sentient principle', an 'immaterial, undivided substance that could "feel" stimuli and necessarily directed the appropriate response', and this became 'the seat of overall control and integration of body function', as Lawrence summarizes it.[41] Foucault's discussion of Whytt adds a key term: 'This very distinct property of both "the faculty of feeling and that of moving" which permits the organs to communicate with each other and to suffer together, to react to a stimulus, however distant – is sympathy'. Such sympathy 'exists in the organs only insofar as it is received there through the intermediary of the nerves; it is the more marked in proportion to their mobility, and at the same time it is one of the forms of sensibility'.[42] Hence, as Bruhm puts it, 'Physical sentience became the raw material of sympathy – that joining together of all aspects of the body in fellow-feeling'.[43] And Foucault adds that, for these physicians, this 'internal sensibility' of the system is particularly likely to be manifested in brain and womb, the organs that maintain 'most sympathy with the whole organism',[44] reinforcing the sense that the gendered aspects of all this are highly significant.

'Sympathy', such a key player here, has earlier roots. In seventeenth-century medicine, it was already being criticized for postulating 'action at a distance', and for implying 'mysterious affinities' between organs[45] – an interesting combination of attributes, given the later emergence of the tensions between 'sensation' and 'sympathy'. Whytt tries to re-establish the notion on firmer foundations. In formulating his 'sentient principle', he claims that 'we know certainly, that the nerves are endued with feeling, and that there is a general sympathy which prevails through the whole system; so there is a particular and very remarkable *consent* between various parts of the body'. Thus, he adds, 'every sensible part of the body has a sympathy with the whole'.[46] This imagining of the feeling body and its internal relations and interconnections in the language of 'consent' is striking, and commentators, in turn, produce rhetorical flourishes to capture it; thus Foucault refers to Whytt's 'nervous system' as 'the body's sensibility with regard to its own phenomena, and its own echo across the volumes of its organic space'.[47] Perhaps Roger French's use of 'awareness' gets us closer: Whytt's principle of 'general sympathy' was 'not a mechanism of bodily co-ordination but ... an "awareness" of the sensible parts of the body by each other'.[48] So there is a reflexive grasp here, a kind of body consciousness whereby the separate constituents can somehow grasp a sense of the whole, perhaps indeed constitute themselves *as* a whole, through this awareness. It may be that something of this can be captured by the more recent concept of 'body-image'. Simon Williams claims that 'The lived experience of emotion ... is mediated through body-image':[49] sensations, tactile impressions, visual images, give us a sense of the relations between the body and its surrounding spaces, the 'echo across the volumes of its organic space' referred to by Foucault. One of those who pioneered this concept, Paul Schilder, calls it 'the body schema ... the tri-dimensional image everybody has about himself', adding that it involves representation but is not reducible to it.[50]

In the light of this, one can note that the 'particular and very remarkable *consent*' that Whytt observes does indeed seem to refer to something like a 'shared image', as though each part of the body, in its awareness of the whole of which it is part, reflexively produces a sense of this whole *as* image. An even more vivid – and, to our eyes, strange – way of expressing this can be found in this excerpt from one of Whytt's physician contemporaries, Jerome Gaub, describing 'neural man'. This 'person' (or perhaps entity, or principle), is:

> ... distributed throughout the entire body and so intermingled with each of its parts that if separated from these parts it could present a simulacrum or skeletal image of a man. Furthermore, this structure of nerves is no less animated from within by its motive power than it itself stirs up the rest of the body's inert mass throughout which it extends. In this sense it represents a kind of man within a man.[51]

This is an arresting image of man *as* image, of a simulacrum of the body that can be produced from anywhere within the body yet also apart from it, the simulacrum as the idea of the image that is impossible to place, immanent within the body yet an emanation of it: the anywhere and nowhere of the image, that, in a sense, we now take for granted. What challenges us is the literalness of this image of an image; that it is somehow image *and* organic, latent in all parts of the body as the carrier or manifestation of the body's sense of itself. And it turns out that this self-aware body is now one that is not only open to its own gaze, but to that of the other, and Whytt himself draws out the intriguing implications: 'there is a still more wonderful sympathy between the nervous systems of different persons, whose various motions and morbid symptoms are often transferred from one to another, without any corporeal contact.'[52] Whytt's idea that this image can carry a 'wonderful sympathy' by some direct transference between bodies, without physical contact, seems even more mysterious. The claim that we can influence one another's feelings seems uncontentious enough; the idea that the specific *content* of these feelings can be transmitted directly, body to body, let alone in these necessarily specific images, is something else again.

Changing imaginations

We can get a better understanding of the process involved here if we introduce the concept of the imagination, for in effect what we are encountering here is a transition between an early or pre-modern perspective on the status and powers of the imagination and a modern one. On the earlier model, what appears in the imagination mimetically affects the body; the imagination is a perceptual mechanism for the transmission, via 'impression', of sensation. As late as 1797, an entry in the *Encyclopaedia Britannica* appealed to this notion of a 'sympathetic imagination' as the explanation for bodily deformity ('monsters'), citing an old example from Malebranche of a pregnant woman who had watched a criminal's limbs being broken; as a result, her infant's limbs were found to be broken in the same way. The entry could then claim that 'the view of a wound … wounds the person who views it,'[53] or, as Logan puts it, 'The material effects of this sympathetic mimesis are dramatized in the body of the child'. So, on this model, 'any distinction between realities and representations is lost, as representations have the ability to cross over into the status of realities', since what matters is that the idea or image be 'vividly present', whether or not the object is.[54]

We have to be careful in locating where precisely the difference between this and the modern imagination lies. After all, 'vivid presence' is also what the contemporary reader or filmgoer experiences when reacting emotionally to something known to be 'unreal'; fictional figures can engage our imaginations, and move us. The real difference comes from the twin requirements, in the former model, that the imagination operate in a strictly mimetic manner, and that this occur in ways that are continuous with the organic mechanism of body reactions generally. The 'impression' left by a sensation in the imagination – resembling, say, that left by a stamp in a bed of wax – is then copied, transferred from the imagination to some appropriate organ of the body, via the nervous system. Citing Alexander Crichton's *An Inquiry into the Nature and Origin of Mental Derangement* (1798), Logan suggests that internal impressions reproduce, via nerves, the effects of external impressions, and that this thereby 'provides an explanatory underpinning for the belief that the physical effect of an idea is identical in kind to the physical effect of the thing for which it substitutes'.[55] And this essential continuity in kind between the imagination and the nervous system doubtless enhances the plausibility of Gaub's account from earlier in the century, whereby nerves and organs can somehow bear the 'impression', as image, of the body as a whole. And this model has wide ramifications. The idea of 'involuntary mimesis' could provide a clue to nervous disorders, through the suggestion that 'retained impressions' of unfortunate and repeated sensations could worsen the original effect.[56] And, more speculatively, unconscious imitation could trap the 'man of feeling' into an unacceptable perversion of himself: 'Imitation of feeling is by definition affectation', as Van Sant puts it.[57] Novelists like Richardson, Fielding and Sterne were widely criticized for encouraging such imitation, albeit unwittingly.

And the alternative? This focuses rather more on the relative independence of the imagination, as a faculty or capacity. In particular, the imagination becomes a capacity for diverging from mimesis, realizing the non-mimetic in the mimetic, introducing difference into the same, hence anticipating Romantic ideas of creativity; but it does this *within* the mind, or as an aspect of it. What the imagination loses, in direct contact with the physical world, it gains in greater autonomy. But there is also an element of obscurity, both because of its link with that other nebulous entity, the mind, and because, in the eighteenth-century context of its origin, all this tended to remain at best implicit in what continued to be the culturally dominant stream of sensationalist empiricism. And a perhaps unexpected corollary of all this is that it reveals sensationalist empiricism itself – heir to the Scientific Revolution, the epistemological cutting edge of advanced ideas of progress and Enlightenment – as having striking continuities with the *older* model of the imagination; indeed, it is arguably unable to come up with an adequate theory of 'imagination' at all, reducing it, essentially, to a mechanical, combinatory response to the input of sense data.

The emergence of the newer model can be associated with a greater emphasis on the imagination in relation to sight, with the status of the latter as the dominant sense being asserted all the more strongly as the 'civilizing process' gradually enforced greater distrust of those senses that seemed to testify to a potentially 'excessive' presence of the body (touch and, particularly, smell). Not only did the visual image come to seem the basic raw material of the imagination, but we can see that the balance of distance with proximity, detachment with vividness and immediacy, that we associate with the visual sense, seem to be particularly suited to the discourse and experience of sympathy and sensibility. For contemporaries, no doubt, it was often the immediacy that was emphasized. Thus for Samuel Johnson, and many others, suggests Van Sant, 'sympathetic feelings, which require vividness and proximity, arise through an act of the imagination largely dependent on sight'.[58]

This is not straightforward, however. Here it would be useful to consider the claim running through Van Sant's invigorating account that the culture of sensibility incorporated two identifiable strands, one emphasizing the sense of sight and the significance of the visual, and the other the sense of touch, which was closely linked to the cult of feeling. She argues that this second theme has a certain priority: 'Sensibility defines all sensory and emotional experience as forms of touch … Interest in scenes of suffering shifts from the spectatorial event to the experience of that event in the body of the spectator'.[59] The 'embodiment' of feeling entailed the proximity of touch. And just as we know that 'seeing' has a powerful resonance in our culture, so too does 'touch': Ahmed reminds us that 'What connects us to this place or that place, to this other or that is also what we find most touching; it is that which makes us feel'.[60] And the 'makes us' again conveys this metonymic, causal dimension, the sense of links in a chain. It may be that after the era of sensibility, 'touch' came to be relatively devalued, but it retains powerful cultural resonance.

While this is a useful corrective to the tendency to neglect this dimension, it may be more accurate to suggest, rather, that there is a *tension* between these two strands. This is another aspect of the tension that has been outlined above, underlying the contrast of spectacle with sensation. Indeed, Van Sant points out that while Locke and his followers tried to explain sight in the language of sensationalist materialism, so that sight is, in effect, a form of touch, nonetheless it is not *experienced* as such, so that 'descriptions of the mind's way of dealing with sensory material still use the visual term *image*'.[61] If one becomes aware of this tension, then the strains and incongruities in empiricist texts as they endeavour to incorporate the language of image – and, more generally, of mind as it reflects on, and manipulates, imagery – can become peculiarly vivid: it is as if the imagination, as the power of mind to engage with the visual, is being called into being even as it is denied theoretical status. The problem of capturing reflexive image-making in the metonymic language of causation clearly has widespread ramifications.

Attempting to draw all this together, we can say that early modern ideas of a 'sympathetic imagination', with the power to directly transmit the image of the shape and form of one body into the shape and form of another (as with 'monstrous births'), are increasingly challenged by a radical reshaping of the imagination into a 'faculty of mind', now equipped with powers that can seem more limited, but actually open up the whole zone of the imagination for intense artistic and scientific creativity, and for structuring the inputs of experience. This, in turn, implies a radical bifurcation of 'sympathy'. It is no longer a diffuse sense of wholeness, an overall feeling transmissible in a quasi-physical way to others, or a term for the transmission of pockets of nervous energy within the body, ensuring links and coordination. Either it becomes *simply* a feeling, the result of 'nervous powers', the energy of sensation, reacting to sensory impressions made on the body, particularly through touch, with representation dissolved into mechanical transmission; or it becomes a feeling that necessarily and crucially involves the imagination, as well as the body, with an emphasis on the visual sense, but now an imagination that incorporates the internal power of image-making, and a vicarious 'imagining' of the other with feelings that are already worked up as representations. In the latter case, 'mind', as judgement and imagination, plays a relatively autonomous role, described in terms of faculties of the self, whereas in the former case it becomes essentially reducible to effects of sensationalist physical and psychological processes.

In short, while the suffering victim, as object of our sympathy, should be both seen *and* felt, as it were, there seem to be two different ways of making sense of this, ways that rarely become directly *in*compatible, but are rarely easily compatible either; and the tension here defines the whole culture of sensibility. On the one hand, we encounter the circuit of sensation; on the other, the spectacle of sympathy. These strands are emergent, overlapping, but real enough, in their differential impacts. It is the stresses produced by the coexistence of these strands that gives a distinctive flavour to so many of these texts, whether in science or medicine (Whytt, Gaub), philosophy (Hartley, Hume), social or moral theory (Smith), or literature (Hays, Richardson, Sterne), even while some of these authors seem to be more clearly on one side or the other of the division (hence the strategy, adopted here, of contrasting Hume and Smith). It is 'sensibility' that holds together – but cannot fuse – these two strands. As they become more distinct, so sensibility itself, in its eighteenth-century sense, which only ever *was* this precarious coexistence, fades away, or, more accurately, becomes dispersed into strands that reflect this origin, while also being transformations of it: sensationalism, sentimentality, and 'civility' (as conventional manners, increasingly divorced from its role as signifier of under-lying feeling).

But let us now turn to another term from the early modern, one that has come back into prominence in our own time ...

Towards affect

From private feeling to public display of emotion, 'sensibility' thus designates a whole cultural orientation, one never free of tensions. The term itself develops from within the confusing undergrowth of feeling-terms that are a feature of the early modern development of a more secular and neutral set of concepts out of theologically inflected ones. Words like 'affection' and 'sentiment' bridged the gap between thinking and feeling, and 'affect' has a role here too. 'Affection' has a long theological history, from Augustine and Aquinas, generally designating the 'higher' faculties, the activities of the soul, potentially related to reason, and the 'passions', and contrasting with the 'lower', animal 'appetites'.[62] Affects are related to this, but with more fluidity and flexibility; and they do indeed continue to exist, in this rather vague and under-specified way, until being revived, at least in academic circles, in recent decades.

The dictionary offers further clues here. In effect, there are two core meanings for 'affect', as a verb: to act upon, have an effect on, disturb (Latin *afficere*), and to put on an appearance, make a pretence of, profess (*affectare*, related to *afficere*). Hence the nouns 'affect' and 'affection', which can refer to a state of body and/or mind, but also, related to the second meaning, an 'affectation' (with 'affected' being related to either). Once again, the realization, manifestation or appropri-ation of 'affect' in its context raises the issue of theatricality and display, making out and making up. As expressed, given form, affect becomes both excessive to meaning and inadequately captured by it, with theatricality as the code through which this tension is 'managed'. Thus the relation to 'affectation': one is drawn towards something, has a tendency in a certain direction, hence changing one's external appearance or behaviour, however unconsciously. In this sense, affect raises the whole issue of 'expression' as a relation of inner content to public form. And here, one can already see a gulf opening up: for this second dimension has – ostensibly at least – been lost in the contemporary 'affective turn', with its emphasis on psychological or even physiological states, manifestations and processes, and the possibilities of direct interpersonal transmission, essentially unmediated by cultural expression.

This contemporary prominence of the term has, rather intriguingly, involved a return to a thinker who preceded the heyday of sensibility, namely Spinoza, whose alleged materialism, and assimilation of God and Nature, led to his near-universal condemnation in his own time. Proponents of the affective turn have generally invoked him as the founding father, and ground their use of 'affect' in an interpretation of his work, particularly emphasizing the alleged 'autonomy' of affect.[63] It would consequently be of interest to see whether Spinoza can accommodate such a reading, or whether his own work, too, reveals something of the tensions mentioned above, and revealed in the apparently minor differences between Hume and Smith that nevertheless have such profound implications. In doing this, the influential interpretation offered by Deleuze, which has been basic to the contemporary appropriation of Spinoza's ideas in this field, will be both drawn on and, in part, challenged.

We can approach Spinoza's perspective on affect by starting from the linked term, 'affection'. Here, an old use of the word, given in the dictionary, is for it to refer to a contingent, changeable state or quality of something, a use clearly linked to the first meaning of affect indicated above, to act on or influence. An affection, then, would be the state or feature of something that results from the impact of something else. At the most basic level, in Spinoza's system, the modes (individual manifestations of substance) are defined through their capacity to manifest such states and, therefore, their relations to other such: 'By mode I understand the affections of a substance, or that which is in another through which it is also conceived.' One might add that the distinctiveness of Spinoza already emerges on this, the first page of the *Ethics*, in the way a quasi-physical description is replicated in conceptual, relational terms, revealing his key assumption that there is but one, unitary substance (albeit differentiated into modes), described under the attributes of Thought and Extension: in effect, one world, perceived under two perspectives. And this is also clear in what these affections are further said to entail, in practice. A physical object or other body, he writes, will produce an 'impression' on another, leaving 'traces', adding that 'the affections of the human body whose ideas present external bodies as present to us, we shall call images of things ... and when the mind regards bodies in this way, we shall say that it imagines'.[64] Hence we find that the imagination, as the foundation of thought, is present with affection, as the condition of embodiment (extension), at the very origin of experience.[65]

At this point, Spinoza introduces a distinction between affection and what seems to be presented as a distinct *form* of it, affect: 'By affect I understand affections of the body by which the body's power of acting is increased or diminished, aided or restrained, and at the same time, the ideas of these affections.' If, in the case of the diminution of the capacity for action, the body can be said to experience passions, it is nonetheless the case that affect is presented as a process or passage that is also active, an act.[66] Thus, when an affection makes us feel sad, it decreases our power of action; when it makes us feel joy, it increases it. Indeed, joy and sadness best express the duality here, and indeed are said to be two of the three basic affects.[67] Offering a clarification or expansion of this, Deleuze suggests that if an affection (*affectio*) is a 'corporeal image', then 'From a given idea of an affection there necessarily flow "affects" or feelings (*affectus*)'. Such feelings are a new kind of affection, incorporating a relation to an earlier state. 'Our feelings are in themselves ideas which involve the concrete relation of present and past in a continuous duration: they involve the changes of an existing mode that endures.'[68]

One could say that there are two aspects to this: there is the initial impact *on* the body, along with the response *of* the body, mapped as 'feeling'; and then there is the fact that this involves a process of change, and that this, too, is inherent in the response. Part of what we are doing, subjectively or unconsciously, when we register a feeling, is that we are noticing this element of contrast. Thus Deleuze suggests that affect 'is experienced in a lived duration that involves the difference between two states'.[69] It might be tempting to gloss this as a simple cause/effect relation, but this is misleading: it suggests that affect is merely another state, separate but resulting from the initial affection. For Spinoza, within the rationalist tradition, 'cause' is far broader, and can include internal relations of implication and expression. As the process whereby the body 'makes sense' of the *affectio*, the *affectus* incorporates it, orients us towards it, all of which is implicit in 'responding' to it.[70]

In the light of this, we can consider a conclusion drawn by Deleuze in the shorter and more influential of his two books on Spinoza: 'Hence there is a difference in nature between the *image affections* or *ideas* and the *feeling affects*, although the feeling affects may be presented as a particular type of ideas or affections ...'. There is a palpable tension here, bursting through in the phrase 'difference in nature', pointing up the awkwardness of the deviation from Spinoza indicated by the first part of the formulation. Hitherto, the two pairs of terms – affections and affects, ideas and bodies – have been shown to be closely interrelated and overlapping, both in Spinoza and in Deleuze's exposition. But now it seems as though affect has broken free, into its own independent sphere, lack of authorization from Spinoza's text notwithstanding. The ground for this move, though, has been laid in what has been quoted above. The contrast between *affectio* as a state and *affectus* as change, process or *duration* (Deleuze's preferred term) is further emphasized by the emphasis on affect as 'purely transitive', and 'experienced in a lived duration', and this is clearly the core of this, pointing indeed to a further significant shift of emphasis. Now, we learn that these states, these 'image affections', are 'not separable from the duration that attaches them to the preceding state and makes them tend towards the next state'.[71] Affect is here seen as having the potential to subsume the sphere of image affections in an enveloping ontology of process.

In due course, this fusion of affect and process will turn out to be the crucial aspect of Deleuze's philosophy as it has come to influence the debates in the 'affective turn' of our own time. In this powerful synthesis of Spinoza and Bergson, we will be presented with an overall picture of a reality in which everything is always becoming, in processes whereby the virtual, in becoming actual, reveals itself through the 'affect' that manifests the transition yet is lost in the very actualization of the virtual state, and that always subverts any images or representations that purport to capture it; and in this perspective, 'affect' has lost its connection with images, and even feelings, its 'autonomy' manifest as a directly visceral transmission of energies and intensities between bodies. In so doing, this perspective loses sight of the embeddedness of affect in a relation with affection, with states of the body, thoughts and feelings, a relation which many of Deleuze's formulations, at this early stage in his career, would seem to imply,[72] as we have seen.

Affect, imagination and reason

To pursue this, let us return to Spinoza, and consider this passage: 'Since man ... is conscious of himself through the affections by which he is determined to act, then he who has done something which he imagines affects others with joy will be affected with joy, together with a consciousness of himself as the cause ...'.[73] The first part of this implies that the positive or negative energy involved in the passage or transmission of image affection into feeling affect is inseparable from an emergent sense of self: in becoming aware of the feeling, I also become aware of myself-becoming-aware, even if this sense of myself as a subject of experience has, so far, no content beyond the experiences themselves. Here we can recall that the image affection is *already* a relation, between the impact of the other and the body that receives the impact, even if the impression left, as image, is necessarily partial, only seen from the viewpoint of the recipient. As Brian Massumi puts it, the initial affection is 'immediately, spontaneously doubled by the repeatable trace of an encounter …', making memory possible, and 'it is only when the idea of the affection is doubled by an *idea of the idea of the affection* that it attains the level of conscious reflection'.[74] For Antonio Damasio, this 'opens the way for representing relationships and creating symbols' – in particular, that of the self.[75]

The flow of images at the heart of this, and the reference to the imagination in the second part of the Spinoza quote, require further consideration. The imagination manifests itself in the transience and contingency, but also the vivacity and intensity, of the images that constitute it; above all, it registers *presence*. Even though the object itself may be absent, to imagine it is always to register it as present: 'even though things do not exist, the mind still imagines them always as present to itself, unless causes occur which exclude their present existence'.[76] And here we can bring in the link to affect again. Since affects involve increases or decreases in energy, just as the imagination can fluctuate in the vividness of its images, so the relation between them can have important implications.[77] Spinoza remarks that when, in the light of reason, the mind understands something to be necessary, 'it has a greater power over the affects, or is less acted on by them',[78] whereas conversely, with the imagination, where 'presences', things or spectres, have all the power of 'presence', albeit with a more uncertain ontological status, our feelings are more strongly affected. Following Spinoza, Deleuze adds that 'the active feelings born of reason … are in themselves stronger than any of the passive feelings born of imagination', and since 'an active joy always follows from what we understand',[79] this provides a stimulus to further thought and the production of rational ideas, which bring further pleasure in train. This process of active reasoning starts from uncovering what we have in common with the other, enabling us to go beyond the limitations of the image that merely reflects its impact on us, and produces positive affect; and this can, in turn, spur us on to understand disagreements, disparities and negative affects, even though we would normally, of course, want to avoid the latter.

In particular, we can now consider pity – that form of negative affect intimately related to feelings for the other. 'Pity is a sadness, accompanied by the idea of an evil which has happened to another whom we imagine to be like us',[80] and compassion could be described as the 'habitual disposition' that can result from this. This requirement of similarity may be less restrictive than it seems: we have already seen that although reason begins locally, as it were, in similarities between two bodies, the rise in pleasurable affect that results from the understanding gained will drive an expansion of the range of 'similarity' to incorporate more and more of what would initially have been seen as insuperable differences. In the course of this, *all* parties will be affected and transformed. Thus we see the rationale for the claims of Moira Gatens and Genevieve Lloyd, in developing the implications of Spinoza's thought, that affective ties are central to the social, that 'Our identities are constituted through sympathetic and imaginative forming of wider wholes with others …', and indeed that these encounters are 'better understood as collective *transformations* of previous identities rather than the exclusion or overcoming of difference'.[81] Our feeling for, and imagining of, the other, can thus be strengthened by reason, in an evolving process. And Spinoza himself draws the conclusion that 'one who is moved to aid others neither by reason nor by pity is rightly called inhuman'.[82]

All this apparent harmony, in the logical unfolding of Spinoza's system, does not, however, conceal a degree of turbulence underneath the placid surface. When Spinoza writes that 'if we imagine someone like us to be affected with some affect, this imagination will express an affection of our body like this affect', we encounter an implicit complexity of contagious transmission between and across image/affect, self/other and mind/body boundaries that defies any simple idea of causal direction. Add to this that imaginings are always 'present', even when the object that originally impressed the image affection no longer is, and we can see how a whole series of imaginary and affectual identities, identifications and relations become possible, with conflict being, in practice, as likely as harmony. Following on from the excerpt quoted and discussed above, Spinoza himself points out that 'it can happen that the joy with which someone imagines that he affects others is only imaginary',[83] since actually he is being a burden – a rather rare example of Spinoza showing how the relative independence of the imagination, even as passive, can lead to problems, given the possibility of reactivating past traces, and the resultant possibility that the one-sidedness of image affections could be a source of later self-deception.

Indeed, we could go further. While we have learnt that the active pleasures of reason overcome the passive pleasures of imagination, it is not so clear that this provides sufficient initial motivation to get things moving, as it were: given that the pleasures of the imagination are presented as being those of passivity and of presence, life experienced in the fullness of the here and now, why move away from this at all? Whatever the answer, it is clear that thought as reason is posited in Spinoza as an active power, with both the imagination and extension, by implication, positioned as passive, as in the status of the image affection, apparently needing the energy of affect to realize its potential;[84] and it is hard to miss a gender shading in all this.

We are, then, called on once more to return to the imagination and its relation to reason. Caroline Williams is right to claim that Spinoza presents the imagination as 'a form of corporeal awareness connecting the body's affects to understanding,'[85] but we have seen grounds for thinking that this is by no means straightforward. What we find here is what Spinoza calls 'knowledge of the first kind, opinion or imagination,'[86] and whatever its limitations, this is the foundation of the edifice, giving us 'a way of directly determining the resemblances between two bodies, however disparate they may be', in Deleuze's words,[87] thus enabling us to progress towards reason. But it may be worth considering the possibility that this sense of knowledge as a hierarchy could coexist with the idea of 'separate spheres' of knowledge, each with their conditions of plausible application. Unusually, Spinoza offers an example that could be said to point in this direction. When we look towards the sun, we imagine it to be quite close; and even when we come to learn its true distance, unimaginably further away, this does *not* affect its location as we imagine it.[88] And he adds, intriguingly, that this is also true for 'other imaginations by which the mind is deceived … they are not contrary to the true, and do not disappear on its presence'.[89] Indeed, he makes the arresting claim that 'the imaginations of the mind, considered in themselves, contain no error'.[90] Imagination gives us the truth of the phenomenal realm, where experience is *our* experience, written on the body *and* imagined in relation to the other as relation (rather than 'in itself'); and hence this hints at the possibility of a theory of everyday popular consciousness, a phenomenology of experience that would run alongside official reason, and would, potentially, have its own integrity.

But all this would be very alarming for Deleuze. Rei Terada characterizes Deleuze's interpretation of Spinoza's image affections as follows: 'Literally impressions in the body, affections imply that encounters with other bodies, and, moreover, between parts of one's own body, are in themselves semiotic. They infect all of experience with interpretation, and thus are portrayed as corrupting.'[91] When Deleuze says of knowledge based on images that 'Such knowledge is not knowledge at all, it is at best recognition,'[92] he does indeed seem to go beyond Spinoza, who – as Deleuze himself recognizes elsewhere – explicitly counts this as a 'first' form of knowledge. So here, in this further deviation from Spinoza, we can see how this can link up with the two earlier features of the analysis presented by Deleuze, Massumi and the radical theorists of affect: if affect can be presented as not only autonomous, and, ambitiously, as a manifestation of the primacy of process in our grasp of reality, then this can be reinforced by its emancipation from the corruptions of everyday discourse.

Overall, then, Spinoza could be said to prefigure themes of the era of sensibility, including the mutual – if problematical – imbrication of feeling and imagination,[93] and we can observe that his contribution is presented in a very one-sided way by contemporary affect theorists, keen as they are to downplay the relation between affect, imagination and culture. While Spinoza's own work manifests the two separable strands identified earlier in this chapter, we can now position contemporary affect theory as successor to *one* of these, the sensation strand, just as it loses touch with the central themes of the second strand, around the social dynamics of sympathetic engagement with the other. Indeed, present-day affect theorists frequently write in the very language of Hume's sensationalism. To take one example, Teresa Brennan's claim that 'In the last analysis, words and images are matters of vibration'[94] could have come straight out of Hume. And we might, finally, suggest that the purported emancipation of 'affect' from difficulties of cultural meaning and interpretation might leave it open to dialogue with contemporary developments in relevant areas of scientific understanding, notably neuroscience – just as it would be vulnerable to a naïve and uncritical acceptance of the fads and fashions emanating from those quarters, having deprived itself of any adequate means of understanding its own status and involvement in *cultural* processes that also incorporate those sciences themselves.

Let us end, though, in the year 1784, when a commission of investigation, in Paris, examined the claims of Franz Anton Mesmer to be able to channel 'animal magnetic fluids' via a rod, and his use of this to produce 'cures' for a variety of ailments. Our source here, Jessica Riskin, suggests that Mesmer applied the central credo of sentimental empiricism too literally: if feeling was an arbiter of truth, the manifestations of what people 'felt' must be reliable testimony. His patients duly writhed, groaned, and 'dramatized the process of feeling', in turn 'dramatically' manifesting the effect/affectation dynamic of affect mentioned at the beginning of this chapter. Mesmer claimed that all this was a manifestation of an ethereal 'fluid of sensibility', pervading the universe, and to deny this was to 'undermine the authority of sensation'.[95] In countering this, the commission came up with what seemed, to many at the time, the equally outlandish claim that the imagination was a mental faculty, hence an *internal* source of influence that could, in bizarre ways, have physical effects. What we find here, then, is a crisis in the whole underpinning of 'sensibility', symbolizing the ongoing collapse of its precarious coherence, with feeling and imagination threatening to fly apart, or recombine in new forms, and hints of unconscious processes and their 'hysterical' manifestations prefiguring developments to come …

6

Unconscious Arts of Memory

We move on. If the writing, art, theatre, and the whole cultural experience of life from, roughly, the 1740s to the 1790s has a distinctive 'feel', compounded of the frequently fractious relations between reason, feeling and imagination encompassed by the term 'sensibility', then anything from, say, the 1840s to the 1860s onwards, for a century or so, reveals a different pattern of experience, and a different cultural configuration through which this is expressed and articulated.[1] In a self-consciously 'modern' age, 'consciousness' itself, in relation to the unconscious and the involuntary, becomes of central concern, linked to the problematical processes of memory, both individual and cultural, through which it develops and changes;[2] and with these processes seen increasingly in evolutionary terms, as adaptation and struggle, with 'memory' and 'heredity' always liable to slide uneasily together, the distinctive inflection of the late-nineteenth-century cultural imaginary comes to the fore. What is revealed, then, is a significant cultural shift, an evolving relation between the experience of rapid change and assumptions about mind, will and consciousness in their temporal unfolding and their capacity for revealing internal tensions and rifts.

Writing of French culture, in the early decades of the century, Reddy identifies a distinctive 'internal space' emerging in perceptions of the self, 'a space where moral uncertainty and ambiguity' take over, 'a disordered terrain of impulses, moods, bodily influences, fears, and illusions'.[3] While a fertile area for artists and novelists to explore, this ensured tensions both in personal life and social relations. Consciousness and knowledge do not run seamlessly together; indeed they can fly apart. The body is inherently difficult to read, its truths obscure. In the British context, Logan claims that 'George Eliot's bodies are unable to express the truth of their feelings, because they no longer know what it is'; sensations have become 'more opaque, or elusive; it requires effort to recover their significance'.[4] Bell notices a growing awareness that 'there is an intrinsic opacity to self-reflection', in turn echoed in 'the opacity of social process'.[5] The relative simplicity of the eighteenth-century sincerity/hypocrisy nexus gives way to more complex possibilities of self-deception, which may defy introspection. The eighteenth-century blush can reveal embarrassment, shame and the possibility of hypocrisy; the nineteenth-century blush can reveal – what? If the agent's motives are inscrutable to self as well as other, we are truly in uncharted waters; it becomes all the more important to understand them even as it becomes all the more difficult to do so.

We can put all this in more abstract terms. The self as a project, oriented to the future realization of its objectives, in the light of its interests, is bound to be inherently flawed if it cannot gain adequate knowledge of its motives, and cannot control, harness and direct them adequately. This self-opacity can stem from the self's own conflicts of interest, motive, impulse and feeling, and the tensions in both seeing and presenting itself in a certain way, in the light of social conventions and expectations, and also from the problems of incompleteness and projection inherent in the paradox of self-reflection; and these can operate together. And given the difficulties here, such a self is bound to be attuned to the likelihood of past influences, and the need to recall them. The possibilities and limitations of memory, situating the individual in time, hence possessing a history, become central to the culture and to the novel, linked to the problems of recall, revelation and interpretation. In short, the effective exercise of will requires an awareness not just of the context of action but an ability to formulate one's interests and have sufficient awareness of motives to be able to act rationally in pursuit of them. 'Given the cherished notion of a unified self, a conscious and voluntary agent, evidence that subjects harboured knowledge unavailable to their ordinary conscious state was extremely threatening', claims Jill Matus, and hence 'fanned ideas about the self as multiple and undermined the notion of will and consciousness as the prime movers in behavior.'[6] As a further corollary, the imagination tends to lose its role as mediator between 'inner' and 'outer' worlds, becoming seen as a source of disturbance and disruption, albeit with potential as a specialist resource for art, culture and entertainment.

In effect, we can map here the emergence of two sets of distinctions, while remembering that they are not necessarily clearly articulated either in the writings of the period, or in the experiences in which they are embodied: namely, voluntary/involuntary, and conscious/unconscious. And there are good reasons for this lack of distinction. Knowledge, especially self-knowledge, and the effective exercise of will are not unconnected. Indeed, as soon as the drive to master slides into the drive to know, as it must, the positioning of the involuntary *as* unconscious becomes a logical move: the unconscious as a sort of space of the self, variously behind or beneath, but also 'inside' it, not just an external determinant. This, in effect, breaks up the category of the involuntary: some aspects, coded as purely physical, are excluded from mind altogether, whereas others are incorporated, as its 'unconscious' aspects. If I 'involuntarily' give off signs of myself, these now invite a deeper reading, testifying to obscure depths, in varying degrees inaccessible even to myself. As we will see, the bifurcations implicit here run through, and arguably undermine, even the most influential system of thought to originate from all this, that of Freud.

This shift is indeed momentous. The eighteenth-century tendency to equate consciousness and mind, with memory seen as a relatively simple power of recall, together constitutive of self-identity over time,[7] gives way to a model of mind in which dreams, fantasies and memory itself become evidence of layers of mind that can even come to be seen as possessing a hereditary element, and which can manifest itself in our actions in the present. Thus Laura Otis has located a 'theory of organic memory' in late-nineteenth-century culture, which 'placed the past *in* the individual, *in* the body, *in* the nervous system', so that people were said to remember 'their racial and ancestral experiences unconsciously, through their instincts'.[8] Consciousness emerges as a precarious layer of awareness against a background of the tumult of the past, with unrecognized affects, emotionally charged images, resonating powerfully in the here and now; and given that memory incorporates past associations of events and ideas, at the mercy of this unconscious turbulence, this makes its distortion and unreliability almost inevitable. The transcriptions in memory get jumbled, or actively reworked, through the imagination; and the intensity of such memories can give pleasure or pain, irrespective of origin, although the 'intensity' can seem to testify to the reality of the origin. And what psychoanalysis will come to offer here is not the notion of the unconscious as such – that has already had its place prepared, its consequences outlined, and indeed its name, before Freud – but the idea that the unconscious has an *active* agency, that its 'doings' are not random, and that therefore a concept like 'repression' must be fundamental to how it operates. In short, as Michael Davis puts it, the unconscious becomes not just an absence, but 'an active force in its own right'.[9] We can say then that if 'sensibility', in the *broad* sense of the term, is a sensory awareness of immersion in the world, then 'consciousness' involves the mind's focus on this, a more situated awareness, responsive to the impact of modern experience, with the unconscious positioned as hidden presupposition, present as troublesome liability but also as a possible creative resource, an ambiguously placed internal 'other'.

Science and mind

In an age when controversy raged over the position of science in culture, with positivist and materialist proponents of a 'unified science' of the human and natural worlds endlessly lambasted by their critics, it is easy to lose sight of the shared premises in the way these debates, and the nature of science itself, both drew on, and influenced, the cultural currents just outlined. Sally Shuttleworth's broad claim that in this period 'the mind and body are regarded as an indivisible circulating system' involving 'a flow of psychological and bodily energy', in turn serving as a model for the 'social body',[10] is one that few would have disagreed with, though not all would have chosen to go on to cast this in the fashionable language of those two pillars of nineteenth-century scientific innovation, electromagnetism and thermodynamics. In human physiology, what was now seen as the unacceptably vague notion of 'sympathy' had increasingly faded away under the impact of the discovery of the reflex response and the autonomous nervous system – both well-established in the first few decades of the century – with the implication that reflex action and the muscular system governing facial expression entailed a separation between action and conscious will. Body acts and gestures became automatic manifestations of self-preservation, and possible evidence of 'primitive ancestry'. The body tells two distinct stories, as it were: voluntarily, in the brain; but also involuntarily, via the spinal system.[11] With Helmholtz and others discovering the electrical basis of the nervous system, with nerves transmitting electrical impulses along neural pathways, so memory came to be seen as 'intense or repeated electrical flows' down them, dynamic flows of association rather than a random collection of impressions.[12] By the later decades of the century, Rae Beth Gordon suggests that habits were seen as equivalent to 'the automatic responses exemplified by nervous reflex and by unconscious mental processes',[13] and she provides a fascinating analysis of the ways in which these assumptions were manifested in the performance styles, the movements and gestures of artists in cabaret and popular entertainment, and the interactive influences between these and the sciences of the time.

Here, we can introduce the ideas of George Henry Lewes, an influential figure respected in Victorian culture as a wide-ranging interpreter of science and general polymath, remembered today mainly as the long-term companion of George Eliot. For Lewes – along with Carpenter and other leading psychologists – unconscious mental processes were not reducible to mere automatism, but involved autonomy and creativity. Lewes challenged any tendency to equate 'conscious' with 'mental', and 'unconscious' with 'physical'. He 'brought the unconscious and the bodily into the conception of mind', as Matus puts it,[14] hence adopting a holistic approach. Far from being reducible to brain, the mind extends beyond it to include 'all Sensation, all Volition, and all Thought: it means the whole psychical life; and this psychical Life has no one special centre ... it belongs to the whole, and animates the whole'.[15] Consciousness thus becomes effect or result rather than cause; emotions and sensations can affect conscious thought without being present to it; but all are part of a system of psychic processes.

In exploring this, Lewes seeks to go beyond the interest in rushes of energy, focusing rather on the significance of imagery, casting his approach within a broadly evolutionary framework, but in such a way that the underlying structure retains a certain priority over the temporal frame. 'Images being the ideal forms of Sensation, the Logic of Images is the first stage of intellectual activity', he argues; hence 'The first attempts to explain a phenomenon must be to combine the images of past sensations with the sensations now felt, so as to form a series'.[16] The image organizes sensory material, hence 'primitive' thinking relies on it; but it retains its crucial significance as, in effect, mediating between the senses and abstract thought. Images can, indeed, operate independently of the latter, being open to combination and recombination. Since consciousness and the unconscious are essentially continuous, images may be a direct manifestation of the unconscious, and Davis adds:

> The imaginative linking of two seemingly unconnected ideas in fact manifests a connection between them in the unconscious mind, which draws on memories no longer available to consciousness. The vivid immediacy of image-based memory, once in consciousness, powerfully grips the individual's existence.[17]

This could almost be Proust; and the emphasis on pattern and relationship, while not strictly incompatible with the associationism of nineteenth-century psychology, in the tradition of Locke and Hume, does seem to point beyond it.

Energy and image: the force of nervous energy, of shock and sensation, produces effects that are *unpredictable*, and precipitate or permit the unfolding of unexpected unconscious patterns, connections between images. The presence of mind necessarily complicates cause and effect. Lewes distinguishes here between a 'resultant' – the regular, predictable effect produced by agents that are alike in nature – and an 'emergent', the outcome of a combination of disparate agents, such as is inevitably present in the processes of consciousness and the unconscious, mental and physical, and which is in principle unpredictable.[18] He writes: 'the emergent is unlike its components in so far as these are incommensurable, and it cannot be reduced either to their sum or their difference'.[19] The imagination, working through images, is always 'emergent', never reducible to predictable cause and effect. More concretely, an episode from *Middlemarch* can be taken to exemplify this. George Eliot is describing the impact of Rome on Dorothea: the fragments of the past 'at first jarred her as with an electric shock', and then, 'Forms both pale and glowing took possession of her young sense, and fixed themselves in her memory even when she was not thinking of them, preparing strange associations that remained through her after-years'.[20] Here we see a dramatic disjunction between the 'electrical' cause and the images that result, and stay present, albeit unconsciously, long after the original cause has disappeared, with their own distinctive implications for her life, and linking her to 'Rome' in a web of meanings that take us out of any circuit of sensation altogether. Retrospectively, indeed, the 'cause' becomes oddly disjunctive, more a marker of the discontinuity than an active determinant. In short, we can recognize something of the tensions that surfaced in the texts of Hume and Smith, albeit in the distinctive inflection of a later age.

But, we have introduced George Eliot, so let us delve further – this time, into *Daniel Deronda*, and the way it is structured by the tensions between sensation and sympathy in this new context.

Gwendolen in distress

After Gwendolen has decided, for reasons obscure, to keep the necklace that her new friend Daniel Deronda had returned to her, the author observes: 'There is a great deal of unmapped country within us which would have to be taken into account in an explanation of our gusts and storms.' This 'unmapped country', then, is not just 'out there', passive and inert; it intervenes in the events in the 'mapped' country we think we are familiar with. And Gwendolen is more than usually troubled by these gusts and storms. Subject to capricious fears, inexplicable fits of dread, the very experience of space threatens her: 'Solitude in any wide scene impressed her with an undefined feeling of immeasurable existence aloof from her, in the midst of which she was helplessly incapable of asserting herself.'[21] Open countryside, the expanse of sea, figure her own self, in its boundlessness, allowing for no clear line between 'interior' and 'exterior', and extending way beyond her own comprehension. In the light of this, it seems hardly surprising that Davis can characterize the unconscious as 'a mode of interaction between inner and outer'.[22]

There is also the matter of keys. Gwendolen is obsessed by locked boxes, signifying controlled boundaries.[23] Indeed, locking and unlocking, and the key as the vehicle for doing either or both, play a significant part in her life, just as they do in the life of Daniel, but in reverse fashion. For her, keys are for keeping things locked away; for him, they are for opening things up. Most vividly, there is the panel in the drawing room, which sends Gwendolen into one of her fits of alarm when she first encounters it. Unlocked, it reveals the picture of 'an upturned dead face, from which an obscure figure seemed to be fleeing with outstretched arms';[24] she hastily has it locked, and tries to ensure she keeps the key. The image itself, detailed with such brevity, strikingly encapsulates and prefigures so much, in the plot and in her future life; it will frequently recur, to traumatize her at 'key' points, and will have its most dramatic 'realization'[25] when she is stranded in the yacht, in the immensity of the sea, witnessing the white face of Grandcourt – her hated, drowned husband – bobbing dead in the water.[26]

Images and keys play out an uncanny *pas de deux* in Gwendolen's life: images that demand and defy keys, keys that cannot unlock what was never properly locked in the first place; and, anyway, what is the image that can be 'unlocked' by a key? They play across a profound discursive tension. And 'image' also conjures up the mind itself, the obscure images that trouble our dreams and demand elaboration, just as it condenses the whole idea of the unconscious and its demand for the psychoanalysis that will, ostensibly, provide its 'key'. Learning of her husband's earlier liaison with Lydia Glasher, and speculating that Gwendolen had learnt of her existence, Daniel 'thought he had found a key now by which to interpret her more clearly', a comment given further, authorial emphasis elsewhere in the text, in the claim that 'all meanings, we know, depend on the key of interpretation', whether we are dealing with words, or the feelings manifest in the body (such as the 'dubious flag-signal'[27] of the blush). And – whatever the problems with keys in general – this is a key that Gwendolen most certainly does not possess, or cannot use: she is endlessly inscrutable to herself.

It is also true, though, that she connives in her own state of lack of self-knowledge, wilfully keeping herself locked up, keeping disturbing secrets locked away, even as this strategy is bound to fail. In the tableau scene, where an excerpt from *The Winter's Tale* is being presented, the panel mysteriously flies open, transfixing Gwendolen in horror,[28] and although the miscreant – a younger sister – returns the key, the damage has been done: the eternal return of the original traumatic encounter is guaranteed, for 'something has been opened here that defies rationalization or even interpretation', as Carolyn Williams suggests.[29] Later, she keeps a small knife locked securely in a drawer, fantasizing the murder of her husband, afraid of her own feelings, her deepest impulses; in the yacht, she even drops the key in the water. But he dies anyway; and the circumstances leave her possibly complicit in his death …

Let us now take up the case of the 'poisoned diamonds'. When Lydia Glasher sends the necklace – originally given her by Grandcourt – to Gwendolen, she encloses a note, condemning her for breaking her promise not to marry him. Thus invested with the power of the curse, the diamonds produce terror, a fit, followed by 'a nervous shock' when Grandcourt enters, so that 'she screamed again and again with hysterical violence'. So, 'Truly here were poisoned gems, and the poison had entered into this poor young creature'.[30] And the necklace retains its malevolent power: opening the jewel-case later, she has a 'shivering sensation'; on another occasion, she is described as 'hurting herself with the jewels that glittered on her tightly-clasped fingers pressed against her heart'. The jewels not only symbolize, but enforce, the life of 'poisonous misery'[31] she lives with Grandcourt.

What we find here is that it is not just emotions, like despair, but also structural features of relationships, such as power, that can be embedded or embodied in physical objects, which thereby both encompass, and go beyond, the role of signifier, carrying the more obscure dimension of the figural, poised uneasily between signifier and signified, metaphorical and literal. George Eliot is constantly interested in the obscure realm of cause and effect where thoughts can be manifested in objects, half-formed intuitions over here can have effects over there, and unconscious pathways can be just as efficacious as intentional ones; the possibility that 'undisclosed, half-conscious forces shape the future too',[32] as Gillian Beer suggests in her exploration of this theme. Gwendolen's 'sensational' response here reflects the discontinuity and disproportion between cause and effect, and indeed the excess of effect over cause; in these circuits of sensation, effects are *always* to be found, and cannot be read off in any automatic way from causes, whether or not the latter involve conscious intentions. In this case, her guilt, her feelings of remorse, are fundamental to her reaction. Here also, the jewellery can meet the 'upturned dead face': object and image, both embodying power in the very disruption of meaning.

But they meet also in the theme of return: in the case of the jewels, the letter itself, and the curse it contains, are explicitly repeated late in the novel.[33] And, in a novel that is full of circulating necklaces and rings, this whole episode is, structurally, a repeat: as we have seen, Gwendolen has already received a previous turquoise necklace, redeemed for her by Daniel after she had lost her money at the gaming-table, and again with an accompanying note, and again causing her distress and embarrassment.[34] This jewellery, too, returns to give her further trouble, this time with Grandcourt.[35] Pawning his own ring at Cohen's, Daniel meets Mordecai, Mirah's brother, an event crucial to the resolution of the story; and it is when Mirah's father steals Daniel's ring and Mirah realizes what has happened that his declaration of love for Mirah is finally prompted.[36] Ordinary objects, invested with sensational power, precipitate sensational events ...

Other episodes in the novel help to bring out this logic of sensation. Of the effect of the Rector's speech on Gwendolen, demanding that she take Grandcourt's marriage proposal seriously, we are told: 'The ideas it raised had the force of sensations.' Her response is immediate, at the level of feeling, yet this response is simultaneously described as 'ideas'. In their affective power, ideas too can *be* sensations. Hence can the channels of influence be both invisible and immediate. And although the 'ideas' may be invisible, their sensational manifestation is quite otherwise: Gwendolen is described as becoming 'pallid' as she listened, and the Rector noticed the 'strong effect' his words had produced. And if ideas can be sensational, so, of course, can emotions. Later, having been scolded by Grandcourt, she retires to her dressing-room, pale and agitated, afflicted by 'hideous' mental images: 'Even in the moments after reading the poisonous letter she had barely had more cruel sensations than now; for emotion was at the acute point, where it is not distinguishable from sensation.'[37] The body thereby becomes 'expressive' even despite itself, in ways involuntary and revealing. Hence, overall, Ann Cvetkovich can suggest that Eliot operates in this novel by 'converting sensational events into sensational psychological dilemmas',[38] which are in turn rendered even more 'sensational' by being made public, both as embodied effects and affects, and in terms of broader consequences.

Is Gwendolen 'traumatized' by all this, then? It seems reasonable to say so.[39] A reference at one point to her 'hidden wound'[40] would certainly fit our contemporary trauma discourse. Most significantly, we find the idea that trauma involves uncontrollable, and frequently unpredictable, repetition, with the corollary that the *first* episode only becomes clearly traumatic in retrospect, through the subsequent repetitions – as with the image of the dead face. Gwendolen herself comments, with resignation, near the end: 'Things repeat themselves in me so. They come back – they will all come back.'[41] The word 'trauma' would have been available to Eliot, and the concept was beginning to occur in discussions of the effects of railway accidents, though had not attained the fashionable status – and theoretical baggage – it was to acquire in our time.

The language of affliction that was of course more widely used was that of hysteria, and we can now turn to that.

It is clear from what has been said above that Gwendolen has a very unstable sense of self, plagued as she is by disturbing visions, agoraphobic responses to space, uncertainties over her own boundaries, and unpredictable emotional outbursts and breakdowns which forever threaten the conventions of civility and her own ability to manage her self-presentation and her relations to others. Indeed, these social dynamics seem to be central to aspects and episodes where the hysteria label is explicitly invoked. For example, Daniel's departure, after comforting her following Grandcourt's death, produced 'hysterical crying', precisely, we are told, because 'The distance between them was too great'.[42] All this fits the model of hysteria as uncontrollable emotional outburst, histrionic display, excessive feeling. But it cannot be left there, for another, rather contrasting 'symptom' is also to be found – one which, however, also fits in with what was becoming the pervasive cultural stereotype of hysterical behaviour.

When her mother finds her, in the episode just mentioned, after Daniel has left, she is initially 'sitting motionless' with 'cold hands'. This reminds us of the tableau scene: here, she does indeed emit a 'piercing cry', but maintains her immobile posture, with only her eyes, dilated in fear, suggesting her fate as 'a statue into which a soul of fear had entered'.[43] The statue becomes 'an image of her own private hysteria', suggests Vrettos,[44] but a very *public* image. This is not, now, the inability or refusal to communicate through excess, an explosion 'outwards', but the opposite, a withdrawal 'inside', into muteness and immobility. And this second version of the hysterical spectacle appears to position the subject or victim decisively as the hapless object of the spectatorial gaze. For Jacqueline Rose, the narrator herself adopts this spectatorial position, together with the potential for a moralizing distancing that this implies. Gwendolen 'disturbs' the gaze, hence must be punished: 'The hysterisation of the woman resides in this scenario, generated by the very form of the narrative itself.' Yet this in turn reproduces the conditions that produce the 'disturbance' in the first place, namely Grandcourt's tyrannical mastery working hand-in-hand with Gwendolen's remorse so that 'mastery and hysteria go together, with the second unleashed by the overcontrolled assertion of the first'.[45] The attempts to control Gwendolen, to *know* her – whether by Grandcourt, the narrator, or even the reader – thus drive towards their own failure, producing either hysterical outbursts or stasis. And there are hints in the novel that if this drive to transparency threatens to succeed, it is at the cost of spectralizing its victim, leaving nothing but a lifeless image; returning in the boat with the dead body of her husband, Gwendolen herself is described as 'pale as one of the sheeted dead'.[46]

Rose's approach is insightful, but ignores the broader dimensions of theatricality implicit in the spectacle of hysteria and the role of tableau in this novel. We now know that initially *Daniel Deronda* seems to have been planned both as novel and as play;[47] and we know that in 1871, just before beginning to collect material for the project, Eliot went to see *The Bells*, a melodrama in which tableau plays an essential part.[48] It seems reasonable enough for David Marshall to claim that *Daniel Deronda* 'considers its own theatrical status as it dramatizes characters who play-act on stage and in life; and it rehearses the problematic ways in which people become spectators to the spectacles of others'. The whole novel is replete with images and tableaux to challenge the reader's imagination, and that do indeed interrupt and challenge the narrative flow, and the very power of narrative to contain or tame them, just as we are reminded that we continue to see others as '*tableaux vivants*' about whom we must make up stories, in 'the theatrical distance that separates us'.[49]

Gwendolen's hysteria, and her propensity to visions and fantasy, cannot, it seems, ultimately be contained by narrative. Emphasizing that Gwendolen's hysteria challenges the narrative structure, Vrettos argues that her ability to make her 'inner visions' come true, 'to see her wishes take shape outside her body', constitutes 'a spiritual and prophetic dimension to her character that is in conflict with the novel's authorized spiritual voice'.[50] The obsessive visions are an important aspect of the 'inward' version of hysteria, but they have intriguing consequences, in that her visions, like her wishes, seem to possess the power of prefiguring the future; and in that they become true, their realization involves their externalization. In *The Bells*, the murder of a rich Jew returns to haunt the murderer, years later, on a stormy night like that of the murder: he 'sees' a tableau of the crime, with him in it, so his interiority is exteriorized in the staged projection of his own past crime.[51] Here, the tableau is retrospective, as it were; in the novel, it is rather that Gwendolen sees the scene, *wishes* the scene, of Grandcourt's death, sees the upturned face, and herself as guilty party, fleeing – and then it comes about.

Williams instances other examples from the novel, such as Daniel meeting Mordecai at Blackfriars Bridge, dramatically visualized in powerfully descriptive prose as a melodramatic tableau.[52] Here, the self meets that other that it has craved, has longed for, and thereby discovers also itself, in transfigured form. As Williams suggests, such scenes of recognition are also scenes of self-reflection, 'the other face uncannily figuring the self as something seen outside itself

... interiority is suddenly extroverted and objectified as representation'.[53] In these visions, prefigurations are also projections, recognition: the same in the other. And here again we find disturbance; for in referring, in the context of this episode, to 'images which have a foreshadowing power', Eliot is ostensibly referencing a more 'respectable' aspect of visions, presenting Mordecai as a 'visionary' in an Old Testament sense, one for whom special visions 'were the creators and feeders of the world'[54] – yet are Gwendolen's visions so different? Perhaps hysteria is not so 'other' after all ... Hysterics, it seems, are never mere victims – they can also be disturbing, questioning presences.

Daniel's sympathies

Several occasions on which Gwendolen's reactions are explicitly described as 'hysterical' involve interactions with Daniel, and it is worth considering how these self/other dynamics affect him. Rose suggests that for Daniel, 'the search for a sureness of identity relies on the disturbance of the woman to give it form';[55] and recalling also his rescue of Mirah from suicide, one sees what she means. Again highlighting the gender dynamics, Cvetkovich argues that his sympathetic encounters with women 'reveal his desire both to rescue them and to identify with them'; while the former makes him the 'patriarchal savior', the latter positions him as resembling them, and hence 'Sympathizing with them allows him ambiguously to do both ...'.[56] That the identification route poses problems for Daniel – just as experiencing identity in terms of a self/other oscillation does for Gwendolen – is clear in his response to her 'confession', near the end: stretched to the emotional limit, we are told that he is 'pierced', indeed 'completely unmanned', clearly at some risk of the hysteria that problematizes gender identity even as it positions the victim as feminine. Intriguingly, Gwendolen seems to pick up the other alternative in him here, reading him as manifesting a compassion which 'seemed to be regarding her from a halo of superiority'.[57] Are these the only alternatives present here, then: sympathy as identification, threatening hysterical excess, or sympathy as superiority, manifested in an arguably patriarchal compassion?

An observation by Marshall may help here. Gwendolen shows signs of being able to grow through her troubles, of hope for the future, when she 'begins to view herself by trying to enter into the sentiments that Deronda feels in trying to imagine her feelings'. This puts the emphasis not on identification with the other but on a kind of reflexive awareness that is made possible by taking

the place of the other, by viewing oneself *as* other; Deronda becomes Adam
Smith's 'impartial spectator' for her, encouraging – by his very presence, and
by enabling her to think *about* herself *through* him – the qualities of imagination and judgement.[58] And Cvetkovich, too, seems to notice some of this:
his apparent suffering gives *her* strength; he helps her 'not by counselling her
but by providing her with an image of how her own suffering affects him. His
helplessness diminishes her own sense of futility, so that sympathy works by
drawing some dividend from incapacity ...'[59] She develops a greater capacity to
'stand outside herself', get some distance, some perspective. And an important
aspect of this is that her 'theatricality' need no longer exist at some distance
from her, as an 'act' she 'puts on'; rather it can reside *in* the distance *from herself*
that makes it a constitutive part of any viable spectacle of sympathy. While
noting that Daniel's long-lost mother, the Princess, is ostensibly anti-sympathy
in orientation (and 'teaches him his difference as well as his identity'),[60] Marshall
points to how she implicitly understands all this, with her 'sincere acting',[61] which
does not mean that she is false, but rather that she stands for the view that 'the
relations of sympathy' are 'inherently theatrical relations'.[62] Because, with her,
'experience immediately passed into drama, and she acted her own emotions',[63]
she implicitly realized the element of distance in sympathetic engagement with
the other, as it was already incorporated in her own ability to 'act herself'.

Sympathetic engagement, then, involves imagination as well as feeling:
Daniel, we are told, revealed 'a subdued fervour of sympathy, an activity of
imagination, on behalf of others'.[64] Such sympathy is expansive, outgoing,
extending one's own capacities as self. Elsewhere, Eliot herself asserts that
'The greatest benefit we owe to the artist, whether painter, poet, or novelist, is
the extension of our sympathies'.[65] And Daniel points to the dangers when 'all
passion is spent in that narrow round, for want of ideas and sympathies to make
a larger home for it'. It is clear that this involves the challenge of an encounter
with difference. To his mother, he says that he has been trying for years 'to have
some understanding of those who differ from myself'; and tramping the streets
of the Jewish quarter leads to 'rousing the sense of union with what is remote'.
He tries to surmount prejudice, and realizes the power of stereotypes: 'a little
comparison will often diminish our surprise and disgust at the aberrations of
Jews and other dissidents',[66] we are told, in a formulation that may well suggest
to the present-day reader that the author is only partly successful in her own
efforts in this direction.[67]

And here we are entering the central theme of the later part of the novel, in
which Deronda's search for the 'larger home' enforces an encounter with his own

hitherto unsuspected Jewish ancestry and a resulting commitment on his part
to the Jewish cause. It is a commitment in which he does, nonetheless, propose
to retain some independence of judgement; he will not slavishly follow these
beliefs and customs, but will maintain his grandfather's ideal of 'separateness
with communication' – which sounds like a possible recipe for life in a multi-
cultural society – while accepting that his 'first duty' is to his own people.[68] And
it is here that a large part of the enduring challenge of the novel itself resides.
Can 'sympathy' survive this transition to a world of competing nationalities and
ethnicities? Can the model of the 'impartial spectator' retain any purchase here?
If the 'larger home' is identified with a *particular* group, does it not shrink back
again, diminish into narrowness and exclusivity?

Now aware of his Jewish origin, we learn, in a passage worth quoting in full,
that Deronda had now found '... his judgement no longer wandering in the
mazes of impartial sympathy, but choosing, with that noble partiality which is
man's best strength, the closer fellowship that makes sympathy practical', hence
'exchanging that bird's-eye reasonableness which soars to avoid preference and
loses all sense of quality, for the generous reasonableness of drawing shoulder
to shoulder with men of like inheritance'.[69] This eloquently encapsulates all the
issues. The target here is a form of sympathy that had earlier afflicted him, a
wide-ranging, disengaged and diffuse sympathy that, in seeing all sides to every
question, leaves us indecisive, unable to act, to make particular moral choices
and commitments;[70] he had succumbed to 'that reflective analysis which tends
to neutralise sympathy'. Whatever Eliot's intentions here, the 'impartiality' being
criticized is clearly distinct from that of Adam Smith's 'impartial spectator',
who is constructed as perfectly capable of exercising judgement, making the
necessary discriminations, partly because in this case 'judgement' is linked
to imaginative involvement and feeling. Given Deronda's problem – that he
wanted to be 'an organic part of social life', not a 'yearning disembodied spirit' –
the solution presented is that he identify with the group that he finally feels able
to recognize as 'my hereditary people', an identity that has 'given shape to what,
I believe, was an inherited yearning'.[71]

What is implied here, then, is that the restless search, the willingness to
expand horizons, engage with difference, must in the end result in the act
of identification, an identification with 'identity' itself, in all its inevitable
particularity, whether as individual or group. The nineteenth-century (organic)
language of heredity, of race, is not the essential point – we can replace it with
the (cultural) language of ethnicity, if it makes us feel happier; it is this idea of
a necessary, fixed mooring point, as a condition for sympathetic engagement,

that is so crucial here – and troublesome. The problem is with the idea that identifications entail identity, that 'belonging' has to be seen *as* identity, and that only on this basis can the necessary sympathetic discriminations be made, even though one might reasonably fear that the resulting sympathetic acts are likely to be too subject to the norms and interests of the specific group – which, of course, is precisely the situation that the 'impartial spectator' was designed to deal with. Thus Audrey Jaffe argues that Deronda's 'complete' sympathy is thus engaged 'only when identity has been evacuated of everything but the self's projections ... only when identity equals identity politics: when self and other merge because they are already merged into an imaginary unified identity', an identity *already there*, so that 'sympathy turns happenstance into fate and makes choices seem to be determined by the promptings of some unalterable essence at the self's core'.[72] And the point Davis makes about Deronda here would therefore be of wider import: '... this liberation of sympathy is also, necessarily, a limitation of its scope: it involves an assertion of specific cultural identity which implicitly excludes from its principal focus those who do not share it.'[73] And it is perhaps the tragedy of the modern world that George Eliot's model has proved to be more *descriptively* prescient than Adam Smith's. 'Identity politics', as a basis for wider sympathetic engagement, is necessarily broken-backed.

But it would be a pity to conclude on this note. After all, elsewhere, as we have seen, Eliot provides many positive insights that could lead in a significantly different direction. In particular, there is an episode – little remarked on, in the secondary literature – that could be seen as a paradigm case of sympathetic engagement, and one that does not require any of this paraphernalia of identity: the episode where Deronda takes Mirah, after her attempted suicide, to the Meyricks, who welcome her – a complete stranger, and a Jew – to their home. While not desperately poor, they are certainly not rich, yet welcome her unreservedly, and look after her while she finds her feet again.[74] She can thereby gain – or regain – a sense of belonging: a sense that comes both from the warmth of the love of a particular, small family group, and also resonates beyond this, as a sense of belonging once again to the world, to life itself. And none of this depends on the dynamics of identification and identity, the dualism of self and other, inside versus outside, that is clearly the danger implicit in the way Deronda's search is presented. 'Belonging', one might suggest, subsumes identity, rather than being subordinate to it, since 'belonging' incorporates the sense in which identity can never be reflexively self-sufficient, can never be sufficiently 'known' to itself, and must indeed presuppose a domain that goes 'beyond', that can 'only' be felt, symbolized, projected as figuration.[75] It is this that the Meyricks offer Mirah – and the modern world.

Tea and cake

At this point, we can turn to Proust, and pursue him into the depths of what he calls the *mémoire involontaire*, the 'place' where the past is 'hidden somewhere outside the realm, beyond the reach, of intellect, in some material object (in the sensation which that material object will give us) of which we have no inkling'.[76] Undercutting conventional distinctions between realism and modernism, the continuities with George Eliot will be readily apparent, particularly in the sense of mind as deeply embedded in time, as temporal in its very structure, and emerging out of this shadowy background of the unknown and the involuntary. In Eliot, the term 'unconscious' occurs, infrequently, more often used as adjective;[77] this is also broadly true of Proust's novel.[78] But in an interesting formulation, he refers to the 'thoroughly alive and creative sleep of the unconscious ... in which the things that barely touch us succeed in carving an impression, in which our hands take hold of the key that turns the lock, the key for which we have sought in vain'.[79] Here, the idea of the unconscious as a positive force in artistic creation comes to the fore – perhaps, indeed, as the 'key' to it. At the same time, this 'place' is only accessible fortuitously, not deliberately, and the key is the encounter with some object or event that may appear to have no inherent interest in itself. And what we find here, suggests Walter Benjamin in his reflections on this, is that 'the materials of memory no longer appear singly, as images, but tell us about a whole, amorphously and formlessly, indefinitely and weightily'. And, with regard to the memory, 'whereas an experienced event is finite – at any rate, confined to one sphere of experience; a remembered event is infinite, because it is only a key to anything that happened before it and after it'.[80]

And how does all this work? One starts with a vivid sensation, but then the mind tries to take on the search for meaning. It then runs headlong into the paradox: to seek, consciously and deliberately, is *not* to find. In his most sustained account, in the famous episode of the dunked *madeleine* that brings a childhood memory vividly to life, Proust writes:

> I ... examine my own mind. It alone can discover the truth. But how? What an
> abyss of uncertainty, whenever the mind feels overtaken by itself; when it, the

seeker, is at the same time the dark region through which it must go seeking and where all its equipment will avail it nothing. Seek? More than that: create. It is face to face with something which does not yet exist, which it alone can make actual, which it alone can bring into the light of day.[81]

Thus does the questing mind fall headlong into the problem of reflexivity: it is itself what it seeks to find, it is its own 'dark region', and the 'finding' becomes inseparable from the projection of the creative act, 'forming', shaping, the unknown, figuration as inseparable from discovery. What makes memory possible, memory as deep recall, is also what makes it unverifiable *as* memory.

But the further details of this process are also intriguing. The narrator tells us that he can feel something inside his mind attempting to rise, something 'anchored at a great depth'. He continues: 'I can feel it mounting slowly; I can measure the resistance, I can hear the echo of great spaces traversed. Undoubtedly what is thus palpitating in the depths of my being must be the image, the visual memory', which is trying to follow the original sensation of taste into his mind. This must be an 'old, dead moment which the magnetism of an identical moment has travelled so far to importune, to disturb, to raise up ...'.[82] And it is then that the memory returns ...

There is an illuminating tension in the language here, as though figuration is itself challenged in thus giving an account of its own emergence. We have the physical presence of some powerful object or creature, raising itself from the immensity of the depths; then we encounter the magnet, doing the raising; and we learn that what will emerge from all this is actually an *image*, not at all what the rest of the 'imagery' might have led us to expect. This, in effect, maps – figures – the disjunction at the heart of the process, or the *two* disjunctions. First, the tension between active and passive, between mind as *producing* the 'memory' or *retrieving* it as something that is always 'already there'; and, second, going beyond this, the transition from 'sensation' to 'image', the shift from a strong sense of a physical striving, by some 'thing', possibly animate, to the 'mere' visuality of the image, as one-dimensional, as 'picture'. This maps the sense of 'shock' itself, the simultaneous exteriority of cause and immediacy of effect, 'simultaneous' yet – as was suggested by Lewes – excessive or incommensurable the one with the other, both crossing and marking the gap in the circuit. But it also maps the inner logic of this, the resulting gap *in* mind, in memory, recording the metonymy of cause and the elaborations, both metaphorical and metonymic, *within* the field of memory and the unconscious that is thereby continually constituted and reconstituted through the impact of the 'outside' and the efforts of the conscious mind to retrieve this. Hardly surprising, perhaps, if this entity, this 'presence' that surges up, seems to be both physical *and* ethereal, both object *and* image: truly the spectral presence of an 'old, dead moment' … What is crucial is that this establishes memory, in its capacity as *mémoire involontaire*, *as* unconscious, as a 'separate sphere', constituted fundamentally by images and nebulous forces, and accessible – but only with difficulty – through mapping the superimpositions and displacements, the analogies and 'correspondences',[83] that both enable and challenge our interpretation of such material, and our theoretical efforts to harness it.

In this particular case, the initial sensation was one of *taste*, the *madeleine* in the tea: it was this that produced the 'exquisite pleasure … something isolated, detached, with no suggestion of its origin'. And it is the final recognition of this as the *madeleine* his aunt had given him long ago that made old Combray 'spring into being', in all its plethora of detail.[84] This immediacy of effect, this experience of 'time regained' as 'time abolished' seems connected to the *non-visual* aspect of the original sensation, and this calls for further examination. Most generally, indeed, it is *scent* that is involved, the 'objective' correlate of the sense of smell,[85] despite the *result* being intensely visual – visual images being the key content of the *mémoire involontaire* as we actually *recall* it. Taste and smell, suggest Proust, 'bear unflinchingly, in the tiny and almost impalpable drop of their essence, the vast structure of recollection'.[86] Reflecting on this, Benjamin describes scent as 'the inaccessible refuge of the *mémoire involontaire*', claiming that it is unlikely to associate itself with a visual image, only with the same scent, and speculating that this is because scent can drug or anaesthetize the sense of time: 'A scent may drown years in the odour it recalls [evokes]'.[87] Here we see, in an association of two experiences of scent, the relation of 'evocation' between them whereby they can be paradoxically identified, thus abolishing time, in the very presence of the 'pastness' of the past. And this in turn can be mapped onto the crucial dis/continuity here, the fact that a sensation of scent provides memory as a panorama of visual imagery, a memory which 'reacts back' so as to apparently incorporate scent and everything else: 'Combray' in its entirety.[88] And Benjamin adds that whereas smell holds memories tenaciously, memories do not hold smells[89]…

Taste and smell are perhaps the most intense, the most 'embodied' of the senses; at the other extreme, sight is a sense of distance and detachment, its picturing power aligning it more with thought. It is the former senses that give experiences their distinctive 'flavour' or 'aroma': they mark experience indelibly *as* experience, in its subjectivity. But above all, they carry the 'presence' of experience. Conversely, the encoding of sight in the visual image renders it subtly timeless, at least in that it can be readily separated from experience as such (as in the photo).[90] So, although the image as picture is what is 'conjured up' in recollection, from the unconscious, it is smell, scent or sound that provide the trigger, the engine, of the process of sensation and its transmission, and it is they that have to be 'reproduced', *in the present*, to give the moment of plenitude, of epiphany.

Some of this is further elaborated at the end of Proust's long journey, in the final volume, *Time Regained*. Approaching the Guermantes mansion, in a mood of black despair, virtually giving up hope of ever being able to convert his material (destined to become the novel) into a work of art, the narrator stumbles over paving-stones; immediately, he experiences what he describes as 'unquestionably the same' happiness as he had during the *madeleine* episode, and several times since, although the details are of course different (this time it is memories of Venice that are brought back). And then, waiting in the library, a second episode: a servant knocking a spoon against a plate brings back a memory of a railwayman hammering at a wheel. And this is followed by a third.[91] This speeded-up process, together with his determination to make the most of it, leads Proust not only to a more comprehensive memory of the past, but to reflect on this, and, in the process, regain some confidence in his vocation.

The crucial passage of reflection comes when he comments on the limitations of ordinary experience: everyday reality disappoints because 'when my senses perceived it my imagination, which was the only organ I possessed for the enjoyment of beauty, could not apply itself to it, in virtue of that ineluctable law which ordains that we can only imagine what is absent'. Yet, conversely, if a sensation, like the spoon or hammer sound, is 'mirrored at one and the same time in the past, so that my imagination was permitted to savour it, and in the present', where the 'actual shock to my senses'[92] could be said to add to the 'dreams of the imagination' the idea of 'existence' such dreams usually lack, then this subterfuge permits the isolation of 'a fragment of time in the pure state'.[93] What we find here, what returns, is not an echo or a duplicate, but 'that past sensation itself', which now 'sought to re-create the former scene around itself'.[94] Experienced in this way, the sound or scent is 'real without being actual, ideal without being abstract', and immediately the 'concealed essence of things is liberated, along with the "true self"'.[95] Thus, as Charles Taylor observes, this 'Proustian epiphany' only occurs when a *recurrence* of the original event, or something sufficiently similar, triggers it: the epiphany 'has to be framed *between* an event and its recurrence, through memory'.[96]

An illuminating discussion by Deleuze can be useful here for grasping what is involved in this 'return' of old Combray. Arguing that what is essential in involuntary memory is 'not resemblance, nor even identity … but the internalized difference, which becomes immanent', he suggests that the Combray encountered here is Combray 'in its truth … in its internalized difference, in its essence. Combray rises up in a pure past, coexisting with the two presents, but out of their reach.'[97] This, one could say, is Combray as 'present' in its difference from the present it once was, as experienced, and from the presence of experience now. This reminds us of the 'pastness' of the past as virtuality, inaccessible to voluntary memory, but always 'present', nonetheless. The twin impoverishments of everyday actuality and detached intellectual abstraction can both be transcended in a thoroughgoing moment of epiphany which, although brief in itself, can have lasting results …

We saw, in the first episode, that the non-visual senses, taste and smell, are crucial to the return of 'old Combray', in all its plenitude; in this second account, we learn that the imagination is, too. It mediates present and absent, bringing the past into presence. The 'subterfuge' of this conjunction of these two disparate realities – 'dreams' and 'actual shock' – produces existence as the presence of the past as 'virtual'. At the same time, the imagination has a synthesizing power: it gives us a sense of relations, of wholes. Is this sufficient, here, to account for the fact that the memory returns in this full density of associations? In Proust's account, it is shock, sensation, which appears to be the active force here, that seeks to 're-create the former scene around itself'. As a further reflection on this, perhaps we might have recourse to another influential thinker of the decade or two preceding Proust, the psychologist William James.

A critic of empiricism, James argues that when the mind perceives a group of objects, it does not experience a fragmented '*cluster of feelings*' but rather a '*feeling of the cluster* of objects, however numerous these may be.'[98] If the mind produces an image of the manifold of experience, feeling responds to this as a *singularity*, as a feeling of the whole; the image-forming capacity of mind – the imagination in the broad Kantian sense – provides us with the material to which feeling responds, the whole *as* and *in* feeling. So this worked-up picture or image is *felt* as embodying relationship, homologous to the original situation, hence as *memory* rather than as pure creation. Davis further claims that, in James, 'feelings exist in fluid relation to each other, rather than as discrete entities';[99] hence each 'segment' of the 'stream' of experience is not felt in isolation because it is inseparable from a 'staining, fringe or halo of obscurely felt relation to masses of other imagery'.[100] Experience is grasped in a way that is not only inherently relational, but also temporal. And this perspective seems to lead not only into Proust, but into Bergson and Virginia Woolf as well …[101]

Resistance and recognition: The artistic encounter

It will be apparent that this Proustian account of memory is constantly at risk of sliding memory into creativity; the boundaries that separate recollection and recreation seem very flimsy. Indeed, by the time we reach the events at the Guermantes mansion, near the end, this close relation has become near-explicit; there is, at the very least, an essential homology between these two processes, and this is worth pursuing, this time from the standpoint of art.

Here, in the discussion of how the raw material of experience is transformed in artistic creativity, we can recall that it is the very *resistance* that is initially encountered that guarantees the most important insights, 'those which life communicates to us against our will in an impression which is material because it enters us through the senses but yet has a spiritual meaning which it is possible for us to extract'. So, the task, adds Proust, is 'to interpret the given sensations as signs',[102] just as it is the 'material pattern', the 'outline of the impression … made upon us' that remains as the token of truth. 'Only the impression … however faint its traces, is a criterion of truth.' And this comes to us as force, as impact, not chosen by us, sensations encountered fortuitously, products neither of our volition nor of pure reason: 'The book whose hieroglyphs are patterns not traced by us is the only book that really belongs to us.'[103] And this is 'the inner book of unknown symbols' we explore in the unconscious, a book in which we have to try to read the symbols for ourselves, individually, 'for to read them was an act of creation in which no one can do our work for us or even collaborate with us'.[104] Thus can sensation, beyond memory, become art.

On this account, it is the presence of the impression *as* impression, as trace, carrying a sense of otherness, of an *impact* on the self from outside, that gives it its truth. And this is further manifest – as we saw in the *madeleine* episode – in the difficulty of its 'coming to the surface', the sense of physical struggle involved. Given this emphasis on the intensity of the experience in itself, any problem of 'deciphering hieroglyphics' seems rather secondary. And this has implications for the apparently important role of the imagination. Having been conjured up to bridge the gap between the original sensation and the current one, so as to present us with the immediacy of memory, the imagination then implicitly disappears again, in the *forcefulness* of the identification. Yet we are told here, several times, of *signs*, and of symbols: these would seem to call for an active *decipherment* of the book of hieroglyphics, clearly a role for the imagination. On the one hand, the language of impression, sensation, force, materiality;

on the other, that of interpretation, decipherment, meaning. We are not so far from Hume (and his critics). And although we appear not to have encountered the spectacle of sympathy as such, there is something here that might make it worthwhile for us to pause, for a moment's reflection.

These experiences of memory, of sensation, in their vividness, 'out of time': these are clearly to be contrasted with experiences *in* time, particularly the time of routine, everyday life, the zone that can be recorded, but only as fragmented and filed away, as *mémoire volontaire*. This is the zone of 'utilitarian, narrow human purpose'.[105] So one could say that the time of *mémoire involontaire* and creativity is the time of the recognition of the integrity of the otherness in experience, the 'time of encounter', emancipated from human interest as such – 'interest' as that which appeals to our needs and desires as constituted selves. This is, necessarily, time as the moment of communication, of engagement with otherness as the difference of other beings. A little-noticed passage from the *madeleine* episode brings this into sharp relief. Bearing in mind that objects, as signs, can embody unsuspected past relations and dimensions, Proust alludes to the 'Celtic belief' that the souls of those we have lost are held captive inside some animal, plant or object, and can only be released with the permission of the latter: 'Then they start and tremble, they call us by our name, and as soon as we have recognised them the spell is broken'.[106] This passage must clearly have been noticed by Deleuze, who writes: 'It is as if the quality enveloped, imprisoned the soul of an object other than the one it now designates'.[107] This charismatic point of recall or creation is actually an *encounter*, then, an affirmation of shared belonging.[108] And this now reminds us of another author, already familiar to us here: Benjamin. It is worth reproducing the quote at length:

> Experience of the aura thus rests on the transposition of a response common in human relationships to the relationship between the animate or natural object and man. The person we look at, or who feels he is being looked at, looks at us in return. To perceive the aura of an object we look at means to invest it with the ability to look at us in return. This experience corresponds to the data of the *mémoire involontaire*.[109]

When Benjamin also tells us that '... we designate as aura the associations which, at home in the *mémoire involontaire*, tend to cluster around the object of a perception',[110] then again, we seem very close to Proust. And Benjamin goes on here to discuss Baudelaire, reminding us of the latter's 'forest of symbols' that look at us with 'familiar glances'.[111] He even adds that 'The deeper the remoteness which a glance has to overcome, the stronger will be the spell that is apt to emanate from the gaze'.[112] Aesthetic engagement is an encounter, in which the element of distance is irreducible.

We can now return to memory, and its relation to the element of artistic creativity outlined here. What is crucial is the distinctive relation to time in the Proustian novel. As Proust writes, he is situated in a present that refers to what happened in the past, to what 'must have' happened then, so as to have brought him to his present position, the position he now writes from, from whence he refers back to the past point of origin, before writing, and to the later points of dramatic revelation that both reconstruct the writing and drive it forward. Given the time that has elapsed in the writing, the distance from the origin, the 'founding moment' or the series of revelations, the actual process of writing maps the very processes of literary creativity and of remembering on to one another, through the very redoublings and recurrences, the recognitions and encounters, that constitute both procedure and subject-matter of both. Of course, the work is characterized as a novel, not as autobiography, but the way these constantly run together or overlap, or run alongside as powerfully homologous,[113] exemplifies this superimposition of creativity on to memory whereby two ultimate incommensurables nonetheless make each other possible – along with the Proustian project of the modern self.

Memory, feeling and modernity

In Proust, all this is linked to a distinction – left implicit, most of the time – between the everyday world of the *mémoire volontaire* and this world of *mémoire involontaire*. In the former, the past is made 'arid' by the intellect, and voluntary memory is merely like 'turning over the pages of a picture-book', so that everyday images are 'desiccated and insubstantial'.[114] Ordinary sensations are really just patterns of homogeneous elements, however individually distinct and distinctive each may seem. In Benjamin's hands, this becomes a theoretically developed, full-scale critique of modernity, but it also reminds us that a theory of memory itself may have to be part of its own subject-matter, itself potentially time-bound.

Erlebnis, the experience of the moment, experience as discontinuous and available to be filed as accessible memory, is contrasted with *Erfahrung*, tradition-bound experience, 'less the product of facts firmly anchored in memory than of a convergence in memory of an accumulated and frequently unconscious data'; and Benjamin adds that 'Where there is experience in the strict sense of the word [*Erfahrung*], certain contents of the individual past combine with material of the collective past'. The latter implies that societies in which collective experience, ritual and tradition enter into and reconstruct the very way individual life itself is experienced, must have a different relation to time and memory, such that even the distinction between two domains or types of memory cannot be taken for granted. This cannot be explored here, but what does emerge is that, in Benjamin's words, following Proust, 'only what has not been experienced explicitly and consciously, what has not happened to the subject as an experience [*Erlebnis*], can become a component of the *mémoire involontaire*'.[115] Thus, the modern self emerges as disjunctive: consciousness and recall exclude one another – save only in the imaginary or aesthetic plenitude of the Proustian epiphany – and, since past and present cannot cohere, experience is fractured.[116] Modernity designates the time of the past as absence, of the subject as never truly self-present. And, as Ian Hacking rather poetically puts it, 'There is one feature of the modern that is dazzling in its implausibility: that the forgotten is what forms our character, our personality, our soul'.[117]

An underlying implication here is that affect cannot be stored: all that can be stored is the 'memory', the representation, of it. The feeling is dissipated, *as* feeling, or energy, in the very experience of it. Feeling *is* presence, in the here and now; it *makes* experience 'presence'. I do not remember past feelings; I only remember *that* I had them. This makes it all the more likely that the Proustian 'deep' memory is actually a process – or moment – of unconscious *re*creation, a reconstruction from the collapse of the internal barriers in the mind, from that moment when the 'shaken partitions'[118] give way, with the resultant or accompanying sensations, or affects, in the present. And here we can revisit a controversy in psychology from Proust's own time (and unresolved since). It has often been assumed that emotions can be lodged in the unconscious, that indeed 'nothing is truly forgotten'. James, however, denied the existence of emotional memory: what surges up is actually a *new* episode of feeling.[119] Most pointedly, the psychologist Claparède, from the same period, claimed that 'For me, it is impossible to *feel* an emotion as *past*'. He adds: 'One cannot be a spectator of one's feelings; one feels them, or one does not feel them; one cannot imagine them [image them, represent them] without stripping them of their affective essence'.[120] This may need some amendment – in some situations, at least, we can be aware *that* we have certain feelings – but the main point is plausible: attempting to grasp the feeling *as* feeling is to lose it in the grasping of it; to record it, or reflect on it, is *already* to have moved on. And Ruth Leys observes that Freud seems to agree – generally, at least – with Claparède on this 'absolute irreducibility between affect and representation'.[121] Since, for Freud, 'Strictly speaking ... there are no unconscious affects',[122] it is ideas, wishes, fantasies, or, in most general terms, representations, that get repressed, and that are worked on by the unconscious processes of displacement and condensation, so that the resulting 'symptoms' in the present, which carry the affect, the emotional charge, can be apparently unconnected with whatever past 'event' was in some distant sense the cause. And this temporal hiatus provides the constitutive challenge for psychoanalysis itself ...

All this serves to deepen and extend our understanding of the paradox of reflexivity in this arena of emotional life in modernity. Can I reflect on myself, in my past *and* present, *in* the present, without losing that affective tinge that marks *any* experience as distinctive? This sense of disjunction between present and past both deepens the paradox of reflexivity, and is deepened by it: the affect, the distinctiveness of the experience of the past, is lost to me, just as my own position in the present gives me a necessarily partial view. The bounded self, exposed to the shocks of experience, finds its own past an increasing problem, returning as it does in mysterious residues and triggering opaque effects, posited as challenges to our ability to 'exercise control'. And the present is not sufficient to itself: it leaves traces, after-effects, after-affects, just as these are also latent in it.

The Freudian moment

The most sustained effort to reflect on these 'unconscious arts of memory', emerging out of this preceding background – and not necessarily resolving the tensions revealed there – is, of course, that of Freud, and it seems appropriate to conclude this chapter with a brief consideration of his work here. We can begin from an interesting observation by Peter Brooks, who suggests that the second half of *Daniel Deronda* reflects a shift of emphasis from 'seeing' (visions, fantasy) to 'listening' (narrative), and that both Eliot and Freud insist that an account or encounter 'get beyond the spectacularization of symptoms, that it becomes a listening to the body rather than simply a viewing of it'.[123] This again raises the issue of 'memory as representation', and its relation to affect.

In Freud, 'affect' exists in dynamic contrast to 'idea': but the German *Vorstellung* can also be translated as presentation, representation (and the French translation is usually *représentation*). A key passage, preceding the assertion of the impossibility of unconscious affects, can be quoted here:

> An instinct can never become an object of consciousness – only the idea [*Vorstellung*] that represents the instinct can. Even in the unconscious, moreover, an instinct cannot be represented otherwise that by an idea. If the instinct did not attach itself to an idea or manifest itself as an affective state, we could know nothing about it …[124]

In interpreting this, we can remember that while Freud's earliest position, adopted in the programmatic 1895 manifesto *A Project for a Scientific Psychology*, is one of wholehearted adoption of the materialist inheritance of the science of his time, with the mind as a system of neural networks, in which the binding and unbinding of 'nervous' energy provided the dynamic force, he had already moved well away from this by 1905.[125] We find, by then, a distinction between *Instinkt*, as innate to, and essentially identical among, members of a given species, and *Trieb* (often, but not consistently, translated as 'drive'), which is indeterminate as to object and aim, and individually variable; indeed, the latter is really about the *pressure* exerted, rather than the direction. This distinction plays a crucial part in opening up the possibility of 'mind' as an arena of relative autonomy and an appropriate topic for investigation by the new perspectives of psychoanalysis, but is not without its own problems.

Bearing this in mind, we can return to the above quote. How, then, is 'drive' related to 'affect'? In their analysis, Laplanche and Pontalis describe affect as 'expressive' of drive or instinct, 'the qualitative expression of the quantity of instinctual energy', its 'subjective transposition',[126] which seems apposite enough, albeit vague; in Kavka's version, 'The quantity of an affect is simply its intensity, while the quality refers to its positive or negative valence, pleasure or pain', and tension is central to it.[127] It has no representational content: ideas or memory traces can be attached, detached, or reattached. Hence affects have 'ideational representatives' (*Vorstellungrepräsentanzen*) to which they can become fixated, and it is these that constitute the core content of the unconscious.

All this serves to remind us of the underlying structural tension, and suggest that it may be unresolved. On the one hand, we have the language of drive and compulsion, of force and energy, in this distinctively Freudian version of the circuit of sensation, which does indeed allow for the circulation of energy among the sectors of the psychical apparatus; and on the other hand, issues of representation, meaning, and cultural translation, the decoding of thought, dream, and fantasy, whether conscious or unconscious, and without any promise of resolution. Translating the language of drive into the more clearly cultural language of desire does not resolve this, for this merely perpetuates the necessary indeterminacies of the former in the language of the latter. If affect is allowed to be unconscious – and, more particularly, if instinct or drive are allowed to be unconscious – then the relative autonomy of the unconscious, and the existence of the psychoanalysis that has postulated it as its subject matter, come under threat: the unconscious would collapse back into 'nature'. And here, in the uncertain status of the unconscious, the apparent incommensurability of 'affect' and 'representation' (or 'idea') can be brought into focus. If affect is unconscious, body is brought *too close* to mind, threatening to overwhelm it; affect has to be kept 'sufficiently' separate, to one side, and triggered as *effect*. Yet this too presents problems: the risk of *too great* a separation between the economic point of view on one hand, and the dynamic or topographical on the other, threatening to fracture Freudian 'metapsychology' by taking the economic out of the mental apparatus altogether, and leaving many of the crucial insights and applications of psychoanalysis, particularly when they involve crucial reference to affect – as in the case of trauma – largely broken-backed. And it may be that the grandeur and power of the Freudian system – along with its irresolvable problems – is inseparable from this aporia at its core.

An implication of this is that trauma and hysteria – presented in psychoanalysis essentially as cause and symptom – may rather be seen to reflect and embody the two incommensurable wings of this Freudian project, along with the underlying tensions of the relations between sensation and sympathy. And it is to them that we now turn.

7

Trauma Trouble

We increasingly inhabit, it would seem, what has variously been described as a 'trauma culture' or a 'wound culture',[1] just as, a century ago, 'hysteria' seemed to play an equally prominent role. The terms 'trauma' and 'wound' can both carry physical and emotional meanings, and the implication that their use points to some essential dynamic in modern culture is worth exploring. Mark Micale, indeed, goes so far as to suggest that 'more and more, trauma and modernity emerge as mutually constitutive categories'.[2] In exploring what this might mean, we will show how the articulation of sympathetic engagement can readily call on the language of trauma, a language that is readily sensationalized (and indeed can readily seem 'hysterical'). This suggests the possibility that trauma and hysteria can be seen as two relatively independent yet clearly related structures of feeling, and that, when examined further, they may reveal an underlying pattern, as manifestations of an underlying cultural configuration.

We can start to expand what the notion of a 'trauma culture' might entail by suggesting that the decay of the social as a basis for allegiance and cohesion finds individual identity moving towards a basis in traumatic abjection, the wound that can never heal because it is constantly recreated as the badge of individual difference. The internalized figure of the social, source of the superego, gives way to the amoral experience of the wound, the negating disfigurement that grounds identity as repetition, the craving for the proof, the ever-transient proof, of feeling in its sensational mode. The display of self through role, involving public projection through codes of civility, increasingly cedes place to the display of self in and as feeling, as sensation or impulse. Approbation in the displayed performance of role gives way to shock at the displayed intensity of the injured, traumatized self, secure only in its hurt, the melodramatic re-enactment of its flawed individuality. Mark Seltzer points to 'the public fascination with torn and opened bodies and torn and opened persons, a collective gathering around shock, trauma, and the wound'; in effect, a 'pathological public sphere'.[3]

In personal terms, trauma becomes the slash across the face of identity. When Audrey Jaffe refers to 'desire for a self that isn't picture perfect: a self that one can call one's own',[4] one can see this as working in a circular way. A need for imperfection, as a badge of distinctiveness, a marker of individual difference, is followed by the rejection of this, a need to aspire to something better, to identify with the ideal; and then, an implicit realization that perfection is just too difficult, hence a flight back to the real. We can all be marked by inadequacy, pain, by the stigmata of experience; and, if strongly so, then our demands for attention and sympathy can be presented as all the greater, all the more legitimate. Excess of the one produces excess of the other. Trauma *makes* us real, dramatizes and projects the flaw that marks our identity, makes it 'traumatic'. One could say that the flaw in identity culture is the flaw in identity itself, the imperative that identity *be* flawed. Not only do we thereby gain a sense of self in an era of individualism – my flaw is *my* flaw – but we gain a project, something to work at, both a source of, and imperative toward, self-improvement, coupled with the opportunity to blame others for our failings, and the implication that we are *entitled* to sympathy. My flaw can be a legitimate mark of my self-esteem; non-recognition of it by others is a lack of respect.

Thus does trauma culture emerge as a possible 'structure of feeling', a sensibility based on the isolating experience of the wound, of flawed identity, a sensibility that can nonetheless be an intriguingly *social* phenomenon. As such, it seems to have substantially replaced the more obviously other-directed sensibility of the 'Age of Sensibility' itself, operating as it did through a framework of civility and appropriate displays of concern, with a focus rather on the claim to authenticity of one's own imperfect condition. If, in the eighteenth century, to be human was to be able to respond to the suffering of others, it can seem in the twenty-first century to be more a matter of the assertion of a claim *on* others, the ability to carry conviction as a bearer of trauma. To bear – and bare – the wound is to make a claim to status, to be a full stakeholder in the culture. No celebrity autobiography or interview is complete without the centrepiece story of 'trauma overcome', the wound displayed for all to see. Roger Luckhurst comments on how the revelation of a hidden trauma 'organizes the autobiographical narrative, the revealed secret becoming the pivot for every public act'.[5] Jill Matus suggests a comparison from a rather more recent period, that of George Eliot, to indicate the distance traversed here. In suggesting that, through her suffering and remorse, Gwendolen in *Daniel Deronda* can become a better person, Eliot emphasizes 'the responsibility and agency of the wounded subject', her obligations to others. It was 'less a "wound culture" than a conscience culture'.[6]

But if we find ourselves here, in the culture of trauma, in the presence of abjection, whether of body or self, we also move in the opposite direction. Dominick LaCapra perceives a tendency 'to convert trauma into the occasion for sublimity, to transvalue it into a test of the self or the group and an entry into the extraordinary'.[7] To survive abjection opens the portals of the sublime. In this context, an affirmation of identity becomes all the more effective, carried as it is by the scar of a trauma marked by this powerful fusion. We may encounter what he calls 'a fidelity to trauma, a feeling that one must somehow keep faith with it'.[8] We can treat it with a degree of awe. And perhaps the combination of abjection and the sublime, in the context of suffering, points to another dimension too, for we have encountered it before: it can embody the sentimental. Through trauma, do we perhaps find ourselves in the presence of a sentimental attachment to the integrity of the body and the truth of personal identity, in a postmodern context of nostalgic mourning for the unattainable?

Just as the earlier periods raised questions of integrity and hypocrisy, of concern as 'real' or as 'feigned', of the possibility that the display of concern could become a form of self-serving self-indulgence, so similar concerns can be raised with the culture of trauma, but with a different focus, this time on the authenticity of one's proclamation of one's own suffering persona. Karyn Ball points to the way that suffering can be viewed as 'moral capital', and trauma thus becomes 'an envied wound because it is seen as vouchsafing moral authority', an envy that contributes to 'the banalization of trauma as a new kind of commodity fetish'.[9] And we may also be able to share the experience vicariously; hence 'the reader or viewer of stories or films about traumatic situations may be constituted through vicarious or secondary trauma', as Ann Kaplan puts it.[10] Thus we encounter the self-reinforcing link between trauma, status and identity in the apotheosis of an individualism based on powerful feeling, swinging between the priority of one's own feeling, and mimetic victim-identification: simultaneous extremes of sensation and sympathy, respectively. Individual distress and cultural anxiety fuse powerfully in a sensational context that casts doubt on the viability of any attempt to distinguish between 'real' and 'vicarious' trauma, just as it also pushes us into needing to make the attempt. When everyone becomes victim or survivor, what price the 'real' trauma of shell-shock victims, war disablement, serious sexual abuse? And how can any of this be rationally evaluated, when all we have are subjective feelings and the language of emotional hurt?

Shells, shards and shocks

At this point, it would seem useful to consider what could indeed be taken as paradigm cases of trauma. While the modern use of the term developed in the context of medical discussions of 'railway accident neurosis'[11] in the late nineteenth century, it is really with the epidemic of 'shell shock' cases in the First World War and the aftermath that the issues came powerfully into focus.[12] The general assumption that emerged was that soldiers who suffered from the condition had been unable to discharge powerful emotions directly, so these had been 'somatized', transformed into bodily symptoms, accompanied by mental dissociation or amnesia, with the result that the patient could not consciously remember the horrifying events that were at the source of the trauma; only their bodies 'remembered'. Controversies raged over appropriate treatment: was greater 'distancing' needed, hence cognitive control and conscious reintegration of the memory, or was emotional discharge, 'abreaction', more likely to lead to cure? Our central concern here, however, is with the condition itself, and we can draw on useful accounts left us by two of the doctors most involved at the time, William Brown and Charles Myers. They outline the symptoms and their own use of hypnosis to try to probe them more deeply.

Brown tells us of a case where a soldier/patient:

> ... begins to twist and turn on the couch and shouts in a terror-stricken voice. He talks as he talked at the time when the shock occurred to him. He really does live again through the experiences of that awful time ... In every case he speaks and acts as if he were again under the influence of the terrifying emotion.[13]

Myers noticed that patients might move in and out of these experiences, at times showing awareness that they were in hospital, but not when in thrall to the experience itself. When his attention was drawn to the resulting inconsistencies in his behaviour and responses, a patient replied: 'Can't help it. I see 'em and hear 'em (the shells).' Patients' thoughts repeatedly returned to the trenches, seeming to repeat the traumatic past in the present tense. Their attention could be gained for a few minutes, but then answers to questions seemed to become absurd. 'How old are you?' got the answer: 'It passed my right ear.'[14]

The reflections of Ruth Leys on these examples are helpful. She suggests they reveal 'an intensely animated, present-tense miming or emotional reliving of the alleged traumatic scene ... in the absence of self-observation and self-representation', so that the subject 'did not appear to be a spectator of the (real or fantasized) emotional scene but was completely caught up *in* it'. Indeed, there seemed to be *no* 'subject', able to 'see or distance himself from his emotional experience by re-presenting that experience to himself as other to himself'.[15] In effect, 'normal' spectatorial distance is not available to the traumatized subject, whether the distance that makes representation possible as such, or the ability to achieve such degree of distance from one's own experience as is inherent in reflexivity, in representing oneself to oneself. The experience of feeling, experience *as* feeling, flies into a relation of mutual exclusion with representation, with catastrophic implications for the coherence of the self. As LaCapra suggests, trauma 'brings about a dissociation of affect and representation: one disorientingly feels what one cannot represent; one numbingly represents what one cannot feel'.[16] Neither experience nor representation can remain unaffected by this: given the impossibility of the distance that keeps them separate yet related, they collapse into each other, and the form this takes is *repetition*. Hence repetition emerges as the mode of existence of unrepresentable experience in its impact on body and self. Clearly the implications of this need further development.

For a start, this carries with it the collapse of any possibility of the subjective *integration* of experience – experience as the experience of a 'subject'. At this limit point, experience remains subjective, but 'subjective' becomes a strictly adjectival or functional term: subjectivity without a subject, so to speak; it is 'registered', there is awareness, but there is no clear sense of the subject as a continuous 'position', manifested in a relatively integrated sense of selfhood, as the embodiment of subjectivity, its experiential core. Hence the absence of reflexivity, of self-awareness. Luckhurst provides a useful formulation: 'The traumatic instant cannot be experienced as such, because the trauma both distends the subject and bursts the bounds of what constitutes "experience".'[17] *What* is registered here has two aspects: it is intensity, force, the purity of the impact, the shock of the alien; and it is what, in its later returns, manifests as *affect*, powerfully in and of the present. This, then, is the *difference* of force, what is ungraspable in impact in the form of representation – sensation in its pure state. Referring to the wound more generally, Sara Ahmed reminds us that it functions 'as a trace of where the surface of another body (however imaginary) has impressed upon the body, an impression that is felt and seen as the violence of negation'.[18]

Returning to the shell-shock victim, who 'sees' and 'hears' the shells, we can say that neither from his own point of view, nor from ours, is he referring to a *representation* of an exploding shell (like a picture of it, on the wall). Whatever *we* may think, it is experienced as 'real enough', for him, as manifest in his dramatic responses. And as for the latter, we can recall that Leys referred to 'present-tense miming', the sense in which reality is being *enacted* here; but again, this may be our way of characterizing what is happening, but it wouldn't be his. We need to remember that his *fear*, and any other emotions present here (such as surprise) are not 'acted' – they are real. If we call this 'acting out', it clearly incorporates real emotion. This also reinforces the suggestion of James and Claparède, mentioned in the previous chapter, that emotions exist *in the present*, however much we might legitimately say that they are activated by memories of the past, from the past. And this bifurcation is itself testimony to the 'reality' that is involved here, reality as experienced by a subjectivity that is split or fragmented, hence a 'subjective experience' that cannot be clearly located by or in a subject.

What most obviously distinguishes the flashback from ordinary memory is its *insistence*, its repetitive reappearance under its own volition, so to speak. Cathy Caruth suggests that the flashback, in its powers of return, cannot be thought of 'simply as a representation'; it is an interruption to representation, rather than an instance of it. With the flashback, she adds, 'the outside has gone inside without any mediation'. Hence trauma emerges as 'the literal return of the event'.[19] For Caruth, and others who share this perspective, Luckhurst suggests that the traumatic memory is 'a shard of the event itself', and trauma can be characterized as 'that which cannot be processed by the psyche yet lodges within the self as a foreign body ...'.[20] It constitutes an absence or gap at the heart of identity: that is, a terrible presence (the 'shard') that is also an absence (of sense, representation).

In exploring this, we enter highly controversial territory. In particular, Caruth's repeated claims about the 'literal return of the event' in trauma, such that this 'insistent return' makes it 'absolutely *true* to the event',[21] has been widely criticized, and it is not hard to see why. Most research suggests that flashback memories are not inherently more reliable than other kinds; and widely publi-cized controversy has swirled around so-called 'recovered memory syndrome' and the use of data based on this in court cases.[22] For example, 'flashbulb' memories are often said to have a rather dramatic, highly lit quality, as if being not so much a literal representation of reality (which would mean what, exactly?) as a cinematic re-creation of it. And this cinematic quality reminds us that the fundamental epistemological quandary remains: the intensity of a 'memory' cannot guarantee its truth value; nor, if we take the statement literally, can there be any '"literal" return of the [traumatic] event'.

And yet: there is that 'shard', the apparent dissociation that indicates the immediacy, the alien presence, experienced *as* alien, impossible to assimilate but *there*, present *as if* a shard of reality. It is real, in that it occupies the place of the real, in the absence of the normal signifying, representational capacity of the subject; the real is present, all-too-present, in the absence of its normal distance. 'A shard, embedded in the mind': a powerful image, but the very language conveys the tension of our (in)ability to grasp what seems to be going on, for we seem to be firmly impaled on the horns of the classic mind/body distinction, not to mention the inside/outside boundary problem; and it is from this doubly impossible place that the trauma victim appears to address us. The shard, embedded, faces both ways: the outside becomes simultaneously inside; a channel of communication is set up, but in such a way that nothing, no message, can cross it – save only, perhaps, the 'message' of shock, of 'impact in itself', ungraspable and unrepresentable to the subject but present in its effect, its effect as affect.

Clearly the language here seems essentially causal, and one can understand the temptation to rewrite it in narrowly physical, ostensibly scientific, terms. Even contemporary neuroscientists who attempt this, however, still tend to resort to terms like 'mind' and 'consciousness',[23] and in this respect, they are, as we have seen, in an eminently respectable tradition, going back to the eighteenth century. There are both shifts and continuities in the scientific language, but what remains consistent is the apparent impossibility of fulfilling the aspiration of more positivist-oriented scientists to 'cleanse' this language of everyday 'impurities'. What we encounter here is the cultural reality of language: concepts that may appear flawed or contradictory, on reflective analysis, nevertheless have a dynamic life in their contexts of use. They *do* things, they blaze tracks and connections, and resonate with powerful imagery. In this case, what we find is the physical and figural power of the language and experience of sensation, reconfigured for the age of trauma. The language of the circuit of sensation helps us to grasp the sense of forces, intensities, of causes and effects, causes evident in affects, that draw mind, body and technology into chains of linkages *and* interruptions, shocks and traumas, that dramatize and energize the whole pattern of experience. And when he refers to 'a gap between impact and understanding, influx and assimilation', and hence 'a fundamental tension between interruption and flow, blockage and movement',[24] both presenting a challenge to coherent narrative and yet demanding it, Luckhurst pinpoints this very clearly.

Concepts like 'sensation' and 'trauma' indeed derive their power from the ambiguity of their 'place' or 'origin': mind or body, representation or reality, sign or substance. They remind us that the favourite dichotomies of Western culture are not so much boundaries to work within, as challenges to be overcome. This boundary-crossing would conventionally be seen as the core of the figurative; but this is a feature of language, and to see it in these terms is to locate it *inside* one term of these powerful dichotomies, when the whole point of it is that the power is derived from the 'between', from the 'impossible place' between two incommensurables that can never, strictly speaking, be said either to 'meet' or to be 'separate' from one another, as two of a pair. In her discussion of American fiction, Laura di Prete hints at this when she argues that 'to represent trauma, language needs to be both literal and figurative and not either one or the other'.[25] This is the realm, or the power, of figuration, or the figural, as it both generalizes and grounds the figurative, trying to crystallize, to focus, the twin mysteries of difference and power, as a kind of action or gesture that uses figurative language, imagery, to map the impact of the difference of power itself. And of course all this remains theoretical, interpretive: the awareness of the traumatized victim cannot encompass it.

The shard, then, provokes crises at the boundaries, both inside/outside and active/passive. 'The problem that the trauma poses', suggests Seltzer, 'is a radical breakdown as to the determination of the subject, from within or without: the self-determined or the event-determined subject; the subject as cause or as caused; the subject as the producer of representations or their product ...'[26] The self-determined subject is able to make rational choices and realize them in action, achieving results: generalized, as the central value of a culture, we can see here the whole framework of the project of modernity. Yet this coexists in a state of some tension with what is also – in part – a product of that same orientation, namely the recalcitrance of experience, the insubordination of the event to the imperative to control, and the inevitable element of passivity, of receptiveness, in our orientation to the world. Hence the sense that there is 'always more causality than we can process', as Kirby Farrell puts it, so that we find 'a disturbance in the ground of collective experience'.[27] Once again we notice that recalcitrance of effect to cause that is one aspect of *shock* in the culture and experience of modernity. The self-determined subject becomes subject to circumstance, at the mercy of the unexpected which is nevertheless ever-present. If shock parries this, trauma capitulates to it, as it were, with the repetitive processes and unexpected effects of modern mechanisms of reproduction and representation inscribing the potential for trauma at the core of the experience of subjecthood.

This can lead us into a further consideration of the relation between trauma and time. A useful starting point is provided by Caruth's suggestion that consciousness works 'by placing stimulation within an ordered experience of time', so that, conversely, trauma is 'a shock that appears to work very much like a bodily threat but is in fact a break in the mind's experience of time'.[28] Certainly the idea that time has a close, indeed internal, relation to subjectivity – even though the latter is commonly figured as an 'inner space' – has been fundamental to Western culture as it has developed in recent centuries. Modern selfhood can be seen in terms of 'depth', integrated 'vertically' (consciousness, the unconscious), mapped into temporal succession and development; in effect, time is drawn on to provide internal coherence to the sense of self-identity. Experience, one might say, involves registration in time. Experience is 'of the present', the *now*; and being registered as 'now' constitutes it *as* experience, for me, just as it makes memory possible, memory as the registered images that, in being recalled, can stimulate affect in the present. This registration process, in the act of separating image from affect in sequencing, constitutes experience in its temporality, gives us what we mean by 'time' in this context: time as narrative. Hence time as registration has something abstract about it, and proce-dural: registration implies classification; experience is already registered *as* an experience of a particular type, place and time. This combination of attributes helps us grasp the way Proust and Benjamin can link this experience of time to features of modern life and, in particular, how they can present 'voluntary' memory as an attenuation, an impoverishment, of 'lived' experience. The process of registration of experience in a sense destroys it as lived experience; as experience minus affect, it becomes representation.

This registration process is what is disrupted by trauma: experience can no longer be known as such, as it cannot be comprehended in time. The Proust–Benjamin distinction between voluntary and involuntary memory collapses; as a necessary constituent of our normal sense of experience, the trauma blasts its way through this, too. Caruth suggests that what matters here is not so much the quantity of stimulus but 'fright', a stimulus that comes on too quickly; we are unprepared, so 'the threat is recognized as such by the mind *one moment too late*'. Hence the threat, not really 'experienced', lacks registration in time; and this grounds its return, in the form of flashbacks and nightmares.[29] We can go on from this to suggest that it is helpful to see trauma as a temporal dislocation that grounds not a literal return (*à la* Caruth) but the repetitive return of an inability to achieve distance, marked in the breakdown of the distinction between experience and representation. Leys expresses it thus: 'The experience of the trauma, fixed or frozen in time, refuses to be represented *as* past, but is perpetually reexperienced in a painful, dissociated, traumatic present.'[30] So the relation between past and present is crucial in trauma, as is the relation between representation and experience, the power of affect serving as the linkage here. We encounter a simultaneous collapse of present into past (memory as flashback), and of past into present (affect can only be lived in the present), which is *also* a collapse of experience and representation into each other, together producing the powerful reality-effect, the sense of trauma as a 'shard' or fragment of the real. And trauma, destroying the experience of time, leaves us with its own eternal return, as repetition.[31]

From trauma to hysteria (and back again)

Freud's own direct response to shell shock emphasized an 'economic' conception – the quantity of shock overwhelms the defences – but also with hints of the 'time lag' conception just outlined, whereby the shock happens so suddenly that it catches the subject unaware.[32] This is not, however, his only theory of traumatic neurosis, and the best-known of his earlier ones is not easily compatible with it.[33]

This alternative model has become particularly influential through its association with the concept of 'deferred action', *Nachträglichkeit*, referring to the 'belatedness' of trauma, the delay between the original event and the onset of symptoms. This carries with it a 'retroactive' effect: only after these subsequent developments can the origin be seen as 'traumatic' at all, leading to the possibility of the endless, retrospective re-writing of life narratives. Trauma, on this model, is constituted by a particular relation between two events, neither of which is inherently traumatic in itself. A simplified version of a typical instance would run as follows. A young child either has, or fantasizes, a sexual encounter with an adult; at the time, this appears to have no significant effect, it leaves no residue. Much later, post-puberty, a second experience occurs, which may appear to have no relation to the earlier one, and may indeed have no apparent sexual connotation at all. It nonetheless evokes the first, through some more-or-less obscure association, and it is only now that a traumatic response kicks in, one that can indeed, through the workings of the unconscious, be subsequently repeated (and subject to symptomatic elaboration). The first event, subject to repression, can now become all the more difficult to retrieve, and traumatic 'memories' become all the more problematical.[34]

It is not difficult to see why this account would present problems as a *total* theory of trauma. It never really fitted the railway accident trauma of the second half of the nineteenth century, but it was shell shock that produced the major crisis. In these cases, the element of belatedness may still be present, but generally over a significantly shorter time scale, and is difficult to connect with issues of childhood sexuality and repression. Also, this earlier model implies a degree of internal complicity in the production of trauma, if only in the sense that it is the subject's own processes of repression and 'deferred reaction' that convert an experience into *trauma* in the first place. It is difficult to see any equivalent in the case of the shell-shock victim – or certainly not to anything like the same extent. Yet it is undoubtedly the case that both theories have not only been profoundly influential in our whole approach to trauma, but also seem to reflect some of the most fundamental problems of trauma itself. In short – and going beyond the details of Freud's own work – we can say that this matters because it presents us with the likelihood of an aporia, or structural tension, at the very heart of trauma theory. Seltzer has suggested that trauma functions as 'an internal alien entity within psychoanalysis itself: as an internal limit or boundary'.[35] What we find here may be two significantly different types of trauma, or perhaps two ends of a continuum, linked to different experiences, though both raising problems of time and representation, and therefore raising questions about memory, and history itself. But we also encounter the possibility that 'trauma' may not be a unitary phenomenon at all.

It is worth remarking here that there has always been an alternative tradition of thought in this area, albeit far less well known, or developed. This takes off from the concept of 'dissociation'.[36] The central claim, or implication, is that 'mind' and 'consciousness' have to be co-extensive; there is, in short, no place for an 'unconscious'. If a trauma is the consequence of the failure of the shock defence, then what happens here is that part of the mind is split away, 'dissociated' from the normally functioning part – or what is left of it – and takes up some of its 'space', bringing along its own fraction of consciousness. This could be said to present a 'horizontal', rather than a vertical, conception of mind, and clearly allows for the possibility of alternative or multiple sites of consciousness; these can be present alternately or collectively ('multiple personality disorder'), occupying the same body, hence as separate 'selves' or 'persons', linked only in this 'external' way, leading to this sense of fractured incoherence that incapacitates the victim and puzzles the spectator (or therapist).[37] It is as though the body has become the site of warring factions, rather than the active, coherent 'embodiment' of identity, and the trauma is manifest in the existence of time as repetition and recurrence, rather than continuity of development. All this seems to fit shell-shock cases well enough, just as it may seem less useful for the other end of the trauma spectrum. So let us now consider the possibility that different theoretical perspectives do indeed address significantly divergent notions of 'trauma' itself.

On one model, then, trauma can be presented as potentially unknowable because endlessly displaced through symbolic representation, endlessly elaborated through the language of the unconscious, to the point where one can wonder whether it has an origin at all, indeed, whether it is really there; every apparent 'original cause' could turn out to be merely another elaboration. While, in theory, accurate recall may be possible, as a real discovery of origin, this postulate is continually subverted in practice by the interminable elaborations, transferences and deferrals. Trauma thus manifests *too much* distance: this is trauma as absence, manifest only in its effects. Indeed, it could even be that 'one of the signs of the presence of trauma is the absence of all signs of it', as Thomas Elsaesser suggests.[38] In effect, on this model trauma is supposed to ground or underlie hysteria and its diversity of symptoms, but all too often collapses into it. And running through this, the question of whether or not the victim is in any way implicated in the production of the condition, and in what sense, can always in principle be raised, since issues of guilt, shame and repression are always liable to be present. Empirically and therapeutically, this is the arena of the sexual neuroses and of sexual abuse scenarios, up to and including the contemporary cases of 'recovered memory'[39] and the controversies around this. Freud's earlier theory fits in with this tradition, the concept of the unconscious seeming to be highly appropriate for probing the phenomenon.

On the other model, though, trauma emerges as unknowable to the victim, as it blasts through the boundaries of mind and reality that make our normal faculties of cognition and memory possible; yet this can go hand-in-hand with a certain obviousness to therapist or theorist, precisely because it abolishes distance, refuses mysterious chains of symbolic association, and seems to allow no obvious place for an unconscious.[40] (This does not, of course, make it any the less recalcitrant to therapy.) In place of the unconscious, we find the phenomenon of dissociation, with an implied absence of any coherent, integrated sense of self. There is not normally, therefore, an intractable problem of locating a cause, an origin, since this is trauma as presence, the wound revealed, displayed and expressed, the wound as eternal return. There is no obvious sense in which we can say that the victim is implicated; indeed, the language of 'wound' may suggest an aetiology of accident or disease. If there is any relation to hysteria at all, it is expressed in affective numbness rather than a florid excess of symptoms; and indeed, any such relation seems to be accidental rather than inherent. This is the arena of railway shock, through shell shock, to more recent cases of battlefield trauma (Vietnam, Iraq and 'Post-Traumatic Stress Disorder'[41]). Freud's later theory would fit in here.

As stated above, these are models: neither in theory nor in reality are matters so straightforward. Hysteria has raised its unruly head; and while further consideration of this, the twin that has always accompanied trauma, must wait a little longer, one can point to some obvious features of it that are relevant here. If the logic of hysteria is one of endless displacement of symptoms, including displacement into the social relations in which it is embedded, notably in 'transference' in the patient–therapist relationship, so that any original cause can become all the more obscure, then this can, in turn, easily 'infect' what lies beyond – including the second type of trauma. After all, shell shock was surrounded by medical, psychiatric and social controversy from the start; the complex dynamics between doctor and patient allowed plenty of scope for 'suggestion', and the possibilities of hysteria and hysterical simulation could never be ruled out. It was very difficult to be clear as to the 'objectivity' of the symptoms. In military hospitals, whether particular doctors and patients were of different ranks and from different class backgrounds could crucially affect interaction, diagnosis and therapy. One might suggest that even the most apparently physical of symptoms are always in some degree *learnt*, even though that does not, of course, rule out the possible presence of an underlying trauma that might merit reference to psychological or neurological description.

Beyond that, the whole notion of a 'trauma culture' tends both to reflect and promote a tendency to assimilate the two models. Trauma can simultaneously be individualized and medicalized, while being embedded in networks of sympathetic engagement, spectacle and sensationalism. And we can note the range of terms used to characterize the symptoms and their potential for transmission, not just in the case of trauma, but in hysteria too. These range from infection and contagion, through imitation, mimesis and identification, with repetition playing a key part; these are terms that can overlap but nevertheless mark ends of a spectrum, terms that slip and slide in their usage, whether by doctors and patients, or in the culture more widely. Clearly these are in some sense distinct, even if frequently assimilated in the cultural imaginary. So a phrase like 'the contagious similarity of the crowd'[42] can serve to characterize 'mass hysteria', including the possibility that cases of trauma can be seen in these terms, while simultaneously leaving pointedly obscure the dynamics of any possible process of transmission that could be present here (cause or copy; feeling or fashion).

We have in effect been sliding towards hysteria, and must now consider it more explicitly. These points about the terminological and conceptual fluidity of the conditions being pointed to here, and their apparently easy capacity for transmission, can be amply illustrated from the period of a century ago when 'hysteria' had been the preferred, fashionable label for a range of apparently disparate conditions. A widespread middle-class fear of crowds, seen as embodying the ready communicability of currents of irrationality and emotional excess, can be exemplified in the psychologist Gustave Le Bon's claim that crowd sentiments could possess 'a contagious power as intense as that of microbes'.[43] Illness and suffering were constituted as a public spectacle that itself contributed, through a pervasive mimicry, to the spread of these conditions, implying 'a state of suggestibility in which viewing, hearing or reading about a disease aroused corresponding symptoms', as Angela Vrettos puts it.[44] The early sociologist Gabriel Tarde went so far as to proclaim in 1890 that 'Society is imitation'.[45] After all this, it is hardly surprising that hysteria comes into focus as 'the quintessentially contagious affliction', and that public spectacles were seen as 'breeding grounds for hysterical contagion'.[46] Pointing to its intimate connection with the culture of the time, and its relation to creativity in the arts, Mark Micale can even suggest, sweepingly, that 'Shapeless and ever-changing, unfixed and undefinable, open to interpretation, a signifier without a signified, hysteria *is* Modernism'.[47]

Not surprisingly, the symptoms of hysteria provoked constant debate and controversy. It seemed endlessly protean, and as Freud and Breuer observed, no sooner has one symptom disappeared than another takes its place, though several can be present simultaneously.[48] And some of the symptoms seem contradictory. We can attempt to make some sense of their significance by suggesting that they occur in three registers, although any specific symptom may occur in more than one: (1) excess, volatility, hyperactivity, convulsions; (2) withdrawal, passivity, exhaustion, muteness; (3) duplicity, game playing, masquerade, apparent malingering, mimesis. It will be apparent that the first and second registers are in some sense contrasted; and that the third could be seen as being on a different level, parasitic on the other two. It has something second-order, reflexive, about it. While the first two could be possible symptoms of 'real' illness, this is less obviously the case with the third. And it is an awareness of the implications of the third – particularly when taken in conjunction with the other two – that informs some of the most insightful remarks of commentators, past and present. From the eighteenth century, the physician Sydenham claimed, of hysteria, that 'few of the maladies of miserable mortality are not imitated by it';[49] and in 1875 Paget, another doctor, coined the term 'neuromimesis' for this aspect of it. This idea is also captured in Micale's formulation, whereby hysteria is the 'masquerading malady', with no essence of its own; it is 'an image made in the image and likeness of other images'.[50] For Elisabeth Bronfen, hysteria negotiates the interface between 'mimesis, imagination, representation, and deception', coming to be seen more and more, in the nineteenth century, as 'the inextricable knot between an expression of passion and a simulation of passion, where the body reproduced the texts it read or converted itself into a text of sorts'.[51] Showalter concludes: 'Hysteria is a mimetic disorder; it mimics culturally permissible expressions of distress.'[52] And it would be hardly surprising if something of this remains today, even if the label itself is no longer fashionable.[53]

Thus the third register of hysteria presents it as unconscious mimicry, copying symptoms, as if to question its own status as illness, implicitly subverting it, perhaps even raising questions about 'symptoms' and 'illness' as such. It is the illness that parodies illness: mimetic illness that cannot be true illness but does not seem to be mere pretence or deceit, either. It *manifests* a condition – or, perhaps more accurately, a relationship – even as it comments on it, if only through mimicking it. It subverts its own 'identity' as something different, distinctive, and thereby questions identity as such. It suggests a sense in which the subject is *implicated* in the production of symptoms without, for all that, being *responsible* for them. It can serve as a paradigm instance of what Baudrillard calls simulation. This is not 'dissimulation'; rather it 'threatens the difference between the "true" and the "false", the "real" and the "imaginary." Is the simulator sick or not, given that he produces "true" symptoms? Objectively one cannot treat him as being either ill or not ill ...'[54] And it is important to maintain the rigour of this position: as also with trauma, unless the subject is reflexively unable to grasp their situation, so that no question of conscious intentions or motives can be raised, the question of deceit will inevitably be back on the agenda. Since the lines here are in practice very difficult to draw, the extent of controversy swirling around is hardly surprising.

Hysteria, then, is always dramatic, and shows a tendency to mimic 'other' patterns of behaviour, along with itself. It suggests, indeed, the possibility that a theatrical mimicry could be central to modern modes of self-construction and self-presentation. We can complement this, though, by introducing another emphasis. Referring both to stage and fiction, Vrettos remarks that audiences are 'invited to participate vicariously in the drama of disease, negotiating the territory between sympathy and detachment';[55] and Bronfen suggests that the hysteric fell ill 'owing to an abundance of feeling, an excessive sympathy with her environment, an uncurbed empathy for all that would move her body and soul

– but a flow of organic and psychic energy that formed a closed circuit'. These uses of the language of sympathy and empathy are significant here; indeed, Bronfen characterizes hysteria as a disorder of 'sympathy gone awry'.[56] But it is important to take the 'closed circuit' as referring to a *relationship*, not just to one person (indeed, 'sympathy' would seem to imply this). Thus Vrettos documents the way the relationships of care and nurturing (motherhood, nursing), very firmly institutionalized as feminine by the Victorian period, came to be seen as inherently liable to hysterical distress and excess, the skills of these emotional tasks being inseparable from their uncontrollable bodily manifestations in a circulating economy of feminine affect. Femininity itself always teeters on the edge of hysteria, threatening 'a disconcerting emotional spectacle'.[57] Gender is clearly as central to the way the spectacle of sympathy has been reconstructed by the late nineteenth century as it was earlier, and hysteria comes clearly into view as its 'pathological' other face.[58]

In its modern form, as a diagnostic category applied to a range of forms of distressed behaviour, characteristically gender-related, hysteria was indeed born as twin to sensibility and sympathy. It does indeed remind us of the problem of sensibility itself: ambiguously positioned as 'feeling', facing inwards to the self, its intentions and motives, and outwards, to the other, to the social world of convention and civility, with the body as the problematical boundary between these, sign as much as substance, manifesting 'feeling' as the repository of all these representations, signs and messages. Unable to stand outside this, hysteria explores the multitude of bodily significations – including the doomed attempt to withdraw from all embodied signification – available when the superimposed dualities of mind/body and self/other fracture and recombine in ways that defy conventional reading and yet must, for all that, be read. The other thereby speaks in and through the hysteric's body, so whose body results – and whose voice? As we saw in the previous chapter, much the same could be asked of Gwendolen, after all, constantly haunted by fears and fantasies projected outwards, by images that can swing between inner and outer worlds, at the mercy of emotional currents that make her as unreadable to herself as she frequently is to others. In this context, then, the hysteric's attempt to communicate, to relate to others, can manifest itself in 'the hysterical tendency to experience and present oneself as other than one is', as Bronfen puts it.[59] Hence the characteristically histrionic behaviour, and hysteria as mimesis, the other collapsing into the same, relationship into identity, identity as a parody of itself. Hysteria is an excess of sympathetic engagement, caught in the nets of identity as identification, swinging between mimetic excess, florid demonstrativeness and an anti-mimetic refusal, frozen into withdrawal. The hysteric can be 'someone who imposes his or her presence, but also someone for whom things and beings are present, *too* present', and who communicates this 'excessive presence', as Deleuze adds.[60]

We can also approach this from another direction. It is very easy to assume that sympathy for the other entails would-be identification with the other; that the sympathetic pole of sensibility requires this sharing of sentiment that would enable one to make this leap of identification. But while this has been central to assumptions about sympathy that have been widely held since the eighteenth century, we have seen that there is good reason to believe that it is, at best, only part of the picture, and misleading overall. Now we can be clearer about the problems that result. In the discussion of Adam Smith, it was suggested that sympathy is not about 'grasping the other', as identification, but rather 'imaginative engagement with the other's situation', involvement in the predicament of the other. Yet it is not easy to separate the two, and a resulting over-involvement, 'identifying' with the other, threatens a slide into hysteria, a transgression of boundaries, whereby the self simultaneously incorporates part of the other while simultaneously trying to defend itself against the threatened implosion. Sympathy *for* the other becomes confusion *with* the other.[61] This produces a necessarily unstable series of oscillations between uncontrollable incorporation and expulsion – a point, or process, of incoherent identity that renders any consistent subject position impossible. To understand the other, on this model, is to translate bodily signs into language or text, into meaning; but these are then re-somatized, as it were: I can only grasp the other *as* other, as mind 'in' body, by reproducing it, in *my* body, where its alien presence can only be manifest as *symptom*, as illness or hysteria. And, in the effort to expel this alien intrusion, mimetic approximation produces hysterical excess: over-identification explodes into a reverse reaction, whether as withdrawal or attempted expulsion.

The issue of identification is also relevant in considering hypnosis, a much-favoured treatment for hysteria a century ago, an apparently appropriate therapeutic style that manifests both sympathy *and* power over the other, through suggestion.[62] Just as the hysteric can seem to be taken over by voices and behaviours not her own, so in hypnosis she really *is* subject to such a takeover. Hypnosis undermines the self in its ability to exercise self-control, as an essential stage in the cure: the patient's ability to exercise judgement, gain perspective and distance, is lost. In this sense, hypnosis can be positioned as structurally equivalent to hysteria conceived as sympathy in its extreme mode, as identification with the other. This, too, could be said to involve a kind of power, as subordination to the other: the aspiration to identify to the point of 'sharing the pain' involves a degree of collapse of self into other, a surrender of the capacity for judgement, vicariously *becoming* other. Here we encounter the grounds for drawing hysteria and hypnosis together, the structural foundation of their historical convergence: for the hysteric, whether or not subject to hypnotism, acts *as if* 'possessed', torn between active and passive, self and other, just as the hypnotized subject does. It follows that an element of splitting or dissociation is present in both, since there is both an identification with the other, *and* an obedience to the other's commands.[63] 'Identification' itself becomes tension-laden, conflictual.[64]

So where does this leave hysteria – and its relation to trauma? Whatever the traumatic origin, this cannot account for the excess of symbolism, both in the elaborations of hysteria itself, and in its attempted appropriation by analyst or theorist: in this sense, hysteria and trauma are conceptually distinct, pointing in different theoretical directions, whatever their links in practice. Hysteria reminds us of the performative, the expressive, of the impulse to elaborate, endlessly defer and extend the initial cause – if indeed there is one. It invites controversy around simulation and fabrication, and places any original trauma firmly in a cultural context of personal interaction, of engagement with the other. And mimesis, raising the issue of identity, comes into focus as the danger at the extreme end of the sympathy continuum, where over-identification looms. Indeed, hysteria implicitly questions the cultural emphasis on identity itself, suggesting it is never a natural or unproblematical state, that perhaps statements or aspirations to identity are only ever panic affirmations, inherently hysterical. Worrying about identity, especially one's own, is always a move in the hysteria game ...

But we cannot leave it there. We must note Bronfen's claim that hysteria is 'not just an illness of imitation and of sympathy' but 'the somatic voicing of traces' of traumatic impact, whereby 'body symptoms *stand in for* a disorder that cannot be located in the body, even as its message can be articulated only by proxy in the register of the body'.[65] This is an intriguing claim, suggesting that recourse to trauma, in understanding hysteria, is both unavoidable and deeply problematical. This trauma, she argues, can be seen as 'a snarled knot of memory traces, which as a wandering foreign body haunts the psyche' – clearly an appropriate successor to the 'wandering womb' of ancient theories of hysteria – and hysteria itself emerges as a strategy of 'multiple self-fashionings' over this traumatic kernel or impact, in itself a 'figuration of nothing'. The memory traces of that impact can be endlessly elaborated, as though independent of it. 'The implication is that the psychic gap, the nothing (of which the hysteric makes so much ado) is a representational impossibility even as it is precisely what makes representation possible …'[66] The hysteric – and her doctors – can endlessly repeat the elaborations of this absence, this gap, even as they can never recover any 'primal scene'; for it is the very *gap* between any original sensation, the sensation *in its impact*, and its subsequent appropriation *as meaning*, within networks of representation and signification, that is what is 'repeated' here. Hysteria calls on trauma, even as it elaborates the impossibility of its access.

Hysteria, then, cannot just be about mind, language, imitation, communication. There was also the *globus hystericus*, a widely noted physical symptom at the time: the lump rising in the throat, threatening the capacity for speech; the very embodiment of unutterable sensation, the trauma as the ever-shifting source, present but never properly 'there', defying articulation …

Repetition, trauma and the time of modernity

It will be sufficiently clear from all this that the very language through which hysteria is constituted discursively both reflects and perpetuates fundamental uncertainties over its nature, its aetiology and its place in culture. And the latter is always basic to it: hysteria always seems inseparable from its mode of dissemination, its symptoms simultaneously referring to the body and communication with others. The problems here seem to coalesce round two terms in particular (and related synonyms): 'contagion' and 'imitation'. The former has connotations of physical immediacy, direct contact, and the involuntary; it can be used to refer to person-to-person transmission of disease, and the figurative extensions always carry something of this with them. 'Imitation', on the other hand, seems more to do with copying, role play, the activity of the imagination, with no physical contact at all. *Ideologically*, assimilating these perspectives frequently occurred, as we have seen, and could perhaps be convenient, enabling notions of danger, disease transmission, etc. to be combined with the more conscious, deliberate-sounding process of imitation so as to permit attributions of moral responsibility and blame; but conceptually, the tensions here have remained unresolved. The use of a term like 'mimesis' does not necessarily help, but it gives a clue to an underlying problem, in that both contagion and imitation can have what appears to be the same effect: namely, the reproduction of 'the same'. In this respect, hysterical mimicry seems to be undecidable between the two alternatives. But now, we can remember that the reproduction of 'the same' is just as fundamental to trauma. This suggests that, just as contagion seems to place us in the circuit of sensation, and imitation, with its links to the imagination and to questions of identity and difference, suggests the realm of spectacle and the engagement with otherness, so their convergence on mimesis, the repetition of identity under the aegis of 'the same', hints at an ultimate point of fusion or indeterminacy.

Clearly this requires further discussion. In his thoughtful account, Seltzer notices a tension, a 'radical uncertainty', about 'the relation between repetition and representation – between the passive action of acting addictively and serially and the active passivity of deriving identity from repeated processes of identification ...'.[67] The active/passive dynamic, and the 'repeated identifications', might make this seem particularly relevant to hysteria, but less so for trauma; and anyway Seltzer is primarily mounting an analysis of serial killing. Nevertheless, he sees the latter, too, as an appropriate product of a 'wound culture' (and with a parallel chronology to trauma, both emerging with the late nineteenth century), and what he points to here may be relevant. There is, he suggests, a tension between identity as identification and as seriality. One can say that identification always involves images, of particular persons and places, and this appropriation as image involves a kind of spatialization: it sets a scene, positions identity *as* scene, as tableau. Conversely, seriality is a process of *repetition*: it occurs in time, and incorporates the event as its basic unit, positioning identity as reiterative; and for repetition to occur, scene has to be transformed into event. Identification, as a form of copying, inherently involves representation, and always, in principle, raises questions about copy and original; repetition involves doing the same thing again, uniformity of process, and is not a matter of 'copies' and 'originals', but of singularities and uniformities. Seltzer adds: 'the trauma is something like the compulsive return to the scene of the crime – not merely in that the trauma is the product of its repetition but also in that it is the product, not of the event itself, but of how the subject repeats or represents it to himself.' This, one could say, is the 'belatedness'. There is *a binding of trauma to representation or scene*.[68] Hence the way time and place, event and scene, cause and effect, perception and representation, can all appear either to change places, or, more accurately, blend into one another, problematizing the distinctions themselves. In particular, the 'binding' here has the effect of *fusing* event *into* scene, ensuring the occurrence of scene *as* event.

In a broader context, Seltzer writes that 'Seriality and repetition ... replace the singularity of the event'; but in trauma, repetition does not so much *replace* the singularity of the event as perpetuate it, *in* its very singularity. The event is perpetuated in its intensity, *as* intensity; and it is this intensity that also denies the purely representational quality of the 'scene', which, in being *repeated*, rather than copied, is transformed into event. Here we find the 'flashback'. The traumatic 'real', the reality of trauma, is this collusion between identification or representation, on the one hand, and event, on the other, a collusion constituted as 'repetition'. Hence the status of both event and of representation is challenged here, in that the event remains unique, singular; yet paradoxically it is this unique identity that is repeated, that becomes serial, becomes traumatic figuration. Here, in the most 'traumatic' trauma, where the representation/ reality distinction is confounded, it is frighteningly real figurations that return, and that undermine the capacity for self-awareness and any coherent subject position, any prospect that 'identifications' can coalesce tentatively in reflexive identity. Without this reflexive capacity, selfhood collapses into the endless repetition of addictive acts of identification. If, as Seltzer suggests, 'identity depends on the identifications that threaten to devour identity',[69] then the 'identifications' *forced* onto the trauma victim illustrate this well, as does the appearance of what he calls 'mimetic compulsion'.[70] This term neatly encapsulates the tension present in the phenomenon itself: mimesis, copying, the excess of identification that marks the 'hysterical' extreme of the spectacle of sympathy; and the insistent, persistent, repetitive aspect of trauma as a pathology of sensation, whether suggesting the possibility of a degree of subject complicity, as addiction, or a compulsion that is externally enforced, mapped into the self as seriality, as repetition, crippling it.[71]

All of this seems to have a further resonance in technology, representation and repetition, in relation to reality, as this relationship has developed over the modern period, particularly recently. As Seltzer observes, the notion of trauma is 'premised on a failure of distinction between the figurative and the literal, between the virtual and the real – representations, it seems, have the same power to wound as acts'. It became a commonplace argument in the 1980s that depictions of rape were also instances of it, and that to peruse pornography was itself to engage in a pornographic act. Since then, we have learnt to apply this same questionable logic to paedophilia, in the context of images of unclothed children. Images and representations have become not just depictions *of* the world but interventions *in* it, hence surrounded by powerful taboos. They can be dangerous; they can be traumatizing. Hence the central role of the 'flashback', in all its vividness and force, and its *repetitive* power. Images matter in their *effects* rather than their *meanings*, for *how they act* rather than what they represent. They become fragments of reality itself, 'shards', able to operate across the boundaries, bring the outside inside. Likeness and analogy blend into cause and effect. The technology of image reproduction is thereby assimilated to the technology of reproduction more generally, and the mind, in turn, becomes a receiver and transmitter, in a circulation process in which we can never be sure whether the mind is itself an influencing machine or a machine subject to influence. Hence Seltzer's 'body-machine-image complex', a postmodern version of the circuit of sensation that nonetheless manifests significant continuities with its forebears. And we see what he identifies as the 'binding of trauma to mechanisms of representation and reduplication',[72] adding that questions of identity and identification become 'inseparable from media-facilitated processes of imitation, simulation, and identity-contagion'. On this logic, trauma becomes merely a more extreme version of the repetition that characterizes identity as such, in a culture of 'similarity-effects' generated by the media, whereby 'discrete events blur into "like" events'.[73] Once again, we can see that when the 'scene' of identity threatens to blend into the 'event' of its own ostensible repetition, the potential for trauma becomes omnipresent.

Finally, if we reflect further on this notion of 'repetition', we can see how problematical it can be for a culture premised on notions of progress, whether individual or communal, of 'moving forward', of problems as 'opportunities' for 'self-improvement'. Trauma becomes not only a challenge to this, but can itself also serve as a powerful figure for those repetitive aspects of life that modern culture disavows in its pursuit of its own perfectibility – for the *recalcitrant*, even the potentially *unresolvable* in experience, what it is that may question, even defy, this whole orientation; perhaps even the possibility of identity itself as repetitive,[74] the nightmare of eternal recurrence, of death itself, as the 'unique' event of life that returns us to the fate of Everyman.

All this would imply that the 'culture of memory' as it developed with the nineteenth century would be in a state of crisis, for 'memory', as the orderly storage of the past, would no longer be enough; and this would be because the 'unconscious', as the store of 'deeper' memories, only accessible with difficulty, but nevertheless in principle still accessible, as a repository of *representations*, cannot be the key repository of trauma. And it is trauma that carries the danger of the return of the past in the present, simultaneously returning the present to the past, presenting an uncontrollable repetition of what cannot be remembered but only *re-enacted*, and hence can never be forgotten either, by (and in) the body that carries this 'shard' inaccessible to reflective consciousness. Might one also encounter, lurking here, the uncanny return of what in the nineteenth century troubled the optimistic linear narrative of modernity: the danger of heredity? Doubtless this would take a different form, but one can recall the terror of 'return' itself, the atavism of the heart of darkness, the infernal dance of the primitive other ...

Cultures of trauma, narratives of origin

In the light of all this, we can return to trauma culture, and explore the sense in which that, like trauma itself, manifests a problematic relation to time. Let us start by observing that if you have to identify with your origin, so that it thereby becomes the source of your identity – origin as essence – and if this origin turns out to be flawed, even in some way catastrophic, then trauma becomes constitutive of your identity in the very process by which you recognize it, constitute it as such, this recognition being always and necessarily *belated*. (We weren't *there*, at the origin – only retrospectively can we have been there, 'origin' now constituted as *ours*.)

This origin, belatedly recognized as such, in turn involves its own origin, so to speak: a background against which it is emergent, or perhaps an other that can more actively stimulate it into existence. These features can be identified, obscurely but importantly – and with their own paradoxes – in Western myths of origin, including birth, whether of the individual, the subject or the group (nation), all attempting to show how identity can be conjured out of the undifferentiated, the in-different.[75] One might add that this state of unboundedness is not, of itself, inherently productive of trauma, and it can of course be a source of imaginative inspiration, or nostalgia, as a state that cannot be known as such and can only be 'realized' in affects and figurations that can mobilize considerable cultural power. Nevertheless, in that this is the source of a sense of belonging or embeddedness, a product of reflexive awareness in its inability to grasp the conditions, extent, and context, of its own being, it is not necessarily experienced as benign. It can be deeply disturbing.

But if such a postulated – imaginary – primal state is not inherently destructive, how would it become so? It could be that this very process of *origination* could be seen as traumatic, as entailing the loss of a primal unity or innocent wholeness. Hence, for example, the sexual abuse scenario, when taken to refer to supposed events from 'long ago', is readily available to be interpreted in these terms: the traumatic departure from innocent wholeness and purity into corrupted, crippled adulthood, the trauma repeating endlessly, disabling the capacity for normal relationships ... The traumatic 'wound', the fundamental damage or inadequacy, the cruel hurt, would then indeed be identity-constituting. Furthermore, this trauma that wounds, separates, can also unify, can be a basis of group identity: trauma as absence or loss becoming a powerful vehicle for the presence of communal, affective ties. 'Identification' can involve a fantasy image, a stereotypical construct that can ground and reproduce group identity: hence 'identity politics', which can readily incorporate this sense of profound hurt, linked to past oppression, fuelling the grievances of social solidarity in the present.[76]

Here we are approaching the apparently paradoxical utility of trauma for foundational narratives of identity, whether individual or social, and the way they challenge assumptions about history. If an origin is necessarily problematical and obscure, and if it can be readily simplified into a narrative of trauma, then this trauma of origin, of coming into being without realizing it, presents history itself as the departure from this origin that is doomed to endlessly repeat it, and time as lived (personal or social) becomes the elaboration of projects to defer, ameliorate or sublimate this trauma, but can never escape being structured by it.[77] 'Memory' becomes systematically over-determined, as it were; it becomes both a product of the originating trauma, and also belatedly, retroactively, it reproduces and strengthens it, triggering a repetition of its power *as* trauma. Hence can trauma always be guaranteed to be sufficiently 'traumatic', guaranteed to return, bringing with it the covert potential for investment by the subject and a denial of its own historicity, of the possibility of historical awareness. If this flawed sense of identity comes to be seen as constitutive of it, then this basic trauma renders history itself a repetition of these origins constituted in trauma, and of endless projects to defer, ameliorate or sublimate the trauma.

Magnified in the media and the cult of celebrity – for which trauma and its overcoming constitutes a defining part of the narrative – this all contributes to a crisis of identity, with 'self' and 'other' potentially available for reification through panic narratives of fear and aggression. Individualism encourages us to call on the personally tailored flaws in our identities to help us confirm our sense of ourselves as 'real' – and enable us to make claims on others for consideration and respect. This is virtually a reversal of those earlier eighteenth-century priorities: it is now us, we ourselves, who are entitled to sympathetic consideration, based on being able to establish the authenticity of our claims, rather than primarily owing such consideration to others. Thus trauma emerges both as a cultural resource for contemporary controversies over identity and responsibility, and an embodiment of crisis for the whole culture of memory, progress and self-improvement that gave rise to it, along with its precarious – yet ever-present – potential for 'fellow-feeling'.

Here we can see how the powerful myths of traumatic origin retain their power, and can thereby generate *interests*, among individuals and groups, in maintaining this. Such myths of origin, frequently linked to the doings of charismatic founders, ultimately reflect the contradictions in our thought about the notion of 'origin' itself, as suggested above, so that this element, apparently timeless and inevitable, can be mapped on to the historically contingent, obliterating the distinction between the two, to powerful ideological effect. Let us take one example. The fact that the Serbs were decisively defeated by the Ottoman Turks at the Battle of Kosovo in 1389 has been subsequently reinterpreted, through generations of Serbs, as the traumatic origin, the birthplace and birth event, of the Serbian nation. Here again we encounter the assimilation of time and place in the ritual intensity of repetition, and the use of the myth to serve the ideological interests of dominant groups in Serb culture, along with its role in outcomes such as the Balkan Wars of the 1990s that *reinforced* the sense of traumatized identity – while doubtless making it all the more likely that others, such as the relatives of the victims of the Srebrenice massacre (1995), will have opportunities to enact a similar traumatic cycle in the future. And behind this, of course, looms what has come to be seen as the ultimate horror in the European history of trauma: the Holocaust. As Leys puts it, 'trauma has come to stand for an entire post-holocaust, post-Vietnam crisis of truth and history, in which not only the actual victim of trauma but everybody in the postcatastrophic condition is trapped'.[78] What price the optimistic promise of modernity when the catastrophe has always already happened, and all that remains is traumatic re-enactment, mournful resignation, or playing in the ruins (the postmodern option)?

Trying to get some critical leverage on all this, LaCapra argues that a trauma culture confuses two separate dimensions. He makes a distinction between a transhistorical or structural sense of trauma, and a historical one, or between what he calls 'absence' and 'loss' respectively. 'Absence' invokes a metaphysical sense of history as the absence of wholeness, a fall into imperfection, yet perhaps offering the hope of a utopian outcome in the future; conversely, 'loss', the historical sense of trauma, points to contingent specifics, to particular causes and effects, to rights and wrongs where there are victims and perpetrators – the arena of moral engagement and political intervention. Eliding one into the other, he argues, variously increases the likelihood of misplaced nostalgia, utopian politics, endless melancholy, or interminable mourning;

running specific individual or historical problems into timeless metaphysical ones confuses and inhibits the possibility of well-judged interventions in actual, concrete situations and problems.[79] This is a valid and useful distinction indeed; but the whole weight of the analysis developed here shows how difficult it is to make it in a culture of trauma in which powerful ideological currents conspire to obscure it and underlying structural factors question its absolute validity in the first place. So we need to pursue this further.

Referring to trauma as 'worryingly transmissible', Luckhurst reminds us of the way symptoms can appear to 'leak' not only between patients and doctors – again, like hysteria – but 'between victims and their listeners or viewers who are commonly moved to forms of overwhelming sympathy, even to the point of claiming secondary victimhood'.[80] Trauma can thus be diffused outwards, and witnesses themselves can appear to 'appropriate' it. Indeed, it is not difficult to think of cases where being present at terrible events could well leave a traumatic residue; but of course this can present severe moral and legal problems for any attempts to distinguish between more deserving and less deserving cases, as it were.[81] In a culture of trauma, transmission can magnify the traumatic in trauma, sensationalizing even occurrences that might not have seemed intrinsically to be cases of 'trauma' at all. Clearly this illustrates the potential for over-identification in the spectacle of sympathy. But it also suggests that what is sometimes criticized as an allegedly 'superior' or excessively 'detached' position occupied by the spectator offering sympathy may also be a structural feature that enhances the possibility of effective assistance by maintaining a degree of distance, a certain kind of insurance against 'catching' the condition. And in a trauma culture, such a safeguard tends to get lost, particularly since a more participatory emphasis – 'we are all fellow-sufferers' – can work powerfully in the opposite direction. The tentative distinction between fellow-feeling as a necessary grounding for sympathy, permitting an active and specific engagement with others in particular situations where they may need help, and sympathy as a kind of automatic, unthinking identification, thus tends to be elided in the rush to share the pain …

One might add that theorists, too, can be influenced by this. Here we can revisit the work of Cathy Caruth – but in this context, more critically. Trauma, she writes, is 'always the story of a wound that cries out', that 'simultaneously defies and demands our witness', hence showing that 'one's own trauma is tied up with the trauma of another'.[82] So far, this might seem to be an eloquent summary of the moral and aesthetic challenges that trauma can pose to historical understanding and artistic representation, but not more than that. The drift of her argument goes further, however. In that it both 'defies' and 'demands' witness, she concludes – crucially – that trauma poses a 'danger' of contamination of listeners or viewers and that this is 'also its only possibility for transmission'.[83] Trauma defies representation, knowledge; in this sense it can only be 'known' as *shared*: to know the hurt is to feel it. We seem to be back with the over-identification pole of the sympathy dynamic. Bracketing her work with that of the neuroscientist Bessel van der Kolk, Leys argues, in her critique, that their theory is 'designed to preserve the truth of trauma as the failure of representation – thereby permitting it to be passed on to others who can not only imaginatively identify with it but literally share in the communion of suffering', so that 'the truth of the past will be performatively communicated to the collective through the suffering of those who "listen" but were not there'. Thus Leys points to – and criticizes – the widespread assumption that 'the trauma experienced by one generation can be contagiously or mimetically transmitted to ensuing generations' so that 'each of us can be imagined as receiving a trauma that we never directly experienced'.[84] This is important, because while nobody can deny the potential for – and indeed, the *need* for – sympathetic engagement with trauma, this does not have to be reduced to helpless immersion *in* it, or, in consequence, agonizing over the impossibility of representing it. Whatever the considerable merits of Caruth's approach for probing the experience and ontology of trauma itself, her further explorations here do indeed seem to be less an analysis of 'trauma culture' than a symptom of it ...

What we can take from all this, though, is the implication that a 'trauma culture' does not thereby become a culture that lacks debate *about* trauma; on the contrary, debate and controversy are central to it, and always have been. Hysteria was accompanied by endless controversy over its meaning, causes, and significance, and this has been no less true of trauma, in all its forms. A culture of trauma can include copycat trauma, the 'contagion' of trauma as fashion, along with textbook cases of 'genuine' trauma – and all these have obscure boundaries, and provoke controversies, but none of it is all-conquering. Along with the sensationalism of trauma and the potential for its vicarious transmission comes an awareness of the essential *unreliability* of memory, the tension of the dual origin ('belatedness'), the competing interests involved in trauma claims: all these can shift the terrain of debate, provide new challenges for feeling, judgement, and imaginative engagement with the plight of the other; and they do not inhibit such debate. And we have seen grounds for arguing that neither talking about trauma, nor representing it, are reducible to transmitting it, or sharing it, unsettling[85] though such engagement necessarily must be – and how could it be otherwise?

But let us end by pointing to another issue. The 'sensational' aspect of shock is always liable to shatter our defences. This may always, in principle, be liable to produce trauma (on the model of shell shock). But it may also be a resource for art. Benjamin refers to Baudelaire, who speaks of a duel in which 'the artist, just before being beaten, screams in fright. This duel is the creative process itself.'[86] Proust had to search for inspiration; the trauma victim has it imposed on him. But Proust's inspiration, like trauma, comes when *it* wants, not when *he* wants. Then, like hysteria, it reveals a process of working through, the elaborations and displacements of creativity. The original insight, like the origin of trauma, can get over-determined, overlaid, even lost, in the 'work'. And if the trauma sufferer can be pushed this way and that, even incapacitated, in art it is perhaps the very tension *between* these dimensions – cause and meaning, origin and transformation, passive and active – that characterizes the myth of the creative, charismatic artist so central to the modern aesthetic tradition and that, in turn, drives the individual artist on. And if art, too, is not subject to conscious control, this could also plausibly apply to its effects – which might give modernists pause, in their obsessive quest to 'shock' their audience, suggesting questionable theories both of artistic creativity and of reception. Art and trauma both reveal the deep conflicts that characterize the modern world in its uncertainties about its own relations to what it is, its origins – and its results.

8

Sympathy, Sentiment and Media Spectacle

We live in a culture of spectacle, intensified by developments in mass media technology, and it is often implied that this is radically new; yet, as has been seen in earlier chapters, there is a sense in which a 'culture of spectacle' was central to the onset of modernity in the eighteenth century. The emergence of a public sphere, in necessary interdependence (and tension) with a 'private' one, was impossible without the spectacle of feeling that both embodied the potential for a managed display in private and paradoxically thereby ensured its 'publicity', with the private as a rehearsal for the public and vice versa, as modes of theatricality. How does one recognize the private, without giving it an image, a 'public face'? Thus Habermas, leading theorist of the eighteenth-century public sphere, offers a formulation that makes the issues sound very contemporary for today: 'Subjectivity, as the innermost core of the private, was always oriented to an audience [*Publikum*].'[1] There is at least some continuity here: the eighteenth-century spectacle can be related to the present by asking how the early twenty-first-century spectacle of sympathy engages with new modes of publicity, of presence and distance, and the projection, interpretation and transmission of 'feeling'. And we can remember that the 'public' context is not just one of feelings and appearances but of talk, reflection and discussion, and it is in the relation between these – between what is 'present', included and evident, and what is 'absent', whether excluded, occluded or overlooked – that helps to pinpoint in all this a potential sense of community, and for the sympathetic engagement across boundaries that is what really gives meaning to 'community' beyond the existence of discrete, embedded groups and societies.

In the light of this, we can reflect briefly on the notion of spectacle, where there are, again, continuities as well as discontinuities as cinema, film and screen came to replace theatre, play and stage as scenarios and figurations of the world and our involvement in it. Spectacle is the mode of appearance of the world, its display before a subject, made real for the subject by the framing that draws attention to it as if to a cinematic image. It is the world that displays its own mediated qualities, with its successive 'frames' as static moments in a process that does not negate the possibility of reflexive appropriation by the subject, indeed could be said to invite it, through the relation between static frames and processes of change, the resulting gaps and discontinuities within experience. Spectacle should not, then, be restricted to the moment of passive appropriation, subject and object positioned in timeless abstraction; 'spectacle' should include this as part of the unfolding, the incorporation of the reflexive difference, participation rather than identification.[2]

In the era of omnipresent screens and digital interfaces, of 'reality television' and live, breaking news, we find two particularly significant transformations. Events that are 'distant', whether in spatial or temporal terms, seem to become vividly 'present', hence conveying a sense of 'mediated intimacies', with space and time becoming emergent properties of interactions themselves, constituting presence *for us*; and, along with this, the experience of the 'truth' that we witness blends reality seamlessly into simulation, with no clear distinction between the boundaries. Nor does this *necessarily* seem to matter. In a world where reality and simulation become indeterminate, the vicarious becomes our mode of experience, the appropriate form of experience for a world of/as spectacle.

We can say, then, that the mediated screen becomes a permanent interface that enforces this sense of the present as recontextualization, but never does so without remainder, without tension: there is a jarring of contexts, informed by the body's differentiated experience. The 'distance' senses (sight, sound) can live easily enough in the new regime of extended presence, but the remaining senses are thereby subordinated or displaced, and hence the overall feeling of 'embodiment' cannot remain constant. If context becomes relative to presence, it does so with this element of simulation, and any sense of relationship or 'community' that evolves in response to this is necessarily reshaped by it. The mediated screen, enforcing a crossing of the boundaries it simultaneously enforces and disavows, is both a medium, and a figure, for the space of public/private dilemmas and the relation to otherness. Thus reality becomes performative, in line with our experience of it becoming vicarious, as the inheritance of theatricality disperses itself into these differentiated modes of mediated culture.

The upshot is that we live in a world where ontological issues around reality and representation have increasingly thrust themselves on our attention. If, as suggested, this does not necessarily matter, there is one area in which it would seem crucial: our capacity to relate to the other's suffering. From this point of view, whether a 'disaster' on the television screen is a scene from a disaster movie or a real-world news broadcast is a crucial distinction to be able to make, and it seems to become more difficult to make it, in a world where it has become increasingly easy to 'stage' news items and where the technology of doctoring or 'touching up' images has become so sophisticated, *and* the knowledge that this happens has become so widely diffused. The risk here is that if, in the context of news, the promotion of spectacle *in itself* comes to take priority over questions of the truth-value of whatever the spectacle purports to be about, or to refer to – whether for commercial motivation, or interest in entertainment for its own sake – then any distinction between a real world where action is deployed and the representations that provide the information to guide this would be threatened with collapse.[3] Such ontological uncertainty would favour a merely voyeuristic appropriation, and this would make it more likely that an exclusively or narrowly aesthetic response to the world – encompassing both entertainment and art – would come to take priority over issues of moral and political engagement. Such, indeed, has been the argument of many of those who have characterized these developments in terms of 'postmodernism', whether viewed favourably or critically.

This clearly poses a problem for the fate of the 'spectacle of sympathy' in our times, but we will have to consider it in the light of the approach developed here, suggesting that 'cultural aesthetics' is a framework that *encompasses* moral response, rather than appearing to preclude it, and that this has been latent in the relation between aesthetics and morality in the modern period. It has also been implicit in this approach that we need to be critical of attempts to separate contemporary ('postmodern'?) developments too easily from what can be too readily dismissed as merely of 'historical' interest – that 'postmodern', if the term has any useful application, really just draws our attention to the reflexive mode, or reflexive aspects, of the modern.[4] And it is now time to suggest that the three main kinds of problem posed for the possibility of sympathetic engagement with the plight of the other have not changed in themselves over the period since the eighteenth century: how to gain the necessary kind of attention in the first place; how to be convinced of the genuineness of the suffering and hence of the witness to it; and how to maintain an appropriate distance, neither excessive (an aesthetic focus on the spectacle of suffering in itself), nor too close (sentimentality), thus precluding appropriate moral or political response. At the very least, the sense of 'community' involved here must not be pre-given, fixed, for that way lie the temptations of identity and identification as an approach to the other, who must be reduced to 'the same' if a candidate for sympathy, or else rejected as too incomprehensibly different. In effect, the existence of a sufficient resolution of these problems such that a 'spectacle of sympathy' becomes possible could *itself* be said to constitute the public sphere. These problems may have altered in form, intensity, or relative importance, but they are still recognizably central to contemporary debate, and a reconstructed sense of the public sphere, including a revised sense of 'presence' and a greater sensitivity to the openness of boundaries, would not alter this.

The challenge here is suggested by Chouliaraki's claim that 'Under conditions of mediation, we should think of cosmopolitanism as a generalized sensibility that acts on suffering without controlling the outcomes or experiencing the effects of such action'; it is a 'disposition to feeling' that incorporates the possibility of action at a distance.[5] How this might be possible clearly requires further discussion.

The spectacle of sympathy in the age of the mass media

The devastating Pakistan floods of 2010 were given extensive television coverage, generally with a focus on the distress caused to particular families or communities among the millions displaced; but some images were rather different. They gave panoramic views of areas of land, extending as far as the eye could see, completely covered by water, with a few trees, the remains of a few houses or telegraph poles – all that could be seen against the quiet, still, watery background. Such images generally did not show people at all. These images were simultaneously distancing, anonymous, disengaged; they invited contemplation; they often – dare one say – conveyed a kind of beauty, occasionally with hints of the sublime. These images embody an aestheticization of the spectacle of suffering, partly by removing any specific images of human suffering altogether, or by absorbing them into this apparently timeless, de-historicized background. And this is a clue to another feature: we have been here before. In her wide-ranging discussion of the presentation of suffering on the media, Chouliaraki refers to the comparably catastrophic Bangladesh floods of 2002. Here again we encounter the use of long shots portraying a static composition, such long shots working to universalize, producing spectacles that could be attributed to a range of other world locations, thus abstracting from particularities of time and place. It is all very aesthetic, turning reality into a 'tableau vivant', inviting 'not engagement with but gazing at the spectacle of suffering', and thereby breaking any 'emotional connectivity' with suffering itself.[6]

It may be that, in this particular context, this effect is mitigated – these images do not generally stand alone, but occur as part of an unfolding story, with other images conveying the suffering more obviously. But there have always been those who have been perturbed by the way we can be lulled, seduced by aesthetic qualities, aesthetic form, distracted from the content. There is a fine line here. On the one hand, a focus on the aesthetic can relativize, or distract from, the distinction between truth and fiction; we respond to the art as such, whatever its relation to reality, and in this sense its status as possibly representational drops out of the picture, as it were. On the other hand, 'emotional connectivity' on its own, is also not enough, as it leaves us trapped in feeling, rather than being able to *react* to feeling, harness it, as a basis for judgement and action. So from this point of view, the mediated spectacle of sympathy *needs* a degree of representational distance, hence potential truth value, just as it needs to engage feeling: the two together can be a basis for that form of 'engaged judgement' that makes a sympathetic response *meaningful*.

There is a certain convergence here with the worries that have often been expressed about the impact of technology in this area. For its critics, suggests Chouliaraki, 'The *capacity* of technology to deliver immediacy is simultaneously the *failure* of technology to establish connectivity'. Technology interposes itself, converts authentic presence into spectacle, and leaves us trapped in the intimate space of reception. Like art, it reduces the distance between truth and fiction and risks reducing its audience to admiration for it – or annoyance with it – and indifference to its content. One might say that 'If looking *through* the screen immerses spectators in suffering ... looking *at* the screen reminds them of the reality of the medium that disseminates suffering as spectacle and fiction'.[7] Whereas art *encourages* the latter, draws attention to itself *as* art, this is not generally true of technology;[8] nevertheless, awareness of it, of its presence as a medium of transmission, cannot sink to zero, so the paradox remains. And here, we must ask a key question: what *exactly* is the problem here; why is this paradox necessarily a problem at all? We have, after all, seen reasons to relativize the concept of presence, to free it from unattainable ideals of 'authenticity', and to defend a perspective on 'spectacle' that does not necessarily reduce spectators to uncritical passivity and narcissism. In the light of this, the 'now you see it, now you don't' characteristic of media technology merely serves to remind us of the irreducible tension between *feeling* and *watching*, hence feeling and reflexive judgement, that has to be drawn on to understand the very possibility and potential of a 'spectacle of sympathy' in the first place. Thus we can agree with Chouliaraki that 'a space of public action towards distant suffering may be constituted in the process of mediation itself'.[9]

Let us take another case: this time, a specific image that has become relatively well-known, one from Africa, showing a vulture perched near a little girl in the Sudan who had collapsed from hunger. The vulture is clearly eyeing its potential lunch; the little girl, barely more than an infant, looks naked, alone, helpless, unprotected.[10] And this raises an issue about the responsibility not only of the viewer in general, but of the specific viewer who was also the photographer, Kevin Carter, later winning the Pulitzer Prize for his efforts. Jacques Rancière puts it succinctly: did the photo justify itself by shattering the 'wall of indifference', or was Carter, in turn, a 'human vulture', with his gaze 'enthralled by the aesthetic intensity of a monstrous spectacle'?[11] Should he have acted to save the girl? We know that Carter himself was not immune to these doubts; he killed himself a year later.[12] Actually, the child was near a feeding station, and was apparently then fed, but none of this is evident in the photo; a photo necessarily cuts out context (and history). Clearly this image is 'sensational' in both senses of the term – not a claim that could really be made of those long-shot images of the floods referred to earlier. In their discussion of it, however, Arthur and Joan Kleinman point to another, ideological dimension: for them, there is an implication that 'unnamed Africans' cannot protect their own; action therefore has to come from outside, a continuation of neo-colonialism. The demand for foreign aid, even foreign intervention, 'begins with an evocation of indigenous absence, an erasure of local voices and acts'.[13] As we will confirm, a political dimension is always irreducibly present, just as its implications are always controversial. For now, one can simply observe, in defence of Carter, that a gap between representation and action is not *itself* a problem; indeed, as has been argued here, it counts as a necessary condition for seeing a problem *as* moral, and permitting appropriate action. This is the legitimacy of witness, after all, which has been central to the possibility of the spectacle of sympathy from Adam Smith onwards.

The otherness issue returns in our third example. This is not a well-known image, for reasons that will become apparent. This time, the reader is invited to look at the image first, and only then read what follows. (For this reason, the image itself is given no descriptive caption at this point.)

As a context, we can take Susan Sontag's critique of Virginia Woolf's argument, in *Three Guineas* (1938), that photographs of the horrors of war can and should have an immediate effect on anyone of normal sensitivity, even across a gender divide in which men – who wage war, after all – may be less likely to be upset by images of its results. Such photos should induce an immediate horror of war, and a determination to avoid it. For Sontag, this just

© Kenneth Jareke/Contact Press Images

won't do. Woolf's pictures – of the atrocities perpetrated by Franco's army in the Spanish Civil War – are of a *particular* war, and a particular *way* of waging war. For Woolf, 'war is generic, and the images she describes are of anonymous, generic victims', and to read in the pictures 'only what confirms a general abhorrence of war is to stand back from an engagement with Spain as a country with a history. It is to dismiss politics …'[14] Wars, and victims, have identities; how one looks at a picture is crucially affected by one's politics, which side one is on – hence the caption, or the context, is as crucial as the image. Identical photos, with different captions, were used by both sides in the conflicts of the Balkan Wars of the early 1990s to justify claims of atrocities perpetrated by the other side. No one views pictures 'innocently'. Sontag concludes: 'No "we" should be taken for granted when the subject is looking at other people's pain.'[15]

Recent allusions to this controversy have tended to take Sontag's side; but there is a lot at stake here, and perhaps we should pause. Woolf's argument implies a version of the belief in a 'universal language' of images that was widely discussed in relation to early film: images can have transcultural meaning as immediate expressions of, and triggers of, emotions and feelings. This is characteristically linked to an assumed circuit of sensation, as indeed it is in Woolf. She is quoted as arguing that a photo is 'a crude statement of fact addressed to the eye', which in turn is connected to the brain, and the brain with the nervous system:

'That system sends its messages in a flash through every past memory and present feeling'.[16] While critical of this approach, Rancière sums up its implications cogently: 'The classic use of the intolerable image traced a straightforward line from the intolerable spectacle to awareness of the reality it was expressing; and from that to the desire to act in order to change it.'[17] This whole structure of assumptions runs deep in modern thought, since the Enlightenment, and connects with significant ideological emphases on individualism and the shared humanity of 'human rights'. This can overlap with another body of ideas that can easily come into conflict with it, as it does here: an assumption that individual views, even feelings, are essentially expressive of specific, group-focused cultural identities (whether of class, gender or nationality). This seems to be Sontag's position: to engage with these images is to engage *as* a combatant, on one side or the other. This position at least has the virtue that it allows for issues of meaning, of interpretation, to be raised; it disputes the bio-psychological determinism implicit in the other model, even if it seems to be at the cost of a social determinism. And one might want to insist – *contra* both positions – on the presence of a reflexive indeterminacy in the interpretation of the image that seems to be implicit in the whole logic of a 'spectacle of sympathy' as it has been encountered since the eighteenth century.

It is time to mention that the photograph here is of the charred head of an Iraqi soldier inside his burnt-out vehicle, a victim of the massacre at Mutlah Gap, when a US division caught and destroyed a convoy of one thousand vehicles retreating from Kuwait in late February 1991, during the First Gulf War, incinerating them with vastly superior firepower.[18] In terms of the above debate, one might note that just as one might anticipate *an* emotional response – or an element of one – to the image, there is no *specific* response that has to be present; indeed it might be a mixture: horror, anger, pity are all possible. This indeterminacy in the circuit of sensation has always been a problem, whether for those who adopt it as a scientific framework or hypothesis or for those who fear its consequences in 'sensationalism': the *appropriation* of sensation, its shaping – a condition for its availability for interpretation – is always at issue. Here, a perceptive observation from elsewhere in Sontag's book may be useful. Noticing that 'For the photography of atrocity, people want the weight of witnessing without the taint of artistry, which is equated with insincerity, or mere contrivance', it follows that photos of suffering should not be beautiful, as this 'tends to bleach out a moral response to what is shown'. Conversely, 'uglifying' is more appropriate, indeed more 'modern'.[19] If, in turn, this is to produce 'horror', then more is needed again: a transgressive crossing and de-formation of categories manifest as a powerful *presence*; an encounter with life-in-death perhaps, the human as charred, monstrous, the accusing gaze of sockets that were once eyes ... And horror, too, is a matter of aesthetics, an aesthetics beyond good form, good sense, beyond the object *as* art – aesthetics as *embodied* response. Nor is such a response in any way incompatible with either sympathy or anger.[20]

Whether a political dimension is implicit in our *response* to this image, it is certainly crucial to the context: one involving the limited availability of the image. At the time, it was shown once, in one (British) newspaper; and no other comparable image of the massacre was shown at the time, anywhere.[21] Indeed, it was remarked then, as it has been since, that the First Gulf War seemed to be a 'war without bodies'. John Taylor points out that a war apparently without bodies is 'an imaginative and bureaucratic feat achieved by direct omission (as in censorship), by metonymic transfer on to objects such as machines, and by the media's adherence to polite discourse when reporting state killing on an unknown scale'.[22] Of course, *some* bodies get shown, and Jean Seaton adds the pertinent comment that 'With the actual sensation of death kept at arm's length, the true-life horror on the screen occupies a no man's land between fiction and experience'.[23] Yet this uncertainty does not necessarily militate against an emotionally engaged response, as we saw in the discussion of eighteenth-century debates over theatre and tableau.

Implicit here is the theme of 'otherness'. Taylor remarks that overseas reports of horrors and disasters concentrate on 'the essential strangeness of victims, whether they invoke revulsion or invite compassion',[24] and invariably involve stereotypes of otherness, the primitive, and the 'naturalness' of disasters in 'backward' countries.[25] Sontag, too, notices the way notions of propriety get mixed up here: 'The more remote or exotic the place, the more likely we are to have full frontal views of the dead and dying'. Conversely, 'our' dead are individuals, and entitled to respect,[26] rather than instances of the anonymous mass of distant others. What we find, then, is that 'othering' techniques serve to increase distance through anonymity and stereotype, just as it is no answer to say that the absolute closeness of identification can rectify this. Sympathy can only emerge, 'mediate', when allowed space between excessive closeness (identification, sentimentality) and excessive otherness (abstraction or anonymity on the one hand, stereotyping on the other). One implication of this is that we must break with the conventional television politics of pity, producing narcissistic emotions that encourage us only to care about those perceived as sufficiently 'like us': intimacy minus real concern, in effect.[27]

Sontag's own *earlier* view seems to be the exact opposite to Woolf's Enlightenment optimism: the mediated image becomes necessarily divorced from any link to action, the spectator anaesthetized by the 'image glut'. Her later critique of Woolf, as just recounted, was now linked to a critique of this earlier view: both are too mechanistic, ignoring the complexity of the relation between image, reason and action. Now, she suggests that it is not so much the quantity of images, but the position of the spectator, that can pose a problem: 'It is passivity that dulls feeling',[28] a sense of the inability to make a difference that inhibits appropriate response. This raises the whole issue of what has come to be known as 'compassion fatigue', though this can comprise several elements – 'blocking out', denial, as well as numbness – and, as with Sontag, can swing between emphasizing the quantity of images and the passivity of their reception. Susan Moeller, who helped put the notion into circulation, argues that 'Compassion fatigue is the unacknowledged cause of much of the failure of international reporting today'.[29] This seems to throw the spotlight on to the theme of attention, linked to consumerism, or, more directly, to advertising. Indeed, all news is advertising, at least to the extent that it has to sell itself, through its content, to be noticed, and hence is inherently part of the drive to sensationalism. Trying to influence people's response to suffering is like selling them something: trying to persuade people to act or contribute money is analogous to asking them to spend it on buying things. This can be linked to the increasingly commercialized intimacies of present-giving: sponsor a child, a *named* child; give a gift to a charity in the guise of a gift to a relative. From this point of view, the idea of 'compassion fatigue' adds nothing to the known logic of advertising. The *repetitive* production of images may well induce a loss of effect; as with anything, you can have too much. Changing fashions can also come into it. All this relies on the assumption that the repetition is of something that is indeed *the same*, or sufficiently so, and this is where the battle for attention rages: is a particular image *sufficiently* different, or *sufficiently* extreme, to escape the trap?

One might suggest that, in practice, one of the most characteristic and successful ways of meshing all this together, of harnessing the potential willingness to make donations with the commercial and entertainment aspects into a 'spectacle of sympathy' as a communal event, is surely the telethon. Arguing that 'television will only be experienced by its audience as making a moral demand when and if it is able to impress some kind of *sensation* of a demand', whereby the 'sensation' of news can be made to stir feeling in its audience, Keith Tester sees the telethon as a way of resolving this by combining news coverage with spectacular entertainment and audience participation

– making a virtue out of necessity, as it were – and showing that something *can* be done to bridge the distance, to 'make a difference', particularly if it becomes socially acceptable, even desirable, to contribute. Audiences know what is expected of them; 'compassion' becomes bite-sized, individually manageable, yet collectively impressive. The sums raised can indeed be huge, whatever their ultimate effectiveness. This presents an interesting perspective on 'compassion fatigue', in that these telethons can become recurrent, even institutionalized: 'telethons are able to secure recurrent investment *precisely because of their predictability*', as Tester puts it.[30] *This* predictability becomes the comforting predictability of ritual, as it were.

Morally, of course, it is easy to be sceptical about all this. It is as though we are offered moral absolution, in return for money – and if we accept the deal, in these terms, we fail to get it. Only unmotivated, spontaneous giving (an expansion of feeling towards the other) or well-motivated giving (doing good because it is good) can really count. But the latter – rule-following for its own sake – might be widely perceived as inadequate. It is only when feeling is present that we can respond to the necessary specificity, the particular instance of suffering. This can be *guided* by rules, in turn requiring judgement, but these are really more like generalizations, expectations of responses to types of situations. Telethons and other forms of charitable response and action may be indeterminate between these possibilities – and in everyday life it may not seem important to choose between them, so long as *something* is done – but the more morally respectable options, as it were, are not in any way precluded. If there is a grey area here, it lies in the whole possibility, and the whole problem, of the modern response to distance, to otherness. And as this study has tried to show, the implications of the twin distances here – between spectator and sufferer, and between observation and action – have been crucial for our understanding of the varying modes and impact of the spectacle of sympathy throughout the modern period. If the great eighteenth-century innovation is the constitution of strangers as a potential moral community, through imaginative involvement in literature, urban spectacle, and the public sphere of discussion and feeling, then we are still living with this, its possibilities, limitations and consequences, and it is difficult to see that the contemporary omnipresence of the mass produced and reproduced photographic image necessarily alters this situation in any fundamental way, even though it greatly extends its visibility and scope. If, as Sontag claims, one of these consequences is that 'Being a spectator of calamities taking place in another country is a quintessential modern experience ...',[31] then this indeed remains part and parcel of our modern dilemmas.

Overall, one might suggest that 'compassion fatigue' can be significant not as the cumulative result of a linear process of sensationalism, but as the product of specific *cycles* of sensationalism, when a particular vein has been quarried to exhaustion, with an excess of 'the same' becoming a factor.[32] But, just as there are always new opportunities for sensation (and its recuperation in melodrama), due to the very impossibility of an ever-intensifying linear process of uniform sensationalism, so the potential for sympathetic engagement, too, can break out anew, be replenished. To be effective in this context, sensation must produce a particular kind of attention – it should demand or attract attention, rather than swamp it, leaving us numb, or overwhelmed to the point of trauma or panic. Affect is not engaged to the point of intensity that excludes the mix of imaginative and emotional involvement that constitutes sympathy.

In the course of all this, we may have to consider the issue of authenticity, on any particular occasion – we know that sensationalism can involve exaggeration, even when there is a core of truth. But this is not necessarily a problem; most of us develop the skills to manoeuvre in, and survive, a culture of sensationalism, after all. Just as such a culture manifests a drive to sensationalize, to gain attention, so it also produces an attendant scepticism, a need to distrust it. Nor need this issue necessarily be present in any particular case. To return to the Carter photo, it may be significant that no questions about its authenticity were raised; all the controversy swirled around whether Carter should have taken the photo at all, rather than rushing to ensure the child got rescued and fed – and this, of course, is the classic contemplation/action dilemma that has been partially constitutive of the spectacle of sympathy since its very inception. One can conclude that sensationalism, in itself, is not necessarily a problem, both because of the built-in limitations implicit in *cycles* of sensation, and because it does not just involve feeling, but can be compatible with the exercise of judgement; it can indeed *open up* possibilities for sympathetic engagement.

Sentiment, sympathy and the vicarious

But now, as we move towards the end of the book, let us also move back towards the beginning, and a further encounter with the dilemmas of the sentimental in relation to sympathy, in the light of the 'mediated culture' we have just been discussing. Misha Kavka describes the effect of the 'age of television' on public consciousness in the context of the presentation and reception of Princess Diana's death, using the term 'mediation', defined here in terms of immediacy, of 'presentation' in contrast to 'representation'. Her thesis is that these events show how we can move 'beyond the semiotics of representation to the affect of presentation', so that we can say the audience was offered 'emotional access to a person whom they *feel* as though they *know*', and hence, far from detracting from the emotional impact, the mourning was 'all the more real *because* of this mediation'.[33] Thus we encounter, with television, an 'affect of presentation' whereby we can be 're-moved' by the world, re-engaged in amplified fashion by the power of the media to reduce distance to proximity, bringing events and emotions home to us.

Clearly 'affect' is being used in an inclusive way here, synonymous with 'feeling', and apparently incorporating emotion too, but in a way that *excludes* representation, and this might give us pause. Diana, after all, had a history, and a very public one. She was flesh and blood, but insofar as anyone else knew her, she was also a composite of media images, narratives, rumours, myths and memories; what is brought to this encounter with her, in her death and its aftermath, is already deeply representational, for her and her audience alike. Calling this encounter 'affect' does not magically abolish all this, in the immediacy of the impact of the here and now. At this point, it is useful to draw on an alternative perspective, from Audrey Jaffe, who argues, with reference to feeling, that 'insofar as it is known, it is constituted by representation', hence is 'inseparable from the scenes that may seem merely to provoke it and the signs by means of which it becomes known'.[34] One can complement this with Rei Terada's claims that 'We are not ourselves without representations that mediate us, and it is through these representations that emotions get felt', adding that, in consequence, 'There is no reason to guard mental life against theatricality, to guard emotion against representation, or to worry that layers of mediation diminish emotional intensity'.[35]

This usefully reminds us that what we may be encountering here are the contrasting routes whereby the two configurations traced in this book can produce intensity of feeling. 'Mediation as presentation' clearly corresponds to the circuit of sensation, in its immediacy of impact, whereby the proximity of the image abolishes its own distance in the power of its effect (its affect); 'mediation as representation' indicates the irreducibility of representation, of the image, to any immediate affective consequences, the distancing whereby its status *as image* indicates the presence of an otherness beyond presence, a theatrical space of imaginative engagement within which emotion can be enacted. We could perhaps say that emotion will necessarily involve imagination and representation, but that this is not necessarily the case with affect (depending on how exactly it is defined).

We can now look at all this in the light of the earlier discussion of the sentimental and its relation to the culture of feeling. The sentimental emerges as a paradoxical conjunction of identification with the other and excess of self, resulting in an uncertainty over boundaries, or even their threatened collapse. Imaginatively, this results in an intensification of presence, the expansive 'homeliness' so apparent in sentimental texts and situations; and this in turn incorporates nostalgia as a central mode, coming into focus as the sentimental reappropriation of the past. This covers over the loss of affect in experience itself through a compensatory excess, simultaneously registering loss yet regaining it as presence, in the here and now, with the embodied investment of emotion linked to the power of memory as imagination, as image. The 'homeliness' can involve a potential generosity of spirit that can coexist with what can also be seen, accurately enough, as a self-centred and self-indulgent exhibition of emotion. The two go together, inherent products of the sentimental moment; and all this helps us understand why the stigmatizing response is inherent in the very way sentimentality is constituted, its 'excess' and boundary-crossing, with emotion overflowing 'rational' restraint, necessarily problematical in a culture that self-consciously proclaims its adherence to the latter.

Not only this, but 'excess', of self and feeling, raises questions about 'sincerity', and hence about 'sympathy' itself. One can say that sentimentality is an excess of sincerity, the 'too sincere' that is denounced as 'insincere' and that thereby necessarily questions the whole idea of being 'true to oneself', implying that this mix of feelings and conflicting emotions only achieves authentic, coherent 'selfhood' through sleight of hand. For Terada, 'The distinction of sentimentality – its witless brilliance – is that it exposes the overlap between the genuine and the disingenuous'.[36] It thus interrogates the motives of sympathy even as it may parade its adherence to its virtues. Hence we can see both how sentimentality is indissolubly linked to the discourse and spectacle of sympathy, and how it renders the latter liable to attack at times of militant rationalism – for the terms in which it is characterized inherently involve the notion of excess, along with the idea of crossing boundaries that are not indeed 'there' in any absolute sense, but are produced as an aspect of such 'transgression', or of its denunciation.

What is also clear is the *outcome* of sentimental identification, its symptomatic presence in the uncertainty of the relation between nature and culture, or body and moral or social regulation. Sentimentality may reveal both an insufficiency of the latter, hence an excess of putatively 'natural' emotion, or an excess of such influence, whereby the expression of 'natural' emotion takes the form of intensely cultural, even theatrical, display – nor are the two necessarily distinguishable. Thus, in Greuze, we found excess of body was revealed *as* cultural or gestural excess, its 'naturalness' becoming self-subverting in the very fact of its display as such. Hence both poles become open to criticism, the impossibility of deciding between them only contributing to the distrust.

In drawing us in – whether as full participants or as observers – sentimental situations may also lead us to react to our own emotions, questioning them in their troubling, unthinking immediacy. Here, in her discussion of Diana, Kavka makes an interesting contrast between mourning and shame as audience reactions, the latter arising as a second-level response to the former: 'Mourning is the affect that denies the mediation of Diana, claiming an intimate bond despite her mediation. Shame, on the other hand, is the affect that recognizes her mediation' because it '*exposes* us as mourners who cried real tears for an object judged to be inappropriate.'[37] Mourning denies the mediation that nonetheless brings it about, while shame recognizes this and consequently denies the validity of our reaction. We are forced, as it were, to confront the possibility that vicarious emotional display, in the age of the mass media, may be just as 'real' as what we conventionally take to be the more valid, 'authentic' responses, and we recoil from this. And it is a contention of this book that this is misleading, in that there is a vicarious element in *any* emotion, insofar as it attains public expression, cultural form, as display.

Sentimentality, then, can only show its 'excessive' sincerity through a display marked as vicarious, hence insincere; yet this is a pyrrhic victory for its critics if the vicarious is found to have infected 'genuine' sympathy as well. If one might have said, using Kavka's distinction, that one of these responses recognizes the mediated dimension the other mis-recognizes, its stigmatization of this 'mediation' as vicarious deprives it of the ability to embrace this insight, through sympathetic engagement, instead spinning it inwards, into shame and the consequent denunciation of the sentimental now positioned as unacceptably other,[38] denying the shared feature: precisely the vicarious itself.

It can be argued, after all, that second-order emotion is not necessarily any less 'emotional' than first-order emotion. Some aspects of this are clarified by Terada. 'When we're aware of the second-order nature of emotion we call it "pathos"', she writes, 'and act as if it were something other than emotion.' She suggests, in consequence, that '*pathos* conveys the explicitly representational, vicarious, and supplementary dimensions of emotion', and that 'debates about pathos come to be about the relation between representation and intensity'. The second-order, mediated quality of pathos always seems to engage with the problematic status of the image, never sufficiently present, always too early or too late, not quite here, or there; and, in consequence, 'Parallel to this experience in the image-world is pathos in the emotion-world'.[39] This sense of a degree of image-dependence inherent in 'mediation' reinforces the connotation of pathos, going back to the ancient Greek, of 'something that happens' *to* someone, an element of receptivity to change, an 'active' response that occurs in the register of the passive. Again, if this is particularly clear in the case of the sentimental, this renders it particularly vulnerable to carrying the opprobrium for what is actually an essential continuity with other emotional responses.

After all, what sentimentality and sympathy or compassion have in common is precisely their status as 'witness' emotions, a degree of passivity, impotence or detachment inherent in the difference or distance of self and other, and indeed of identity itself and its mediated manifestation. What separates them, albeit tentatively, is that the sentimental refuses this difference, covers or floods it with its own excess, while sympathy respects it by harnessing it to judgement and allowing the imagination to explore the gap, without negating it. That gap is positioned through the whole culture of representation and its incorporation in theatricality. The vicarious can thus be understood as the experience of the gap between representation and reality, and the difference between sentimentality and sympathy lies in how they 'inhabit' this gap. Sentimentality *exhibits* our vicarious participation in the world, allows us to experience it, *as* emotion; sympathy *distances* us from this world, experiencing this vicariously through imaginative projection, embedded in feeling, enriched by it and extending it.

The vicarious thus comes into focus as the mode of inhabiting the difference between representation and reality that threatens the breakdown of the distinction itself – hence the world of modernity as *mediated* experience. This is the scenario on which the tension between distance and proximity, involvement and detachment, is played out, managed, and dramatized – life as a spectacle of vicarious involvement. If this can be disturbing, it is because we do indeed respond to real-life situations *as if* they are in some sense cultural products. We even respond to our own emotions as if we are witnesses, as if at some level we can *only* be onlookers. At this level, our capacity to sympathize with the other may be inseparable from our ability to sympathize with ourselves, just as, in sentimental mode, our joys and our tears at least *appear* to manifest an identity 'across' boundaries otherwise impossible to cross, in the very immediacy of affective response – an 'immediacy' that remains, nonetheless, clothed in borrowed garb. If the word 'vicarious' is derived ultimately from the Latin *vicis* (via *vicarius*), meaning an interchange, change or alternative, we can perhaps say that it is through our performance of (or in) the vicarious that we survive the 'vicissitudes' of life.

One can further observe that sentimentality always has something of the sensational about it; indeed, it can reasonably be presented as the sensational mode of the spectacle of sympathy. Affect is clearly central to it, but it is affect *on display*, which is what can lead it be denounced as second hand, as 'vicarious'; and it is, one might add, affect in the form of emotion, which is never innocent of these dimensions of the demonstrative, hence inherently public. This also gives us a clue to the mutual attraction of sentimentality and melodrama, the former indeed frequently occurring as an aspect or subset of the latter, linked to the poles of innocence and virtue in the conflict of good and evil.[40] It could even be argued that perhaps it is only in the context of melodrama that the sentimental, as 'excess' of feeling, can plausibly be identified as such, hence reinforcing the potential for the stigmatization of both. As sensation becomes more sensational, so the spectacle becomes more spectacular, and melodrama becomes a characteristic feature of this, a superimposition of one on the other, and all the dramas of our lives – little and large – become available for this process of intensification and magnification.

As affect in a virtual state, sympathy testifies to that latent sense of connectedness, relationship or 'belonging' that emerges into more specific states of feeling as they engage the spectacle of sympathy and the circuit of sensation. Thus Phillips and Taylor suggest that words like kindness, generosity, altruism, benevolence, compassion and pity all implicitly refer to 'the sympathetic expansiveness linking self to other', though an alternative formulation, referring to how sympathy or kindness 'mingles our needs and desires with the needs and desires of others',[41] is perhaps preferable, suggesting that we are *changed* by this, that it involves risks, in that 'self' and 'other' are emergent, rather than presupposed. This 'mingling' testifies to a certain priority of relations over separate entities, suggesting the 'bounded self' as an artificial, secondary construct that is embedded in this, however much it may seek to cut itself off from it. And this is really the point: if there is a sense in which the bounded self is necessary for survival, it needs to be porous, too. It is bounded in action, yet porous in reaction, in its ability to experience the world. As responses, feelings involve an openness, a diffusion of being; this in turn may result in actions, which in turn involve a degree of limitation, a certain impoverishment of feeling, or distancing from it, even in the very move into the external world that is needed in order to 'realize' such feelings. This implies a concentration of attention, and of being itself, as against the receptive diffusion of experience that allows the plenitude of feeling. A culture that gives positive valuation to action over feeling, particularly action purportedly guided by 'reason', will naturally have problems here (problems not unconnected with the gendered dynamics of all this). We can add that if an element of passivity is inherent in both sympathy and sensation, then the shaping of the response, and the further, possibly active reaction *to* the response, is where judgement is involved, in the case of sympathy, and where it may be involved, in the case of sensation (and may, conversely, not be, where sensation works 'contagiously').

Hence, if the spectacle of sympathy can be presented as a spectacular resolution of the tensions inherent in sentimentalism, in its conjunction of the natural and the social, pain and transcendence, image and narrative, good and evil, and its relation to sympathy itself, then it can only be seen to succeed 'vicariously'. Nor can it deny the insight of sensationalism, that there is an excess beyond representation, potential for a 'contagion' of affect 'infecting' the spectator, reinforcing the element of vicarious participation. The imaginative spectacle of sympathetic engagement includes us, as roles, as participants and spectators, just as the resonance of reverberating affects, vivid in their impacts, takes place in some quasi-physical zone that is located as much across as within or between physically separate entities, registered through the senses. Through the spectacle of the mass media, and the excesses of melodrama, the outlines of the two elements of the dual inheritance of the Age of Sensibility – sensation and sympathy – can, therefore, still be made out ...

Corrupt practices

It increasingly seems to be the case, then, that while the spectacle of sympathy, as a cultural configuration, presents tensions that are both internal to it and that result from the interaction with the wider context of modernity, the effects of the mass media, in themselves, are not the crucial factors here. For the major 'external' threats to the possibility of sympathetic engagement, we need to look elsewhere.

We can start by considering the provocative theses put forward by Slavoj Žižek in his book *Violence*. Of central importance is his argument that 'language, not primitive egotistic interest, is the first and greatest divider'; one of the most fundamental forms of violence 'pertains to language as such, to its imposition of a certain universe of meaning', and hence 'verbal violence is not a secondary distortion, but the ultimate resort of every specifically human form of violence'.[42] Language is not corrupted into violence, as it were; violence is of the essence. Žižek is clearly gunning here both for a broad liberal consensus that postulates communication, particularly language, as inherently beneficial, diminishing the likelihood of conflict, and for specifically academic manifestations of this, notably the work of Habermas.[43] Overall, he argues that the evidence 'renders problematic the prevalent idea of language and the symbolic order as the medium of reconciliation and mediation, of peaceful coexistence, as opposed to a violent medium of immediate and raw confrontation'.[44]

Žižek's key move is to link language, violence and desire. The fundamental power of linguistic symbolization involves separation and designation, a violence or 'dismemberment' of the thing, subordinating it to the realm of meaning: hence Lacan's idea of a 'master-signifier', which 'quilts' or sutures the field of meaning, holding it together. Hence a space of discourse is ultimately grounded in this 'violent imposition' which necessarily cannot be grounded in reason: it is a *diktat*.[45] The highest form of this in modernity is the Kantian moral law, the absolute imperative to obey the universal, the unrealizable, which becomes inseparable from *desire* for the universal, a desire so incapable of satisfaction that it is endlessly substituted, displaced, into the specific desires of consumerism, none of which ever really 'satisfies', and thus lead endlessly to further desires. The law embodies the power to define what is 'violent', and we must remember there that the 'highest form of violence is the imposition of this standard with reference to which some events appear as "violent"'. Hence we can see how 'language itself, the very medium of non-violence, of mutual recognition, involves unconditional violence' and thus 'it is language itself which pushes our desire beyond proper limits, transforming it into ... an absolute striving that cannot ever be satisfied'.[46]

Žižek takes his place here as the latest in a long line of pessimistic theorists of the human condition, and modernity itself, running from Schopenhauer, through Nietzsche, to Freud, and on through Lacan. Certainly Žižek's all-encompassing thesis, as it stands, would clearly be fatal to any hopes of articulating a plausible model of sympathetic engagement as anything other than deluded liberal ideological window-dressing[47] for the dark destructive forces of language and the psyche. My book has attempted to show, *per contra*, that between arguing that violence and inequality are inherent in human language and communication, and, conversely, that it is possible to specify a framework that would reveal egalitarian tolerance to be of their essence, there is room for a more historically based identification of specific cultural configurations that can open up various possibilities for communication, some of which may well be contentious, and which will have consequences that can be evaluated in positive or negative terms, along with hints about the circumstances that are likely to realize the one rather than the other. It is within this framework that one can try to map the problems and possibilities of the spectacle of sympathy as a structure of feeling as this has existed since the eighteenth century.

But if this is to be plausible, the most ambitious part of Žižek's account, the critique of language, clearly needs to be answered. For a start, one might observe a slippery quality about his use of 'language' here. It is true that ultimate appeals to the rationality of reason can only return on themselves, so that the justification can only be circular, or ultimately ungrounded (a *diktat*), but this does not in itself necessarily imply or presuppose 'violence', and anyway does not appertain to language as such, the power of which ranges far beyond its use in reasoning. Of course, perpetrators of violence may well appeal to ostensibly 'rational' grounds for the justification of their actions, and this brings us to language itself, more broadly – for language, too, can be *used* to promote violence, either directly or indirectly, but is hardly violence in itself. Language can be dangerous, unquestionably, in various ways, notably through the power of categorization, evaluation and denunciation, and the construction of ideologies. All this is obvious enough (and far from unimportant). But any stronger claims, to the effect that language *is* violence, seem either to be unfounded or else the word 'violence' is being used in a misleadingly broad, metaphorical sense. But this is interesting in itself, this power of language as source of figuration, and it is to this that we now turn.

As has been suggested, Žižek attempts to deal with this problem through a Lacanian-Freudian theory of signification. And here, one can observe that the idea of a 'master-signifier', imposed by force, has all the power of a foundation myth. In such myths, the impossibility of the foundation *ex nihilo* is revealed in the death of the charismatic creator, a death followed by eternal rebirth. In the Freudian version of this – and we can surely, by now, accept that it is indeed another *version*, rather than an *explanation* – paternal authority is that of the Father, the Law, the master-signifier that fixes language to the world in a charismatic act that negates its own impossibility through the eternal recurrence of its death, symbolized by the death of Moses and the heroes who represent this self-creative power of language itself. Even more powerfully, it is death by murder, whether of the original creator or, subsequently, his sons, but this murder – as with Christ – is also, in a sense a self-murder, as if an impossible act negates itself by taking responsibility for negating its own origin. For Žižek, this leaves language itself inherently corrupted by violence, its affective power, dependent on this myth of origin and reproduction, dominating its own power as difference, the creativity of the difference of language itself, of metaphor and figuration. But this very fact converts Žižek's *use* of this myth into another *variant* of it, an example of the power of language as figuration that necessarily implies that this dimension cannot itself be reduced to anything else, including violence, and that Žižek can provide no adequate account of this dimension of meaning and symbol that is coextensive with language and absolutely central to it, language in its inherent capacity to open up the figurative powers of the imagination.

But we can strike a more positive note as well. When Žižek claims that only psychoanalysis can disclose the full extent of 'the shattering impact of modernity – that is, capitalism combined with the hegemony of scientific discourse – on the way our identity is grounded in symbolic identifications',[48] there is a useful insight here. Indeed, it has been an argument of this book that when identity is based on, or assimilated to, identification, our relation with the other becomes always potentially hysterical or traumatic, and this may be particularly true of those to whom we are closest.[49] This in turn can affect other facets of self-identity and the motivational patterns associated with capitalism. One can accept this, without necessarily accepting the trans-historical claims Žižek would make for psychoanalysis, which has indeed been positioned here as a specifically modern project, limited as well as powerful, perhaps the highest form of modernist self-examination in the context of self and identity, even though it cannot escape the reflexive paradox inherent in its constitution in these very terms.

Žižek's reference to modernity as capitalism plus scientific discourse is also a useful cue for further reflection. We can indeed see how the 'everything can be measured' imperative of scientific discourse and practice can sit easily alongside the 'everything has its price' of the capitalist market orientation, and has many similar implications. But in order to pursue this, we need to move on from Žižek in order to bring capitalism itself into focus.

It would be difficult to argue that there are any intrinsic qualities that enable something to be a commodity, subject to market forces, available to be bought and sold, or indeed that there are any that enable it to resist this fate. Nonetheless, the idea of 'intrinsic quality' is important here. One might say that 'commodities' are precisely *not* seen as having 'intrinsic qualities' that make them ends in themselves: rather, they have a utility, they derive their value from human needs or aspirations, and, as such, their values are always relative, hence comparable, and measurable in market terms (money). And really, we need to think not of commodities, as things, but rather of *processes*, the transformations whereby objects, activities, and relationships, can be shaped according to the language and practices of the market. Conversely, when something is seen as, or treated as, having value in itself, as being self-sufficient and self-justifying, then it either escapes the market, or can be seen as justifiably attempting to do so. The corollary of this is that the market presents a threat to it: it is vulnerable, corruptible.

It is interesting that we can so readily draw on the language of 'corruption' in this context, in the broader sense of the term that goes beyond the narrowly legal (giving and taking bribes, nepotism) to include debasement, contamination, defilement, taint, uncleanness, rottenness, putrefaction and decay. Some of this carries strongly organic and visceral connotations: 'corruption' may more neutrally be 'transformation', but it is clearly not a transformation that is good for the body politic. And this language is extensively deployed by Michael Sandel, in his critique of the process whereby 'we drifted from *having* a market economy to *being* a market society', with the resulting 'remaking of social relations in the image of market relations'. He adds: 'To describe what's disquieting about this condition, we need the moral vocabulary of corruption and degradation. But to speak of corruption and degradation is to appeal, implicitly at least, to conceptions of the good life.'[50] His critique incorporates many well-chosen examples of this process and its consequences.[51] One general point that comes through clearly is that if a task is seen as intrinsically worthwhile, paying people to do it may mean they make *less* effort, and this helps to draw out a difference between intrinsic motivations (moral conviction, interest in the task) and external or instrumental ones (money, status, tangible rewards), a distinction that again reflects the contrast between a market attitude to the world and its opposite.[52] One might extend this to a critique of the destruction of professionalism in an era when trust and responsibility are displaced by accountability, supervision and managerialism, and motivation is weakened as the conscientious performance of tasks is replaced by the mechanical repetition of assignments designed to be measurable, ticked off on a list of superficial 'performance indicators'.

One aspect of this, then, is a 'corruption of the subject', a degradation of the quality of motivation, and this is significant because of what it, in turn, liberates: a narrow emphasis on self-interest, whether as defensive or expansive, reinforced by what the system *can* offer, in terms of material reward and competitive self-esteem. This, in turn, has the effect of strengthening the idea that people are essentially motivated by a market-driven focus on economic calculation, deciding what will provide most 'utility', the latter in turn being affected by what others are perceived as wanting, thus contributing to the cultural hold of emulation through fashion, as a central facet of personality.[53] Hence the powerful impetus to ideologies justifying all this as 'natural' and inevitable, evidence to the contrary notwithstanding.

The other side of all this is a 'degradation of the object'. In some cases, after all, to attempt to buy some sought-for good, such as friendship, would destroy or undermine what is sought. Thus, argues Sandel, treating religious rituals, or natural wonders, as marketable is a 'failure of respect'. The sacramental is lost if the access to experiencing it is up for sale. But if nothing is *inherently* beyond the reach of the market, as argued above, then this suggests that what is at stake here is a *relationship*. What matters is that something be *treated* as an 'end in itself' by a subject. In the language used previously, what we have is an *encounter*. Such relations are in turn embedded in, and manifested by, the symbols which thereby both represent and strengthen the relation, or indeed may create or re-create it. The characteristic material symbol here is the gift, which is precisely what defies economic rationale.[54] If we persist in giving gifts, this is because of the symbolic relationship here: gifts 'express' friendship, love, family obligation – something 'beyond' mere money.

This can also be reflexive. Sandel instances an episode of the public performance of Shakespeare in Central Park, New York: there had to be tickets, as space was limited, but these were free, on a first come, first served basis; when some of these were sold on, there was an outcry. The logic is the same: in effect, free public theatre was seen as a communal, civic celebration, 'a gift the city gives itself', hence something that was seen as corrupted when access to it was made marketable. Indeed, the implicit link to citizenship here is fundamental to the sense of 'belonging' that underlies the nature of sympathetic engagement, involving differences across encounters that mark community and communication not as a reaffirmation of identity but a shaping of mutuality and interaction in an overall context of fairness and respect. In claiming that some gifts are 'expressive of relationships that engage, challenge, and reinterpret our identities',[55] Sandel points to the way identities – far from being given, fixed, or presupposed – are emergent properties of the ongoing relations themselves, and that new encounters transform both parties.

Finally, it is important to add that this is neither an appeal to a nostalgic vision of the pre-modern, or to a utopian view of a possible future. Rather, this is grounded in the experience of modernity itself, in the circumstances of its development. Individualism, secularism, industrialism, the decline of traditional class-based sources of cohesion: these are not the problem. It is not these that have threatened the possibilities of sympathetic engagement. The age of the internet makes it abundantly clear that some general 'decline of community' is not what is at stake – what this presents us with is simply the transformation of the conditions under which relationships develop, with new modes of friendship and mutuality, and an emergent sense of 'community' as network. All this provides new possibilities – and problems – for face-to-face interaction, rather than displacing it. Nor is individualism the problem in itself, though as we saw with trauma it can become a key site for modern dilemmas over identity. What *is* a problem, again revealing the centrality of capitalism, is that particular form of it that can be called egoism: the reduction of the other to the status of means to an end, a pursuit of self-gratification as self-realization, and the construction of this as the self-sufficient project of life.[56] At the same time, we can return to Žižek for a caution here: it is not egoism per se, but egoism in relation to envy, emulation, and *ressentiment*,[57] whereby 'self-interest' is indelibly marked by self-deceit and frustration, resulting in anomie, melancholy, addiction, and the other pathologies of object-desire that are inherent in consumerism. We can conclude, then, that the problems confronting sympathy in the contemporary world are not primarily due to the media, or to some generalized 'human condition', but to our embeddedness in ever more aggressive, oppressive and environmentally destructive forms of capitalism in the era of its globalization, along with the character structure it fosters.

Let us end by recalling Emma, from the third chapter. Earlier in the modern era, in another time of political and economic upheaval, Emma struggled to reconcile feeling, imagination and judgement as the basis for a life of good citizenship and personal fulfilment. In a later era, of rampant capitalism, with similar hopes, similar frustrations, and essentially the same weapons, we struggle still.

Postscript: Empathy, Spectacle and Mirror-Touch Synaesthesia

Synaesthesia – the sensation of a sense other than the one being stimulated, such as tasting sounds or colours – has been known about for a long time, while the word itself is more recent, dating from the late nineteenth century. Then, in 2003, came the first report of what appeared to be a hitherto unnoticed variant, quickly christened 'mirror-touch' synaesthesia, with the first reference in a neuroscience journal dating from 2005, since when it has been generating rapidly increasing interest, along with controversy about its interpretation. A conference at Tate Modern in early 2014, entitled 'Mirror-touch: Synaesthesia and the Social', with speakers from neuroscience, psychology, anthropology, film and the visual arts, put it firmly on the cultural map, and served to bring out its wider significance.[1]

Mirror-touch synaesthesia involves feeling touch when seeing another person being touched, a feeling that is experienced as just as real as if it had been the person viewing who had been touched, and is felt in exactly the same part of the body. It is as though the visual and the tactile sensory mechanisms are getting confused, or being triggered in tandem, hence the grounds for seeing this as another form of synaesthesia. The person being viewed may be physically present, or may be seen on a screen, so mediation does not seem to affect it. In the great majority of cases, it must be a human person who is being seen; if it is a puppet or inanimate object that is being touched, this will not have the same effect. But here, we can add that there is nothing inherently fixed about the clear distinctions we conventionally draw between the senses anyway: this is really a product of the eighteenth century. It has indeed been suggested that the infant experience of the world is strongly synaesthetic: clear sensory boundaries develop gradually, influenced by culture. Indeed, synaesthesia brings into play a vivid experience of sensory immersion, of existence in a world that is almost one of sensory overload, with the body as an interchange of messages between and across the senses.[2]

The particular conjunction of senses in mirror-touch makes it particularly challenging. We can recall here the eighteenth-century controversy over the relative weight of sight and touch as foundations for human interaction and social life. Sight is a distance sense; touch is about proximity and intimacy. If the boundary between these senses is disrupted, so too is our relation to the world. We become open to it, our boundaries more porous. The world draws closer, drawn onto our body as we are drawn into it. As our relation to the other becomes more intimate, the possibilities and problems of identification loom, impacting our sense of self. Here, it is worth pointing out that if, in the great majority of cases, the other in question is definitely human, then the fact that for a minority this need not be the case is also significant. Possibilities for imaginative relationships with non-human, animate or inanimate others seem to be opened up. New perspectives on our ability to react to works of art, be 'moved' by them, come into focus. In short: do we encounter some intriguing, but limited, neurological pathology here, or a challenge to the conventional limitations on our ability to respond to the other, a capacity for radical engagement that is latent in all of us?

We can, after all, be 'touched' emotionally. We can relate this to the ability of some mirror-touch synaesthetes to respond to violence that they see on screen, or in real life, by feeling pain themselves. There is also evidence (both from first-person accounts and psychological experiments) that mirror-touch synaesthetes are more sensitive to other people's emotions: they can react to bodily signs and cues that most of us miss. In this case, it is as though the cultural shaping and projection of emotion, its framing as spectacle, is bypassed by the affective immediacy of sensory transmission. And if we position the body here as a kind of screen, through which we try to decode the other person's inner emotional state, so that we can assimilate this to the mediated image of the body, we can move towards a question that leads into the broader significance and implications of all this: are we affected by the emotional cues, or the sight of touch itself, *through* the screen, with the screen as a channel, or is it the *image* of touch, *on* the screen, that matters here? Is it an affective pulse, a physical transmission of energy, that is involved here, or is there an engagement with the image, involving the image-making capacity of mind, our imaginative grasp, that is in play? The omnipresent screen (television, film, video, computer, smartphone) hence becomes a physical 'embodiment' of these possibilities, an interface across which messages pass constantly, in whatever form, image and text, with an impact that has been explored particularly in contemporary Deleuze-influenced film theory.[3] Naturally all this is a site of controversy: some scientists postulate a neuronal 'empathy circuit' as the basis for human social emotions, while critics of this emphasize our imaginative capacity to 'put ourselves in the place of the other'.[4]

Clearly we are on familiar ground here. Lurking behind the novelty, we find the old tension between the two strands, going back to the eighteenth century, that has been the central theme of the second half of this book. The characteristic language of sensationalist empiricism resurfaces, with terms like 'vibration' in widespread use in neurological accounts, and elsewhere, as writers struggle to find the appropriate expressions for the causal dynamics of the 'affective currents' postulated here. In art, Kandinsky, himself a synaesthete, used this language of 'vibration' and 'resonance' – a language that seems highly appropriate for describing the way sight itself seems to operate *as if* a form of touch in these cases. But if this language of the circuit of sensation is allowed to sweep all before it, then some of the wider implications claimed here for our understanding of empathy will become more difficult to sustain. For this, we need to draw on the alternative conceptual structure of the spectacle of sympathy, as theorized by Adam Smith and others, with their emphasis on the imagination, rather than the Humean tradition.

There has been an important shift in the language of the debate, however: now, as already hinted, it is empathy that has, in recent decades, replaced sympathy as the preferred term. Hence we need to reflect again on the relation between these, touched on briefly in the Introduction. As the translation of a term from late nineteenth-century German psychology, *Einfühlung*, 'empathy' seems to have occurred first in 1912, but even by mid-century had barely spread beyond this original psychological domain. An interesting case can be cited from the 1947 edition of the *Shorter Oxford Dictionary*, which, along with its more standard definition, gives this as another meaning of synaesthesia: 'Agreement of the feelings or emotions of different individuals, as a stage in the development of sympathy.' This is exactly the situation where, today, empathy would be invoked (just as it hints at the very real difficulties that would be involved in trying to distinguish them). The ostensible rationale for this shift is conceptual clarity: empathy refers to imaginatively entering into the situation of the other, hence gaining a better *grasp* of their feelings or perspectives, while sympathy is an immediate emotional response, characteristically of sorrow or pity, whereby we appear to *share* those feelings.

There seems to be more to it than this, though; lurking behind sympathy is the ever-present danger of sentimentality which, as we have seen, is both stigmatized and an omnipresent temptation in the culture. 'Empathy' is there, in part, to keep it at bay; and 'sympathy' effectively becomes the sacrificed term, to make this possible. Looming up here is the artificial tyranny of the of the 'reason' v. 'emotion' dichotomy, so important to the ideological self-image of modern Western culture, and the associated cultural devaluation of that immediacy of emotional response that 'the sentimental' seems to imply. And this, together with the difficulty in practice of separating out these terms, is the reason why this book has maintained 'sympathy' as the umbrella term, in accordance with the underlying pattern that this cultural history reveals, while simultaneously seeking to bring out the tensions *within* this pattern and the way it has been theorized. And, in the light of all this, it might be unsurprising if 'empathy', in turn, as the aspiring successor to 'sympathy', might be found increasingly to embody the tensions between the two traditions, those of the circuit of sensation and the spectacle of sympathetic engagement, stemming from Hume and Smith, discussed in this book. In particular, the approach to empathy suggested in the preceding paragraph would be threatened by any wholesale appropriation of empathy by neuroscientific discourse, since this would be likely to lose sight of the issues that are *not* adequately theorized within the sensationalist tradition.

While these continuities are undoubtedly there, it might be good to speculate beyond these, and feel our way into other aspects, new possibilities opened up here, ways of thinking about all this that may bypass the dilemmas referred to. That was a deliberately loaded way of putting it: we 'feel our way' into problems, situations, relationships, artworks – and into the potential that synaesthesia may possess for disrupting conventional boundaries between literal and metaphorical. The senses have, after all, long been powerful sources of imagery, and synaesthesia, as an overt crossing of boundaries, is even more so, since it maps on to metaphor itself, as the boundary-crossing dimension within language, and questions whether this homology testifies to a certain priority of *relationship* itself, over 'entity'. Something of this is present in Goethe's colour wheel, where specific colours are tied to particular emotions. I may be 'touched' by your concern, and vice versa, metaphorically, just as we may literally touch each other, but with mirror-touch synaesthesia, the situation changes: although seeing an act of touching becomes feeling the act, you are not literally touching me, but neither are you metaphorically touching me. The distinction between metaphorical and literal becomes unclear; the sensory dislocation troubles our ontological certainties. And if I can 'feel' your emotion, I can be 'touched' by you in a sort of literalization of the metaphor. Clearly we are in the world of Baudelaire's 'correspondences', where '*Les parfums, les couleurs et les sons se répondent*'.

None of this takes us far from empathy, and the challenges posed for our understanding of it. In the poem just cited, Baudelaire tells us how 'man' passes through forests of symbols, which *'l'observent avec des regards familiers'*. Here *they* – whatever exactly 'they' may be – are looking at *us*, in a reversal of what we conventionally think of as the spectatorial attitude. Yet the possibility of this reversal, along with problems this might pose, has always been there in the implications of empathy. Do we open ourselves *to* the other, or project ourselves *into* the other? The latter possibility, that imaginative projection may be more like a form of imposition, which is then misread as 'other', can be found in various contexts. We may, for example, project our feelings into an artwork, and then imagine that, in responding to the result, we are responding to qualities of the artwork itself. At the same time, the mirror-reversal of this – being overwhelmed by the other, taken over by it – is hardly the answer. What seems to be called for here is a move beyond the active/passive dynamic, in relation both to empathy and to spectatorship, into a mode of reciprocity or participation that accepts the inevitability of the fact of *encounter* itself: an aesthetics of the creative encounter, or indeed aesthetics *as* creative encounter.[5] Being touched, being moved – to what extent this comes from self *or* other would always have an element of the essentially unknowable; and a culturally embedded aesthetics would seem to be the appropriate mode of theoretical exploration here.

Empathy and spectatorship are thus drawn more closely together, with mirror-touch synaesthesia now serving not only as a metaphor (for these relationships, these connections), but as a model for how we should approach these issues, how we should conceive of them and practice them – a model for new ways of seeing, positioning seeing as an embodied experience of participation in a creative encounter with otherness, a process in which distinctions between literal and metaphorical shift and slide, just as language, too, becomes situated, embodied. Our very notion of language as a mirror or reflection of reality becomes elided into a model of language – and art – as process, continuation of reality by other means, in other dimensions, ensuring that our capacity to grasp it reflexively is also, inevitably a contribution to changing it.

But all this is very speculative – a good place to end.

Notes

Cloying Sentiments

1   C. Davies, 'Jokes on the Death of Diana', in T. Walter (ed.), *The Mourning for Diana* (Berg, 1999), p. 258.

2   L. Grant, 'I'll second those emotions', *Guardian*, 30 December 1997, p. 10.

3   D. Aitkenhead, *Guardian*, 16 July 1998.

4   D. H. Lawrence, *Phoenix: The Posthumous Papers of D. H. Lawrence* (Heinemann, 1936), p. 545.

5   J.-P. Sartre, *Being and Nothingness* (Routledge, 2003 [1943]), Part IV, 2:iii, esp. pp. 625–32.

6   Ibid., pp. 632, 629, 632, 630.

7   G. Little, *The Public Emotions: From Mourning to Hope* (ABC Books, Australian Broadcasting Corporation, 1999), p. 22.

8   Cit. ibid., p. 24.

9   T. Walter, 'The Questions People Asked', in Walter, *Mourning*, pp. 19–21. See also A. Kear and D. L. Steinberg (eds), *Mourning Diana: Nation, Culture, and the Performance of Grief* (Routledge, 1999), another wide-ranging collection, and M. Merck (ed.), *After Diana* (Verso, 1998).

10   J. Wolffe, 'Royalty and Public Grief in Britain: an Historical Perspective 1817–1997', in Walter, *Mourning*.

11   The concept of 'structure of feeling' is generally derived from the work of Raymond Williams, where it is, however, relatively undeveloped and unclear. For discussion, see P. Filmer, 'Structures of feeling and socio-cultural formations: the significance of literature and experience to Raymond Williams's sociology of culture', *British Journal of Sociology* (2003), 54:2.

12   Davies, p. 259.

13   Cit. Walter, 'Questions', p. 31.

14   B. Babcock (ed.), *The Reversible World* (Cornell University Press, 1978), p. 32.

15   Little, p. 5.

16   Walter, 'Questions', p. 26.

17   I. Jack, 'Those Who Felt Differently', *Granta* (1997), 60, p. 17.

18   Cit. Walter, 'Questions', 26.

19   D. Knight, 'Why We Enjoy Condemning Sentimentality: A Meta-Aesthetic Perspective', *Journal of Aesthetics and Art Criticism* (1999), 57:4, pp. 418, 419. This

argument is of course using the critic's own assumptions about the sentimental against him, without necessarily assuming their validity in themselves.

20 E. K. Sedgwick, *The Epistemology of the Closet* (Penguin Books, 1994), p. 180 (see also pp. 152–4).

21 Grant, p. 10.

22 K. S. Gruesz, 'Feeling for the Fireside: Longfellow, Lynch and the Topography of Poetic Power', in M. Chapman and G. Hendler (eds), *Sentimental Men: Masculinity and the Politics of Affect in American Culture* (California University Press, 1999) p. 43.

23 K. Sánchez-Eppler, 'Then When We Clutch Hardest: On the Death of a Child and the Replication of an Image', in ibid., p. 70.

24 *The Letters of Charles Dickens* (Clarendon Press, 1965), vol. 1, p. 327; and see I. Newman, 'The Alleged Unwholesomeness of Sentimentality', in A. Neill and A. Ridley (eds), *Arguing About Art: Contemporary Philosophical Debates* (Routledge, 2002), pp. 326–7, where the episode is discussed.

25 Grant, p. 10.

26 For a discussion of the sentimental in relation to sensationalism and popular culture, see my *Sensational Subjects: The Dramatization of Experience in the Modern World* (Bloomsbury, 2014), Ch. 2; and, for the sentimental in relation to melodrama, Ch. 8.

27 See R. Barthes, *A Lover's Discourse* (Vintage, 2002), pp. 13, 175, 177, for provocative comments on these themes.

28 Grant, p. 10.

29 E. S. H. Tan and N. H. Frijda, 'Sentiment in Film Viewing', in C. Plantinga and M. G. Smith (eds), *Passionate Views: Film, Cognition and Emotion* (Johns Hopkins University Press, 1999), pp. 53, 55.

30 Aitkenhead.

31 R. C. Solomon, *In Defence of Sentimentality* (Oxford University Press, 2004), p. 7.

32 E. Wilson, 'The Unbearable Lightness of Diana', *New Left Review* (1997), 226, p. 140.

33 M. Chapman and G. Hendler, 'Introduction', in Chapman and Hendler, pp. 2, 9.

34 G. Hendler, 'Bloated Bodies and Sober Sentiments: Masculinity in 1840s Temperance Narratives', in Chapman and Hendler, p. 125.

35 Ibid., pp. 128, 130.

36 L. Boltanski, *Distant Suffering: Morality, Media and Politics* (Cambridge University Press, 1999), p. 101.

37 Men cry about 'important' things, like politics and football …

38 A further complication can be added here. In her recent work, Lauren Berlant argues that 'starting in the 1830s an intimate public sphere of femininity

constituted the first subcultural, mass-mediated, market population of relatively disenfranchised people in the United States', a feminine sphere which would open up opportunities for both the exploration *and* the commercial exploitation of feeling; see *The Female Complaint: The Unfinished Business of Sentimentality in American Culture* (Duke University Press, 2008), p. xii and *passim*.

39   S. L. Stratton-Pruitt, 'Murillo in America', in S. L. Stratton-Pruitt (ed.), *Bartolomé Esteban Murillo (1617–1682): Paintings from American Collections* (Kimball Art Museum and Henry H. Abrams, 2002), p. 94. For reception in America, see also M. E. Boone, *Vistas de España: American Vistas of Art and Life in Spain, 1860–1914* (Yale University Press, 2007), Ch. 2.

40   X. Brooke, 'Seville and Beyond: The Taste for Murillo's Genre Painting across Europe', in X. Brooke and P. Cherry (eds), *Murillo: Scenes of Childhood* (Dulwich Picture Gallery and Merrell Publishers, 2001), p. 63.

41   P. Cherry, 'Murillo's Genre Scenes and their Context', in ibid., p. 13.

42   A. Bermingham, Introduction, to A. Bermingham (ed.), *Sensation and Sensibility: Viewing Gainsborough's* Cottage Door' (Yale University Press, 2005), p. 8.

43   Cherry, p. 27.

44   A. E. Pérez Sánchez, *Murillo* (Electra, 2000), p. 55.

45   For *Uncle Tom's Cabin*, see D. S. Reynolds, *Mightier Than the Sword: 'Uncle Tom's Cabin' and the Battle for America* (Norton, 2011); L. Berlant, 'Poor Eliza', *American Literature* (1998), 70:3, pp. 635–68, and reproduced in her *The Female Complaint: The Unfinished Business of Sentimentality in American Culture* (Duke University Press, 2008), and T. F. Gossett, *Uncle Tom's Cabin and American Culture* (Southern Methodist University Press, 1985); for *A Christmas Carol*, see P. Davis, *The Lives and Times of Ebenezer Scrooge* (Yale University Press, 1990), and F. A. Guida, *A Christmas Carol and Its Adaptations: A Critical Examination of Dickens's Story and its Productions on Screen and Television* (McFarland and Company, 2000).

46   H. B. Stowe, *Uncle Tom's Cabin* (Wordsworth Editions, 1995), pp. 20–1, 124–5, 130–1. Since there are numerous editions and imprints, I will also give chapter references: IV, XIII, XIII.

47   C. Dickens, *A Christmas Carol* (Wordsworth Editions, 1993), pp. 60–2, 41–2. Again, I will also give chapter references (Dickens calls them 'staves' [st.]): 3, 2.

48   *Cabin*, pp. 317, 319–20, 342 (Chs XXXII, XXXII, XXXV).

49   *Carol*, p. 20 (st. 1).

50   L. Merish, *Sentimental Materialism: Gender, Commodity Culture, and Nineteenth-Century American Literature* (Duke University Press, 2000), p. 153.

51   H. B. Stowe, 'House and Home Papers' [1865] in her *Household Papers and Stories* (AMS Publishers, 1967), p. 82.

52   *Cabin*, p. 124 (Ch. XIII).

53 Merish, p. 143.

54 *Cabin*, p. 131 (Ch. XIII).

55 *Carol*, p. 54 (st. 3).

56 Merish, p. 150.

57 L. Wardley, 'Relic, Fetish, Femmage: The Aesthetics of Sentiment in the Work of Stowe', in S. Samuels (ed.), *The Culture of Sentiment: Race, Gender and Sentimentality in Nineteenth-Century America* (Oxford University Press, 1992), pp. 213, 214.

58 K. Sánchez-Eppler, 'Bodily Bonds: The Intersecting Rhetorics of Feminism and Abolition', in ibid., p. 112.

59 *Cabin*, Ch. XVIII; and see the discussion in Wardley.

60 Wardley, p. 216.

61 Merish, pp. 138, 165.

62 Sánchez-Eppler, 'Clutch Hardest', p. 74.

63 A. Jaffe, *Scenes of Sympathy: Identity and Representation in Victorian Fiction* (Cornell University Press, 2000), p. 44.

64 *Carol*, p. 25 (st. 1).

65 *Cabin*, pp. 319, 344, 390, 344, 313, 345 (Chs XXXII, XXXV, XLII, XXXV, XXXI, XXXV).

66 There is an apparently endless supply of circulating female hair in *Cabin*: remember also the strand found in a locket on St Clare after his death (p. 296, Ch. XXIX).

67 *Cabin*, pp. 362, 130 (Chs XXXVIII, XIII).

68 *Carol*, pp. 29, 18 (st. 1).

69 Jaffe, pp. 36, 38.

70 E. Barker, *Greuze and the Painting of Sentiment* (Cambridge University Press, 2005), p. 11.

71 *Carol*, p. 89 (st. 5).

72 J. Tompkins, *Sensational Designs: The Cultural Work of American Fiction 1790–1860* (Oxford University Press, 1985), pp. 134, 135.

73 *Cabin*, Ch. XXVIII.

74 R. Barthes, p. 63.

75 J. Culler, *Flaubert: the Uses of Uncertainty* (Cornell University Press, 1985), p. 226; and see pp. 226–8 generally.

76 A. Vrettos, *Somatic Fictions: Imagining Illness in Victorian Culture* (Stanford University Press, 1995), p. 100.

77 M. Noble, *The Masochistic Pleasures of Sentimental Literature* (Princeton University Press, 2000), p. 65.

78 S. Clark, *Sentimental Modernism: Women Writers and the Revolution of the Word* (Indiana University Press, 1991), pp. 10–11.

79 J. Kristeva, *Powers of Horror: An Essay on Abjection*, (Columbia University Press, 1982), p. 4.

80 Ibid., p. 11.

81 Clark, pp. 22, 10.

82 Ibid., p. 20.

83 Kristeva, p. 3.

84 Sedgwick, pp. 142–3: the book links this to gay contexts and controversies

85 *Cabin*, pp. 362, 264 (Chs XXXVIII, XXVI).

86 M. Noble, 'The Ecstasies of Sentimental Wounding in *Uncle Tom's Cabin*', *Yale Journal of Criticism* (1997), 10:2, pp. 296, 299.

87 Barthes, pp. 189, 160.

88 R, Barthes, *Camera Lucida* (Vintage, 1993), pp. 21, 27, 73; and see pp. 25–30.

89 Noble, 'Ecstasies', p. 305.

90 See M. Noble, *The Masochistic Pleasures of Sentimental Literature* (Princeton University Press, 2000), Ch. 2; and G. Bataille, *Eroticism* (Marion Boyars, 1987).

91 Tompkins, p. 176.

92 See, for example, Susan Warner's *The Wide Wide World*, and Martha Finley's *Elsie Dinsmore*, both from roughly the same period as *Uncle Tom's Cabin*. On Warner, see Tompkins, Ch. 6, and Noble, *Masochistic*, Ch. 3; on Dinsmore, see Noble, Ch. 2; and see Noble, Ch. 4, on Stowe.

93 L. Bersani, 'Representation and Its Discontents', in S. J. Greenblatt (ed.), *Allegory and Representation* (Johns Hopkins University Press, 1981), p. 150.

94 Jaffe, p. 32.

95 Solomon, p. 9.

96 Sánchez-Eppler, 'Bodily Bonds', pp. 99–100.

97 Barker, p. 11.

98 Sánchez-Eppler, 'Bodily Bonds', p. 99.

99 Sedgwick, pp. 143, 150.

100 J. Elison, *Cato's Tears and the Making of Anglo-American Emotion* (Chicago University Press, 1999), p. 196n. 19.

101 Tan and Frijda, pp. 48, 52.

102 J. Howard, 'What Is Sentimentality?', *American Literary History* (1999), 11:1, p. 71. The point is made in a discussion of Adam Smith.

Sensibility and Sympathy in the Theatre of Tears

1 A. Radcliffe, *A Sicilian Romance* (Oxford University Press, 1993 [1790]), pp. 7–8.

2 A. Vincent-Buffault, *The History of Tears: Sensibility and Sentimentality in France* (Macmillan, 1991), p. 53.

3   For a general account, see G. J. Barker-Benfield, *The Culture of Sensibility: Sex and Society in Eighteenth-Century Britain* (Chicago University Press, 1992).

4   C. Campbell, *The Romantic Ethic and the Spirit of Modern Consumerism* (Blackwell, 1989), p. 41.

5   For a brief account, see E. Barker, *Greuze and the Painting of Sentiment* (Cambridge University Press, 2005), pp. 207–8.

6   D. J. Denby, *Sentimental Narrative and the Social Order in France, 1760–1820* (Cambridge University Press, 1994), p. 115.

7   J. Elkins, *Pictures & Tears: A History of People Who Have Cried in Front of Paintings* (Routledge, 2001), p. 124.

8   Elkins argues (Ch. 7) that we have 'lost' the eighteenth century – we can no longer engage with sentimentalism. The problem here, though, is that while there has clearly been a major shift in aesthetic style and fashion since then, and this is significant for our understanding of different modes of expression and representation, it does not necessarily follow that there are no underlying continuities and patterns. He focuses particularly on the manifest interest Greuze shows elsewhere in depicting adolescent girls on the cusp of womanhood, his 'attraction to underage girls who have recently been deflowered', and argues that his philosopher defender Diderot shares this fascination (pp. 113–14, 131; and Barker broadly endorses this: see pp. 1–4, and 242n. 11). Again, one might observe that the fact that *we* cannot handle this, that it disturbs our convictions about childhood innocence and brings into play our moral panic over paedophilia, shouldn't blind us to continuities: the sentimentalist linkage of purity, innocence and loss can easily be mapped onto the theme of sexuality and the loss of virginity; our contemporary version reinterprets all this in a different register, but the similarities are there.

9   Barker, pp. 237, 238.

10   Denby, p. 86.

11   A. Bermingham, 'Introduction', in A. Bermingham (ed.), *Sensation and Sensibility: Viewing Gainsborough's* Cottage Door (Yale Center for British Art, 2005), p. 1. The rest of the essay explores Gainsborough's art as an exemplification of sensibility in the British context.

12   In Ann Radcliffe herself, for example. A. Milbank refers to the 'sequence of alternating frantic chases and frozen tableaux' in *A Sicilian Romance* (Oxford University Press, 1993 [1790]), Introduction, p. xv.

13   D. Diderot, *Entretiens sur le Fils naturel* (1757), p. 88, cit. M. Fried, *Absorption and Theatricality: Painter and Beholder in the Age of Diderot* (California University Press, 1980), p. 95.

14   Fried, pp. 78, 92.

15   C. Williams, 'Moving Pictures: George Eliot and melodrama', in L. Berlant (ed.), *Compassion: The Culture and Politics of an Emotion* (Routledge, 2004), p. 105.

16 Denby, p. 76.

17 Williams, p. 112.

18 D. Diderot, *Lettre sur les sourds et muets*, p. 64, cit. Fried, p. 91.

19 Fried, p. 91.

20 Using Brecht, Barthes argues, in his account of tableau, that there is indeed no overall 'final' meaning, in that 'all the burden of meaning and pleasure bears on each scene, not on the whole': R. Barthes, 'Diderot, Brecht, Eisenstein', from *Music Image Text* (Fontana, 1977), p. 72. Hence the maximum of meaning is concentrated in the instant depicted. See also discussions of Diderot and the later history of tableau in M. Meisel, *Realizations: Narrative, Pictorial, and Theatrical Arts in Nineteenth-Century England* (Princeton University Press, 1983), pp. 49, 84–6.

21 Barthes, pp. 70, 71.

22 Cit. ibid., p. 71.

23 Williams, p. 112. The best overall account of melodrama remains P. Brooks, *The Melodramatic Imagination* (Yale University Press, 1976). See also the discussion of melodrama in my *Sensational Subjects: The Dramatization of Experience in the Modern World* (Bloomsbury, 2014), Ch. 8.

24 S. Manning, 'Sensibility', in J. Keymer and J. Mee (eds), *The Cambridge Companion to English Literature 1740–1830* (Cambridge University Press, 2004), p. 89.

25 Campbell, p. 134.

26 We can let Emily St. Aubert's father, in Ann Radcliffe's *The Mysteries of Udolpho*, speak for this complaint: he warns that sensibility 'is a dangerous quality, which is constantly extracting the excess of misery, or delight, from every surrounding circumstance' (Oxford University Press, 1986), p. 79.

27 Diderot, *Entretiens*, p. 102, cit. Fried, p. 94.

28 Fried, pp. 68–9, 68, 104, 104–5.

29 Barthes, p. 70.

30 J. Caplan, *Framed Narratives: Diderot's Genealogy of the Beholder* (Manchester University Press, 1986), p. 4.

31 Caplan, p. 16.

32 Diderot, 'Eulogy of Richardson', 1761, from *Diderot's Selected Writings*, ed. L. G. Crocker, (Collier-Macmillan, 1966), p. 110, cit. in Caplan, p. 99.

33 Charles Taylor links this to the Enlightenment project whereby 'the enlightened trail-blazer of the present most often knowingly sacrifices his own well-being to that of future generations': *Sources of the Self: The Making of the Modern Identity* (Cambridge University Press, 1989), p. 331.

34 Caplan, p. 20.

35 Diderot, 'Eulogy', cit. ibid., p. 8, amended trans.

36 Caplan, pp. 20, 22–3, 23.

37   J. Schulte-Sasse, 'Afterword', in Caplan, pp. 107, 104, 108, 108.

38   Barker, p. 238.

39   Diderot, *Selected Writings*, p. 110, cit. Schulte-Sasse, p. 99.

40   M. Hays, *The Memoirs of Emma Courtney* (Oxford University Press, 1996). Since
     very few will be familiar with it, I include a brief plot synopsis, as follows. Emma
     is writing to her adopted stepson Augustus, son of the object of her unrequited
     love, Augustus Harley, in response to his request for an account of her life and
     her relations with his father. In doing this, she quotes copiously from her old
     correspondence with Augustus, and with a friend, the philosopher Mr Francis.
     Emma met Augustus by chance, after seeing a portrait of him at his mother's
     home, and engages in a vigorous pursuit of him; early promise gave way to
     silence and coldness on his part; it later transpired that he had married and had
     a son. Finally accepting the futility of her passion for Augustus, and in desperate
     financial straits, she marries another, who proves unfaithful and shoots himself.
     Augustus dies in an accident, after explaining himself and admitting his love for
     Emma on his deathbed.

41   On the 1790s, see Barker-Benfield, Ch. 7, including pp. 365–8, on Hays specifically.
     It is of course true that Wollstonecraft's *Vindication of the Rights of Woman* (1792)
     is the major work here, and there is a tendency to belittle Hays in comparison:
     for example, Barker-Benfield claims that Hays 'cobbles together' a celebration
     of feminine sensibility with Wollstonecraft's 'devastating critique' of it (p. 366),
     a comment that ignores the way the ambitious fusion of themes in the *Memoirs*
     both develops and extends Wollstonecraft's more theoretical approach. See also,
     on the broader issues, K. O'Brien, 'The Feminist Critique of Enlightenment', in M.
     Fitzpatrick et al. (eds), *The Enlightenment World* (Routledge, 2007).

42   Since it is of course Emma who articulates all this, in the course of the novel, I
     will generally refer to views as 'hers'; for reasons implied above, we can generally
     assume them to be those of Mary Hays, as they evolved in her past and in the
     writing of the novel. This of course raises tricky issues around authorship and the
     fictional subject, returned to later.

43   *Emma*, pp. 95, 96.

44   Ibid., pp. 99, 129, 129.

45   Ibid., p. 146.

46   W. M. Reddy, *The Navigation of Feeling: A Framework for the History of Emotions*
     (Cambridge University Press, 2001), p. 164.

47   Vincent-Buffault, p. 41.

48   J. Todd, *Sensibility: An Introduction* (Methuen, 1986), pp. 5–6.

49   J. Mullan, *Sentiment and Sociability: The Language of Feeling in the Eighteenth
     Century* (Oxford University Press, 1988), p. 16.

50   Denby, pp. 25, 51.

51 *Emma*, pp. 150, 156. The first encounter with the portrait is mentioned on p. 59.

52 Ibid., pp. 25, 84.

53 Ibid., pp. 169, 82. See also references to the 'distempered imagination' at pp. 77, 97, 118, 169.

54 Letter to *Monthly Magazine*, May 1797, cit. in G. Kelly, *Women, Writing, and Revolution* (Clarendon, 1993), p. 109; and see Ch. 3 for a general account of the politics of Hays's writing.

55 *Emma*, p. 82.

56 The epistolary mode of much eighteenth-century fiction has been widely noted. What Lois Bueler claims in relation to Richardson's fiction – 'that a letter has both the immediateness of drama and the recursive possibilities of narrative' – would have obvious application here, too; see *Clarissa's Plots* (Delaware University Press, 1994), p. 149. See also T. Castle, *Clarissa's Ciphers: Meaning and Disruption in Richardson's* Clarissa (Cornell University Press, 1992), pp. 16–18, 41–6, 154–6.

57 *Emma*, pp. 28, 41.

58 Denby, p. 206.

59 *Elements of Criticism* (Kincaid, Bell, Edinburgh, 1762), vol. I, p. 114.

60 M. Bell, *Sentimentalism, Ethics and the Culture of Feeling* (Palgrave, 2000), p. 48. The book is a most thoughtful and wide-ranging discussion, taking these themes on into modernism.

61 Reddy, p. 164.

62 M. Sutrop, 'Sympathy, Imagination, and the Reader's Emotional Response to Fiction', in J. Schlaeger and G. Stedman (eds), *Representations of Emotion* (Gunter Natt, 1999), p. 34 and *passim*.

63 Bell, p. 159.

64 T. Rajan, 'Autonarration and Genotext in Mary Hays's *Memoirs of Emma Courtney*', *Studies in Romanticism* (1993), 32:2, p. 149.

65 See *Emma*, pp. 83, 149, 163–4, 179, for examples.

66 P. M. Logan, *Nerves and Narratives: A Cultural History of Hysteria in Nineteenth-Century British Prose* (California University Press, 1997), p. 59; and see Ch. 3 for further discussion.

67 *Emma*, p. 7.

68 Logan, pp. 71, 72. Claudia Johnson's claim that female suffering cannot be articulated by heroines at this period because 'under sentimentality the prestige of suffering belongs to men' is clearly relevant here, and suggests a further level of gender complexity to be returned to shortly; see her *Equivocal Beings: Politics, Gender, and Sentimentality in the 1790s. Wollstonecraft, Radcliffe, Burney, Austen* (Chicago University Press, 1995), p. 17.

69 *Emma*, pp. 8, 86.

70 Logan, p. 65.

71   Ibid., pp. 42, 9.

72   Here, it seems appropriate to allude to the episode in *Uncle Tom's Cabin* when
     Senator and Mrs Bird are discussing the newly passed legislation that would make
     it a criminal offence to harbour a fugitive slave. The Senator, who always rejects
     'sentimental weakness' in his senatorial speeches, argues that 'we must put aside
     our private feelings' and not let them affect our judgement. His wife refuses to
     engage at this level at all, saying she 'hates' reasoning, especially on such topics,
     as it ignores what is the 'plain right thing'; instead, she asks him whether he
     would actually turn away a 'poor, shivering, hungry creature', suggesting that he
     wouldn't, that she knows him better than he knows himself. And of course she
     turns out to be right – the fleeing Eliza is given refuge and helped on her way.
     (H. B. Stowe, *Uncle Tom's Cabin*, Wordsworth, 1995, Ch. IX, pp. 83, 75, 76, 75.)
     In his discussion, Bell tries to show that it is feeling, not reason *divorced* from it,
     that is crucial; one might add that it calls for an account of judgement that is not
     reducible to either (pp. 121–3).

73   *Emma.*, pp. 140, 145.

74   Ibid., pp. 3, 138.

75   Ibid., p. 143.

76   Ibid., pp. 144, 85, 144, 144, 32.

77   Ibid., p. 113.

78   Here one can mention Johnson's convincing identification of the 1790s as a
     period which 'unsettles customary definitions of gender and sexuality both
     between and *within* the sexes' (p. 17) while perhaps indicating reservations about
     her narrower claim that the apparent 'sentimentalization' of culture was really
     a '"masculinization" of formerly feminine gender traits' now only valued when
     'recoded as masculine' (p. 14). This seems to imply a rather gender-determinist
     model of 'sentiment' as a homogeneous terrain which, insofar as it is occupied by
     one sex, must necessarily be vacated by the other, and in turn downplays both the
     subtlety of her own analyses and the possibilities for gendered experimentation
     within and beyond the established framework, as indeed we find not only in Hays
     but – in different ways – in Jane Austen (of whose work she is well aware: see the
     Afterword). See also G. E. Haggerty, *Unnatural Affections: Women and Fiction in
     the Later Eighteenth Century* (Indiana University Press, 1998).

79   *Emma*, pp. 98, 96, 96, 158.

80   Mullan, pp. 239, 240.

81   Mannng, p. 87.

82   A. Vincent-Buffault, pp. 32, 37.

83   Denby argues that the sentimentalist virtue/villainy pairing can be readily
     superimposed on the Enlightenment reason/obscurantism one (pp. 88–91, 95);
     and see Reddy (Part II), on sentimentalism in the French Revolution.

84   See J. A. Van Sant, *Eighteenth-Century Sensibility and the Novel: The Senses in
     Social Context* (Cambridge University Press, 1993), Ch. 2, and L. Boltanski, *Distant
     Suffering: Morality, Media and Politics* (Cambridge university Press, 1999), pp. 6–7.

85   Denby, p. 96.

86   Van Sant, p. 33.

87   Ibid., p. 53.

88   1778; cit. in ibid., p. 57.

89   For a pertinent discussion of Sterne, exposing some of the paradoxes in 'charity',
     see R. Markley, 'Sentimentality as Performance: Shaftesbury, Sterne, and the
     Theatrics of Virtue', in L. Brown and F. Nussbaum (eds), *The New Eighteenth
     Century: Theory, Politics, English Literature* (Methuen, 1987).

90   Sarah Fielding's letter to Richardson about her reaction to *Clarissa* can be
     taken to typify this: 'When I read her, I am all sensation; my heart glows; I am
     overwhelmed; my only vent is tears ...' (cit. Van Sant, p. 116.)

91   From c. 1790; cit. Van Sant, p. 51.

92   Van Sant, pp. 63–4; and see L. Jordanova, *Sexual Visions: Images of Gender in
     Science and Medicine from the Eighteenth to the Twentieth Centuries* (Harvester
     Wheatsheaf, 1989), Chs 2, 5.

93   Brissenden cheekily compares the two Jane Austen sisters, Elinor and Marianne,
     in *Sense and Sensibility*, to Sade's Juliette and Justine: R. F.Brissenden, *Virtue in
     Distress: Studies in the Novel of Sentiment from Richardson to Sade* (Macmillan,
     1974), pp. 273–6. (See also Part One, Ch. 4, and Part Two, Ch. 5, for related
     examples.) For discussions of Richardson's *Clarissa*, see also ibid., Part Two, Ch. 1;
     Van Sant, Ch. 4; Mullan, Ch. 2; and J. Todd, *Sensibility: An Introduction* (Methuen,
     1986), Ch. V.

94   L. Hinton, *The Perverse Gaze of Sympathy: Sadomasochistic Sentiments from
     Clarissa to Rescue 911* (State University of New York Press, 1999), p. 46; and see
     Ch. 1 generally.

95   Van Sant, p. 74.

96   Cit. in ibid., p. 95.

97   L. Haakonssen, *Medicine and Morals in the Enlightenment: John Gregory, Thomas
     Percival and Benjamin Rush* (Editions Rodopi, 1997), p. 217.

98   H. Arendt, *On Revolution* (Penguin, 1990 [1963]), pp. 80–90.

99   Ibid., pp. 86, 85, 85. Whether the latter comment is fair to Rousseau is debatable
     – see the next chapter of this book – but his influence certainly tended in this
     direction.

100 Ibid., pp. 85, 89, 89.

101 Boltanski, p. 6.

102 Arendt, p. 89.

103 The revolutionary, Siéyès, cit. ibid, p. 75.

104 Arendt, p. 89. This argument, generalized, is of course an important basis of the critique of the 'project of Enlightenment' and its legacy. A useful review of these issues is T. Osborne, *Aspects of Enlightenment: Social Theory and the Ethics of Truth* (Routledge, 1998).

105 Boltanski, pp. xiii–xiv.

106 Denby, p. 96, 243.

107 Ibid., p. 13.

108 The conventionally philosophical or political focus in Enlightenment studies has not helped clarify this relationship with the culture of sentimentalism. Some effort in this direction can be found in more recent works such as D. Outram, *The Enlightenment* (Cambridge University Press, 1995); R. Porter, *The Enlightenment* (Palgrave, 2001); and M. Fitzpatrick et al. (eds), *The Enlightenment World* (Routledge, 2007). The most thoughtful and balanced source on this remains Taylor, *Sources*, esp. Chs 17, 19.

109 One might also observe another outcome, that the theme of endurance and the transcendence of suffering as a crucial source of identity and insight – but in resolutely secular terms – becomes a powerful stream running into Romanticism and beyond. See, for example, S. Bruhm, *Gothic Bodies: The Politics of Pain in Romantic Fiction* (Pennsylvania University Press, 1994).

110 Taylor, pp. 297, 301.

111 Diderot, 'Eulogy', cit. Caplan, p. 8, amended trans.

112 *Emma*, p. 155. (For the other episode, the death of her father, see p. 33.)

113 No doubt, in the eighteenth-century context, the most appropriate manifestation of this mutuality would be *shared* tears, and there are indeed two such episodes in the novel: with Mrs Harley (p. 92), and with Augustus (p. 57).

114 Bell, p. 5.

115 *Emma*, p. 89.

Sympathy Theory

1 R. C. Solomon, *In Defence of Sentimentality* (Oxford University Press, 2004), p. 69.

2 L. Boltanski, *Distant Suffering: Morality, Media and Politics* (Cambridge University Press, 1999), p. 37.

3 H. Ferguson, *The Science of Pleasure: Cosmos and Psyche in the Bourgeois World View* (Routledge, 1990), p. 188, in a summary of Adam Smith's view.

4 D. H. Lawrence, *Phoenix: The Posthumous Papers of D. H. Lawrence* (Heinemann, 1936), p. 545.

5 D. H. Lawrence, *Phoenix II: Uncollected, Unpublished and Other Prose Works of D. H. Lawrence* (Heinemann, 1968), p. 187.

6   E. K. Sedgwick, *The Epistemology of the Closet* (Penguin Books, 1994), p. 143
     (in italics).

7   M. Midgley, 'Brutality and Sentimentality', *Philosophy* (1979), 54, pp. 385, 386.

8   E. S. H. Tan and N. H. Frijda, 'Sentiment in Film Viewing', in C. Plantinga and
     M. G. Smith (eds), *Passionate Views: Film, Cognition and Emotion* (Johns Hopkins
     University Press, 1999), p. 49.

9   D. Knight, 'Why We Enjoy Condemning Sentimentality: A Meta-Aesthetic
     Perspective', *Journal of Aesthetics and Art Criticism* (1999), 57:4, p. 418.

10   Boltanski, p. 101.

11   In *From Passions to Emotions: The Construction of a Secular Psychological Category*
     (Cambridge University Press, 2003), p. 17, Thomas Dixon argues that this
     dichotomy is becoming well established during the first half of the nineteenth
     century, replacing the more fluid approach of the preceding period. He adds that
     the category of emotion is an invention of the early nineteenth century, with
     notions like 'passions', 'affections' and 'sentiments' falling out of favour (p. 3). See
     also Chs 1, 8.

12   T. L. Beauchamp, 'Editor's Introduction' to D. Hume, *An Enquiry Concerning the
     Principles of Morals* (Oxford University Press, 1998 [1751]), p. 26.

13   M. Bell, *Sentimentalism, Ethics, and the Culture of Feeling* (Palgrave, 2000), p. 1.

14   M. Z. Rosaldo, 'Toward an Anthropology of Self and Feeling', in R. A. Schweder
     and R. A. LeVine (eds), *Culture Theory: Essays on Mind, Self, and Emotion*
     (Cambridge University Press, 1984), p. 143.

15   Bell, p. 19.

16   Ibid., p. 13.

17   C. Taylor, *Sources of the Self: The Making of the Modern Identity* (Cambridge
     University Press, 1989), p. 390.

18   D. Hume, *A Treatise of Human Nature* (Oxford University Press, 1976 [1739–40]),
     p. 417.

19   Bell, pp. 9, 207.

20   W. M. Reddy, *The Navigation of Feeling: A Framework for the History of Emotions*
     (Cambridge University Press, 2001), p. 222; and see pp. 94, 111. This book
     makes a stimulating and ambitious – if only partially successful – attempt to fuse
     cognitivist psychology with cultural history.

21   Rosaldo, p. 143. Martha Nussbaum, too, argues that the embodiment of emotions
     does not preclude them from being in some sense 'intelligent' and 'cognitive'; see
     her *Upheavals of Thought: The Intelligence of Emotions* (Cambridge University
     Press, 2001), p. 25 and *passim*.

22   S. Williams, *Emotion and Social Theory* (Sage, 2001), p. 59; and Chs 2, 4, give a
     helpful account of some of these issues.

23   R. Solomon, p. 23.

24   Reddy, pp. 94, 128–9; 321–2; 111, 128, 330. Again, J. M. Barbalet gives a useful account in *Emotion, Social Theory, and Social Structure* (Cambridge University Press, 2001), Chs 1, 2, but this rationalist bias is at times evident.

25   C. Campbell, *The Protestant Ethic and the Spirit of Modern Consumerism* (Blackwell, 1987), Ch. 4.

26   Ibid., pp. 69, 76, 73–5. A corollary, for Campbell, is that emotion may not be 'truly genuine', but may be 'artificially stimulated for the pleasure it yields' (p. 134), which was of course implied by critics of sentimentalism, and seems to rest on the assumption that emotion has to be purely 'natural' if it is to be genuine; the plausible alternative, that it can be – and perhaps always is – culturally shaped and influenced, seems to be left out of the equation, in favour of a model that seems, as I go on to suggest, both implausibly deliberative and too purely self-motivated. Re-cast, the claim would, however, usefully indicate the significance of the birth and development of a 'culture of the vicarious'.

27   As theorized by A. Giddens; see his *Modernity and Self-Identity* (Polity Press, 1991).

28   S. Ahmed, *The Cultural Politics of Emotion* (Edinburgh University Press, 2004), pp. 7, 6.

29   N. Crossley, 'Emotions and Communicative Action', in G. Bendelow and J. J. Williams (eds), *Emotions in Social Life* (Routledge, 1998), p. 28.

30   Solomon, pp. 24, 251.

31   G. Bateson, *Steps to an Ecology of Mind* (Paladin, 1973), p. 456.

32   J. Austen, *Sense and Sensibility* (New American Library, 1961 [1811]), p. 8.

33   Solomon, p. 243.

34   Ahmed, pp. 2–3.

35   Ibid., pp. 10, 11, 11, 191.

36   Hence connecting with the 'expressivism' that Taylor sees as so central to the development of the modern self

37   N. Denzin, *On Understanding Emotion* (Jossey Bass, 1984).

38   Reddy, p. 110.

39   So, that sense of impact, of being swamped, that point of excess that is also a point of *difference* can be read in two 'different' ways, with contrasting implications: as the point of intensity on the circuit of sensation, and as the looming up of figuration, the picturing of difference across boundaries, central to the spectacle of sympathy. On the concept of a 'circuit of sensation', see Ch. 1 of this book.

40   D. J. Denby, *Sentimental Narrative and the Social Order in France, 1760–1820* (Cambridge University Press, 1994), p. 31.

41   Bell, p. 44.

42   For accounts that reflect this changing emphasis, see K. Haakonssen (ed.), *The Cambridge Companion to Adam Smith* (Cambridge University Press, 2006); C. L.

Griswold, *Adam Smith and the Virtues of Enlightenment* (Cambridge University Press, 1999); and Boltanski, Ch. 3.

43 Hume, p. 363.

44 A. Smith, *The Theory of Moral Sentiments* (Liberty Fund, 1982 [1759, rev. edn 1790]), pp. 10, 43.

45 A. Broadie, 'Sympathy and the Impartial Spectator', in Haakonssen, pp. 164, 165.

46 M. Sutrop, 'Sympathy, Imagination and the Reader's Response to Fiction', in J. Schlaeger and G. Stedman (eds), *Representations of Emotion* (Gunter Natt, 1999), p. 37.

47 Smith, p. 21.

48 Ibid., pp. 12, 11.

49 Ibid., pp. 9, 10, 12.

50 Ibid., p. 317.

51 J. Howard, 'What is Sentimentality?', *American Literary History* (1997), 11:1, p. 71.

52 C. L. Griswold, 'Imagination: Morals, Science and Arts', in Haakonssen.

53 At this point one might observe, as mentioned in the first chapter of this book, that the widely used distinction between sympathy as 'feeling for' and empathy as 'feeling with' is rather unhelpful, sliding a difference of degree into separate concepts, and downplaying the unavoidable element of 'distance' in the latter in order to berate the former for its alleged aura of patronizing superiority. Ahmed is surely right that empathy 'sustains the very difference that it may seek to overcome' in that 'subjects "feel" something other than what another feels in the very moment of imagining they could feel what another feels' (Ahmed, p. 330). I argue below, using Smith, that a more structural approach can sideline this difficulty.

54 J. Derrida, *Of Grammatology* (Johns Hopkins University Press, 1976 [1967]), pp. 190, 185, and see pp. 182–92, 343. Building on this, see also R. Terada, *Feeling in Theory: Emotion after the 'Death of the Subject'* (Harvard University Press, 2001), Ch. 1. This approach to Rousseau also implies that his critique of the theatre is not a critique of *all* theatricality, but rather a call for a kind of theatre that engages the imagination and hence liberates a potential for passionate response.

55 Smith, pp. 9, 27–30.

56 Of course, we need to remember an alternative view, stemming from the Christian tradition, which emphasizes precisely our capacity to share each other's pain, on the analogy with Christ's suffering. This has considerable resonance in the modern period; perhaps the most powerful philosophical formulation is in Schopenhauer, for whom the will is the source both of our individuality and of our suffering, and *Mitleid* (pity, compassion) is the crucial moral response to this. This does not necessarily contradict Smith, of course, who is using 'pain' in the more literal sense, but it does involve a difference of emphasis.

57   See D. M. Morris, *The Culture of Pain* (California University Press, 1991), and
     S. Bruhm, *Gothic Bodies: The Politics of Pain in Romantic Fiction* (Pennsylvania
     University Press, 1994), Chs 1, 2, for a penetrating discussion of 'imagining pain'
     in eighteenth-century culture. All recent discussions draw heavily on E. Scarry,
     The Body in Pain (Oxford University Press, 1985).

58   On the significance of the contrast with 'sensation' here, see Ch. 1.

59   Smith, p. 29.

60   Ibid,. p. 33.

61   D. Hume, Letter to Smith, 28 July 1759, in *The Letters of David Hume* (Oxford
     University Press, 1932), vol. I, p. 313. The issue is discussed in Broadie, pp. 170–4,
     whose approach differs from that taken here.

62   Smith, p. 46n. 2.

63   And one has to point out that 'disinterested' is not the same as 'uninterested'. (One
     should not have to point that out, but alas one must.)

64   Griswold, *Smith*, p. 121.

65   D. Diderot, *Oeuvres esthétiques* (Garnier, 1968), p. 189, cit. and trans. J. Caplan,
     Framed Narratives: Diderot's Genealogy of the Beholder (Manchester University
     Press, 1986), p. 10. See also Smith, p. 143.

66   Of course, we need to remember in all this that it is always possible for the
     response to be *un*sympathetic. Arguably Smith, with his emphasis on the moment
     of reflection, can give a better account of this possibility than can Hume.

67   Hence, as Griswold puts it, in his discussion of Smith, 'The imagination provides
     for the "appearance" of selves on the stage' (*Smith*, p. 342).

68   Broadie, p. 177.

69   Smith, p. 23.

70   Ibid., pp. 24, 24, 147, 147.

71   Ibid., pp. 190, 191.

72   It is not surprising that the distinction between the virtues here is markedly
     gender-coded, in Smith: see p. 190. This aspect is discussed in H. Clark, 'Women
     and Humanity in Scottish Enlightenment Social Thought: The Case of Adam
     Smith', *Historical Reflections* (1993), 19.

73   Smith, pp. 113, 113, 130–1.

74   Ibid., pp. 130, 134.

75   Ibid., p. 137.

76   Ibid., p. 159.

77   J. Mullan, *Sentiment and Sensibility: The Language of Feeling in the Eighteenth
     Century* (Oxford University Press, 1988), p. 48. In his thoughtful attempt to tease
     out the differences between Hume and Smith (Ch. 1, esp. pp. 53–6), Mullan
     writes: 'Hume generalizes the model of particular contact or connection to explain
     all social relations; Smith insists on all specific interactions or conflicts being

referred to an abstract and universal standard' (p. 55). The former claim seems sound, but not the latter.

78 Griswold, 'Imagination', p. 38.

79 Griswold, *Smith*, p. 135.

80 Smith, p. 320.

81 This is an appropriate point to remark on a degree of convergence with Kant here. In the notoriously tricky §40 of the *Critique of Judgement*, Kant argues that the *sensus communis*, too, faces both ways: it is a 'public sense', reflective and critical, involving the 'communicability of our feeling'; it is also that 'internal feeling' itself, an awareness of feeling, 'sense' as the 'effect that mere reflection has upon the mind; for then by sense we mean the feeling of pleasure'. It involves a public face of feeling as an interplay of imagination and understanding (a 'sensibility') that can properly be characterized as 'aesthetic'. One might – with some trepidation – gloss this as the claim that 'communicability' is due to this capacity of aesthetic judgement to respond to the homology of reflexivity whereby the formal properties of self-awareness are present as essential preconditions for any actual communication between subjects, as subjects of experience, just as this homology itself, within and between subjects, is present *in* experience as *feeling*. (Quotes are from the J. C. Meredith trans., Oxford University Press, 1952, pp. 151–4.) See also R. A. Makkreel, *Imagination and Interpretation in Kant* (Chicago University Press, 1990), Ch. 8.

82 Smith, pp. 326, 131.

83 See Broadie, pp. 179–86, for a useful account.

84 Ibid., p. 175. One might observe here that the idea of the Enlightenment as dogmatically rationalist is valid up to a point, but, as suggested in the previous chapter, there is another strand – one that incorporates a positive relationship with sentimentalism (as brought out in Denby). This is the strand emphasized in the account of Smith given here. See also I. Wilkinson, *Suffering: A Sociological Introduction* (Polity Press, 2005), Ch. 5, for a good review of these issues.

85 Griswold, *Smith*, p. 300.

86 Griswold, 'Imagination', p. 39.

87 Boltanski, p. 41. At the same time, Boltanski's account separates Smith too strongly from sentimentalism (Chs 3 and 5 respectively).

88 Smith, p. 22, as summarized earlier in the first paragraph of this section, above.

89 Boltanski, p. 49.

90 Smith, p. 51.

91 Ibid., pp. 61, 61, 64, 64, 57.

92 Ibid., p. 62.

93 There is a remarkable (and generally unremarked) similarity with the themes of Rousseau's critique of modernity here, despite other obvious differences of

perspective. One of the few scholars to emphasize the relative coherence of
Rousseau's system is Nicholas Dent; in his *Rousseau: An Introduction to His
Psychological, Social and Political Theory* (Blackwell, 1988), he presents the
problem concept *amour-propre* as referring to the need to be a 'human presence'
for others, the need for esteem, so it is an inherently social and moral dimension
of the self; as such, it can become 'inflamed', obsessive and excessive, when
over-stimulated by the pressures of modern competitive society (pp. 20–5).
Conversely, 'pity' offers the prospect of 'human relations not perverted by the
demands of "inflamed" *amour-propre*' (p. 97). In Rousseau's own writings, see,
inter alia, the extended footnote to the First Part of the *Discourse on the Origins
of Inequality* [1755], and *Emile* [1762], sec. iv. An older work, Ernst Cassirer's *The
Question of Jean-Jacques Rousseau* (Indiana University Press, 1963 [1932]) is also
worth consulting.

94 Smith, p. 337 (my italics) and p. 50.

95 Ibid., pp. 183, 158; and see also pp. 51–3, 181–3, developing the critique.

96 Griswold, *Smith*, pp. 262, 128; see also pp. 222–5, and 'Imagination', pp. 42–5.

97 Smith, p. 50; and, for the other issues raised in this paragraph, see pp. 83–5, 34–8.

98 Smith draws a distinction between resentment and 'envy', the latter always being
unjustified; see pp. 44–5, 244. On resentment, see also pp. 75–6, 83–4. It may be
that in our contemporary age, when there is a widespread perception that wealth
and celebrity have no connection with merit whatsoever, the distinction between
resentment and envy breaks down, with sympathetic engagement replaced by
voyeuristic distraction, but this is not the place to pursue this. See my *Sensational
Subjects: Modernity and the Dramatization of Experience* (Bloomsbury, 2014),
Chs 5, 6.

99 This is developed in an interesting way in Boltanski, Ch. 4. One should add
here that, despite his insights, Smith's own political position remains relatively
conservative, even in the context of his time.

100 Smith, p. 143, Hume, p. 604; and Smith, p. 140.

101 Hume, p. 481.

102 Griswold, *Smith*, p. 128.

103 This has frequently been noticed by critics, e.g. see L. Merish, *Sentimental
Materialism: Gender, Commodity Culture, and Nineteenth-Century American
Literature* (Duke University Press, 2000), Ch. 1. It is a fair point, but the task
here is to uncover the deeper pattern, rather than the specific options opened up
within it, and this is clearly what Hume and Smith are at least trying to do.

104 There is a rough, undeveloped equivalent of this figure in Hume, in the form of
'general rules'; see Hume, pp. 583–4.

105 Smith, pp. 136–7, 36, 235.

106 Hume, p. 481. He also implies that since abstraction and self-interest are not

sufficient to generate an involvement in 'the good of society', sympathy must have a crucial role (p. 577).

107 M. J. Ferreira, 'Hume and Imagination: Sympathy and "the Other"', *International Philosophical Quarterly* (1994), 39:1, pp. 55, 56, 56.

108 D. Panagia, 'Inconsistencies of Character: David Hume on Sympathy, Intensity and Artifice', in C. V. Boundas (ed.), *Deleuze and Philosophy* (Edinburgh University Press, 2006), p. 96.

109 Again, this has been widely noted by critics. Thus Merish claims that Scottish Enlightenment theorists mention the plight of recipients of sympathy while 'abjecting them through a symbolics of race, class, and gender difference, encoding differences of social status that both elicit and regulate the flow of sympathy', so that such sympathy presupposes significant inequalities of wealth and status (Merish, pp. 38, 39). Again, a fair point, but not the whole truth, as the argument here hopefully shows.

110 Among recent contributions, one might cite Richard Sennett's argument in *Together: The Rituals, Pleasures and Politics of Co-operation* (Allen Lane, 2012) that the twentieth-century emphasis on 'solidarity', with its tendency to polarize an 'us' versus 'them' mentality – which can easily slide into an individualistic 'you are on your own' version – distorted the potential of 'co-operation' as a model for working with others. Coming from a very different theoretical perspective, Giorgio Agamben's work again shows the power of such mechanisms of exclusion of the other, though he is concerned to show a sense in which the excluded other is simultaneously 'included', as a necessary component of the political order and the hierarchy of power. Taking the inmates of 'camps', from the Holocaust to Guantánamo, he shows how they are constructed by this logic of power as 'unpersons' in a 'zone of indistinction', both 'beneath' power yet essential to it. See his elaboration of this in *Homo Sacer: Sovereign Power and Bare Life* (Stanford University Press, 1998), and *State of Exception* (Chicago University Press, 2005). While there is, of course, more to these arguments, they all show that modernity has long exercised the power to expel and exclude, and that the rhetoric of identity and identification has played a key part in this.

111 Hume, p. 619.

112 T. J. McCarthy, *Relationships of Sympathy: The Writer and the Reader in British Romanticism* (Scolar Press, 1997), p. 153.

113 Ferreira, p. 56.

114 Something of this is also present in Rousseau, for whom the individual's 'benevolent sentiments' reveal 'his creative and restorative care and power, are an expression of ... positive life and expansive force', and 'pity' is 'a mode of unfolding of sensibility, which allows for the possibility of loving, beneficial passions', as Dent puts it (pp. 162, 122).

From Sensibility to Affect?

1   A. J. Van Sant, *Eighteenth-Century Sensibility and the Novel: The Senses in Social Context* (Cambridge University Press, 1993), pp. 91, 94, 95.

2   M. Hays, *The Memoirs of Emma Courtney* (Oxford University Press, 1996 [1796]), pp. 99, 99, 92, 92.

3   C. Lawrence, 'The Nervous System and Society in the Scottish Enlightenment', in B. Barnes and S. Shapin (eds), *Natural Order: Historical Studies of Scientific Culture* (Sage, 1979), pp. 25, 29. For general treatments of these ideas, see also H. Ferguson, *The Science of Pleasure: Cosmos and Psyche in the Bourgeois World View* (Routledge, 1990), Ch. 9, and G. J. Barker-Benfield, *The Culture of Sensibility: Sex and Society in Eighteenth-Century Britain* (Chicago University Press, 1992), Ch. 1 and *passim*. These ideas spread through Enlightenment Europe: see J. I. Israel, *Political Enlightenment: Philosophy and the Making of Modernity 1650–1750* (Oxford University Press, 2001), Chs 25, 27, on the decline of Cartesianism and the triumph of Newton and Locke; and J. C. O'Neal, 'The Sensationist Aesthetics of the French Enlightenment', *L'Esprit créateur* (1988), 28:4.

4   A. Smith, *The Theory of Moral Sentiments* (Liberty Fund, 1982 [1759, rev. edn 1790]), p. 43.

5   D. Hume, 'Of Tragedy', in *Selected Writings* (Oxford University Press, 1996), pp. 126, 129, 129.

6   D. Hume, *A Treatise of Human Nature* (Oxford University Press, 1976 [1739–40]), p. 605 (see also pp. 576, 593, for similar formulations).

7   Smith, p. 14, my italics.

8   See, for example, *Treatise*, pp. 576, 317–19, 385–6.

9   See ibid., pp. 317, 605.

10   Smith, pp. 10, 11.

11   Hume, *Treatise*, pp. 317, 319, 385–6, 576.

12   L. Hinton, *The Perverse Gaze of Sympathy: Sadomasochistic Sentiments from Clarissa to* Rescue 911 (State University of New York, 1999), p. 23.

13   Hume, *Treatise*, p. 319; and, on ideas and impressions, pp. 1, 6, 8.

14   This produces a significant issue for interpreting Hume on sympathy, in that he argues that we are most immediately sympathetic to those who are most like us, and who are closest to us (ibid., pp. 581, 604) – a view that, as we have seen, provides grist to the mill of critics of the sympathy discourse generally. I argued, in the previous chapter, that it is possible to read Hume differently, since he also emphasizes the 'expansive' capacity of sympathy, able to respond across boundaries and distances; but there is undoubtedly a tension in his work here, one that reflects deep strands in eighteenth-century culture.

15   Ibid., p. 365.

16   Smith, pp. 110, 110, 111, 112.

17   C. L. Griswold, 'Imagination: Morals, Science, and Arts', in K. Haakonssen (ed.), *The Cambridge Companion to Adam Smith* (Cambridge University Press, 2006), pp. 36, 37.

18   D. Marshall, *The Figure of Theater* (Columbia University Press, 1986), p. 172.

19   J. Mullan, *Sentiment and Sensibility: The Language of Feeling in the Eighteenth Century* (Oxford University Press, 1988), pp. 43, 45.

20   Here, we are getting close to Campbell's thesis about the origins of modern consumerism in *The Romantic Ethic and the Spirit of Modern Consumerism* (Blackwell, 1987).

21   L. Merish, *Sentimental Materialism: Gender, Commodity Culture, and Nineteenth-Century American Literature* (Duke University Press, 2000), p. 50.

22   C. L. Griswold, *Adam Smith and the Virtues of Enlightenment* (Cambridge University Press, 1999), p. 109.

23   Conversely, the model of mimetic identification can readily incorporate rejection of otherness, since the notion of 'mirror identity' as fantasy wholeness is inseparable from the rejection or repression of threats to this precarious status.

24   For a brief account of theatricality in relation to mimesis, see M. Potolsky, *Mimesis* (Routledge, 2006), Ch. 4.

25   We can remember here that Smith and Hume knew one another, and seem to have been on good terms. They had no particular reason to advertise their differences, even when they were aware of them, and Smith seems to have absorbed much of his older colleague's general philosophical framework. Nor was this Smith's main focus, after all. So teasing out differences here is inevitably speculative – the emphasis being, of course, on the underlying cultural assumptions and implications, rather than the philosophy as such (let alone the biographical aspects).

26   Hume, *Treatise*, pp. 7–8. On 'impression' in Hume, see J. Matz, *Literary Impressionism and Modernist Aesthetics* (Cambridge University Press, 2001), pp. 19–25.

27   It is this sense of relationship that a Hume-based perspective has trouble grasping, and arguably this undermines any account of judgement – which involves thinking of something *as* something – stemming from it: see B. Stroud, '"Gilding" or "staining" the world with "sentiments" and "phantasms"', in R. Read and K. A. Richman (eds), *The New Hume Debate* (Blackwell, 2007, rev. edn), p. 28.

28   G. Deleuze, *Empiricism and Subjectivity: An Essay on Hume's Theory of Human Nature* (Columbia University Press, 1991 [1953]), p. 49, italics in original. In this early work, Deleuze misses a few tricks: 'intensity', later a key term in his system, is barely mentioned here, even though Hume gives ample opportunity for us to use it; he does however refer at times to 'vividness' (pp. 128–9, 132–3). However,

Deleuze offers a powerful reinterpretation of Hume that proves fundamental to his own thinking. See also J. Roffe, 'David Hume', in G. Jones and J. Roffe (eds), *Deleuze's Philosophical Lineage* (Edinburgh University Press, 2009), and J. Bell, *Deleuze's Hume: Philosophy, Culture and the Scottish Enlightenment* (Edinburgh University Press, 2009).

29   D. Panagia, 'Inconsistencies of Character: David Hume on Sympathy, Intensity and Artifice', in C. L. Boundas (ed.), *Deleuze and Philosophy* (Edinburgh University Press, 2006), pp. 94, 95, 95.

30   C. L. Boundas, 'Translator's Introduction' to Deleuze, p. 12; see also pp. 16–17, on intensity.

31   See G. Deleuze, *Difference and Repetition* (Continuum, 2004 [1968]), p. 182. In this, perhaps his major philosophical work, Deleuze makes significant use of 'intensity', and is aware of its links to 'sensibility' and Hume's thought, which he continues to cite with approval. He might also have added, in the spirit of Hume, that the pleasure in sympathy is produced in the succession of alternating relaxations and intensive contractions (p. 95). On intensity in Deleuze, see also C. Colebrook, *Gilles Deleuze* (Routledge, 2002), pp. 38–9; and J. Williams, *Gilles Deleuze's* Difference and Repetition: *a Critical Introduction and Guide* (Edinburgh University Press, 2003), Ch. 7.

32   Van Sant, pp. xiv; 1n. 1, my italics.

33   Still being republished in 1810, this book continued its readership and influence through to the Romantics, including Coleridge.

34   Hartley, pp. 281, 373, cit. Ferguson, p. 180.

35   Mullan, p. 231; and see Ch. 5, *passim*.

36   Barker-Benfield, pp. xvii; see also pp. 4–5, 16–18.

37   S. Manning, 'Sensibility', in T. Keymer and J. Mee (eds), *The Cambridge Companion to English Literature 1740–1830* (Cambridge University Press, 2004), p. 83.

38   A. Vincent-Buffault, *The History of Tears: Sensibility and Sentimentality in France* (Macmillan, 1991), p. 119.

39   *Shorter Oxford Dictionary*, entry for 'electricity'.

40   G. S. Rousseau, *Nervous Acts: Essays on Literature, Culture and Sensibility* (Palgrave, 2004), p. 54. This collection of his essays is an invaluable resource for research on these topics; see esp. Chs 1, 5, 7, 8.

41   Lawrence, pp. 19, 25.

42   M. Foucault, *Madness and Civilization: A History of Insanity in the Age of Reason* (Tavistock, 1967), pp. 152, 152–3.

43   S. Bruhm, *Gothic Bodies: The Politics of Pain in Romantic Fiction* (Pennsylvania University Press, 1994), p. 13; and see Ch. 1, *passim*.

44   Foucault, p. 153.

45 R. Rey, *The History of Pain* (Harvard University Press, 1993), pp. 122–5.

46 *The Works of Robert Whytt* (Edinburgh, 1768), p. 493. These excerpts, and others, are cited in Mullan, p. 229, and Bruhm, p. 12.

47 Foucault, p. 153.

48 R. K. French, *Robert Whytt, the Soul, and Medicine* (Wellcome Institute of the History of Medicine, 1969), p. 36.

49 S. Williams, *Emotion and Social Theory* (Sage, 2001), p. 61.

50 P. Schilder, *The Image and Appearance of the Human Body* (International University Press, 1950), p. 11.

51 J. Gaub, *De regimine mentis* (1747), cit. in L. J. Rather, *Mind and Body in Eighteenth Century Medicine* (Wellcome Institute of the History of Medicine, 1965), p. 64.

52 Whytt, p. 583, cit. Bruhm, p. 14.

53 Cit. P. M. Logan, *Nerves and Narratives: A Cultural History of Hysteria in Nineteenth-Century British Prose* (California University Press, 1997), p. 117.

54 Logan, p. 118.

55 Ibid., p. 119.

56 Ibid., pp. 119–20; Van Sant, p. 28; and see Rousseau, *passim*.

57 Van Sant, p. 121.

58 Ibid., p. 16.

59 Ibid., p. xiii.

60 S. Ahmed, *The Cultural Politics of Emotion* (Edinburgh University Press, 2004), p. 28.

61 Van Sant, p. 92.

62 T. Dixon, *From Passions to Emotions: The Construction of a Secular Psychological Category* (Cambridge University Press, 2003), Chs 1, 2, esp. pp. 17–18.

63 Most influential here is B. Massumi, *Parables for the Virtual: Movement, Affect, Sensation* (Duke University Press, 2002). This book has become a founding text for the 'affective turn', and a prime route for the diffusion of Deleuzian ideas; see esp. Ch. 1, on the autonomy of affect. It is important to add that I consider here only that aspect of affect theory that relates to the sympathy/sensation tension; on the ramifications of affect theory itself, as a continuation of the 'sensation' strand, see my *Sensational Subjects: The Dramatization of Experience in the Modern World* (Bloomsbury, 2014), Ch. 7.

64 EID5, p. 1; EIIP17S, p. 46. The *Ethics* (1677, cited as E) is arranged as a treatise in logic, with sections (I–V) divided into numerous propositions, axioms, etc. I use what seems to be becoming the standard mode of citation, as indicated by the translator to the Penguin edition (1996), E. Curley (p. xix), along with page numbers to this edition; this translation is also available in *A Spinoza Reader* (Princeton University Press, 1994).

65   That these are two sides of a coin is reflected in Deleuze's two accounts; see *Expressionism in Philosophy: Spinoza* (Zone Books, 1992 [1968], hereafter cited as EP), p. 147, and *Spinoza: Practical Philosophy* (City Lights Books, 1988 [1970], hereafter SPP), pp. 3, 73. The latter is the more widely cited (doubtless its brevity may have something to do with it); the former, which can seem rather off-putting for non-specialists, is actually one of Deleuze's more accessible tomes, and very recommendable as a conscientious exposition of Spinoza, as well as being the foundation for Deleuze's later work.

66   EIIID3, p. 70; EIII, Definitions of Affect, III, p. 104.

67   EIIIP11S, p. 77. The third is given as desire (though this seems different in kind from the other two, and will not be further explored here).

68   EP, p. 220 (also SPP, p. 49, a very similar formulation).

69   SPP, p. 49.

70   Referring to Spinoza, Martin Joughin, the translator of EP, suggests that *affectus* comprises both 'affect' and 'effect': 'an affect is "inwardly" directed toward an object as its final cause, an effect "outwardly" caused by an object as its efficient cause – for Spinoza they are only two aspects of the same process', p. 413.

71   SPP, p. 49.

72   Deleuze seems ready enough, at this stage of his career, to see 'affect' as interchangeable with 'feeling', as shown. Joughin notes that Deleuze uses *sentiment* as the word for *affectus* in French, and 'feeling' is the natural translation into English, to which Deleuze seems not to have objected (see EP, pp. 413–14). In his later work, though, 'feelings' will be denounced as too polluted by everyday notions, so that when writing about Bacon's paintings, for example, he will claim that 'there are no feelings in Bacon: there are nothing but affects', or sensations as a directly visceral engagement with the world: see his *Francis Bacon: The Logic of Sensation* (Continuum, 2003 [1981]), p. 39. I discuss this aspect of Deleuze's work in *Sensational Subjects*, Ch. 4.

73   EIIIP30D, p. 86.

74   Massumi, pp. 32, 31.

75   A. Damasio, *Looking for Spinoza: Joy, Sorrow and the Feeling Brain* (Vintage, 2004), p. 215.

76   EIIP44S, p. 59.

77   Spinoza writes: 'An affect … is an imagination, insofar as it indicates the present constitution of the body' (EVP34D, p. 176). This formulation again reminds us of the 'one world, two perspectives' approach, entailing differing characterizations of what is ultimately the same object or event.

78   EVP6, p. 165.

79   EP, pp. 295, 286 (in italics); and see pp. 282–5.

80   EIII, Definitions of Affects, XVIII, p. 107.

81   M. Gatens and G. Lloyd, *Collective Imaginings: Spinoza, Past and Present* (Routledge, 1999), pp. 77, 142.

82   EIVP50S, p. 142.

83   EIIIP27D, p. 84; EIII30S, p. 86.

84   See D. Vardoulakis (ed.), *Spinoza Now* (Minnesota University Press, 2011), for articles discussing aspects of the theory of passions in Spinoza.

85   C. Williams, 'Affective Processes Without a Subject: Rethinking the relation between subjectivity and affect with Spinoza', *Subjectivity* (2010) 3:3, p. 255, an account influenced by Deleuze and Massumi.

86   EIIP40S2, p. 57.

87   EP, p. 278. This is where Spinoza's theory of 'common notions', as the building blocks between imagination and reason, comes into play; see EP, Ch. XVII, and the first few pages of the following chapter, for an exemplary exposition, and one that pays tribute to the positive role of the imagination (whatever the author's criticisms of it elsewhere). More briefly, see SPP, p. 58.

88   EIVP15, p. 118. (The example is also used at EIIP35S, p. 53.) Spinoza is, of course, using imagination to include what we might more naturally call perception, hence anticipating an important hinge of Kant's system.

89   EIVP15, p. 118. It will be recalled that 'imaginations' disappear when supplanted by stronger ones, not when the object itself disappears – hence the potential for memories, fantasies, phantoms …

90   EIIP17S, p. 46.

91   R. Terada, *Feeling in Theory: Emotion after the 'Death of the Subject'* (Harvard University Press, 2001), p. 115.

92   EP, p. 147. What we find here is an early manifestation of what will become even more evident in his later work: his determination to ensure that a philosophical understanding of reality is unpolluted by the fallacies of everyday thinking and the stereotypes of popular culture. In particular, concepts like recognition and representation necessarily make reference to this conservative pattern of conventional, taken-for-granted thinking, and merely reproduce it in philosophical form. See also my *Sensational Subjects*, Ch. 4.

93   It should be added that Spinoza has his limitations, from this angle: there is no real theory of selfhood, nor is there anything of the later sense of the imagination as a distinctive faculty of mind.

94   T. Brennan, *The Transmission of Affect* (Cornell University Press, 2004), p. 71. She adds that 'transmission through physical vibration' is also a social process, vital to 'electrical entrainment'.

95   J. Riskin, 'The Mesmerism Investigation and the Crisis of Sensationist Science', in D. Howes (ed.), *The Sixth Sense Reader* (Berg, 2009), p. 120. It should be added

that 'mesmerism' would nevertheless continue its career well into the nineteenth century, despite the commission's best efforts.

Unconscious Arts of Memory

1 Appropriately, the term 'sensibility' itself falls out of fashion, though uses of it can be found. In George Eliot's *Daniel Deronda*, Daniel advises Gwendolen: 'Try to take hold of your sensibility, and use it as if it were a faculty, like vision' (Penguin, 1995 [1876], p. 452, Ch. 36). This advocates a conjunction of feeling and self-understanding that seems very true to the eighteenth-century tradition.

2 Jonathan Crary claims that 'The problem of consciousness becomes inseparable from the question of physiological temporality and process': see his *Suspensions of Perception: Attention, Spectacle, and Modern Culture* (MIT Press, 2001), p. 56. This book offers illuminating insights on the development of these themes in nineteenth-century culture.

3 W. M. Reddy, *The Navigation of Feeling: A Framework for the History of Emotions* (Cambridge University Press, 2001), p. 212, and Chs 6, 7, *passim*.

4 P. M. Logan, *Nerves and Narratives: A Cultural History of Hysteria in Nineteenth-Century British Prose* (California University Press, 1997), p. 169. See also J. B. Taylor, *In the Secret Theatre of Home: Wilkie Collins, Sensation Narrative, and Nineteenth-Century Psychology* (Routledge, 1988), Ch. 1.

5 M. Bell, *Sentimentalism, Ethics and the Culture of Feeling* (Palgrave, 2000), p. 132.

6 J. L. Matus, 'Historicizing Trauma: The Genealogy of Psychic Shock in *Daniel Deronda*', *Victorian Literature and Culture* (2008), 36:1, p. 64.

7 The Gothic and Romanticism do, of course, anticipate later developments, although the focus on the uncertain boundaries of mind, body, and the other – with the resulting interest in the spectral – and on those between passion and social convention, do not congeal into the patterns apparent later. For various aspects, see T. Castle, *The Female Thermometer: Eighteenth-Century Culture and the Invention of the Uncanny* (Oxford University Press, 1995); S. Bruhm, *Gothic Bodies: The Politics of Pain in Romantic Fiction* (Pennsylvania University Press, 1994); and A. Richardson, *British Romanticism and the Science of the Mind* (Cambridge University Press, 2001).

8 L. Otis, *Organic Memory: History and Body in the Late Nineteenth and Early Twentieth Centuries* (Nebraska University Press, 1994), p. 3, and see Ch. 1.

9 M. Davis, *George Eliot and Nineteenth-Century Psychology* (Ashgate, 2006), p. 147.

10 S. Shuttleworth, *Charlotte Brontë and Victorian Psychology* (Cambridge University Press, 1996), p. 47. For further background on nineteenth-century science and psychology, in addition to other items listed in this section, see R. Rylance,

Victorian Psychology and British Culture, 1850–1880 (Oxford University Press, 2000); A. Stiles (ed.) *Neurology and Literature 1860–1920* (Palgrave, 2008); L. Otis (ed.), *Literature and Science in the Nineteenth Century* (Oxford University Press, 2002); and J. B. Taylor, 'Obscure Recesses: Locating the Victorian Unconscious', in J. B. Bullen (ed.), *Writing and Victorianism* (Longman, 1997).

11 Logan, p. 168.

12 R. Knoper, 'Trauma and Sexual Inversion, circa 1885: Oliver Wendell Holmes's *A Mortal Antipathy* and Maladies of Representation', in Stiles, p. 126.

13 R. B. Gordon, 'From Charcot to Charlot: Unconscious Imitation and Spectatorship in French Cabaret and Early Cinema', in M. S. Micale (ed.), *The Mind of Modernism: Medicine, Psychology, and the Cultural Arts in Europe and America, 1870–1940* (Stanford University Press, 2004), p. 96.

14 Matus, p. 65.

15 G. H. Lewes, *The Physiology of Common Life* (Blackwood, London, 1860), vol. 2, p. 12, cit. Matus, p. 65.

16 G. H. Lewes, *The Physical Basis of Mind* (Trubner, London, 1877; vol. 3 of *Problems of Life and Mind*, 1874–9), p. 169, cit. Davis, p. 153.

17 Davis, p. 154.

18 Davis, p. 112.

19 G. H. Lewes, *Problems*, vol. 2, p. 413, cit. Davis, p. 112.

20 G. Eliot, *Middlemarch* (Oxford World's Classics, 1998 [1871–2], p. 191 (Ch. 20).

21 *Deronda*, pp. 277 and 63–4 (Chs 24, 6).

22 Davis, p. 182.

23 A. Vrettos, *Somatic Fictions: Imagining Illness in Victorian Culture* (Stanford University Press, 1995), p. 63; and see Ch. 2, *passim*.

24 *Deronda*, p. 27 (Ch. 3).

25 M. Meisel uses this concept to refer to the production of 'reality effects' on the stage and in culture generally. See *Realizations: Narrative, Pictorial, and Theatrical Arts in Nineteenth-Century England* (Princeton University Press, 1983).

26 *Deronda*, Ch. 56.

27 Ibid., pp. 434, 57, 420 (Chs 36, 6, 35).

28 In Ch. 6.

29 C. Williams, 'Moving Pictures: George Eliot and Melodrama', in L. Berlant (ed.), *Compassion: The Culture and Politics of an Emotion* (Routledge, 2004), p. 131.

30 *Deronda*, pp. 557, 358–9, 359 (Chs 45, 31).

31 Ibid., pp. 427, 610, 670 (Chs 35, 48, 54).

32 G. Beer, *Darwin's Plots: Evolutionary Narrative in Darwin, George Eliot and Nineteenth-Century Fiction* (Cambridge University Press, 2000), p. 174; and see Ch. 6. See also Davis, pp. 109–12.

33 *Deronda*, p. 424 (Ch. 35).

34 This episode is, in some respects, a structural opposite of the former: the return of something hers v. the gift of something asserted to be not-hers. But then again, what is 'hers' was actually her father's, just as the 'not-hers' was Grandcourt's … For an interesting discussion, see C. Gallagher, 'George Eliot and *Daniel Deronda*: The Prostitute and the Jewish Question', in R. Yeazell (ed.), *Sex, Politics, and Science in the Nineteenth-Century Novel* (Johns Hopkins University Press, 1990), esp. pp. 48–53.

35 *Deronda*, pp. 19–20, 447 (Chs 2, 36).

36 Ibid., pp. 396, 399 and 790, 792 (Chs 34, 68). One can add here that Daniel has previously saved Mirah from drowning, thus initiating the second theme of the novel, since it is through Mirah's Jewish family that he is led to ponder his own obscure origins and open up issues around cultural identity and belonging.

37 Ibid., pp. 142, 589 (Chs 13, 48).

38 A. Cvetkovich, *Mixed Feelings: Feminism, Mass Culture, and Victorian Sensationalism* (Rutgers University Press, 1992), p. 129; and see Ch. 6.

39 Matus mounts an explicit argument to this effect.

40 *Deronda*, p. 564 (Ch. 45).

41 Ibid., p. 770 (Ch. 65).

42 Ibid., p. 702 (Ch. 57). For other such episodes, see pp. 359, 806 (Chs 31, 69).

43 Ibid., pp. 806, 61 (Chs 69, 6).

44 Vrettos, p. 70.

45 J. Rose, *Sexuality in the Field of Vision* (Verso, 1986), pp. 117, 118; and see Ch. 4, *passim*.

46 *Deronda*, p. 686 (Ch. 55).

47 G. H. Lewes, diary entry for 29-6-1873, cit. D. Marshall, *The Figure of Theater: Shaftesbury, Defoe, Adam Smith, and George Eliot* (Columbia University Press, 1986), p. 471.

48 Williams, pp. 106–11. This article provides an insightful account of melodrama in relation both to Eliot and nineteenth-century popular culture more widely. On this, see also Meisel, and J. Litvak, *Caught in the Act: Theatricality in the Nineteenth-Century English Novel* (California University Press, 1992), Ch. 5.

49 Marshall, pp. 194, 231; and see Ch. 8 for an elaboration of these points.

50 Vrettos, p. 75.

51 Williams, pp. 107–8.

52 Ibid., pp. 119–23; and see *Deronda*, Ch. 40 (also Ch. 38).

53 Williams, p. 120.

54 *Deronda*, pp. 471, 684–5 (Chs 38, 55).

55 Rose, p. 119.

56 Cvetkovich, p. 152.

57 Deronda, pp. 693, 694 (Ch. 56).

58 Marshall, pp. 21, and 207–10.

59 Cvetkovich, p. 154.

60 Marshall, p. 217.

61 *Deronda*, p. 629 (Ch. 51).

62 Marshall, p. 227.

63 *Deronda*, p. 629 (Ch. 51).

64 Ibid., p. 178 (Ch. 16).

65 T. Pinney (ed.), *Essays of George Eliot* (Routledge, 1963), p. 270.

66 *Deronda*, pp. 451, 630, 366, 366 (Chs 36, 51, 32, 32).

67 One must, of course, salute George Eliot's bravery in raising these issues at all, in the context of the time: anti-Semitism was staple fare among ruling class and some intellectual circles in Britain (and remained so until at least the 1940s).

68 *Deronda*, p. 725 (Ch. 60).

69 Ibid., p. 745 (Ch. 63).

70 See also Gallagher, pp. 56–8, who links this to Eliot's critical comments elsewhere on 'cosmopolitanism' and the abstract universalism of market forces – criticisms, especially of the latter, that retain their pertinence.

71 *Deronda*, pp. 364, 365, 365, 661, 750 (Chs 32, 53, 63). Deronda is articulating here the characteristic evolutionist perspective of his time, presumably shared by the author. We even learn that he seems to be touching the 'electric chain' of his ancestry (p. 721, Ch. 60), a sort of hereditary extension of the circuit of sensation, reaching through time, and operating unconsciously, albeit open to conscious reinforcement.

72 A. Jaffe, *Scenes of Sympathy: Identity and Representation in Victorian Fiction* (Cornell University Press, 2000), p. 139; and see pp. 138–40, for elaboration.

73 Davis, p. 113.

74 *Deronda*, Ch. 18.

75 See also *Middlemarch*, Ch. 80, where Eliot shows some sensitivity to this.

76 M. Proust, *Swann's Way*, vol. I of *In Search of Lost Time*, trans. C. K. Scott Moncrieff and T. Kilmartin (Vintage, 1996 [1913]), p. 51.

77 *Deronda*, e.g. pp. 653, 316 (Chs 52, 28). For a summary, referencing Eliot's works generally, see Davis, pp. 147–59.

78 Proust was aware of Freud, and apparently sympathetic to the idea of 'repression'; see J. Jordan, 'The unconscious', in R. Bales (ed.), *The Cambridge Companion to Proust* (Cambridge University Press, 2001), p. 104. See also W. C. Carter, 'The vast structure of recollection: from life to literature', p. 37, in the same volume, and R. Mackenzie, 'Proust's "Livre intérieur"', in P. Collier and J. Davies (eds), *Modernism and the European Unconscious* (Polity, 1990), p. 150.

79 M. Proust, *The Captive*, vol. II of *In Remembrance of Things Past*, trans. C. K. Scott Moncrieff (Random House, 1932 [1923]), p. 619.

80 W. Benjamin, 'The Image of Proust', from *Illuminations* (Fontana, 1992 [1929]), pp. 210, 198, also available in *Selected Writings, vol. 2: 1927–34* (Belknap/Harvard University Press, 1999), pp. 247, 238.

81 *Swann*, p. 52.

82 Ibid., p. 53.

83 This term, of course, recalls Baudelaire; see the reflections in W. Benjamin, 'On Some Motifs in Baudelaire', in *Illuminations*, and in *Selected Writings, vol. 4: 1938–1940* (Belknap/Harvard University Press, 2003 [1940]).

84 *Swann*, pp. 51, 54–5.

85 See, for example, the episode of the scent of hawthorn blossoms recalling those in the old church: *Swann*, pp. 164–6, 132–3.

86 Ibid., p. 54.

87 'Motifs', p. 180 (335). Numbers in brackets refer to the *Selected Writings* edition; and words in square brackets indicate translations from this edition, when the difference may be significant.

88 Jack Jordan, in his article (p. 113), claims that it is not a matter of finding the cause of the sensation in either subject or object, but in the fusion of the two; this seems correct up to a point, but rather misses these discontinuities.

89 'Image', p. 209 (246).

90 As a record, filed in conscious memory, a photo can of course carry a powerful sense of 'here and now', relative to when it was taken – but it is not, for all that, either experienced, or a record of experience.

91 M. Proust, *Time Regained*, vol. VI of *In Search of Lost Time*, trans. A. Mayor and T. Kilmartin, revised D. J. Enright (Modern Library, 1993 [1922]), pp. 255, 257–9. (The pagination in the Vintage [1996] edition is different: for these episodes and the subsequent reflections, see pp. 216–225, 232–4.)

92 Ibid., p. 263.

93 Ibid., p. 264.

94 Ibid., p. 267.

95 Ibid., p. 264.

96 C. Taylor, *Sources of the Self: The Making of the Modern Identity* (Cambridge University Press, 1989), p. 479.

97 G. Deleuze, *Proust and Signs* (Minnesota University Press, 2000 [1964]), pp. 60 (in italics in the original), 61. Like Proust, Deleuze takes the forcefulness, the intensity, of the recall as a criterion of its 'truth'; for our purposes, it is the emphasis on 'difference' here that is important.

98 W. James, 'Are We Automata?', *Mind* (1879), 4, p. 7, cit. Davis, p. 139.

99 Davis, p. 139.

100 James, p. 18, cit. Davis, p. 140.

101 One must be careful here. There has been an assumption that Proust must have

been influenced by Bergson's emphasis on time as duration; actually, Proust seems to have kept a certain distance, unimpressed by Bergson's insensitivity to some of his central concerns, such as the distinction between two kinds of memory. See Benjamin, 'Motifs', sec. II.

102 *Time Regained*, p. 273.

103 Ibid., p. 275.

104 Ibid., p. 274. 'Interior' might be a more exact translation than 'inner', keeping a clearer sense of the *spatial* aspect of the word in this context.

105 Ibid., p. 264.

106 *Swann*, p. 50.

107 *Proust*, p. 11. And alluding to Proust elsewhere, he suggests that 'The other is the existence of the encompassed possible', a formulation that neatly encapsulates the tension of imaginative engagement here; see *The Logic of Sense* (Continuum, 2004 [1969]), p. 347.

108 Deleuze argues that the emphasis on 'encounter' permits us to avoid the traps of 'recognition', mere familiarity (*Proust*, p. 27). This contributes to his project of purifying art and aesthetics of the twin corruptions of public opinion and objectivism; avoiding the latter, in particular, involves a stronger separation between art and memory than the approach adopted here. (Ch. 5 of *Proust* is indeed entitled 'The *Secondary* Role of Memory', my italics.) One can therefore agree that 'reminiscence is the analogue of art' (ibid., p. 60) without necessarily implying that the relation of homology implies any necessary inferiority of one series to the other, or even that they can be clearly distinguished in the first place. (See also ibid., pp. 55, 111.) For a critique of Deleuze on public opinion and the traps of representation, see also my *Sensational Subjects: Modernity and the Dramatization of Experience* (Bloomsbury, 2014), Ch. 4.

109 'Motifs', p. 184 (338).

110 Ibid., p. 182 (337).

111 Ibid., sec. XI. The Baudelaire quotes are from his poem *Correspondences*.

112 Ibid., p. 186 (340).

113 Which is why, following what seems to be common critical practice with this author, I have made no careful effort to distinguish between 'author' (of the novel) and 'narrator' (of the story). For some purposes, of course, it might be very necessary to do so.

114 *Time Regained*, pp. 264, 265, 270.

115 'Motifs', pp. 153–4 (314), 156 (316), 157 (317).

116 Benjamin suggests that in Freud, too, consciousness and leaving behind a memory trace are presented as incompatible within the same system: 'consciousness comes into being at the site of [takes the place of] a memory trace'. See 'Motifs', p. 157 (317). See also *The Standard Edition of the Complete Psychological Works of*

Sigmund Freud, trans. and ed. J. Strachey (Hogarth Press, 1953–74), vol. 18, p. 25, on 'excitatory pressures' expiring in the very act of consciousness.

117 I. Hacking, 'Memory Sciences, Memory Politics', in P. Antze and M. Lambek (eds), *Tense Past: Cultural Essays in Trauma and Memory* (Routledge, 1996), p. 70.

118 M. Proust, *On Art and Literature*, trans. S. T. Warner (Carroll and Graf, 1997), p. 19.

119 W. James, *The Principles of Psychology* (Harvard University Press, 1983 [1890]), pp. 1087–8.

120 E. Claparède, 'La question de la mémoire affective', *Archives de psychologie* (1911), 10, pp. 367, 369, cit. R. Leys, *Trauma: A Genealogy* (Chicago University Press, 2000), pp. 95, 96. (Passages in square brackets were presumably added by Leys.) See also her useful discussion, pp. 94–7.

121 Leys, p. 97.

122 S. Freud, 'The Unconscious' [1915], *Standard Edition*, vol. 14, p. 178.

123 P. Brooks, *Body Work: Objects of Desire in Modern Narrative* (Harvard University Press, 1993), p. 255; Ch. 8 develops the argument.

124 Freud, 'Unconscious', p. 177. See also the other metapsychological works of 1915, in the same volume. For an interesting discussion, see M. Borch-Jacobsen, *The Emotional Tie: Psychoanalysis, Mimesis and Affect* (Stanford University Press, 1993), pp. 123–54.

125 For Paul Ricoeur, in *Freud and Philosophy* (Yale University Press, 1970), the *Project* can be seen as evidence of a shift from the language of forces to that of meanings (pp. 130–1); there might be better grounds, though, for arguing that the tension between the two runs right through Freud's work. Indeed, for Misha Kavka, in *Reality Television, Affect and Intimacy: Reality Matters* (Palgrave, 2008), 'Ultimately, affect is the touchstone of psychoanalytic knowledge, the stuff of the psyche that does not lie' (p. 32), though since it is fundamental to psychoanalysis that affect *per se* cannot *tell* us anything it is difficult to know how we could assess the latter claim.

126 J. Laplanche and J.-B. Pontalis, *The Language of Psychoanalysis* (Hogarth Press, 1973), pp. 13, 14.

127 Kavka, p. 31.

Trauma Trouble

1 R. Luckhurst, 'Traumaculture', *New Formations* (2003), 50. See also R. Luckhurst, *The Trauma Question* (Routledge, 2008); M. Seltzer, 'Wound Culture: Trauma in the Pathological Public Sphere', *October* (1997), 80, reproduced (slightly altered) as Ch. 10 of his *Serial Killers: Death and Life in America's Wound Culture* (Routledge,

1998). Luckhurst's book is the most useful overview of the topic in its cultural ramifications (literature, film, art, theory); Seltzer's work offers an insightful cultural theory perspective.

2   M. S. Micale, 'Medical and Literary Discourses of Trauma in the Age of the American Civil War', in A. Stiles (ed.), *Neurology and Literature, 1860–1920* (Palgrave, 2007), p. 184.

3   Seltzer, 'Wound', pp. 3 and 22n. 50.

4   A. Jaffe, *Scenes of Sympathy: Identity and Representation in Victorian Fiction* (Cornell University Press, 2000), p. 176.

5   Luckhurst, *Trauma*, p. 132; and see Ch. 3, esp. pp. 131–3.

6   J. Matus, 'Historicizing Trauma: The Genealogy of Psychic Shock in *Daniel Deronda*', *Victorian Literature and Culture* (2008), 36:1, p. 73.

7   D. LaCapra, *Writing History, Writing Trauma* (Johns Hopkins University Press, 2001), p. 23.

8   Ibid., p. 22.

9   K. Ball, 'Introduction: Trauma and Its Institutional Destinies', *Cultural Critique* (2000), 46, p. 39.

10   E. A. Kaplan, *Trauma Culture: The Politics of Terror and Loss in Media and Literature* (Rutgers University Press, 2005), p. 39; and see pp. 39–44, 88–9, and Ch. 4, *passim*. Her book focuses on the twin issues of witnessing, and working through, trauma.

11   See J. L. Matus, 'Emergent Theories of Victorian Mind Shock: From War and Railway Accident to Nerves, Electricity and Emotion', in Stiles; M. S. Micale and P. Lerner (eds), *Traumatic Pasts: History, Psychiatry and Trauma in the Modern Age, 1870–1930* (Cambridge University Press, 2001), Chs 2, 3; and W. Schivelbusch, *The Railway Journey: The Industrialization of Time and Space in the 19th Century* (Berg, 1986), Chs 7, 9, 10.

12   See R. Leys, *Trauma: A Genealogy* (Chicago University Press, 2000), Ch. III; M. Stone, 'Shellshock and the Psychologists', in W. F. Bynum et al. (eds), *The Anatomy of Madness: Essays in the History of Psychiatry* (Routledge, 1985), vol. 2; Luckhurst, *Trauma*, pp. 49–53; and E. Showalter, *The Female Malady: Women, Madness and English Culture, 1830–1980* (Virago, 1987), Ch. 7.

13   W. Brown, 'The Treatment of Cases of Shell Shock in an Advanced Neurological Center', *The Lancet* (1918), 2, p. 198, cit. Leys, p. 101.

14   C. Myers, 'Contributions to the Study of Shell Shock', *The Lancet*, (1916), 1, pp. 67–8, cit. Leys, p. 101. One might add that the symptoms of war traumas from later periods, e.g. those of Vietnam veterans, seem broadly consistent with this; see Luckhurst, 'Traumaculture', pp. 29–31.

15   Leys, p. 100.

16   LaCapra, p. 42.

17   Luckhurst, *Trauma*, p. 118.

18   S. Ahmed, *The Cultural Politics of Emotion* (Edinburgh University Press, 2004), p. 27.

19   C. Caruth, *Unclaimed Experience: Trauma, Narrative, and History* (Johns Hopkins University Press, 1996), pp. 115n. 6, 59, 59. The latter claim is repeated by her in C. Caruth (ed.), *Trauma: Explorations in Memory* (Johns Hopkins University Press, 1995), p. 5.

20   Luckhurst, 'Traumaculture', p. 28.

21   Caruth, *Trauma*, p. 5.

22   See Luckhurst, *Trauma*, pp. 11–12, 72–4, 122–4, 147, 179–85, for a useful survey. On the controversies, see also Leys, pp. 241–3, and 253n. 35; Kaplan, pp. 25–38, incl. discussion of Freud and neuroscience; and R. J. McNally, *Remembering Trauma* (Harvard University Press, 2003).

23   See, for example, the work of Bessel van der Kolk, who has influenced Caruth: B. A. van der Kolk and O. van der Hart, 'The Intrusive Past: The Flexibility of Memory and the Engraving of Trauma', in Caruth, *Trauma*; and B. A. van der Kolk et al., *Traumatic Stress: The Effects of Overwhelming Experience on Mind, Body, and Society* (Guilford Press, 1999). For a thorough (and devastating) critique, see Leys, Chs VII, VIII. Affect theory, too, draws heavily on neuroscientific sources; for a discussion, see my *Sensational Subjects: The Dramatization of Experience in the Modern World* (Bloomsbury, 2014), Ch. 7.

24   Luckhurst, *Trauma*, p. 79.

25   L. di Prete, *'Foreign Bodies': Trauma, Corporeality, and Textuality in Contemporary American Culture* (Routledge, 2006), p. 8. On this point, she acknowledges the influence of D. Horvitz, *Literary Trauma: Sadism, Memory, and Sexual Violence in American Women's Fiction* (State University of New York Press, 2000).

26   Seltzer, 'Wound', p. 11.

27   K. Farrell, *Post-Traumatic Culture: Injury and Interpretation in the Nineties* (Johns Hopkins University Press, 1998), pp. 5, 3.

28   Caruth, *Unclaimed*, p. 61.

29   Ibid., p. 62.

30   Leys, p. 4.

31   One might note, in passing, a degree of overlap here with the uncanny. Trauma is the other that cannot be recognized as such, the alien in identity, constituting it as repetitive, neurotic, 'foreign' to itself. The obsessive, repetitive power of the returning 'image', experienced as all-too-real, and the disruption or fragmentation of time that is both cause and consequence, is vividly brought out in Toni Morrison's *Beloved*, which also reminds us that there can be a collective, social dimension to trauma, and a potential for 'working through'. For discussion, see A. Gordon, *Ghostly Matters: Haunting and the Sociological Imagination* (Minnesota University Press, 1997), Ch. 4, and Luckhurst, *Trauma*, pp. 90–7.

32   S. Freud, 'Beyond the Pleasure Principle' [1920], secs II, IV, in *The Standard Edition of the Complete Psychological Works of Sigmund Freud*, trans. and ed. J. Strachey (Hogarth Press, 1953–74), vol. 18. This is where Freud introduces his most radical attempt to deal with the problem of repetition itself, the concept of the death instinct, a concept that oscillates in an illuminating if arguably incoherent way between referring to an adaptive 'strategy' of the self in an impossible situation (hence a strategy that is therefore ultimately maladaptive); an aspect of the drive to mastery; and a manifestation of a quasi-organic drive (instinct) to re-establish an earlier state of stasis, in death.

33   A problem recognized several times by Freud himself; see, for example, his comment in the late 'Outline of Psycho-Analysis' [1938], *Standard Edition*, vol. 23, p. 184.

34   This model is implicit in much of Freud's work, but gets perhaps its most explicit formulation in 'The Aetiology of Hysteria' [1896], *Standard Edition*, vol. 3.

35   Seltzer, 'Wound', p. 10.

36   This stems from the work of Pierre Janet, contemporary with the earlier part of Freud's career. See S. J. Lynn and J. W. Rhue (eds), *Dissociation: Clinical and Theoretical Perspectives* (Guilford Press, 1994), esp. Chs 1, 18, 20; Luckhurst, *Trauma*, pp. 41–4, 48; and Leys, Ch. III.

37   On these wider aspects, see I. Hacking, *Rewriting the Soul: Multiple Personality and the Sciences of Memory* (Princeton University Press, 1995), and Leys, Ch. II. See also my *Sensational Subjects*, Ch. 5, relating this to the notion of distraction.

38   T. Elsaesser, 'Postmodernism as mourning work', *Screen* (2001), 4:2, p. 199.

39   On 'recovered memory syndrome', see C. Lury, *Prosthetic Culture: Photography, Memory and Identity* (Routledge, 1998), Ch. 5, and Luckhurst, *Trauma*, *passim*.

40   Of course, one *can* introduce this, using 'castration anxiety', and indeed shell shock was often associated with a range of physical injuries and disfigurements; but, one might suggest, *pace* Freud, that perhaps castration powerfully figures the wound-as-trauma, rather than the other way round; and it is difficult to see that a notion of the unconscious adds anything *essential* here.

41   On the latter, see A. Young, *The Harmony of Illusions: Inventing Post-Traumatic Stress Disorder* (Princeton University Press, 1995).

42   Seltzer, *Serial Killers*, p. 237.

43   G. Le Bon, *The Crowd: A Study of the Popular Mind* (Ernest Benn, 1947 [1895]), p. 126.

44   A. Vrettos, *Somatic Fictions: Imagining Illness in Victorian Culture* (Stanford University Press, 1995), pp. 83, 97.

45   Cit. R. B. Gordon, 'From Charcot to Charlot: Unconscious Imitation and Spectatorship in French Cabaret and Early Cinema', in M. S. Micale (ed.), *The Mind of Modernism: Medicine, Psychology, and the Cultural Arts in Europe and*

America, 1880–1940 (Stanford University Press, 2004), p. 118. On this engagement of hysteria with popular culture, see also F. McCarren, 'The "Symptomatic Act" circa 1900: Hysteria, Hypnosis, Electricity, Dance', *Cultural Inquiry* (1995) 21.

46 Gordon, 'From Charcot', p. 117. One might add that there is plenty of scope here for gendering these perceived dangers: crowds, like bodies, could be seen as overflowing, leaking pollution ...

47 M. S. Micale, 'Discourses of Hysteria in *Fin-de-Siècle* France', in *Mind of Modernism*, p. 90.

48 See their account, 'Studies in Hysteria'[1895], in *Standard Edition*, vol. 2. The symptoms of the celebrated Anna O, for example, included paralysis and loss of feeling on one side of her body, disturbed vision, an odd head posture, coughing, bouts of delirium, hydrophobia, loss of speech (what Breuer called her 'absences' [p. 30]), and strange distortions of language, including childhood words and sounds, foreign phrases, and neologisms.

49 Cit. B. Inglis, *The Diseases of Civilization* (Paladin, 1983), p. 234.

50 Micale, 'Discourses', p. 90.

51 E. Bronfen, *The Knotted Subject: Hysteria and Its Discontents* (Princeton University Press, 1998), pp. 105, 114.

52 E. Showalter, *Hystories: Hysterical Epidemics and Modern Culture* (Picador, 1997), p. 15.

53 Micale notes the emergence of the 'new hysteria studies', and of contemporary disorders that are easily spread by suggestion and imitation, the media playing a key role; see pp. 294 and 4–12 of his *Approaching Hysteria: Disease and Its Interpretations* (Princeton University Press, 1995). This is also noted by Showalter (*Hystories*, pp. 4, 6, 28). This is fair enough, though the latter author has a tendency to classify a whole rag-bag of disorders, physical and mental, as 'manifestations' of an underlying 'essence' of hysteria, claiming that we must 'recognize hysterical syndromes as a universal psychopathology of everyday life' before we can dismantle their 'stigmatizing mythologies' (p. 12). This runs the risk of becoming a further move in the hysteria game rather than an analysis of it.

54 J. Baudrillard, 'The Precession of Simulacra', in *Simulacra and Simulation* (Michigan University Press, 1994), p. 3. See also the stimulating account in R. Butler, *Jean Baudrillard: The Defence of the Real* (Sage, 1999), Ch. 1.

55 Vrettos, p. 83.

56 Bronfen, pp. 115, 113; and see pp. 109–13, tracing the sources of this from the eighteenth century.

57 Vrettos, p. 45; and see pp. 46–7.

58 Generally, men avoided the label, though not always; it could at times be fashionable. In a private letter, Freud even used it of himself: see the *Complete Letters of Sigmund Freud to Wilhelm Fliess* (Harvard University Press, 1995),

p. 325. More usually, the less stigmatizing label of 'neurasthenia' was used for men: the classic case is Proust (see M. R. Finn, *Proust, The Body, and Literary Form* [Cambridge University Press, 1999], esp. pp. 38–41). See also M. Gijswit-Hofstra and R. Porter (eds), *Cultures of Neurasthenia from Beard to the First World War* (Rodopi, 2001); and, for further wide-ranging discussions of hysteria, including gender aspects, see S. L. Gilman et al., *Hysteria Beyond Freud* (California University Press, 1993). Given these gender aspects, together with increasing medical scepticism, and the concentration on shell-shock trauma, 'hysteria' as a medical label was dying out by the 1920s.

59 Bronfen, p. 40.

60 G. Deleuze, *Francis Bacon: The Logic of Sensation* (Continuum, 2003 [1981]), p. 50. Deleuze suggests an internal connection between painting and hysteria; see pp. 50–5.

61 Once again, one notes a certain convergence with sentimentalism here: both involve an apparent excess of feeling. This renders sentimentalism even more vulnerable to ideological attack at times when any 'cult of feeling' is under pressure, the alleged sentimentalist thus becoming available for denunciation as 'hysterical'. The relevant difference here, though, is that sentimentalism is fundamentally an overflowing of feeling for the other *in* a distance it both affirms and mourns, rather than a crisis of boundaries that can potentially cripple the coherence of the self.

62 One might add that hypnosis played a part in cultural life and entertainment generally, as indeed did hysteria; it contributed to a 'spectacle of sympathy' in which the spectacle could clearly win out over the sympathy. This could even be true of the medical environment itself: Charcot's famous demonstrations of the use of hypnosis in the diagnosis of hysteria took place before an audience, and the theatricality of the 'performances' was widely commented on. (See Gordon, 'From Charcot', and Showalter, *Female Malady*, Ch. 6.)

63 And we can recall that while Freud's decisive rejection of hypnosis was motivated not only by his awareness of its therapeutic inconclusiveness – its use seemed merely to result in endless symptomatic repetitions and displacements – but also by his unease at this authoritarian mode of interaction, his own development of the 'talking cure' and his discovery of transference do not of course necessarily resolve either problem. Even on his own account, transference is necessarily the site of a *battle*, and the twin possibilities of psychoanalysis as authoritarian imposition in another guise, or as a process ultimately interminable, loom into view ...

64 It follows that seeing hypnosis purely in terms of mimetic identification is inadequate. Leys refers to a 'profound' identification between hypnotized self and other, and refers to 'the tendency of hypnotized persons to imitate or repeat

whatever they were told to say or do' (pp. 46, 8). But this seems odd. If you are under hypnosis, you do not 'imitate' what you are told to say or do; you just do it. With hypnosis, there is *control* of self by other; referring merely to 'identification' obscures the asymmetry here. Going on from this, one can add that although Leys is surely the most penetrating analyst of the medical and psychiatric traditions of trauma theory and treatment, her central theoretical innovation – analysing trauma in terms of a mimesis/anti-mimesis dichotomy – seems suspect. Presenting trauma through a mimetic theory of hypnosis, she then argues that this in turn produces an anti-mimetic reaction, through theorizing trauma as external impact, rather like an infection, so that, on this model, the subject's integrity can be safeguarded, and the subject can, in principle, remember it and report on it (pp. 9–10, 37, 298–9). But this won't do. Even if hypnosis provides a convincing model for trauma (very dubious), we've seen that hypnosis cannot be reduced to mimesis anyway; it has to incorporate the element of coercion, of external force. And conversely, if this element *is* present, and is necessary for trauma, then it must be present in the anti-mimetic model too (as indeed it is, even in her account), and the latter cannot serve to rescue the 'coherent subject' from the risk of fracture and dissociation. Since an essential feature of trauma is precisely this *absence of distance*, so that the victim can gain no purchase on it, and remains trapped in it, we can now see why posing all this in terms of mimesis v. anti-mimesis is not helpful: this central feature runs right through *both* the alleged alternatives. And, beyond this, it seems that the term 'mimesis' is stretched, in opportunist fashion, to cover far too much, just as 'anti-mimesis' is, in turn, left far too vague. For example, we are informed that the anti-mimetic theory 'also tends to make imitation basic to the traumatic experience', but in a different sense of 'imitation': it is not the mimetic sense of 'immersion' in trauma, but 'hypnotic imitation', whereby the subject remains a spectator of the trauma scene and can report on it (p. 299). At this point, the incoherence of the mimesis/anti-mimesis pair seems to have spread contagiously to imitation, now bifurcated into two senses, neither of which seem to be central to 'imitation' anyway ... All in all, then, to claim that 'both mimesis and antimimesis are internal to the traumatic experience' (p. 40) risks tautology – in terms of the central issues, the terms have not been coherently or usefully distinguished in the first place.

65   Bronfen, p. 117.
66   Ibid., pp. xiii, 35, 35, 36.
67   Seltzer, *Serial Killers*, p. 65.
68   Seltzer, 'Wound', p. 11, italics in original.
69   Seltzer, *Serial Killers*, p. 184.
70   Seltzer, *Serial Killers*, pp. 45, 145; 'Wound', p. 9. See also Leys, p. 37 and *passim*.

71 And if this extreme form of sensation can be characterized as 'sensational', this would of course be even more true in the case of serial killing…

72 Seltzer, 'Wound', pp. 12, 15, 15.

73 Seltzer, *Serial Killers*, pp. 43, 61n. 64; and see pp. 45–6. It needs to be reiterated that the repetition of *content* is crucial for trauma, whereas Seltzer's own argument, emphasizing a 'statistical' notion of the person as embodying 'merely formal' equality, goes in a somewhat different direction.

74 There is an intriguing reminder here of the thesis of Judith Butler (*Gender Trouble: Feminism and the Subversion of Identity* [Routledge, 1990]) that identity is performative, reiterative, 'the stylized repetition of acts through time', hence subverting any notion of a fixed ground of identity (p. 141); one might remark that the *effect* of trauma is to *reintroduce* this fixed ground, as the crippling, disavowed condition of identity itself …

75 See Leys, for a fascinating discussion of this theme as it occurs in Freud (pp. 29–33). She suggests that Freud postulates a state of 'primary identification' that can never be remembered because it precedes the self/other distinction: but if this is the case, who or what is identifying with who or what? It is, rather, a state of undifferentiation, before any question of identification (or mimesis) can arise; such identification can only be emergent, constituted retrospectively.

76 Lauren Berlant is critical of the way some identity politics activists 'assume pain as the only sign readable across hierarchies of social life … know me, know my pain – you caused it'. Hence 'trauma stands as truth'. See L. Berlant, 'The Subject of True Feeling: Pain, Privacy, and Politics', in A. Sarat and T. R. Kearns (eds), *Cultural Pluralism, Identity Politics, and the Law* (Michigan University Press, 1999), pp. 73, 72.

77 Caruth (*Unclaimed*, pp. 62–5) tends to present this as a universal ontological dilemma, rather than as having its source in 'trauma culture' in the sense being developed here.

78 Leys, p. 204.

79 LaCapra, pp. xiv, 46–7, 76–81; and see the illuminating account in Ch. 2 overall.

80 Luckhurst, *Trauma*, p. 3.

81 See Luckhurst, *Trauma*, pp. 29–31, on the example of the 1989 Hillsborough disaster (when 95 spectators died in a football stadium accident), for an elaboration.

82 Caruth, *Unclaimed*, pp. 4, 5, 8.

83 Caruth, *Trauma*, p. 10.

84 Leys, pp. 253, 254, 304; and see her overall critique of Caruth, in Ch. VIII.

85 LaCapra's concept of 'empathic unsettlement' is apposite at this point: see LaCapra, p. 78. His use of – and sensitivity to – 'empathy' is generally compatible with the approach adopted here.

86   W. Benjamin 'On Some Motifs in Baudelaire', in *Illuminations*, p. 159, and in *Selected Writings, vol. 4: 1938–1940* (Belknap/Harvard University Press, 2003 [1940]), p. 319.

Sympathy, Sentiment and Media Spectacle

1   J. Habermas, *The Structural Transformation of the Public Sphere* (Polity, 1992), p. 49.

2   For a more extended discussion, see my *Sensational Subjects: The Dramatization of Experience in the Modern World* (Bloomsbury, 2014), Ch. 6. There is also relevant discussion of the public sphere and the media in Ch. 8.

3   See L. Boltanski, *Distant Suffering: Morality, Media and Politics* (Cambridge University Press, 1999), pp. 154, 173. This book remains the most thoughtful recent exploration of these issues; see esp. Ch. 2, and Part III.

4   The one 'deconstructs' the other, so to speak.

5   L. Chouliaraki, *The Spectatorship of Suffering* (Sage, 2006), pp. 13, 11, 2. It is worth adding that a new book by her that looks highly pertinent to these issues arrived too late for consideration here: *The Ironic Spectator: Solidarity in the Age of Post-Humanitarianism* (Polity, 2013). (Subsequent references to 'Chouliaraki' are of course to the former.)

6   Chouliaraki, pp. 103, 104. Chouliaraki's use of 'tableau' here marks a departure from the eighteenth-century sense, and from its later use, in melodrama. In these areas, the tableau served, through its intensity, to concentrate the meaning of suffering, engaging the spectator emotionally. The properties of the pictorial scene were supposed to *enhance* 'emotional connectivity', not distance us from it.

7   Ibid., pp. 26, 37–8.

8   It is when it is *apparently* true, as in 'special effects', that the involvement of technology with melodrama is potentially at its strongest; but even here, the melodramatic effect is enhanced if the audience is not aware of the impact of the technology as a separate aspect. Really, it is the excessive, 'over the top' aspect of technology that is crucial here.

9   Chouliaraki, p. 189.

10   It appeared in the *New York Times*, 26 March 1993.

11   J. Rancière, *The Emancipated Spectator* (Verso, 2009), p. 99.

12   One should add that there are motivational complexities here, but the photo, and the reaction to it, was clearly a factor.

13   A. and J. Kleinman, 'The Appeal of Experience; The Dismay of Images: Cultural Appropriations of Suffering in Our Times', *Daedalus* (1996) 125:1, p. 7. Their solution is to work through the local; but this, too, presents pitfalls, particularly

the risk of corruption – large quantities of foreign aid disappear into the hands of local elites. The initial problem, clearly, is how to respond meaningfully to this image *without* letting it unwittingly reinforce 'Darkest Africa' stereotypes.

14 S. Sontag, *Regarding the Pain of Others* (Penguin, 2004), p. 8.

15 Ibid., pp. 9, 6.

16 Cit. ibid., p. 23.

17 Rancière, p. 103.

18 For discussion, see J. Taylor, *Body Horror: Photojournalism, Catastrophe, and War* (New York University Press, 1998), pp. 166–7, 180–3.

19 Sontag, pp. 23, 72, 72.

20 One must enter a caveat here. It was suggested, in the discussion of sympathy theory in a previous chapter, that an excessively visceral, 'in your face' effect may bypass the emotional and imaginative involvement needed for the sympathetic response to engage. Context would seem crucial here, and this may well be a factor in the response to the Iraq image. (The situation is clearly different from watching a horror film …)

21 The photo, by Kenneth Jarecke, appeared in the *Observer*, 3 March 1991, with the caption: 'The real face of war'. It did not carry commentary. Some newspapers carried pictures of wrecked vehicles, taken from some distance. For most of the press, brief references to Iraqi casualties were presented in the logic of melodramatic personalization: it was all Saddam Hussein's fault anyway … It should of course be added that the image is readily accessible now, on the internet.

22 Taylor, p. 157. His discussion of this (Ch. 9) is entitled 'The body vanishes in the Gulf War'. This of course provided some basis for Baudrillard's thesis in *The Gulf War Did Not Take Place* (Power Publications, 1995), exploring the logic of simulation. See also D. Kellner, *The Persian Gulf TV War* (Westview, 1992); E. Scarry, 'Watching and authorizing the Gulf War', in M. Garber et al. (eds), *Media Spectacles* (Routledge, 1993), and D. K. Thussu, 'Live TV and Bloodless Deaths: War, Infotainment and 24/7 News', in D. K. Thussu and D. Freedman (eds), *War and the Media: Reporting Conflict 24/7* (Sage, 2003).

23 J. Seaton, *Carnage and the Media* (Allen Lane, 2005), p. 220.

24 Taylor, p. 129; see also Chs 8, 9; and S. D. Moeller, *Compassion Fatigue: How the Media Sell Disease, Famine, War, and Death* (Routledge, 1999), Chs 3, 5.

25 J. Dawes, *That the World May Know: Bearing Witness to Atrocity* (Harvard University Press, 2009), is a sensitive exploration of these themes in the context of the Rwandan genocide of the 1990s – largely ignored or distorted in the Western media – placing an emphasis on the written word, including literature, rather than the visual image.

26 Sontag, p. 63. See also Taylor, pp. 193–6.

27 See Chouliaraki, pp. 13–14, 209–13, for a critique of narcissism and an

over-emphasis on feeling, in particular the tendency to reduce cosmopolitanism to intimacy via psychological identification, and the easy idea of a 'common humanity' which really just reflects this narcissism (p. 210). Conversely, when television news combines emotion with an element of impersonality, maintaining a creative tension between 'feeling' and 'watching', permitting reflexive engagement, cosmopolitanism can in principle defeat narcissism (p. 212). Jean Seaton makes a similar point: '… feeling empathy is sometimes about making spectators feel good about themselves, with the glow of shared humanity substituted for an arduous comprehension of what is different about other people' (p. 285). There is a slight problem with Chouliaraki here: in the book, her perspective on theatricality shifts it too close to emotion, hence threatening to assimilate it to the narcissism/identification model she rightly criticizes. But with Nicholas Abercrombie and Brian Longhurst, in *Audiences: A Sociological Theory of Performance and Imagination* (Sage, 1998), this gets worse, and narcissism and spectacle become two sides of the same coin: 'people see themselves as performers being watched by others; narcissism is the treatment of the self as spectacle' (p. 96), in that it is narcissism that provides the emotional dynamics of spectacle. This is insightful enough, as a description of a central strand of modern consumer culture, but as an all-pervasive perspective on modernity it leaves us without those resources for critique that *also* run deep within the modern, as argued previously (see esp. the chapter on sympathy theory). One might want to suggest that while narcissism implies spectacle, the converse is not the case. On the motivational issue, it is certainly true that there can be an easy slide from feeling good after doing good to doing good *in order to* feel good; thus James Dawes, in *That the World May Know,* points out that 'it is sometimes impossible to distinguish the desire to help others from the desire to amplify the self, to distinguish altruism from narcissism', and quotes a UN aid worker referring to 'the narcissism of righteousness' (pp. 122, 126).

28   Sontag, p. 91. For her earlier position, see *On Photography* (Farrar, Straus and Giroux, 1977), pp. 17–20. This is summarized in *Regarding Pain*, pp. 94–7; for her critique of this earlier position, and a conditional defence of images, see esp. pp. 102–6, although really the whole essay is relevant. Given that her later position could indeed be seen as tending towards a certain social determinism, there is a degree of unresolved tension here. See also Rancière, pp. 103–5.

29   Moeller, p. 2. See also Taylor, pp. 18–26, on Sontag's earlier position, and compassion fatigue.

30   K. Tester, *Compassion, Morality and the Media* (Open University Press, 2001), pp. 57, 122; and see Ch. 5, *passim*. And it is not, of course, just telethons that raise enormous sums. In *The Culture of Calamity: Disaster and the Making of Modern America* (Chicago University Press, 2007), K. Rosario points out that 9/11

produced the greatest charitable outpouring ever in the US: nearly two-thirds of households contributed time, money or supplies, and $1bn went to the American Red Cross alone (p. 197).

31 Sontag, *Regarding Pain*, p. 16. Tester observes that it is difficult to see why compassion fatigue should in principle be a problem at all, unless the idea of some bond of sympathy with the stranger has come to be accepted in the first place, as happened with modernity; and he distinguishes this from traditional notions of charity (pp. 18–21). For a useful review, see also I. Wilkinson, *Suffering: A Sociological Introduction* (Polity, 2005), Ch. 6; he concludes, optimistically, that 'the moral significance of the mass media may lie not so much in their power to exhaust our capacity to feel compassion as in their potential to cultivate it …' (p. 156).

32 See *Sensational Subjects*, Ch. 3, for further discussion.

33 M. Kavka, *Reality Television, Affect and Intimacy: Reality Matters* (Palgrave, 2008), pp. 7, 38, 43. See also pp. 37–46 for the extended discussion of the Diana case.

34 A. Jaffe, *Scenes of Sympathy: Identity and Representation in Victorian Fiction* (Cornell, 2000), pp. 14, 15.

35 R. Terada, *Feeling in Theory: Emotion after the 'Death of the Subject'* (Harvard University Press, 2001), pp. 21, 40. Terada is explicitly invoking Derrida here; and indeed, it is difficult to avoid seeing Derrida and Deleuze as the two heavyweights lying behind these rival perspectives, representation versus presentation, and their ramifications.

36 Terada, p. 71.

37 Kavka, p. 44.

38 As a recent example of this 'othering', we can mention Adam Phillips and Barbara Taylor. In their engaging and timely defence of kindness and associated virtues, *On Kindness* (Penguin, 2010), they nonetheless take time out to make the provocative claim that 'Sentimentality is cruelty by other means' (p. 94) – a claim that comes out of the blue, and is not given any substantive justification.

39 Terada, pp. 13, 5, 5, 13.

40 For the links between the sentimental, the sensational, and melodrama, see also *Sensational Subjects*, Chs 2, 8.

41 Phillips and Taylor, pp. 4, 12.

42 S. Žižek, *Violence* (Profile Books, 2009), pp. 56, 1, 57.

43 In particular, see J. Habermas, *The Theory of Communicative Action* (two vols, Heinemann, 1981, and Polity, 1987).

44 Žižek, p. 51.

45 Ibid., pp. 52, 53.

46 Ibid., p. 55. See also p. 166, on Kant.

47 The 'liberal guilt' thesis has of course been widely argued, and not without reason:

there is plenty for liberals to feel guilty about. See, for example, the essays in L. Berlant (ed.), *Compassion: The Culture and Politics of an Emotion* (Routledge, 2004). Whether the whole potential of the sympathetic orientation can be *reduced* to this functional social-psychological dimension is another matter – this whole book attempts to argue that it cannot.

48 Ibid., p. 70.

49 Žižek is insightful on how 'love thy neighbour' is implicit testimony to the fact that our neighbours are frequently those we hate: see pp. 47, 50.

50 M. Sandel, *What Money Can't Buy: The Moral Limits of Markets* (Penguin, 2013), pp. 10, 51, 187.

51 Thus when day-care centres for young children introduced fines for late pickups by parents, so as to avoid teachers having to stay late, this actually *increased* the number of late pickups. The fines had, in effect, become fees, a change of norm from the moral obligation not to inconvenience teachers to a market relation, paying teachers to stay longer. And discontinuing fines permitted no return to the old ethos; once gone, it was indeed gone. See Sandel, pp. 64–5, 89–90, 119.

52 The classic study is by R. M. Titmuss, *The Gift Relationship: From Human Blood to Social Policy* (Pantheon, 1971), arguing that the commercialization of blood-giving tends to drive out voluntary giving, and that the latter is generally preferable on a range of grounds, including economic efficiency.

53 This is an extension of the line of argument used by Adam Smith (see Ch. 4), generally ignored by later followers who focus exclusively on the economics of his *Wealth of Nations*.

54 The gift makes little economic sense: giving money is almost always more 'rational', more utility-efficient for the recipient (who can get *exactly* what is wanted), and less costly for the giver (in time, money spent on sending it): see Sandel, pp. 98–104. The classic comparative account of the gift is M. Mauss, *The Gift* [1925]; for a more recent review and development, see L. Hyde, *The Gift: How the Creative Spirit Transforms the World* (Canongate, 2007 [1979]).

55 Sandel, pp. 33, 102. Sandel rightly points out that 'fairness', the reduction or elimination of socially engendered inequalities, is a second key requirement for an adequate overall critique of capitalism's implications; see pp. 8–9, 110–13. This cannot be pursued here, except to observe that it would fit in with the Enlightenment critique touched on above (Ch. 3).

56 The classic account of this distinction within the sociological tradition is E. Durkheim, 'Individualism and the Intellectuals' [1898], in *Emile Durkheim: On Morality and Society*, ed. R. Bellah (Chicago University Press, 1973), also in *Durkheim On Religion*, ed. W. S. F. Pickering (Routledge, 1975). Durkheim, in turn, draws on Rousseau's distinction between *amour-de-soi* and *amour-propre*.

57 Žižek, pp. 74–5 and *passim*. See also the discussion of Adam Smith, in Ch. 4, above.

Postscript: Empathy, Spectacle and Mirror-Touch Synaesthesia

1 Daria Martin was the moving force behind the conference, and I would like to acknowledge the stimulus of her own contributions for influencing the direction of my thoughts here.

2 For a useful survey of synaesthesia research, see J. Ward, 'Synesthesia', *Annual Review of Psychology* (2013), 64; on mirror-touch specifically, see J. Banissy and J. Ward, 'Mechanisms of self-other representations and vicarious experiences of truth in mirror-touch synesthesia', *Frontiers of Human Neuroscience* (2013), 7.

3 For an ambitious recent contribution to this, see P. Pisters, *The Neuro-Image: A Deleuzian Film-philosophy of Digital Screen Culture* (Stanford University Press, 2012). Deleuzians, of course, as enthusiasts for the neuroscience links, prefer to see the brain itself as the screen here.

4 See S. Choudhury and J. Slaby, *Critical Neuroscience: A Handbook of the Social and Cultural Context of Neuroscience* (Blackwell, 2012), along with references to this controversy, and Deleuzian film theory, in my *Sensational Subjects: The Dramatization of Experience in the Modern World* (Bloomsbury, 2014), Chs 6, 7. See also the discussion of Spinoza and affect theory in Ch. 5 of the present book. The underlying neuroscientific claim is that mirror-neurons get activated both when experiencing emotion *and* when observing other people's emotional states.

5 This reminds us of Benjamin and aura; see Ch. 6 of this book.

Index

Note: authors of single short quotes are not generally listed here.

www.ingramcontent.com/pod-product-compliance
Lightning Source LLC
Chambersburg PA
CBHW050408280326
41932CB00013BA/1779